Africa Writes Back to Self

Africa Writes Back to Self

Metafiction, Gender, Sexuality

EVAN MAINA MWANGI

SUNY
PRESS

Cover art: Simon Muriithi, "Two Ideas," 9 × 11, oil on canvas (collection of the author). Courtesy of www.insideafricanart.com.

Published by
State University of New York Press, Albany

Printed in the United States of America

For information, contact State University of New York Press, Albany, NY
www.sunypress.edu

Production by Eileen Meehan
Marketing by Fran Keneston

Library of Congress Cataloging-in-Publication Data

Mwangi, Evan.
Africa writes back to self : metafiction, gender, sexuality / Evan Maina Mwangi.
p. cm.
Includes bibliographical references and index.
ISBN 978-1-4384-2681-5 (hardcover : alk. paper)
ISBN 978-1-4384-2682-2 (paperback : alk. paper)
1. African fiction (English)—History and criticism. 2. Self in literature.
3. Self-perception in literature. 4. Sex role in literature. 5. Sex in literature.
I. Title.

PR9344.M83 2009
823'.91409353—dc22 2009005428

10 9 8 7 6 5 4 3 2 1

I dedicate this book to
Geraldine, Betty, Bryan, and Beatrice Mwangi
in appreciation of their love and patience.

Contents

Preface

This book primarily concerns the intersection of metafiction, gender, and sexuality in contemporary African novels, especially those published after the mid-1980s. I argue that the novelists exploit self-reflexive techniques to signal changing circumstances in the society, discuss traditionally taboo issues such as homosexuality, and preserve themselves in the face of censorship. A second concern of the book is the fact that postcolonial theorists have been adept at noting the shortcomings of their approach to indigenous literatures, but they rarely implement their own recommendation. I aim at correcting the impression circulated in mainstream postcolonial theory that African literatures "write back" to the colonial center. I propose that the novels be read as writing back to themselves and to one another.

I am writing from the premise that although postcolonial theories are multiple, they seem to be powered by the now-naturalized notion that African literatures are a response to a singular European *Other* and an insurrection against an external aesthetics. This position ignores the way in which individual local texts address emergent themes that demote the West as the reference point of non-Western cultures. I find this focus on the reactive project of African literature problematic because it tends to silence Africans' articulation of self in favor of the West that postcolonial theory claims to be deconstructing.

In order to be able to read some texts in local languages, I draw my examples mainly from East Africa, an area of African literature that also has been largely ignored. The term *metafiction* is equated with Western aesthetics, but in introducing it I call upon African theorists such as Nadine Gordimer, Said Khamis, and Kyallo Wamitila to locate self-reflexivity in the context of indigenous aesthetics and politics. In Chapter 1, I sketch the genealogy of metafiction in African novels and demonstrate how, through self-reflexive devices, the novels transcend narcissistic wordplay, grounding themselves instead in the gritty political realities of Africa, even if their narratives are seen to be more than singular, representable essences. The second and third chapters illustrate some of the heuristic claims in Chapter 1 by performing close readings of representative works. Chapter 2 studies the intermingling of sex and nationalism via metafiction in the realist African literature in English. Arguing that metafiction is not new in African literature, this chapter shows that texts written as far back as the 1950s are preoccupied with their own canonization in the African and world academies. Sex is evacuated from these texts, but it haunts them as it constitutes a subtle reference point in the novels' participation in debates about what African literature should be. Chapter 3 turns to novels in Kiswahili to show that writers in indigenous languages are more concerned with local issues than with colonialism. I also indicate some of the shortcomings of these novels, written mainly by male artists from a fairly nationalistic perspective.

Chapter 4 proceeds to demonstrate that metafictional elements in the African novel tend to emanate from its connectedness to oral culture, but the novels intensify the metafictional dynamic by departing from particular genres and from the items of oral literature evoked. I seek to challenge the popular misconception that African literature is a continuation of the oral tradition, emphasizing instead the writers' breaks with the oral tradition. In Chapter 5, I refer to different texts and their revisions to examine the palimpsest as a form of metafiction. Related to this "palimpsestuous" nature of the novel (given an individual text's play with other narratives) is the use of painting as a signifier of the events in society. In Chapter 6, then, I proceed to explore the use of the trope of painting. I argue that contemporary African novelists deploy modern painting to deconstruct notions of a static, exotic, and authentic Africa created through the Western gaze. They refer to precolonial art from the perspective of the local cultures rather than from the anthropological perspective of Africa as the Other of the West.

Chapter 7 discusses the use of metafictional devices such as magical realism to present and deconstruct heteronormativity. Critiquing the dominant view of queerness as an imported and "un-African" perversion, the chapter demonstrates the positions of silence and marginality to which nonheterosexual practices are consigned in African societies, and how metafictionality is deployed to give voice to, as well as to critique, queer desire. In Chapter 8, I try to account for the dominancy of the "writing back" to the center theory. Contesting the tendency to flatten African gender theories into a single mass of statements opposed to Western feminism, I present a synthetic summary of the landmark feminist statements to question the foreclosure of indigenous theorizations of gender and sexuality and to deconstruct the tendency to regard African feminisms as a feeble philosophy that needs sheltering from predatory and perverse metropolitan feminist theories.

Overall, this book demonstrates the pervasive presence of metafiction in African novels and argues that African fiction should be read not as exclusively "writing back" to the metropolis but more meaningfully as writing back to itself in order to address issues such as AIDS, sex, and gender alongside classical themes such as colonialism. While figuring a world on the verge of despair and abyss, the narratives I examine are also suspended in hopeful moments.

Acknowledgments

This book could not have been completed without the support of various individuals and institutions. The gestation of the book occurred during my teaching of graduate and undergraduate courses in African literatures and literary theory at the University of Nairobi, Moi University, Ohio University, and Northwestern University. I would like to thank my students and colleagues for their observations and critical engagement.

I enjoyed the mentorship and friendship of many people as I prepared the various sections that make up this book. I cannot mention all of them by name, but I acknowledge with gratitude Ken Daley, Esiaba Irobi, Jules Law, Josie Bloomfield, Martin Müeller, Karen Vedder, David Wachanga, Ben Armstrong, Sandra Richards, Peter Amuka, Paul Breslin, James Ogude, Susannah Gottlieb, K. W. Wamitila, Jennifer Brody, Senorina Wendoh, Betsy Erkilla, Chris Lane, Christine Froula, Brian Edwards, Henry Indangasi, Christopher Herbert, Douglass Mpondi, Susan Phillips, Betty P. Pytlik, Kate Breen, Ciarunji Chesaina, Wen Jin, Julia Stern, Jeff Masten, Steve Howard, Kevin Bell, Janaka Bowman, Jay Grossman, Joyce Nyairo, Vivasvan Soni, Nick Davis, Richard Joseph, Susan Phillips, Tracy Davis, Mary Kinzie, Alex Weheliye, Kasey Evans, John P. Mbonde, Barbara Newman, Regina Schwartz, John Keene, Larry Lipking, Wendy Griswold, Helen Thompson, Kimani Njogu, Carl Smith, Linda Rice, Nathan Mead, Reg Gibbons, J. Roger Kurtz, Simon Gikandi, Carey Snyder, George Gathigi, Paul Edward, Joe MacLaughlin, and my many colleagues at Nairobi, Moi, Ohio, and Northwestern universities who not only gave me moral support but also showed great faith and interest in the project.

I had the opportunity to present some parts of this manuscript at Afrisem, a graduate seminar run by students at the Program for African Studies (PAS) at Northwestern University. I also presented the project at PAS faculty seminars. I would like to thank the then-PAS director, Richard Joseph, student seminar organizers Christina S. McMahon and Emily Callaci, and my faculty colleagues and seminar participants from the wider Chicago area for their critical discussions of the project. Brenna Stuart helped me with the much-needed initial copyediting.

I thank the anonymous reviewers who read the manuscript for State University of New York Press for their intellectual insights and incredibly productive criticism. My friends and colleagues also read the drafts at their various stages and offered invaluable critical comments. I am especially grateful to Paul Breslin, Ernest Waititu, Shingisie Musemwa, Stephen Partington, Paul Wahiu, Larry Ndivo, and Jenie Muchiri for their incisive critiques and advice. I discussed the project with Lila Luce, who recommended invaluable readings. In addition, Jeremy Webster of Ohio University advised me on some ways of reading sexuality, for which I am grateful.

The Weinberg College of Arts and Sciences and the Graduate School at Northwestern University gave me generous travel and research funding, without which I could not have completed this project. I extend my gratitude to Kathy Daniels, Susan Manning, and Wendy Wall for facilitating the availability of these funds. The graduate school further offered me forums in which to discuss this work and to receive commentary from faculty, students, and the general public. The Northwestern University Research Grants Committee has provided partial support for the publication of this book. I gratefully acknowledge this assistance. I am grateful to the staff at the Melville Herskovits Library of African Studies, especially director David Easterbrook, for getting me most of the books I needed. The librarians at the Africana section of the Jomo Kenyatta Memorial Library of the University of Nairobi were extremely helpful with archival materials. I also thank David Mugonyi, Pilli Kamenju, and Rose Mathenge for getting me books from different locations in Africa.

Further, I owe an immense debt of gratitude to Larin McLaughlin, Andrew Kenyon, Eileen Meehan, and their team of editors at State University of New York Press for the dedication and professionalism with which they handled this manuscript.

An earlier version of Chapter 4 appeared in *Gefame: Journal of African Studies* (2006) 3:1 as "Painted Metaphors: The Use of Visual Arts in Contemporary African Novels." I thank the editorial board for permission to reprint the revised version of the article.

I am grateful to Jim Fuhr for indexing and proofreading the book. Many thanks also to Todd Schaffer and Simon Muriithi for generously allowing me to use images from Inside African Art (www.insideafricanart.com) for the cover design.

Evan Mwangi
Evanston, March 2009

Introduction

Writing Back to Self

Since the mid-1980s, African novels have become markedly self-reflexive in the way they rewrite one another and draw attention to their own fictionality. They mark stylistic and thematic departures that deliberately undermine the nationalist and realist impulse that governed earlier writing (Wright 1997; Gaylard 2005). The novels further depart from the tradition of "writing back" to the European colonial center by focusing their gaze on local forms of oppression that are seen to parallel classical colonialism. The hint of interest in gender issues that Neil Lazarus (1990) noted in African novels of the 1970s is developed to a higher level of self-consciousness in the novels of the 1980s. Yet while critics have separately studied gender and self-reflexivity in African texts, the intersection of the two has not been given sufficient attention. Examined here are contemporary African novels that demonstrate perceptible shifts in focus from issues of external colonialism to a more self-reflexive treatment of gender and sexual relations. Although most African languages do not have a word for "gender," and although some African scholars of relations between male and female subjects such as Oyèrónkẹ́ Oyewùmi (1997) and Nkiru Nzegwu (2006) have seen "gender" as an invention of Western epistemologies, the indigenous novels studied reflect and refract prevalent socially constructed hierarchies based on sexual practices. The continued search for the appropriate word for "gender" in various African languages (Mugambi 2007) indicates that contemporary Africa recognizes the centrality of female/male power hierarchies and the need to create a balance between the sexes.

In the novels I examine here, resistance to the West may be seen to reside more potently in the texts' disregard or demotion of the West as the categorical and ineluctable point of reference in the representation and self-fashioning of the Global South; the texts resist the West by erasing it from local discourses on postcolonial cultures, aesthetics, and politics of identity.[1] Staging internal heteroglossia, individual texts are more preoccupied in writing back to themselves and other local texts to address emerging realities and to express the growing diversity of identities in Africa. I argue that postrealist narrative techniques and realism are not mutually exclusive as the metafictional texts deploy these techniques to depict the material realities in contemporary Africa. It is in the metafictional excursions that some of the novels hint to the reader the extratextual realities upon which they are based. By prioritizing metafictional novels, I am not following John Barth's hierarchy that seems to denigrate realism as a lesser form of artistic expression. As I demonstrate, even realist novels have metafictional moments, and most metafictional novels are grounded in factual material conditions in specific locations in Africa.

A corollary argument here is that we need to reexamine the dominant notion in postcolonial studies that African literature "writes back" to the Western metropolis. Some critics have recently become impatient with the "writing back" tradition of the postcolonial theory. For instance, analyzing indigenous scales of beauty in South African Zakes Mda's novels, *The Heart of Redness* and *Ways of Dying*, Rita Barnard gestures toward the need to abandon the "stale old notion of postcolonial literature as 'empire writing back' and accept that the relationships in the texts are not unidirectional" (Barnard 2006, 121). However, this injunction is rarely observed in practical criticism of African literature, where the literature is presented as dominantly an "anti" art in relation to European literature. By demonstrating that the texts are primarily writing back to themselves and to each other, just as the societies signified examine themselves in order to apprehend their contribution to their own predicament, I argue that the novels offer a corrective to the dominant theory in postcolonial studies that African literature's main preoccupation is to subvert the colonial metropolis. To use a Nietzschean term, African literature in the 1980s is not primarily an art of *ressentiment*, reactively directing grudges and hostility at Europe as the cause of all African frustrations. Rather, it is an art of positive self-affirmation that is also not blind to internal causes of malaise within African societies.

The novels engage in a politics that is more scathing in its attack on wayward Africans than on the imperial West. The texts themselves have theorized their role in nations that need to be made aware of their problems and potentiality, indicating that Africans can contribute to a resolution to their own problems rather than blaming colonialists and outsiders for all of the problems on the continent. I attempt to go beyond the regular complaint that postcolonial criticism ignores locally produced texts and popular culture in favor of canonical texts and diasporic and transnational literature issuing from Western academic and publishing venues. Reading metafictional moments in contemporary African novels from a post-Afrocentric perspective, I seek to explain the novels' reconfiguration of priorities in ways that illuminate the use of self-reflexive technique to particularly focus on gender and sexuality. In the process, I explain the local nuances the texts generate as they continue critiquing colonialism and other hegemonic practices.

Granted, Ghanaian novelist Ayi Kwei Armah, whose modernist novels are haunted by the figure of the artist, has Solo, his fictional translator aspiring to be an artist in *Why Are We So Blest?* (1972), suggesting that any artistic intervention in Africa outside of the writing-back-to-Europe tradition is an exercise in artistic futility: "Only one issue is worth our time: how to end the oppression of the African, to kill the European beasts of prey, to remake ourselves, the elected servants of Europe and America. Outside that, all is useless" (1972, 230). I argue here that contemporary African literature is primarily neither a "writing back" to Europe nor an endorsement of Euro-American neocolonialism. It is first and foremost about self-perception.

Despite my skepticism toward postcolonial studies as practiced in Western institutions, this book is not a "writing back" to postcolonial theory. The theory has received energetic critique from within its own ranks, although it appears never in a hurry to adopt its own recommendations.[2] I shall return briefly later in the book to possible reasons the theory would be so obsessed with arguing that cultures of the Gobal South are "writing back to the West." But particularly instructive at the outset is Simon Gikandi's observation in "Globalization and the Claims of Postcolonialism" (2002), that in the era of increased integration of economies and unabated cultural exchanges around the world, analyses of literature in English studies can easily be misapplied to extend Western nationalism to formally colonized regions while invoking the dissolution of African nation-states. Like Revathi Krishnaswamy in "Mythologies of Migrancy" (2005), Gikandi critiques the new focus on cultural production by the relatively comfortable émigré native informants in the West at the expense of the brutal material conditions in the postcolonial nations. A study of locally produced texts, alongside the émigré literature, would help us apprehend the multiple sites of identity formations in Africa.

Given the predominant notion that African literature is about "writing back" to the European canon, my proposal that African arts are primarily writing back to themselves might give the impression that this book is a subversion or parody of Bill Ashcroft, Gareth Griffiths, and Helen Tiffin's well-argued book *The Empire Writes Back: Theory and Practice in Postcolonial Literatures* (2002). It is not. Rather, I am extending the ideas in Ashcroft and colleagues' authoritative and seminal analysis in a direction they have indicated, especially in their discussion of how we can rethink postcolonial studies to pay more attention to local texts and contexts. I am particularly attracted to their prognosis toward the end of their book to the effect that the future of postcolonial studies resides in the consideration of local conditions and the influence of global moments on particular instances and spaces. Noting the shortcomings of postcolonial studies and charting the way forward, they underscore that "as the field has developed over the last decade or so, it becomes clearer that perhaps postcolonial theory needs to be further grounded in specific analyses of the effects of large movements and ideologies on particular localities" (2002, 210). It is in this spirit that I examine local African texts in English and indigenous languages.

In chapter 8 of this book, I critique the usage of the expression "writing back" in postcolonial studies. Suffice it to say here that the expression, as introduced to academic literary criticism by Ashcroft and colleagues, acquires different meanings in a practical examination of postcolonial texts. These include intertextuality between imperial texts and art from formerly colonized regions, the use of English in ways that deviate from Standard English, and the reclamation of subjectivity for the formerly colonized people through a celebration of their liberation struggles. My criticisms of postcolonial theory should not be seen as a rejection of its valuable contribution to the explanation of African literature, especially its critique of Eurocentrism and other European ontological traditions that have powered colonial and neocolonial domination of Africa. I am trying to avoid the Western ethics of reading that privileges non-Western literatures in order to give priority to the very European cultures that produced that ethics. I use and extend postcolonial theory to argue that contemporary African novelists resort to self-reflexive devices to signify a state of being in postcolonial African societies rather than to retaliate against, parody, or negate Western discourses.

To examine African literature outside of the "writing back to Europe" paradigm is to appreciate the borrowings and contestations among local texts and to attend to the contradiction raised by Arif Dirlik in "The Postcolonial Aura," that relations in postcolonial literature are seen as "uniformly between the post*colonial* and the First World, never, to my knowledge, between one post*colonial* intellectual and another" (1994, 342, emphases in original). Following Dirlik, I see the need to study not only the contestations between writers in Africa but the internal heteroglossia within individual texts, where self-mimicry and self-critique are figured through bricolage and self-conscious literary forms that help the narrative undermine notions of a stable unitary self without fetishizing fragmentation and chaos. My main objective in considering contemporary African novels is not only to rethink the dominant paradigm of "writing back" to the West but also to examine the emergent issues that these novels present. I demonstrate that the "writing back to the colonial center" paradigm is undermined by the novels' preoccupation with self-interrogation and by their prioritization of themes other than the relations between the colonizer and the colonized.[3]

What follows in these chapters, then, is an examination of the treatment of gender and sexuality in texts that deploy metafiction as a strategy of narration and self-representation. While reading the role colonialism plays in African self-fashioning, this book primarily focuses on the use of self-reflexive devices in texts seeking to bring up for public debate issues that are considered taboo or not worthy of serious discussion. The stylistic and thematic inward-looking orientation of the novels is not meant to be taken as a reflection of an Africa that is insulated from the rest of the world—the kind of community Karl Marx controversially described as characterizing non-European modes of production prior to colonialism. Even individual texts written in marginalized African languages underline the desire of African societies to reach out to the rest of the world. But these novels reject the undercurrents in postcolonial theory that suggest that European literature is the proper literature (the father figure) to which African literature writes back.

Expanding Fredric Jameson's caveat in *The Political Unconscious* (1981), that some of the novels read today as realist were not written to fit modern definitions of the term, our discussion of self-reflexive narratives is not limited to texts consciously written to fit into the concept of "metafiction" as it is used in the current theorizing of literature. Although metafiction is associated with nonrealist, postmodern aesthetics, some of the novels I discuss here are on the whole realist and modernist; they use metafiction in certain moments of their narration, sometimes to enhance their realism in a way that renders indeterminate the borderline between metafiction and realism. In responding to such novels, I use a mode of reading indirectly allusive to Roland Barthes's rereading of Balzac's "Sarrasine"—an active and a constitutive aesthetic engagement in which the reader uncovers the divisive and multiple layers behind the unitary and centered codes of a realist classic.

Defining Metafiction in African Contexts

In one of his readings of the experimental Kiswahili novels of the 1990s, Zanzibari novelist and critic Said A. M. Khamis (2001) strategically avoids using the term *metafiction* because, as he suggests in the essay, the postrealist fiction in African languages derives from indigenous oral literature rather than from Western postmodern aesthetics. Khamis is articulating a position held by several postcolonial theorists.[4] A participant in self-conscious fabulation in his own novels (written under the name Said A. Mohamed), Khamis suggests that African postrealism is an independent genre developed from indigenous narrative forms. However, it is not lost on the keen reader of his analysis that, although not fully acknowledged, the Western theorization of metafiction forms an important palimpsest in Khamis's readings of Kiswahili novels, including the commentaries on his own writing. For example, in "Fabulation and Politics of the 90s in Kezilahabi's Novel *Nagona*," Khamis describes that novel in terms that echo Patricia Waugh's definition of "metafiction" as "a type of fiction that self-consciously and systematically draws attention to its own status as an artifact in order to pose questions about the relationship between fiction and reality" (Khamis 2001, 124).[5] In reproducing Waugh's definition of "metafiction" word for word without using the term itself or bibliographically acknowledging Waugh, Khamis indexes the problematic relationship between the conventional theorization of self-reflexivity and the African scholar's wish to ground the concept in homegrown aesthetic practices. Without dismissing the applicability of Western concepts, theorists are reluctant to adopt critical terms wholesale to explain African phenomena.

It is therefore crucial to define the term *metafiction* in relation to postmodernism and African literature, not only because postmodernism has a vexed relationship to indigenous African literature but also because of the various shades of meanings the term *metafiction* takes in different contexts.[6] Following Dilip Gaonkar's (2001) and Sanjay Subrahmanyam's (1998) questioning of Wallerstein's view of modernity as a Western virus spreading to the rest of the world, I view metafiction not as an exclusively Western phenomenon but as an aesthetic practice that has grown simultaneously in different parts of the world. Metafiction in African literature is situated, interlinked with similar practices across the globe but entailing unique disruptions of Western postmodernisms.[7] There are, of course, links between the different practices of metafiction, but metafiction in African literature, as in other literatures, is conjectural. It gestures to its own indigenous specific location, even when it is linked to global metafictional productions.

Although seen as an exclusively Western, postmodern term, "metafiction" is what in Kiswahili language would be called *bunilizipiku* (imaginative creation that extends beyond the conventions of fiction, fiction beyond fiction, fiction that outdoes fiction in its fictionality).[8] It involves *bunilizi rejelevu* (Kiswahili term for fiction that refers back to itself, self-reflexive fiction) and *bunilizi ya kihalisiajabu* (fiction with a surrealist feel, magical realist fiction). When the Gĩkũyũ culture talks about "*ng'ano cia mageganiа*" (mind-blowing stories, out-of-this-world narratives) to describe novels such as Ngũgĩ wa Thiong'o's *Mũrogi wa Kagogo* (*Wizard of the Crow*), the language is referring to the same phenomenon of literature that challenges the conventions of realism by drawing attention to its fictional status. Therefore, in an African context, I use the term *metafiction* to describe that form of African literature that is self-conscious, self-reflexive, and self-referential.

Larry McCaffery uses the term to refer to "that type of fiction which either directly examines its own construction as it proceeds or which comments or speculates about the forms and language of previous fictions" or fiction that seeks "to examine how *all* fictional systems operate, their methodology, the sources of their appeal, and the dangers of their being dogmatized" (1982: 16–17, emphasis in original). I extend this definition to consider local conventions of self-reflexivity and the specific political and social nuances that moments of self-reflexivity generate. Metafictional moments in a narrative are those where the text displays an awareness of its own textuality as an artistic creation; metafictional literature advertises itself as art and problematizes its relationship with the reality it purports to represent through language. It blurs the distinctions between creative writing and literary theory and between different genres and modes of transmission. The texts comprising this form of literature sometimes treat issues that would be expected in a critical essay, while using literary form innovatively to draw attention to their status as fictions rather than representations of a tangible world outside of the text.

Some novels use metafiction in a pronounced way, especially when they employ the mise-en-abyme technique, a tendency of the text to mirror itself as another text by replicating the narrator's story as happens in David Maillu's *No!* and *Broken Drum* or Katama Mkangi's *Mafuta* and Vassanji's *The Book of Secrets*, in which the novels are replicated by an embedded manuscript. Others foreground the act of writing itself by citing other oral and written texts or presenting the artist as a principal character in a way that undermines realism. Novels such as David Karanja's *The Girl Was Mine* (1996) and Wairimu Kibugi's *Painful Tears* (1997) may not be included in this category because although treating the theme of writers and writing, they are transparently realist. The writers bemoan the fate of artists in Africa and celebrate the material success of an artist, but instead of subverting the status quo through metafiction, the novels seem to endorse a writer's pursuit of a bourgeois lifestyle and eventual assimilation by the mainstream fraternity of writers and political leaders. I exclude the novels of Amos Tutuola and Shaaban Robert because although ideologically subversive and set in a preternatural fantastic world, these writers are too open in trying to recuperate the logicality of their stories and draw attention to their narratives' isomorphic relationship to an established reality.

Throughout the history of written literature in Africa, novels have commented on their own textuality as works of art, on previous novels, and on the role of art, its producers, and its consumers in society. Although the most intensely metafictional African texts came out in the 1980s, literary self-referentiality precedes this era of tremendous changes in Africa and the world. Sally O'Reilly notes in "Self-Reflexivity" that "metafiction could be said to be as old as the novel itself, as fiction and the act of writing itself are bound up with self-consciousness and representation so, rather than a subgenre, it is inherent in all writing" (2005, 8). For her part, Linda Hutcheon has noted in *A Poetics of Postmodernism* (1988) that although the term *metafiction* is relatively new, coined by William H. Gass in 1970 to describe a novel's tendency to reflect itself more than an extratextual world, the practice of metafiction is "as old (if not older) than the novel itself" (5). African texts such as Grace Ogot's *Promised Land* (1966), the first novel by a black African woman to be published,[9] have deployed metafictional techniques to undermine the precapitalist patriarchy in Africa, while Rebeka Njau's *Ripples in the Pool* (1975) uses similar techniques to figure lesbian identities.[10]

Indeed, written African literature, at least since Olaudah Equiano's slave narrative *Interesting Narrative of the Life of Olaudah Equiano, or Gustavus Vassa, the African*, first published in 1789, has been marked by self-referentiality and indeterminacies.[11] Henry Louis Gates Jr. (1988) relates the deconstructive playfulness of black literature in the Diaspora to vernacular myths from the continent, to modes of self-articulation and self-inscription that the enslaved communities brought with them from the continent. Although it would be wrong and totalizing to argue that the self-referential indeterminacies of black literature have their sources in the Esu-Elegbara of the Yoruba community of West Africa, the influence of orature and local expression has had tremendous effects on the production of metafictional literature.[12] In East Africa, texts in local languages such as Gĩkũyũ and Kiswahili tend to be more self-reflexive than the ones written in English because the texts are more intimate with the local oral literatures.[13] Esu-Elegbara is just one of the multiple sources of the playfulness and trickster techniques of self-representation in African literatures.

Considering the pervasiveness of metafiction that Gates notes in his study of black discourse—a generality that marks even the earliest African texts such as Olaudah Equiano's slave narrative, which was written at the threshold of the novel as a genre—then what is not metafiction? Is metafiction in the African novel different from metafiction in the Western novel? Mark Currie has warned that "since metafiction concerns itself above all with a reflexive awareness of the conditions of meaning-construction, any typological definition of metafiction rooted in objective characteristics or essences will contradict the linguistic philosophy that it attempts to describe" (1995, 15). The easiest antonym for "metafiction" seems to be "realism," but this opposition is underwritten by the very ontological fixedness that metafiction seeks to disrupt. I propose that we view the concepts for what they are, not according to what they oppose. Metafiction is simply what it is (not a reverse of its supposed opposite)—literary moments that are aware of their own textuality.

There is little to be gained from efforts to differentiate "African metafiction" from "Western metafiction," because metafiction is a technique of writing; just as it may not be all that useful to differentiate between, for example, British flashback and Indian flashback, American irony and Cambodian irony, or Canadian sarcasm and Yoruba sarcasm, there is no difference between what might be perceived as "African metafiction" and non-African novels that employ the technique. If we were to step out of this bipolar logic that ironically powers theories of hybridity and cross-cultural engagements, then we would see metafiction as a cross-culturally employed technique that varies in application from one text to another depending on the talents of the writer and the historical, political, and social contingencies that the text seeks to signify. Therefore, readers of this book looking for a discussion of "African metafiction" are likely to be disappointed because, contrary to the impression given by Madelyn Jablon's *Black Metafiction* (1996), no literary technique is specific to any individual or social category. What may be unique is the way a particular literary technique is deployed or constructed through a writer's peculiar use of language in specific circumstances. Even those who do not demur at Rene Etiemble's claim that there are "invariables" available to all global literatures or at Northrop Frye's contention about archetypes shared among all literatures would not avow that certain stylistic devices in themselves belong to a certain set of socially oriented texts. What distinguishes artists and groups of texts from one another is the way they employ a given technique.

In this discussion I argue that even genres such as the epic that are traditionally associated with masculine military exploits have been used in metafictional texts to undermine sexism and militaristic conquest. Therefore, there is no "African metafiction," just as there is no "Illinois metafiction," "London metafiction," "Kawangware metafiction," "Soweto metafiction," "Duke metafiction," or "Paris metafiction"—except perhaps within the politics of naming, hinted at in the preface of Michel Foucault's *Order of Things*, whereby we give names to phenomena in order to localize their power of contagion, although we know such names do not have any meanings outside of language (1970, xv–xvi). I would not claim that there is anything like "African metafiction" except in the simple and inadequate sense of metafiction written by Africans. Unlike a term such as the "African novel" or "African literature," where there are fairly discernible systematic characteristics among texts, despite the fact that some texts defy such categorization, the term *metafiction* can only be used to describe a universal literary technique that is, however, variably deployed in specific African novels to express and refigure different social facts. What should be important for us here, then, are the conventions of self-reflexivity evoked and how self-reference is employed in texts to generate certain meanings and aesthetic effects.

Further, the boundary between metafiction and its opposite is highly unstable, as is the distinction between metafiction and realism. What matters is the particular phenomenon a metafictional moment in the narrative signifies, even if that narrative is not wholly comprised of such moments. That is, metafiction should not be read as an abstraction but as a means of expressing concrete ideas in the narrative, even if the metafictional act signifies abstraction, disfigurement, and incomprehensibility. Although African novels of the 1950s and early 1960s were largely realist in their method of presenting the precolonial, colonial, and neocolonial condition in Africa, they contain metafictional moments that demand to be read in a way that yields different responses from those given them through the privileging of causality and objectivity. Because specific metafictional moments are symptomatic of different social conditions, it is appropriate to depart from the general celebration of unreality, fragmentation, and ambivalence with which metafictional novels are greeted. In the discussion of individual texts, I have tried to focus on how effectively the device has been deployed in order to help readers tease out the repressed social conditions and explain the proliferation of metafiction in African novels since the 1980s. The increased propensity of the device in the 1980s can be accounted for partly by the growing suspicions of the grand narratives of national unity expressed through realist modes in the 1950s, 1960s, and well into the 1970s. But the texts do not disavow nationalism; they seem to be suspicious of the misuse of the claims to nationalism that leave out certain sectors from the national realm.

Teasing African Literature to Define Itself

As a teacher of Anglophone African literature in an American institution, I am perennially haunted by the old question of the definition of African literature: What is African literature? How does it differ from Western literature? These are questions I have also constantly heard in forums on African literature in Africa. The expected answer is a defensive delineation of the differences between the politically conscious African texts and the supposedly disinterested literature of the West.[14] The two questions seem to invariably follow each other. The questions and the sequence in which they are ordered reveal that African literature is still viewed, however unwittingly, in terms of the Lacanian Other—as a not-self or as a surrogate entity that exists only in relation to Western literature.

The project of empowering minority literatures from Africa must start with listening to what those literatures say about art. Various conflicting theories have been offered in an attempt to define African literature as an aesthetic category. Chinweizu and colleagues' notoriously Afrocentric work, *Toward the Decolonization of African Literature* sees African literature as "an autonomous entity separate and apart from all other literatures" (1980, 4).

The authors seem to be more interested in showing the differences between African literature and other literatures and in censuring writers they feel not to be "African" enough for subscribing to supposedly non-African artistic categories. Their critique implies that the critic of African literatures needs to be immersed in non-African cultures to be able to assess the Africanness of texts in terms of how they are different from other categories, especially the Western canon. While Achebe sees no need to be preoccupied with providing clear-cut definitions of the complex and diverse literatures of Africa, or with combining them into a single aesthetic, Ngũgĩ defines African literature as that which is composed and primarily written in an African indigenous language.[15] Again, Ngũgĩ's argument prioritizes an interest in what is not African literature (Europhone literatures) instead of focusing on the Africanness of the text.

Abiola Irele's *The African Experience in Literature and Ideology* (1981) demotes indigenous language from its position as the primary criterion of whether a text is African or not. Irele prioritizes style (regardless of the particular national or ethnic language) in addition to historical and sociological factors that he sees as determining the aesthetic mode of expression of the writing. But his later text, *The African Imagination* (2001), notes the centrality of oral discourse in African aesthetics and points to the need to go beyond texts written in African languages. Irele evacuates white writers from the realm of "African imagination," because they "do not display the sense of connection to an informing spirit of imaginative expression rooted in African tradition," and because "in a formal sense their works are bound just as much to the European literary tradition as are those of metropolitan writers" (2001, 15). To tie imagination to the color of the skin is, to say the least, quite reductive. But we should not be in a hurry to dismiss Irele as belonging to an aesthetic Neil Lazarus (1990), discussing Ayi Kwei Armah's *Why Are We So Blest?*, sees as retrogressive because of its racial essentialism; it is apposite to put Irele's politics of essentialism in context because, I think, he is staging what Spivak memorably called "strategic essentialism," a political positioning that treats diverse groups as a single body to confront a formidable and silencing force such as white imperialism. Because essentialism in itself is not a bad thing as long as it is not put to unscrupulous ends, Irele's kind of strategic essentialism in *The African Imagination*—a simplification of phenomena for the sake of struggle—could be seen as regenerative. It is the kind of thinking we see endorsed by minority writers and theorists as diverse as Spivak, Diana Fuss, Toni Morrison, and Dwight McBride.[16]

Irele's definition of "the African imagination" (with a definite article *the*) seems to be ordered by the very Western academy he is criticizing rather than by what African texts view themselves to be. He appears to be responding to the Western academy's tendency to limit discussions of African writing to expatriate narratives by explorers and missionaries, postmodernist and diaspora novels, or works by white South African postmodernist and liberal humanist writers who, unlike black writers, have supposedly not been energetic and partisan enough in their opposition to apartheid. Nevertheless, strategic as it is in the Western academy, Irele's restrictive and essentialist typology would encounter opposition in postcolonial Africa because it excludes not only immigrant writers from Asia but also respected African writers of European extraction such as Kenyan Marjorie Oludhe Macgoye, Mozambican Mia Couto, and Angolan Pepetela. In their thematic preoccupations and stylistic choices, these non-black writers do not exhibit the weaknesses Irele uses in his criteria to exclude white writing from his idea of "the African imagination." In other words, there is nothing to mark some non-black writers as different from indigenous writers in an either/or dichotomy. The kind of differences the writers may display from "the African imagination" that Irele prescribes can also be found among indigenous African writers. Indeed, a white writer such as Pepetela is closer to the indigenous novelist Ngũgĩ in style and theme than Ngũgĩ is to his Kikuyu compatriot Meja Mwangi or to Achebe. It is in recognition of this instability of the black/white dichotomy in his theorizing of "the African imagination" that Irele (2001, 15–16) qualifies that some Lusophone white writers such as Castro Soromenho and Luandino Vieyra may be considered as part of "the African imagination." It needs to be observed that there are many indigenous writers, even in African languages, who operate outside of the restrictive confines of "the African imagination" that Irele stipulates as the ideal aesthetic for African writing.

In a different context, Amoko (2006) has hinted at the unproductiveness of the prioritized tokenism race and postcoloniality have enjoyed in Western academic venues. It is because of some of its practitioners' uncritical racial essentialism that Irele, in *The African Experience in Literature and Ideology*, accepts the disapproval levied against the negritude movement while at the same time recuperating negritude from its harshest critics:

> But though Négritude was a legitimate reaction, it is probably true that today our need is less to press our claim, however justified, to an original difference, than to begin to restate our common involvement with the rest of humanity. It is precisely in this perspective that our modern literature will derive its enduring interest—in the way it throws a vivid light upon an area of human life and experience which, though circumscribed in its immediate reference, has nonetheless a fundamental correspondence to other areas, in other climes and other times. (Irele 1981, 3)

Irele notes the commonality of black people's experience with slavery and colonialism but resists uncritical essentialism. He accepts Soyinka's rejection of the black/white Manichean opposition and negritude approaches to culture that seem to be apologizing for Africa. Both of Irele's books indicate a sympathetic view of negritude and an attempt to define, along Blyden's lines, the quintessential "African personality" that transcends local boundaries to unite transatlantic black communities.

In "Modern African Literature and Cultural Identity," Tanure Ojaide (1992), following Irele's *The African Experience in Literature and Ideology*, downplays the centrality of the language of composition as the prime focus in deciding the Africanness of a text. Ojaide puts particular emphasis on the moral and utilitarian imperatives of African literature, which he defines as any literature written in a language spoken in Africa, regardless of the origin of that language. Both Irele and Ojaide see African literature as distinct, especially with regard to Western and colonial aesthetics. To move beyond these polemical gestures and statements, however, we need to ask: What do the literatures themselves say about what should be considered African literature? The literatures, as Olakunle George asserts, should be treated as "a mode of theory" (2003, 105), and nowhere is this theorizing more poignant than in metafictional texts. Toward the end of this book, I hope to be able to glean from the novels what they assume African literatures to be.

Politics and Formal Analysis

In *Death of a Discipline* (2003), Spivak has emphasized the need to study non-Western literature primarily as artistic texts. In a narratological and deconstructive analysis of Tayeb Salih's (1969) metafictional novel *Season of Migration to the North* via Freudian psychoanalysis, Spivak privileges the undecidable in the novel's unnamed narrator. She urges us not to read peripheral literatures "with foregone conclusions that deny it literariness" (Spivak 2003, 58). But easily overlooked in the study of postcolonial literatures is the question of form beyond the postcolonial texts' deployment of English in a way that deviates from standard language, as if that is not what all literature is supposed to do—avoid the beaten track through the innovative use of linguistic resources. The neglect of the study of form has been read by Rey Chow (2006, 80), among others, as a political gesture by Western institutions of interpretation, which presume that non-Western writing is not literary but sociological, political, or anthropological. Also frequently unattended to in the study of gender in African literature is the relation between African feminisms and stylistics. African feminists pay attention to form and to the ways textuality is deployed to unmask local patriarchal practices that have encouraged sexism.

Wilson-Tagoe's various gynocritical examinations of Yvonne Vera's fabulist narratives about patriarchy and nationalism in Zimbabwe are exemplary in their historically situated close readings of Vera's layered, intertextual networks, her play with language and orality, and her transgressive cultural translation. According to Wilson-Tagoe, Vera's fiction breaks gender hierarchies, interrogates history from the perspective of marginalized subjects, and reinscribes agency and subjective self-realization for silenced women.[17] Wilson-Tagoe suggests that the fundamentals of the gynocritical approach formulated by Elaine Showalter are applicable to African literatures of the 1980s, especially because Showalter deemphasizes the feminine (emulation of dominant male forms by women writers) and feminist (reactive marginality based on negation of male writing) to focus on the female (women's expression of self). Without attaching as much importance to essence as Showalter did in her politics of representation, and without seeing the feminist as fully divorced from the other three phases of women's self-realization in literature, we see African literature following a similar pattern—the initial imitation of colonial forms, the conscious deconstruction of colonial literature, and the eventual focus on African societies unencumbered by Western expression.

Yet as demonstrated by Rey Chow's and Wilson-Tagoe's stylistic readings, a purely formalistic approach to literature that ignores the sociological and political contingencies ordering the production of art would be untenable in the study of African literature. The literature, to quote Ngũgĩ in *Homecoming*, "does not grow in a vacuum"; it is "given impetus, shape, direction, and even area of concern by social, political, and economic forces in a particular society" (1972, xv). While Ngũgĩ, writing in the 1960s, sees opposition to European imperialism as the major force fueling African literature, new texts show a shift in focus. What emerges from Ngũgĩ's argument is the suggestion that we should pay attention to the extratextual forces that influence the literature or, to use Fredric Jameson's famous phrase in *The Political Unconscious* (1981), to "always historicize" textual strategies in a work of art. Therefore, I follow the example set by Ato Quayson, Olakunle George, Deepika Bahri, Wilson-Tagoe, and Simon Gikandi in their various readings of postcolonial literatures in a way that focuses on form without ignoring the sociological facts circumscribing the production, circulation, and consumption of the literatures. While readings of postcolonial literatures tend to focus on politics and sociological data, these critics have been attentive to the aesthetics of the texts, which they place in their social and political contexts in a manner that illumines both the society and the aesthetic objects.

In searching the embattled emergence of metafiction in African novels, my point of departure is the notion expressed by Russian formalist Victor

Shklovsky, that "art is a way of experiencing the artfulness of an object" ([1917] 2005, 800). For Shklovsky, literary language calls attention to itself in order to estrange the reader from the familiar and offer deeper insights into daily life. As already shown, the notion of defamiliarization is a politically potent concept despite the demonization of formalism as apolitical and inappropriate for the study of politically invested art such as the postcolonial novel. Beyond aesthetic considerations, African writers have used the "unfamiliar," especially in political novels, to avoid retaliation by the state or to talk about taboo issues without offending someone.

Recent studies have shown that from the very beginning the concept of *ostranenie* (estrangement/defamiliarization), given currency by Shklovsky and suggested by Bertolt Brecht's *Verfremdungseffekt* (alienation effect/distancing effect), has always been an active part of politics.[18] Despite the formalist insinuation that literature has little to do with reflecting the society from which it comes, I undertake a reading of textuality that locates the forms writers enlist to historiographic and political impulses ubiquitous in African literature. The social implications of the forms that the writers adopt would be important in helping us understand the societies from which that literature comes. Through metafictional devices, the literature itself insists that it is by its very nature historical and political and treats the interplay of art, history, and politics as an intense dialogue between sublime creativity and mundane social conditions. The texts raise questions about the relationship between literature and social consciousness, especially in the way they thematize the institutions and protocols of literary interpretation and meaning-production.

I allude indirectly to Shklovky's notion of estrangement throughout the study not only because it structures much of the contemporary theorizing of literature but also because metafiction is a form of proliferated defamiliarization. In the search for a genealogy of metafiction in African novels, I also consider Ngũgĩ wa Thiong'o's and Fredric Jameson's separate reminders that all literature is political, not the least texts and stylistic elements that appear to be apolitical. Metafiction as a technical device has been used in different ways to defamiliarize and consequently demystify African social experience and to serve as a forum for political intervention.

African historical and political contingencies shape the way metafiction is applied in the novels. Unlike other linguistic and paralinguistic structures that writers employ to engender defamiliarization, metafiction defamiliarizes the world as we know it by radically undermining the illusion of reality and advertising the means by which it is undermining realism. Here I see metafiction as a means of replenishing the way we perceive Africa through its arts. The delay of perception created by metafiction and other devices of defamiliarization helps us see the world more clearly than if it was directly rendered. In other words, in the African novel, form and political content are inseparable. Stephen Slemon has pointed out that despite its tendency to align itself with postmodern aesthetics, a postcolonial text "retains a recuperative impulse towards the structure of 'history' " (1990, 6). This point is also taken up by Elleke Boehmer, who argues in *Colonial and Postcolonial Literature: Migrant Metaphors* that—notwithstanding the confluence between postmodernism and postcolonialism in their critique of Enlightenment and their production of texts that display fragmentation, playfulness, self-consciousness, and ambivalence—postcolonial art "emerges out of the grit and rank specificity of a local culture or cultures, history or histories" (2005a, 238). For Slemon, even utopian texts from formerly colonized regions would be better read as "grounded in reference" (1990, 6).[19] By using Slemon's endorsement of the referential imperative of nonreferential postcolonial texts while removing from it his suggestion that the postmodern elements in postcolonial texts counter the surplus of imperial ideology in Western literary traditions, the current discussion aims to contextualize literary form within wider sociopolitical concerns that often lie outside of the colonial-anticolonial dialectic, which masks multiple other constructions of the self. I would like to claim metafiction as a politically invested textual practice central to a wide range of thematic and formal issues in African literature.

I find particularly useful Frederic Jameson's observation in "Third World Literature in the Era of Multinational Capitalism" (1986), that non-Western literature constitutes allegories of the state of the nation. While departing from Jameson's prioritization of allegory and nation as the key components of African literature, it is nevertheless productive to read literature as Jameson does—as the interpenetration of the individual self and the much wider collective consciousness.[20] An individual character's experience can be read as symbolic of the events taking place at a national level. This is why the allegorical elements that Jameson notes in his comparison of Western and "Third World" literatures in the era of global capital have become preeminent in the African novel. However, the well-forged isomorphic correspondence between contemporary African art and reality that Jameson's juxtaposition of the terms *allegory* and *nationalism* suggests is absent in metafiction; nor is metafictional literature as didactic and homiletic, in conformity with mainstream national morality, as Jameson's terms imply. It is ironic that, written in the mid-1980s at the height of feminism and poststructuralism, Jameson's misinterpretation of African literature arises mainly from his limited focus on foundational male socialist-realists authors, disregarding emergent women artists and writers operating outside of anti-Western socialism.

Buchanan (2006) has done an exemplary job of recuperating Jameson's notion of national allegory, indicating that Jameson is talking about a national aesthetic form as opposed to a nationalist ideology. Buchanan rightly disputes the idea that the proposition that non-Western writers are nationalistic lies at the center of Jameson's argument. While Jameson seems to be holding up the "Third World" writer's engagement in politics as a good example for the supposedly genteel and politics-averse Western artists and critics, he suggests that the writers deliberately occlude Western readers through the use of ideal readers that would be in radical variance with them. The ideal audience for Jameson's essay comprises Western theorists who collectively feel their (Western) canon is being written back to by an insular anti-Western literature. Contrary to Jameson's insinuation, however, some African literature is transnational in spirit, constantly questioning the validity of national boundaries and forging new alliances with categories that would be viewed as adversaries in nationalist and realist fiction.

The writers seem to be bending backwards to retain non-African audiences; for example, the move to call Ugandan words (Luganda language words, to be precise) "African words" in a glossary appended at the beginning of Moses Isegawa's national allegory *Abyssinian Chronicles* (2001) to explain the non-English words in the novel indicates that it is presuming not a non-Ugandan audience or Ugandan readers not conversant with the language spoken in the Buganda region but non-African readers. This is a novel that mocks the very notion of the nation, although it is set in a particular African nation and reproduces dates that serve as milestones in the construction of the Ugandan nation. Thus we might agree with Jean Franco who, in a study of South American literature, argues that the self-referential literature parodies and pillories the nation; for Franco, in a situation where modernity and repression are mutually enhancing, as in some of the nations governed by autocrats, the nation disappears as the "inevitable framework for either political or cultural projects" (1997, 130). The African metafictional novels, while inspired by specific national histories, are less likely to uphold parochial nationalism.

We should keep within our sights the overwhelming exceptions to Jameson's typology but also consider his view about the political imperative of African literature, which is purposely composed to interpret a certain reality, even if that reality does not conform to any nationalist ideology and does not have to be unitary. Jameson's emphasis on the centrality of form in the definition of African texts is pertinent despite the predominance of political and thematic readings of the African novel at the expense of aesthetics (ostensibly because African literature does not subscribe to art for art's sake). Although metafictional forms are not exclusively African, they have been used in African texts to generate meanings that relate to debates and conditions among the African peoples.

The same argument would apply to postmodernist texts; we should read them in terms of how they relate to and problematize the reality they evoke in their stylistic playfulness. As South African novelist and Nobel laureate Nadine Gordimer argues, even the most modernist and postmodernist art cannot be exempted from politics. In her 1988 essay "Three in a Bed: Fiction, Morals, and Politics," Gordimer sees the inevitability of a relationship between politics and literature:

> When, overtly or implicitly, could writers avoid politics? Even those writers who have seen fiction as the pure exploration of language, as music is the exploration of sound, the babbling of Dada and the page-shuffling of Burroughs have been in reaction to what each revolted against in the politically imposed spirit of their respective times; theirs were literary movements that were an act—however far-out—of acknowledgement of a relationship between politics and fiction . . . it seems there is no getting out of the relationship. (1999, 8)

For Gordimer, then, playful self-reflexive fiction ("fiction as the pure exploration of language") is in itself political. Gordimer's novels that use metafictional devices—beginning with her first novel *The Lying Days* (1953)—are intensely political in their self-reflexivity and play with language and in their references to the mechanics of artistic production and reception. The best metafictional novels from Africa use playful language to signify political conditions in society.

Stirling Grant also warns us against the minimalist pathologization of metafiction as mere narcissistic exercises in the "turning back of the self upon itself" (2000, 80). Grant wants us to see metafiction as more than an obsession with self; it is a form of defamiliarization that foregrounds the realities narrators inspire readers to recognize beyond the narrative. Postrealism has been seen as the staple of minority discourse and associated with nonlinear narratives by women writers and postcolonial subjects; it is regarded as a liberatory mode that disrupts the oppressive logic of realism. Persuasive as this argument may appear, it is hard to see a technique, in itself, as emancipatory. In the course of the discussion, I will demonstrate instances of metafictional excursions that would aid in entrenching stereotypes. What matters is the context in which metafictional techniques are employed.

In a deconstructive analysis of African artistic expression, Nigerian theorist Adélékè Adéèkó (1998) concludes that "irony, self-reflexivity, metafiction, strategic uses of conventions, the conventionality of strategies, and cultural hybridity are rhetorical apparatuses" (1998, 131). Adéèkó demonstrates that these modes of articulation are crucial markers and avenues of the political will in diverse African discourses. In this book I demonstrate that the narratives in African fiction pose the theoretical question of the relationship between fiction and reality in order to affirm at times protean and unfixed identity. Patricia Waugh's definition of metafiction is significant because it seeks to explain the social dimension of metafiction; to her, metafiction is "a fictional form that is culturally relevant and comprehensible to contemporary readers" (1984, 18). It can be best engaged by working out the historical and political circumstances that it signifies and that have given it impetus.

Nadine Gordimer (1999) has stated that even when art has to be political, it is not tendentious. She contends that "the transformation of the imagination must never 'belong' to any establishment, however just, fought for and longed-for" (1999, 15). Metafiction, as a transformed aesthetics, should be judged as an exercise in the kind of regenerative indirection that is expected in all sublime art. Novels that do not meet this criterion, however metafictional they may be, should be viewed as deficient as works of art. This seems to be the argument that Rey Chow presents in her discussion of nonrealist artistic projects in *The Age of the World Target* (2006), in which she draws upon a tradition within Marxism that goes back to Marx and Engel's distinction between art and propaganda in order to underscore the centrality of subtlety even to radical literature and aesthetics. In distinguishing artistic statement from political pronouncements, Marx and Engels startlingly insist on indirection as the key component of revolutionary art. Chow observes that in literature "the modus operandi is not to speak about something expressly even when one feels one must—[but to speak] in a manner quite opposite the clarity and forthrightness of rational argumentation" (2006, 54–55). The argument is not lost on the reader, despite the circumlocution that metafiction generates.

I read metafiction, then, as serving the intrinsic unpredictability of art championed by Chow and, in African literary theory, by Karen Press in "Building a National Culture in South Africa" (1990) and Njabulo Ndebele in *Rediscovery of the Ordinary* (1991). Press and Ndebele variously aver that contemporary African art's reluctance to follow a clearly realist mode or to serve an overt political program does not detract from its forcefulness as a political object. That is, the use of nonrealist modes is not a call for the abandonment of political engagement in favor of hermetic aestheticism. Ndebele underlines that "technique does not mean a rarefied, formal, and disembodied attempt at innovation for its own sake" (1991, 72). The artistic mode is a means of provoking the reader to reassess his or her experience of the world. Critical of fascism in all of its manifestations, Ndebele seems to agree with Walter Benjamin's "The Work of Art in the Age of Mechanical Reproduction" ([1936] 1992), that the forcefulness of a work of art resides less in the overt revolutionary message than in the way it reconfigures form to offer an aesthetic means of staging a new politics. In fact, African literature's departure from the habitualized modes of self-presentation, coupled with a stylistic search for self-renewal, makes it more effective in challenging society to view life from different perspectives. It is not the kind of figural experimentalism that Mario Sironi, an Italian painter and theorist under Mussolin's fascism, calls for in the "The Manifesto of Muralism" (2005). For Sironi, the avant-garde art would be used to support the populist government in power; in contrast, metafictional experimentation in African novels is largely used to demystify fascist and patriarchal projects. African writers are suspicious of government projects, and they conjure up a grassroots resistance against monolithic authorities via montage and artistic forms that blur established boundaries. Further, stylistic innovation does not disqualify self-reflexive art from a reader's materialist and revolutionary critique if the reader deems that to be the best way to engage the fiction. Indeed, the novels provoke, through their very structure, a politically engaged materialist reading.

Toward Post-Afrocentrism: Beyond an Edenic Africa

The argument that African literature writes back to itself in order to address issues of gender and sexuality calls for a transdisciplinary and an eclectic approach that can be termed *post-Afrocentric*. This is a form of discourse envisaged by Tejumola Olaniyan in *Scars of Conquest/Masks of Resistance* (1995) in which colonialism and imperialism are repudiated without precolonial Africa being romanticized as a site of perfection. Straddling Western traditions and African cultural practices in his study of theatre by artists of African descent, Olaniyan not only rejects the Eurocentric approaches to African theatre that denigrate cultural production from non-Western societies but also an Afrocentric position that sees "black aesthetics" as opposed to "white aesthetics." Echoing Bhabha, Olaniyan forges a third space that recognizes the inevitable interimplication between European and African forms and that sees literary production as a process that does not fossilize African literature into a static entity with a supposed culturalist leverage over other social categories. For Olaniyan, post-Afrocentricity distinguishes itself as "a singular insistence on unscrambling and supplanting the excessive Manichaeism that both constitutes the Eurocentric and undermines the subversive potential of the Afrocentric, while both affirming instead the foundational premise of an irreversible imbrication of histories, and therefore cultures and cultural forms" (1995, 4). This is to say that post-Afrocentricity occupies an in-between space in the opposed discourses while remaining vigilant against moves that would dehumanize Africa as a marginalized racial, political, and social category.

Looked at from an Afrocentric position, Olaniyan's formulation can easily be misinterpreted to mean the recuperation of Eurocentric modes or the sanitization of the colonial project. But like Afrocentricity, it is critical of the linear progressive categories of Enlightenment that shored up colonialism, without sparing African practices from critique. Post-Afrocentricity emphasizes "historical specificity . . . in a way that reveals hierarchy between the dominant discourse and counterdiscourse . . . but also emphasizes the most frequently related internal differences within each formation" (Olaniyan 1995, 27). Sandra Richards uses a similar model in the study of African and black diaspora theatre in which she does not seek to privilege Africa as a "site of pristine authenticity" vis-à-vis cultural production outside of Africa (1999, 101). Both Olaniyan and Richards usefully emphasize the importance of gender in post-Afrocentric analyses of black art. I complicate post-Afrocentric discourse further by incorporating in my discussion nonblack writers as part of African literature while retaining a gendered critique of Africanness.

In situating myself within post-Afrocentricity, I am following Edward Said, who argues that while there is a need to shift the academy away from Eurocentrism, it is invalid to replace Eurocentrism with essentialist and parochial positions. Said reminds us that the founding theorists of postcolonial theory, such as Fanon, were suspicious of unchecked nationalism and teleological mind-sets. Said calls for a postcolonial practice that focuses on a deethnicized transnational aesthetics:

> But our point, in my opinion, cannot be simply and obdurately to reaffirm the paramount importance of formerly suppressed or silenced forms of knowledge and leave it at that, nor can it be to surround ourselves with the sanctimonious piety of historical or cultural victimhood as a way of making our intellectual presence felt. Such strategies are woefully insufficient. The whole effort to deconsecrate Eurocentrism cannot be interpreted, least of all by those who participate in the enterprise, as an effort to supplant Eurocentrism with, for instance, Afrocentric or Islamocentric approaches. On its own, ethnic particularity does not provide for intellectual process—quite the contrary. (1991, 26)

Here, Said would prefer an approach to literature that exposes the atrocities of colonialism and neocolonialism while, like much African literature (especially that emerging from Anglophone Africa), accepting the culpability of societies in their own predicaments.

Though made in the post-structuralist and diasporic spaces of the Western academy, Olaniyan's, Richard's, and Said's warning against partisan presentations of a perfect Africa is not new in African literary studies. It is not only heard in South African Njabulo Ndebele's *The Rediscovery of the Ordinary* (1991), but also in the 1970s in indigenous black aesthetics critical circles in Africa. For example, at a black aesthetics colloquium held in Nairobi in 1971, historian Bethwell Allan Ogot argued that for spiritual rebirth and regeneration to happen in postcolonial Africa, black aesthetics should be based on self-awareness rather than self-deception that Africans are perfect vis-à-vis the colonizing cultures of the West. For Ogot, the "view that the African has no sins except those imposed on him by outside forces or their agents in Africa does not do justice to the African himself" (1973, 22). He says that writers and critics of African literature, then, should not promote through stereotypical images in art and its evaluation "the dangerous notion that the African is a creature more sinned against than sinning" (1973, 23).

Therefore, I do not have much sympathy for views such as the one expressed by Nigerian critic Oyekan Owomoyela, where he suggests that talking about the weaknesses in African societies would amount to "corroborating what colonizers had all along said about Africans, and, lately, chastising Africans for blaming all their problems on colonialism and its long-term effects, on neo-colonialism and economic imperialism, instead of accepting the fact of their own incompetence and moral corruption" (2008, 248). To me, Africans have always been criticizing the shortcomings in their own cultures. The fear of what imperialists would think about Africa should not be a major worry. Indeed, the defining characteristic of Anglophone African literature from its inception is its refusal to romanticize Africa, with anticolonial novels such as Achebe's *Things Fall Apart* (1958) also criticizing some of the indigenous practices in precolonial Africa. While I agree with Owomoyela that it would be wrong to entrench colonialist attitudes by showing Africans as inherently corrupt and incompetent, we need to guard against the fundamentalization of anti-Westernism to such an extent that we would be ready to deodorize injustices coming from within sections of the African societies.

Said (1991) further warns us that not all antihegemonic narratives are of equal value as literary texts. Although I analyze some texts that may not be considered classics of African literature, I consider them alongside masterpieces to reveal sublime moments in both groups of the texts. At the same time, I try to unmask some of the hegemonic positions that the texts take on issues of gender and sexuality. While Said tries to achieve his ends by discussing both "Third World" and European texts, I focus on African texts but show how they attempt to transcend local boundaries in a move to forge a sense of cosmopolitanism, even if their circulation is limited to small geographical spaces.

Contrary to the "writing back" orthodoxy that defines postcolonial studies, African literature is what it is not because it is non-Western but because it attempts to assert an autonomy for itself and the postcolonial subjects it figures in its narratives. This autonomy does not mean solipsism or exclusiveness. As we shall see in this discussion, the more localized the African text sometimes is, the more global it tends to be, even using modes that would be considered postmodern. Nor should nonlinkage to the West mean irrelevancy for African literature in Western academies; a literature does not necessarily have to refer to us directly to be of value to us as a community or as individuals. Even when the novels are not fixated on colonialism, they do not condone it or any other form of hegemonic control.

Yet a major problem in African literary studies is the exclusionary predisposition to define literary categories in terms of what they supposedly are not. This leads to the disregard of texts that do not deal directly with Western imperialism and colonialism, despite the fact that imperialism is indirectly represented in texts that do not overtly tackle it as a subject matter. Colonialism is so pervasive in African literature that it will be even where it is not. But once subjected to a Western gaze that seems to expect conformity, despite celebrating difference, the stylistics of African texts are seen to reside primarily in the way they deviate from European aesthetics, a typology that implies that European literature is the benchmark of value from which African texts must deviate to be of appreciable literary worth. While this approach to African literature appears liberating in its critique of colonial and neocolonial practices by the West, it is culturally patronizing and far from representative of arts emerging from Africa.[21] Little wonder that postcolonial theory as practiced in Western academies is, for better or worse, viewed with suspicion in institutions located in geographical areas whose literature the theory seeks to explain.[22]

Admittedly, comparative discussions of African literature are inevitable, especially because of the influence of the West and of English on world cultures and because, as Tejumola Olaniyan aptly notes, African writers "are indebted to Western categories of knowing," even when they seek to counter European epistemological categories (1995, 140). Despite the fear expressed by Aijaz Ahmed (1992) and Arif Dirlik (1994), that the use of postcolonial theory constitutes assimilation into a Western mind-set, discourse can never free itself from binary pairing; comparison and contrast of Africa with the West encroach upon all conversations as rhetorical strategies to emphasize a point of view.[23] But Asian comparativist critic Radhakrishnan is correct when he points out in *Theory in an Uneven World* (2003) that "in a world structured by dominance, comparisons are initiated in the name of those values, standards, and criteria that are dominant" (2003, 74). The émigré postcolonial theorists who dominate the study of Africa in the West have failed to challenge the axiomatized dominance of Western categories of knowledge, because they operate within the dominance of Western culture and seem almost completely incapable of looking at African literatures in their own right.

In their metafictional mode, African texts engage in a linguistically mediated examination of historical moments in society. Germane here is the Heideggerian view that the essence of a work of art is not its "representational" efficacy but its capacity to allow a disclosure of the world. While employing nonrepresentational techniques, African novels reveal certain "truths" about society, including some of the strategies employed to compound the silencing of certain uncomfortable truths. At the same time, because these revelations are not absolutely transparent, metafictional devices momentarily conceal certain truths and relay them to the reader with much more force and point, especially when historical contingencies are factored in during the interpretation of materials. As Gadamer says in his use of Heidegger, understanding is *wirkungsgeschictliches Bewußtsein* (historically effected consciousness). In responding both to African literature and to the way it is interpreted in Africa and elsewhere, it is appropriate to take into account the hermeneutic horizons within which the texts are created, circulated, and consumed, and how they also deviate from those horizons. Although we may not obtain from the texts a cut-and-dry definition of African literature—assuming anybody would desire that of such a diverse literary tradition—metafictional texts give us a sense of what they understand African literature to be. We hope by the end of this discussion that African literatures' self-definition will be apparent.

As I shall show in this discussion, the modern and the avant-garde are not necessarily un-African, as suggested by Achebe and Ngũgĩ in their essays of the 1970s. Discourses on authenticity work to disempower Africa and render it incapable of participating in modernity. Neither is the African novel necessarily realist as alleged by criticism of the 1970s. For instance, reading the fiction produced from the 1950s to the 1960s, Ugandan critic Shatto Arthur Gakwandi contends, in *The Novel and Contemporary Experience in Africa* (1977), that compared with avant-garde nonrealist writing, the realist novel is a far more appropriate mode for writing Africa. He concludes that "realism is the best instrument for analyzing individual behavior and the social patterns in a given society" (126). But the novel has changed to nonrealism as the avenues of realism become exhausted in apprehending the reality of emerging ideas on gender and sexuality. If the novels upon which Gakwandi focuses are probably "shy of experiment" (127), the novels of the 1980s and after tend to use language in a self-conscious manner to critique the nation as the most viable analytic concept and to expose the internal colonialism going on within a unitarian nationalist discourse. I show here that some of the novels from the time period that Gakwandi covers have an experimental strain that draws them toward metafiction, and it is in those moments of metafiction that gender inequalities and possibilities are presented to the reader.

Limits and Diversity

Over three decades since Wole Soyinka cautioned us in *Myth, Literature, and the African World* (1975) against reading African efforts at self-understanding as essentialist acts of negation, postcolonial critics continue to view non-Western literatures as projects in "writing back" to Europe. Soyinka's argument here is that each African culture is peculiar to itself, but it should not be seen as completely different from other cultures for the sake of showcasing its marginalization:

> The African world, like any other "world," is unique. It possesses, however, in common with other cultures, the virtues of complimentarity. To ignore this simple route to a common humanity and pursue the alternative route of negation is, for whatever motives, an attempt to perpetuate the external subjugation of the black continent. (1975, xii)

By "black Africa," Soyinka does not mean an identitarian category founded on skin pigmentation. Later in the book, he criticizes, as V.Y. Mudimbe (1988) has eloquently done, colonial inventions that failed to take into account that sub-Saharan Africa "is still a very large continent, populated by myriad races and cultures" (Soyinka 1975, 97). Throughout this book, I use Africa as a geographical space, not as a single racial category. Following Soyinka's skepticism toward authenticity and essentialism, involving the occlusion of a supposed opposite of Africa, I see the orthodox of "writing back to Europe" as a marginalizing gesture that ignores the African peoples' attempts to dialogue with one another. Despite its veneer of the celebration of resistance, the writing back orthodoxy is a mockery of claims to agency in African cultural production. I focus on metafictional texts because they resist the traditional boundaries between criticism and creative writing, picking up the raging critical debates to comment on or thematize their own compositional mechanics.

It is important to note that any book that seeks to discuss "the contemporary African novel" naturally risks not only overgeneralizing but also suggesting that "the novel" is a Western phenomenon that other cultures imitate or add to, a notion that has been criticized by Chow in *The Age of the World Target*. Chow unmasks the use of the generic term *the novel* to mean "English (and sometimes French) materials," while outside Western Europe the term is almost always invoked with a national or an ethnic qualifier (2006, 78). I am not using "the African novel" in an ethnic or a racial context; I use it as a marker of a body of works written by people of African origin, regardless of their biological race or ethnicity. Neither do I see the African novel as a deviation from (or an addition to) another transcendental category, *the novel*; contrary to conventional postcolonial theory, I do not assume that the African novel is the Other of the European novel, which does not need an ethnic qualifier because it is supposedly *the novel* proper. Therefore, while remaining post-Afrocentric, I try to avoid what Armah (1977) called "Larsony." This, according to Armah in a response to American scholar Charles R. Larson's reading of his novels in the early 1970s, involves interpreting African literature out of context in order to promote Western values and prejudices by making universalizing generalizations or by looking for Western sources for the admirable qualities in an African text.

Needless to say, African texts are too diverse to be comfortably lumped into a single category. Given the breadth of Africa and the diversity of its culture, it is impossible to do close readings of works that cover the whole continent in a single study. By focusing on East African materials in the context of a wider background of African letters, I also seek to undo this literature's relative marginalization in the discussion of African aesthetics. What is clear from the studies that have so far focused on gender and sexuality in Africa and on African postrealist fiction is that they limit themselves either to southern Africa, North Africa, or West Africa.[24] At a personal level, I am taking advantage of my knowledge of several East African languages to explain aspects of the text that may not be immediately clear to readers who do not speak these languages. However, I hope to avoid claims to nativist ontological and experiential advantage that Biodun Jeyifo warns us against in "The Nature of Things" (1990) because even East African literature is itself too diverse for any critic to claim nativist privilege, unless the critic is dealing with a narrow set of texts and authors, a choice that would be viewed, in Africa at least, as ethnocentric. By focusing on the singularity of individual texts within a wider political and cultural context, I hope to emphasize the particularities of the literatures and to avoid generalizations that mar the study of African literatures by taking a few texts as representative of the entire continent's arts.

Chapter 1

Genealogies and Functions of Self-Reflexive Fiction

This is not a search for the lofty origin of the metafictional in African novels. As Nietzsche posits, a pursuit that assumes an exact and a pure essence is impossible. There is no immanent and transhistorical moment in which African literature did not have metafictional components, and the rise of metafictional novels since the mid-1980s cannot be accounted for by a single, self-contained event. It is a product of a plethora of contradictions in which opposite forces (such as the growth of democratic ideals, on the one hand, and the doggedness of autocratic government resisting democratic change, on the other hand) produce similar results in the realm of culture—intensely self-reflexive fiction that openly flaunts its fictional status as art rather than a reflection of a fixed, transcendental reality. This chapter charts the genealogy of metafiction in the African novel and explains the political conditions that gave impetus to its proliferation. I try to locate the gendered dimensions of what David Attwell, in an astute reading of South African literature, calls "the experimental turn" (2006, 169).[1]

I demonstrate that metafiction is overdetermined, in similar terms to those envisaged by Althusser in *For Marx* (1969), by multiple factors dispersed throughout society, including but not limited to its economics and politics. This complex confluence of different forces, some of which are mutually contradictory, accounts for the explosion of metafictional texts; the trajectory of metafictional texts follows contradictory formations, which have nevertheless worked to augment one another in producing more self-reflexive fiction. In the metafictional excursions of African novels, the structural totality that Althusserian Marxism sees as the outcome of "overdetermination" is in the form of an ever-changing absolute dispersal and skepticism toward totality itself.

The augmentation of self-reflexive novels can be explained through an examination of the several developments of the 1970s: the change in the role of cultural nationalism, the improvement in literacy and purchasing power, the dissatisfaction with exclusion from the national canon, the collapse of

African nation-states and, finally, the growth of indigenous publishing, with its attendant use of local languages more closely linked to folklore, which continued into the 1980s.

I examine here the social functions that metafiction assigns itself as a form of political intervention, given that the changes in the canonizing and circulation networks in Africa are politically implicated and have contributed to changes in the self-reflexive tendencies more evidently seen in the literatures of the 1980s. To illustrate these heuristic claims, I respond to the metafictional elements in novels by Helon Habila, Nolizo Mareira, Moses Isegawa, David Maillu, and Francis Imbuga.

Decolonizing the Syllabus in the 1960s

Carol Sicherman (1995, 1997, 1998) offers historically astitute analyses of the developments in the curriculum change in East Africa from the colonial syllabus to a more African-based syllabus. I propose to see the the birth of metafiction in African novels to have started with the nationalistic endeavors to decolonize the syllabus and later to criticize the governments in a disguised way that would eschew censorship. Since the 1960s, the African academy has sought to offer literary courses relevant to local populations and to consciously decolonize the syllabus.[2] In the 1960s, the literature syllabi across Anglophone Africa were criticized for putting more emphasis on foreign (read Western) literature at the expense of texts from Africa, other parts of the developing world, and the Soviet Union This self-conscious literary nationalism that seeks to depose Western texts from positions of privilege and to monumentalize African texts has been the subject matter of many African novels since the 1970s, even when the novels are written in realist representational mode. For example, Ngũgĩ wa Thiong'o *Petals of Blood* (1977) and Nadine Gordimer's *The Lying Days* (1953)—two novels to which I return in some detail in the next chapter—are examples of the creative works that discuss the role of literature, the syllabus, and culturally astute interpretative skills in national politics. In Achebe's *A Man of the People* (1966), the corruption of the national leadership in Nigeria is equated with ignorance about the country's literature, while Westerners are laughed at for imposing their values on local art and African gestures to generate gross and sometimes sexually perverse interpretations.

Echoing the spirit of the Bandung Conference in 1955, in which Asian and African states resolved to be their own masters as opposed to puppets of the West, African universities sought to liberate the canon and the syllabus from Western domination and to establish a self-reliant method of analyzing local and foreign texts, emphasizing African American literature and arts from Asia, the Caribbean, and South America.[3] In Eastern Africa, Ngũgĩ wa Thiong'o, Taban lo Liyong, and Henry Owuor-Anyumba's initiative in the late 1960s to decolonize the canon at the University of Nairobi rapidly spread across the continent, with the literature departments offering more African-centered curricula. These theorists insist that their interest was not adversarial to Western culture; they sought to diversify the syllabus from a concentration of literary texts from a single cultural tradition. In an October 24, 1968, memo to the university authorities, entitled "On the Abolition of the English Department" and published as an appendix to Ngũgĩ's *Homecoming* (1972), Ngũgĩ and colleagues explain that the intention of the drive was to change the "basic assumption that the English tradition and the emergence of the modern West is the central root of our consciousness and cultural heritage" (Ngũgĩ 1972, 146).

More than once later, Ngũgĩ clarifies that the aim of the initiative "was not the abolition of English literature as such, but for the reorganization of the English departments so that they would properly reflect the realities of the twentieth century and the world" (1998, 107). In a 2004 lecture, he further argued that although theorists of African literature emphasized that the aim of the intervention was to get rid of the English Department, "we were calling for a reorganization of the teaching of literature so as to place Kenya, East Africa, and Africa at the centre of the literature syllabus, and then adding to that central concern Caribbean, African American, Latin American, Asian, and European literatures in that order—thus giving an African child the base from which to interact with the globe" (Ngũgĩ 2005, 63). Their position was not then founded on remonstrance against Western aesthetics but on a drive to make the syllabus more diverse, inclusive, and less Eurocentric.

With political decolonization in the 1960s and the consequent anticipated demand for local voices on the cultural and literary scene, publishers had to change their publication priorities. Metropolitan publishers operating in the African markets realized immediately that it would only be a matter of time before the call for the replacement of European colonial literature with an African canon reached a crescendo. The launching of the African Writers Series by Alan Hill of Heinemann Educational Books (London) in 1962 was one of the initiatives that tapped into a growing demand for African writing. The series was particularly effective in popularizing the emergent African novel internationally. The African market for these works comprised only a small percentage of the publisher's revenue.[4]

The African Writers Series produced educational novels tackling political and cultural themes. The canon in the early years of the African Writers Series was more or less nationalistic. A major theme in the early novels in the African Writers Series was colonialism and its effects on African cultures, with the novels published during the mid-1960s focusing on the disillusionment among Western-educated intellectuals with post-independence conditions in Africa. Novels in the series that did not primarily handle these grand themes were allowed to go out of print because they were not widely used in schools. As noted by Susan Z. Andrade, the novelistic genre was at this time dominated by male writers, and the women novelists in existence were overlooked because "novels by women were understood to be uninterested in politics" (2007, 87). Women's novels in the African Writers Series that seemed apolitical went out of print quickly, partly because they were not being accorded enough attention in academic circles.[5]

As its founding editor, Chinua Achebe guided the African Writers Series to produce some of the best-known novels from the continent. Its target market was African schools, with over 75 percent of its sales in African educational institutions. The market and the popularity of the series were fueled by newly established universities at Baden, Legion, and Makerere. The focus on school markets meant that manuscripts with educational themes would be preferred by the canonizing series. Under the rubric of the African Writers Series, canonical African writers such as Ngũgĩ, Alex la Guma, Wole Soyinka, Ayi Kwei Armah, Dennis Brutus, Gabriel Okara, Ama Ata Aidoo, Buchi Emecheta, Okot p'Bitek, and Meja Mwangi were to reach a wider readership.[6] Later in the 1990s, younger writers such as Nigerian Ben Okri were to reject the "African Writers" rubric, opting instead to be published by other metropolitan venues that did not have a special series for African writing. But the African Writers Series had such a canonizing force that incredibly talented writers published outside of the series, such as Abdulrazak Gurnah and Ben Okri, remained obscure in much of Africa despite their recognition in Europe and America.

The Nationalist Canon and Precolonial Art in the 1950s and 1960s

As Nigerian critic Emmanuel Obiechina notes in "Cultural Nationalism in Modern African Creative Literature" (1968), it is expected of any literature emerging from a colonial situation to be nativist. In this literature, according to Obiechina, "there is a fundamental assumption that the African had a civilization that was distinct from all other civilizations and which distinguishes him from all other human beings" (1968, 26).[7] Even when energetically critical of nativism and its essentializing tendencies, Kwame Anthony Appiah indirectly admits in "Topologies of Nativism" that there have been similar stances in other cultures emerging from matrixes of marginalization, as was the case in nineteenth-century Russia between Westerners and Slavophiles (Appiah 1992, 54). Published for educational purposes, the novels of the 1950s through 1960s and 1970s were nationalistic and tried, through a nativist sensibility, to reinstate the subjectivity of the African that colonialism had obliterated.

Even when disenchanted with the postindependence conditions of the 1960s, the writers were not antinationalist; rather, they bemoaned the failure of the nationalist dream. Powerful works in this category include Achebe's *Things Fall Apart* (1958) and Ngũgĩ's *The River Between* (1965), which portray in a realist mode the weaknesses and strengths of precolonial Africa. In Achebe's words, the African writer was attempting to educate the newly independent people about "where the rain began to beat us" (Achebe 1975, 44). Achebe insists that the writer should be at the forefront in helping the community regain its dignity:

> African people did not hear of culture for the first time from Europeans; that their societies were not mindless but frequently had a philosophy of great depth and value and beauty; that they had poetry and above all, they had dignity. It is this dignity that many African people all but lost during the colonial period and it is this that they must regain. The worst thing that can happen to any people is the loss of their dignity and self-respect. The writer's duty is to help them regain it by showing them in human terms what happened to them, what they lost. There is a saying in Ibo that a man who can't tell where the rain began to beat him cannot know where he dried his body. The writer can tell the people where the rain began to beat them. (1973, 8)

By invoking a proverb talking about the beginning of a traumatic event ("where the rain began to beat them"/"where the rain began to beat us"), Achebe tries to restore the verbal art of the Ibo community that modernity has threatened with erasure. But at the same time, he indicates that there were adversities before colonialism in the sense that this proverb predates colonialism. *Things Fall Apart*, the novel Achebe is explaining in this authorial statement, sympathetically shows the many problems the Igbo culture faced before colonialism, including disease, droughts, ritual homicides, and internecine wars. The folk stories that the narrative presents, such as that involving a tortoise that broke its shell as a result of a fall from the skies, indicate that society had its share of "things falling apart" before colonialism. But it had a mechanism of bringing the things together without necessarily achieving an originary harmony. Thus Achebe has no intention to claim precolonial Africa as a perfect paradise. Rather, he wants to show that colonialism exacerbated tensions within a society already in motion toward an indigenous modernity. Through the figures of the philosopher, artist, and organic critic, such as Obierika, Unoka, and Nwoye, respectively, Achebe shows that some members of the society were questioning some of the practices this society privileges, indicating that even before colonialism, the Igbo were at the cusp of questioning their own shortcomings.

In their theoretical essays, Achebe and Ngũgĩ variously seem suspicious of modernist experimentation, which they view as a luxury only a Western writer—celebrating individualism and alienation from society—can afford.[8] In the 1990s, Soyinka was to bemoan, especially in the essay critiquing nativist demands as joining the state in stifling art, prescriptive criticism that devalued art outside of the realist tradition. He sees this kind of criticism as suppressing "forms of literature, or other art forms that may represent reality outside the glossy brochure of the state" (Soyinka 1993, 221). Without necessarily endorsing postmodernist experimentation, both Ngũgĩ and Achebe have expressed admiration for the experimental work of Ben Okri. They have also written metafictional novels since the 1980s, even if they have not endorsed postmodernism.

In the texts produced in the 1950s and 1960s, colonialism is seen as having destroyed the integrated precolonial societies and caused alienation and anguish in the colonial subject. Waiyaki, in Ngũgĩ's *The River Between*, is caught between tradition and modernity, and his attempts to synthesize the two modes of living almost destroy him. The novel's sense of tragedy lies in the character's failure to integrate modernity into African traditions in a society that is still polarized despite the desire for the synthesis of cultural values. This novel also captures the weaknesses of the precolonial Gĩkũyũ society, such as discrimination against women, female genital mutilation, the rejection of its own prophets, and the perennial internecine wars between precolonial communities. Achebe's *Things Fall Apart* also shows that despite colonialism's perniciousness, the African societies contributed to their own disintegration, especially in the way they treated the marginalized sectors of the society. Stylistically, the novels employed folkloric techniques such as song interludes, proverbs, and oral narratives, displaying the beauty of indigenous oral literature and the role of the arts and artists in precolonial Africa.

While the foundational novelists attempt to establish a unitary identity for all Africans, an identity that is threatened by colonial modernity, their works also metafictionally signal how art can be misused by dominant groups to compound the marginalization of the more powerless members of a disempowered community. In *The River Between* (1965), Ngũgĩ presents circumcision songs that regeneratively break down the boundaries between age sets and genders as the society prepares a young generation for transformation into adulthood. But it is also through myths that some of the hegemonic practices in these societies are shored up. For instance, the discrimination against Gĩkũyũ women is rationalized through narratives that present women as poor managers of livestock and oppressive leaders. In the novel, the principal character's father inducts him into manhood through narratives of the tribal nation that justify the economic marginalization of women. One of the myths even claims that wild animals were once women's domesticated livestock, but the women could not manage them. From the man's patriarchal perspective, women are dictatorial and would make poor leaders (15). Through the chauvinistic enunciations of a sympathetically drawn character, Chege, Ngũgĩ subtly indicates the potential abuse of traditions by even progressive characters to roll back freedoms of the disempowered in Gĩkũyũ culture.

It is also through orature in the form of circumcision songs that women are compelled to express their support for female genital cutting. The novel presents them as dancing with grace in support of their own oppression. The songs present the subaltern speaking through her body and voice to aggrandize her own marginalization in a patriarchal society. This is best captured in the women's participation in the literary components of the ceremony:

> Men shrieked and shouted and jumped in the air as they went round in a circle. For them, this was the moment. This was the time. Women, stripped to the waist, with their thin breasts flapping on their chests, went round and round the big fire, swinging their hips and contorting their bodies in all sorts of provocative ways, but always keeping the rhythm. (41)

Ironically, the songs are not mere expressions of the women's masochistic collusion with patriarchy but enunciations of positive agency as well; Muthoni has rebelled against her Christian fundamentalist father to undergo a tribal rite of passage.

Muthoni is not alone in the sense that the novel notes that some of the girls participating in this event have perhaps run away from parents who are opposed to female circumcision. The oral art creates an illusion of freedom, in which women feel as if they have become emancipated by deconstructing racial hierarchies and the "otherwise strong cultural code" (41). They are unaware that this deconstruction is only a one-night event to be followed by a lifetime of pain and perhaps death, as happens to Muthoni. The carnivalesque discourse, implied by Achille Mbembe's deployment of Bakhtin's notion of the subversive power of Menippean aesthetics, deconstructs colonial power in African self-fashioning—but in this instance it also intensifies the enslavement of the subaltern, especially the female who thinks she achieves self-fulfillment through genital cutting. Ngũgĩ's narrative thus "writes back" to colonial laws that arrogantly banned local practices such as initiation rites, but the story also criticizes the use of art to silence women in precolonial cultures.

Important to note is that the European missionaries opposed to female genital cutting are not interested in empowering African women but in fighting what they consider pagan practices that have no biblical parallels. They are using the ploy noted by Partha Chatterjee in *The Nation and Its Fragments*, whereby the Europeans present themselves as chivalrous saviors out to liberate the colony's women from its oppressive males but are indeed only interested in entrenching and rationalizing imperial domination (1993, 622). Spivak exposes a similar colonist gambit in "Can the Subaltern Speak?," where British colonialists who ban oppressive traditional practices see themselves as "white men saving brown women from brown men" to legitimize a different and harsher form of repression of the local subjects (1985, 121). Spivak's variant repetition, in close proximity, of phrases in scare quotes contrasting "white men" and "brown men" as supposed liberators and oppressors of Indian women, respectively (Spivak 1985, 121, 127), rhetorically underlines her indignation at the exploitation of the plight of women by colonialism to justify the subjugation of the Global South. Her rhetorical repetition also signifies that while she would welcome any move that unshackles women from indigenous oppression, she is all too aware that the white men have no interest in liberating Indian women; they are invested in wresting power from Indian men for the purposes of entrenching European hegemony in the colonized world.

In the context of Ngũgĩ's *The River Between,* the missionaries are more interested in imposing their religion on the Africans; they have no primary interest in women's welfare. It is for this reason, perhaps, that the novel makes Muthoni die from her genital wound, even when she is taken to a modern missionary hospital for treatment. The novel makes us dissociate ourselves from Joshua, Muthoni's Christian father, for his failure to bless the girl before circumcision as required of him by tradition. It is both Joshua's negligence of his parental duties and the failure of colonial modernity to liberate women despite its pretensions to modernizing Africa for the Africans that would account for Muthoni's death.

Local Resistances to the Nationalist Canon in the 1970s

In the heady days of postindependence nationalism of the 1960s and 1970s, African art had to be "serious," and supposedly mundane topics such as sex were therefore suppressed in favor of grander nationalist themes, such as decolonization. Works that deviated from this norm would be regarded as unfit to be read in polite society. But the radical anti-neocolonialism novels that Neil Lazarus (1990) notes to have characterized the 1970s were accompanied by works that sought to be different from the canonical political novels. David Maillu playfully named one of his texts *Unfit for Human Consumption* (1973b), and another of his works advertised in its title that it is about the *Kommon Man* (1975), complete with a misspelling, to align itself against the university-educated elites.

The indigenous publishing that thrived in the 1970s was to provide an alternative canon, especially in Nigeria, Ghana, and Kenya. This popular literature was primarily for local audiences and focused on more day-to-day experiences such as romance, robberies, and poverty in urban centers. While cultural nationalism helped expand the body of works thought worth reading in schools and for social and political regeneration, the canon's scope still fell largely within the parameters of anticolonial nationalism; the texts studied in school remained those that treated the theme of colonialism, the liberation struggle, and the aftermath of flag independence. When attention was paid to style, the interest was limited to how the novels approximated precolonial expression as a form of symbolic resistance to the colonial canon.

In contrast, literature of a nonpolitical nature was rarely studied as part of African literature; it was seen as foreign, even when there was nothing alien about it, and even when it was published by back-street publishers without as many links to the West as the Western-published anticolonial novels by Achebe, Ngũgĩ, and Sembene Ousmane.[9] Because of the power of the academy when it comes to canonizing and monumentalizing art, only the heavily anticolonial texts have been accessible to the Western-based postcolonial theorists of African literature. Meanwhile, the marginalized novels and writers tried to resist this nationalist canon by parodying it; it is no wonder that Okot p'Bitek's *Song of Lawino* (1966)—a long, dramatic poem about the conflict between African traditions and modernity that is powered by a call to restore vanishing African traditions—spawned imitations, some of which were sexually lurid. A case in point here is Maillu's dramatic poems such as *The Kommon Man* (1975), *After 4:30* (1974), and *My Dear Bottle* (1973a), which, though quasi-nationalistic, are more focused on mundane issues such as prostitution, crime, and drunkenness. The novels of disillusionment were accompanied by narratives of urban culture in which the writers, while not nostalgic about rural life, presented the challenges of the city, such as rising crime rates and slum life. The contrast between the city and the village was emphasized, with the writers drawing attention to the characters' acceptance of their uprootment from their rural origins. The figure of the prostitute, symbolizing the nation, is a recurrent motif in these novels that also capture the problems of urbanization and the tension between the city and the rural life.[10]

Further, the 1970s witnessed more publishing opportunities in sub-Saharan Africa. The newly independent governments set up publishing units to produce educational materials. The national universities set up in the 1960s, at the onset of independence, were also bearing fruit; the locally trained graduates were not only venturing into writing but also providing a market for books. The enrollment in colleges shot up dramatically in the 1970s to over 600,000 in 1980. By 1995, the figure more than doubled to 1.75 million in 1995 (Mama 2005, 98). The universities were more regional and national than universal in their political and intellectual orientation. This translated into the demand for, and the consequent production of, a literature that was more inward-looking, as opposed to the universalist colonial literatures affecting cosmopolitanism while promoting European interests. Emphasizing this spirit of autonomy, indigenization, and nationalist anticolonial aesthetics, Chinua Achebe complained in a 1974 essay, "Colonialist Criticism," about the Eurocentric use of the term *universal*, "as though universality is a bend in the road which you may take if you travel out far enough in the direction of Europe or America, if you put adequate distance between you and your home" (Achebe 1975, 9). He rejected the term in the "discussions of African literature, until such a time as people cease to use it as a synonym for the narrow, self-serving parochialism of Europe" (1975, 13).[11] However, in the monumentalizing critical texts by indigenous theorists, the *local* and the *antiuniversalist* art was largely seen to be anticolonial and nationalist because of the urgent work that had be done to correct the distortions that colonialism had caused in African nations.

The oil boom in Western Africa and the coffee boom in East Africa during the 1970s, not to mention rising rates of literacy, created a market for locally published, popular books that, though sometimes political, were more interested in such mundane issues of life as romance, sex, crime adventures, unemployment, and prostitution. The popular literature of the 1960s and 1970s, which was largely produced by small publishers without much of an international network, and which targeted unsophisticated local readership, displays metafictional impulses that signal the lived experiences and contradictions in society. The novels indicated an awareness of their low artistic qualities. They playfully registered their recognition of a lack of sophistication in their own narratives, mocking the reader for reading socially unsanctioned literature, especially because the books were published on poor paper and were badly bound.[12]

A case in point is Maillu, who between 1973 and 1977 churned out popular small volumes that portrayed the sleaze, corruption, and urban problems in the 1970s. Unlike writers such as Achebe, Ngũgĩ, and Ousmane, Maillu's work was self-published and was read clandestinely because of its tendency toward pornography and escapism.[13] Some of the books were small in size and could be carried easily to work to be read surreptitiously. Maillu explains in an interview in Bernth Lindfors's *Africa Talks Back* (2002) that the smaller size was to shield the reader from the inconveniences of the larger volumes circulating from more established outlets: "As an artist, I liked it in the sense that it's a handy book that you can put in your shirt pocket. It doesn't feel like a book at all. Having educated myself, which meant having to carry lots of books around, I found larger sizes very impractical" (Lindfors 2002, 158). Trivial as physical size may appear in considering the efficacy of a work of art, Maillu's mini-novels write back to the "big" African books by coupling metafictionality with sexual presentations to signify the rottenness and emasculation of the nations in the 1970s.

In "East African Popular Literature in English," Lindfors notes that Maillu's books are not only "topical and moralistic, [but] they teach as they entertain" (1979, 113). However, because of their sensational nature, Maillu's novels were not canonized by the African academy and were seen in certain quarters as perverted. Like his other works in this series, *No!* (1976) self-consciously mocks its readers for reading it in government offices instead of doing their work. Strikingly, Maillu's justification for writing racy fiction, probably for money, is through a sexual metaphor: "Maillu's literary products are not necessarily profit-motivated. The author himself has quipped that if a man met a very rich and beautiful girl and married her, people who see her do not remember that he married her for her beauty; they will always say that he married her for her riches" (Wanjala 1980b, 23).

In *No!*, a melodramatic mini-novel about abuse of office, corruption, violence, and sex, Maillu not only shows how self-reflexivity can be an unproductive, narcissistic, and hedonistic act in an individual character, but also how a similar self-awareness can be a regenerative narrative project. The story is farcical and contains an equally absurd story within a story, but the readers of the fictional ludicrous narratives read and interpret them seriously. One of the stories within the story criticizes similar stories that people are reading in offices, instead of performing their civil service duties. This signals to the actual readers, who could be doing similar things to the unethical readers in the stories, that they have not been invited to be participants in a farce; the frame story is meant to be taken as a serious indictment of a society that critiques its own cavalier playfulness. In the novel, farcical and narcissistically self-reflexive characters are doomed to death, while the novel itself uses a narrative within a narrative to validate its claim and to counter the monolithic structure of power that signifies the pervasive moral despondency in the East Africa of the 1970s. Published in the popular Comb series, which capitalized on the coffee boom of the

1970s, the novella is a potboiler about sexual exploits in a degraded civil service. The narrative is as vulgar as its characters and the story within a story that it carries.

Simple in execution, *No!* is the story of Washington Ndava, an immoral senior civil servant who not only cheats on his wife but also sleeps with the spouse of his subordinate, Mbithi. He is caught in Mbithi's house and attacked viciously in a dramatic scuffle that witnesses the loss of his ear and penis. The narrative stages a number of intensely metafictional acts. The short story about Dikison Ngoloma that Janifa, Ndava's wife, reads as her husband leaves for the fatal sexual orgy, replicates the life of immorality led by Ndava, whom the novella proper is about. Diki of the story within the story parallels Washington of the novell. There are many other parallels: Telesia, Diki's wife, in the embedded story replicates Janifa; Sofi reflects Brigita while the crying babies in reality and fiction, Ndinda and Ndindi, respectively, echo each other. This playful establishment of a relationship of mutual similitude between the novella and its embedded narrative serves to strengthen the novella's claim about the corruption and ineptitude of a bloated civil service.

In the novel, Ndava is self-conscious in a narcissistic, self-destructive way. The novella launches the narrative by declaring him "an artist of life" (7). He views existence as an art where one creates the illusion of respectability only in order to cheat on one's spouse and to steal from public coffers without being discovered. He speaks English with an exaggerated self-consciousness that embarrasses even native speakers of the language: "He loved employing very unusual words, such as *meritorious, heterodox, precocious, jocund, reconnoiter*, and so on" (8). These words are empty expressions with only an ironical relationship to the conditions in the society presented, where anomalous, aberrant, and uncreative practices are the order of the day—especially in Ndava's civil service:

> That was the game in most of the civil service offices—drinking tea, hugging women, knitting, gossiping, reading papers, talking politics, and spending hours and hours talking about opportunities and business. The best place to work when you are lazy is in the civil service, being a government servant. (37)

This is veiled as a statement from a magazine short story that Janifa, Ndava's wife, is reading when her husband goes off to Mbithi's house. The story underscores the vulgarity and helplessness of ordinary people in a country whose civil service is crumbling as they watch.

The futility of self-aggrandizement in a morally decayed society is expressed through Ndava's suicide and through the sense of inaction that governs the society. Wives in the novella and in the story within the story know that they are being cheated on but can do nothing about it. Mbithi, the junior civil servant, is fully aware that his boss is corrupt and that he sleeps with his wife, but he cannot report him to the authorities because that would create more problems for him. The novella seems to be calling for a shift from accepting the single voice of the government by instantiating other voices that complement each other to end corruption and immorality.

Indigenous Publishing and Literature in Local Languages

In a 1989 essay entitled "From the Corridors of Silence," Ngũgĩ gives a rough outline of African literatures from the 1950s to the 1980s, forecasting a growth of writing in local languages if the literature is to come out of what he considers its "linguistic exile." For Ngũgĩ, African literature before the 1980s is trapped in a prison because, like its imprisoned and exiled writers, the literature is not accessible to the indigenous majority. Emerging from the era of disillusionment of the 1960s into a period of struggle to reconnect art to the desires of the majority, African writers in the 1970s and 1980s are, in Ngũgĩ's view, more optimistic in tone but "hampered by the very linguistic prison they had been thrown into by their colonial legacy" (Ngũgĩ 1993, 108). Ngũgĩ sees the literature of the 1990s to be interested in breaking out of the "linguistic prison" through their use of indigenous languages and consequent accessibility to the nonliterate majorities (Ngũgĩ 1993, 108). The writers have not necessarily adopted the Marxist utopia that Ngũgĩ prophesies here, and a lot of literature emerging from Anglophone Africa from the 1980s is still in English, with the poet Susan Kiguli using the image of the mother tongue in her poetry in English as a metaphor for women's automated acceptance of oppressive patriarchy. However, the growth of writing in indigenous languages, though not as intensive as Ngũgĩ would want, has contributed to the self-reflexivity of the texts.

I return to a reading of Kiswahili novels in Chapter 3, but let it suffice here to note that the economic and political pressures of the 1980s saw the establishment of local branches of multinational publishing firms, the rise of new publishing units, and the collapse and merger of publishing companies. Official records indicate that in 1983 there were 818 publishers in Africa, but according to publishing scholar Ruth Makotsi (1988), the figure could be as high as 4,000, of which 50 percent are commercial publishers. These publishing venues, such as East African Educational Publishers, which is an offshoot of Heinemann, published novels in local languages alongside works in English.[14] The literature in local languages complemented books published by missionary presses since the beginning of the twentieth century, but its main focus was not to celebrate Christian modernity by combating what missionaries considered African superstitions. Rather, the indigenous-language literature of the 1980s aligned itself with African traditional cultures and was critical of Western practices in Africa. Published by private firms, the literature was, unlike the earlier realist and nationalistic vernacular literatures produced by state and missionary presses since the 1950s, critical of the nation-state.[15] While the colonialists and missionaries had promoted publishing in local languages since the 1910s, writers such as Ngũgĩ and Zimbabwean Charles Mungoshi were to retrieve the languages from the ghetto they had been relegated to as tools of balkanizing the continent along ethnic lines. Although he had turned to English to avoid ethnic ghettoization by the colonial government in the 1970s, Mungoshi translated Ngũgĩ's *A Grain of Wheat* in Shona in the 1980s to valorize the Zimbabwean war of independence that most white settler writers had demonized as an act of terrorism and anarchy.

In the same period, women writers started focusing more on gender issues in their writing. The level of literacy among women had risen appreciably, and the internationalization of the feminist movement was beginning to have an effect on African literature. With the Women's Decade summit taking place in Africa in 1985, gender was to become a central issue for both male and female writers. Nonrealist techniques would become particularly useful in the gendered interventions for women's rights because, as María Ruth Noriega Sánchez has noted in her study of magical realism, the nonrealist techniques are invested in "a political dimension and subversive potential" that is useful to women writers, especially minority women, who want to express their marginality while at the same time challenging their exclusion from mainstream politics and culture (2002, 31). For Sánchez, women writers find nonrealist forms "a suitable literary mode to convey the contradictions and complexities of their lives, which realism cannot adequately contain" (2002, 32). Thus the 1980s witnessed a tendency toward the use of metafiction as a means of challenging the conventional perception of history, unsettling the understanding of reality and offering the possibility of radically changing the social realities that marginalized important sections of society.

Some male writers' attempted, with varying degrees of success, a departure from the traditional subordination of women's issues to nationalistic loyalties. The preoccupation with using cultural nationalism to address Western readers in the 1960s subsided in the 1970s and 1980s, and the literature became more and more self-reflexive. Literature in the local languages borrowed more directly from oral literature. Ngũgĩ's *Caitaani Mũtharaba-inĩ* (1980), translated as *Devil on the Cross* (1982), not only uses the polyphonic Gicaandi artist to structure its narrative but also examines, by gesturing toward the narrator's unreliability, the gendered implications of a male artist telling a woman's story. In the most intensely metafictional moment in the novel, it equates itself with a futuristic oral composition by its character Gatuĩria, a composition in which the multiple desires of the nation are to be voiced. It is to be remembered that Gatuĩria is an alienated student of Western music, but as long as he uses the knowledge he acquired in the West for emancipatory purposes, he is seen as an important force in fighting injustices in Africa. Thus the national oratorio he intends to produce approximates the novel more closely than the indigenous Gichaandi performance that the frame narrator produces in the novel.[16]

In Ngũgĩ's metafictional prose in Gĩkũyũ, the artist characters—such as the Gicaandi narrator and Gatuĩria in *Caaitani Mũtharaba-inĩ* and Nyawira in *Mũrogi wa Kagogo* (2004) [*Wizard of the Crow*]—either speak the indigenous language with a foreign accent or articulate their positions in hybrid languages that demolish the boundaries between nation-states in the Global South. Even if, based on criticism of African literature, it might appear as though the Africanness of the literature resides in its thematic and stylistic tensions with European literature, stories written in local languages, such as Grace Ogot's *Miaha* (1983a) [*The Strange Bride*] and *Simbi Nyaima* (1983b), address issues other than colonial conflict in narratives that are more inward-looking in their examination of gender issues. Even during the colonial era, while foundational works in English addressing Europeans were sometimes radically oppositional in relation to Europe, writers in African languages were incidentally more moderate, urging their readers, in a language the colonialists were supposed to not understand, to take advantage of European modernity. This was probably because the writers, trained in missions, were very much part of the European library.

Disillusionment Unabated

It is apparent that even the most dictatorial regimes in Africa, such as that of Robert Mugabe in Zimbabwe since 1980, have been overwhelmingly popular with the indigenous populations because of their invocation of anticolonial rhetoric. Writers have tried to educate the people to come out of the nationalistic mold by demoting anticolonial themes and drawing parallels between the present condition and colonialism. Even the apartheid regime in South Africa is spared blame from all of the problems in the new democracy. Like literatures that emerged from newly independent sub-Saharan African nations in the late 1960s and 1970s, postapartheid literature contains a sense of disillusionment with the emergent dispensation of wealth. The black communities are still mired in poverty, and various forms of crime are on the rise. There is no nostalgia for apartheid days, but the texts depict unhappy moments in which the new dispensation is still oppressive to certain categories in society. What marks the South African novel of disillusionment from its equivalent in sub-Saharan literature are the overtly self-reflexive techniques through which it presents a desire for more freedoms and fear of new forms of hegemony. Written in an age of poststructuralism and intense globalization, the novels self-consciously acknowledge other novels of disillusionment from the rest of the continent and the novels of liberation in South Africa. Novels by Nadine Gordimer, Zakes Mda, J. M. Coetzee, Andre Brink, Ahmad Essop, Mike Nicol, Phaswane Mpe, Christopher Hope, and Achmat Dangor present the compromised freedom in much more self-reflexive terms than similar novels from the rest of the continent, where this sense of disillusionment started earlier.[17]

Brenda Cooper and Maggie Ann Bowers are among the scholars of nonrealist fiction who have suggested that the nonrealist style offers the writer leeway to criticize authoritarian regimes and eschew the censors. Cooper perceptively observes that a nonrealist fictional mode of expression such as magical realism "at its best opposes fundamentalism and purity; it is at odds with racism, ethnicity, and the quest for the tap roots, origins, and homogeneity" (1998, 22). The mode has been put to use to depict and undermine the totalitarianism of dictatorial regimes in Africa and to disrupt nationalistic and gender chauvinism. The end of the Cold War in the 1980s ushered in an unprecedented wind of change in African nations. The period witnessed a rise in demand for political accountability, pressure for an end to authoritarian, one-party states, and a clamor for more democratic space. Most of the governments gave in to this pressure, but despite their embrace of the rhetoric of liberal democracy, they remained authoritarian while claiming to allow competition in order to reduce accountability. Termed "semi-authoritarian" by political scientist Marina Ottaway (2003), these regimes are extremely dangerous to freedom of expression because they allow a free press to function to some extent to encourage the existence of rival political parties and to allow a semblance of dissenting voices while keeping a close eye on any radical political formations. Under such political circumstances, authors would be innovative as they exploited new freedoms, but at the same time they used experimental techniques to eschew the authoritarian side of Janus-faced governments paying lip service to democracy while abusing its most basic tenets.[18]

The desire for a pluralistic government was expressed through narratives that were multifaceted and plurivocal in their structure. For instance, written in Gĩkũyũ and borrowing from oral literature and community theatre techniques, Ngũgĩ's novel *Caitaani Mũtharaba-inĩ* (1980, *Devil on the Cross*, 1982) signifies in its very structure the societal desire for a break from authoritarian rule. Although his *A Grain of Wheat* (1967) and *Petals of Blood* (1977) display intensely multivocalized narrative perspectives in which the events are relayed to the reader through the consciousness of multiple characters, *Caitaani Mũtharaba-inĩ* is much more plural and open-ended in its incorporation of characters' voices, presenting itself as a collectivity of voices making up a society struggling against neocolonial exploitation.

By the late 1960s, the sub-Saharan African governments were rolling back the freedoms promised at independence earlier in the decade. When Wole Soyinka explained, in a paper entitled "The Writer in a Modern African State," presented at the African-Scandinavian Writers' Conference held in Stockholm in 1967, that writers from already-independent nations could indeed envy South African writers under apartheid because the latter, despite the bleak conditions in which they operated, had "still the right to hope" (1968, 15), he underlined the sense of disappointment with the political dispensation in the newly independent nations. At least the South African writer had hoped that conditions would improve after apartheid was dismantled, but the writers in the independent nations had come to realize that there was no substance in the constitutional independence of the nations. Governments were trampling underfoot the rights of the majority.

It is this sense of disillusionment, disappointment, and hopelessness in the face of a failed nation-state that is characterized by murders, injustice, rape, and human rights abuse—a common sentiment since the mid-1960s—that a character in Francis Imbuga's play about a miniature play within a play of the same title, *Betrayal in the City* (1976), captures.[19] In the play, Mosese, an intellectual jailed on trumped-up charges because of his political involvement against a postindependence dictatorship, explains the bleak circumstances facing the nation by invoking the earlier days of adversity when there was hope that conditions would improve:

> It was better while we waited. Now we have nothing to look forward to. We have killed our past and are busy killing the future. Sometimes I sit here and look far into the past. There I see my mother slaughtering the biggest family cock. Once every year she slaughtered a senior cock to mark the birth of Christ. Our children will never have such memories. Now there is blood everywhere. Cocks are slaughtered any day, many times a week. (Imbuga 1976, 33)

The ultimate sovereignty of the African government as presented in the play is the power to destroy and imprison bodies, especially the bodies of intellectuals challenging the government's legitimacy. Opening and ending the play with a scene at an antigovernment playwright's graveside, Imbuga frames the succession of scenes in the play where state hoards shoot at an unarmed public and force some citizens, including the fictional playwright, into the ultimate subjection of death. In a context of absolute intolerance, violence, and incarceration of intellectuals, Imbuga's play survived the censor by presenting itself as not a piece of writing but as a jocular drama about another play that never sees the light of day. The highly accomplished play remained in the school syllabus well into the 1980s and influenced younger writers who used the novel within a novel technique, as Imbuga did with the play within a play technique, to handle political themes and to eschew retaliation from the government. Although ideologically naïve and transparently realistic in their presentation of an artist's struggles toward a bourgeois stature and/or recognition by the male national and corporate leadership, the *Künstlerroman* attempts by David Karanja (*The Girl Was Mine*), Stephen Mugambi (*Wait for Me Angela*), and Wairimu Kibugi (*Painful Tears*), which all use the novel within a novel technique, are more likely to have been influenced by the play within a play theatre by Imbuga, Athol Fugard, and John Ruganda than by postmodern or magical realist aesthetics.

As seen in Imbuga's play *Betrayal in the City*, the 1960s and 1970s were decades of disillusionment with constitutional independence, unaccompanied by the expected substantial freedoms and economic amelioration. Emmanuel Obiechina observes that the most outstanding feature of the novels written in this period is the "uncompromising way their authors attack the post-independence elite in Africa" (1990, 123). Poverty, poor governance, coups, and countercoups in the first decade of independence had taught the African writer a lesson in not being too hopeful about the capacity of the African elites leading the countries to a better life. The radicalization of the African academy in the 1970s also saw the production of literature that was scathing in its criticism of the state, as well as of the intellectual community that had failed to expose the weaknesses of the state.

Frantz Fanon's theory of neocolonialism is reflected in some of the novels coming out of the 1960s and the 1970s, even if their authors do not necessarily adopt Fanon's model of violence as the way out of the crises or do not focus on trauma and psychological details. Writing in the early postindependence era, Fanon (1925–1961) provides a powerful and preconscious explanation of the betrayed freedom that African states experience at the hands of the new leaders. In *The Wretched of the Earth* (1963), Fanon presages a local elite that, in an attempt to outdo the former European colonizer in exploiting local populations, employs cruder forms of repression than the classic colonialist.[20] Well into the 1980s, some novelists influenced by Fanon expressed that sense of disappointment with the new leadership, comparing colonialism to the brutalities and corruption of the new leadership.[21]

Suffice it to note that even before the death of Nigerian poet Christopher Okigbo in combat during the Biafra war of the late 1960s, a death that became the subject of novels such as Ali Mazrui's *The Trial of Christopher Okigbo* (1971), the writers were aware of the role of the artist and the student of literature—and the constraints facing them—in changing the sorry state of African nations.[22] Achebe's *A Man of the People* (1966) bemoans the use of the carnivalesque discourses of orature to entrench dictatorship in Nigeria, while his *Anthills of the Savannah* (1988) uses oral literature to underline the extent to which a writer should go in the physical combat for social justice. Self-reflexively, Achebe figures the writer as the "anthill of the savannah" who would survive the physical battles against oppression. The destruction of literary texts and the desecration of intellectuality by military and authoritarian regimes are important motifs in such novels as Mary Karooro Okurut's *The Invisible Weevil* (1998), Chimamanda Ngozi Adichie's *Purple Hibiscus* (2003), and Marjorie Macgoye's *Coming to Birth* (1986). While the theme of disillusionment with the modern state continued in the 1980s and 1990s, the mode in which it was presented changed into highly self-conscious metaphors of rottenness and the disintegration of African nations. Engagement with the politically charged novels of disillusionment is featured in later novels as symbols of the ideological maturation of characters.[23] Further, while the radical novels of the 1970s were more open in their expression of disillusionment, the novels of the 1980s expressed their sentiments in labyrinthine narratives that not only heightened the sense of alienation and fragmentation of self pervading the society but also signaled some hope for more democratization and acceptance of nonofficial senses of reality and history. The earlier literature tended to blame colonialism and the West for the conditions in Africa; the later literature started to examine how the local communities contributed to their own predicament.

Eschewing Authoritarian Regimes in the 1980s and 1990s

The use of fabulistic techniques affords the writer a rare opportunity to be critical of intolerant regimes in an aesthetically sophisticated way that would also confound the censor. In their critical readings of fabulistic novels of the 1980s and 1990s, Khamis and Wamitila have noted the influence of mutually conflictual factors—political liberalization and the fear of intolerant regimes—as some of the motivators for self-reflexive narratives. Khamis (2001) argues that the shift from socialist ideology in Tanzania in the 1960s and 1970s was accompanied by a new kind of freedom that did not require writers to toe the government's social-nationalist line. He notes that earlier silent censorship did not permit the writers to "widen the range of dialogue and discourse or deviate from the 'commonly accepted paradigm' and political consensus" (2001, 119). For Khamis, the liberalization policies, the attendant widening of democratic spaces, and the abandonment of rigid socialist *Ujamaa*[24] policies inaugurated the first decade of independence in the 1960s: "Instead of being mere passive defenders of the nationalist agenda, [Tanzanian writers] are becoming more and more eager to venture into forbidden grounds or simply chose no longer to glorify the shameful" (2001, 119–20). Thus the spirit of the 1980s has engendered a more experimental literature that is not invested in the simplistic communication of the nationalist agenda.

Yet this experimentalism echoes Julius Nyerere's *Ujamaa* policy of self-reliance, but without its original dogmatism. Kezilahabi's *Mzingile* (Labyrinth) and *Nagona (Self-consciousness)* involve Nyerere-like skepticism toward Western philosophies as a viable means of enabling independence and progress in Africa. The narratives rely on myths from the Ukerewe ethnic community on an island in Lake Victoria to suggest ways in which Africans can prioritize their own indigenous knowledge if they are to apprehend their tangled postcolonial identities. In these myths, moments of self-reliance (such as the mythical Kakulu growing crops that provide food for everyone in his community, or his mother's ability to give birth to him without anybody's help, or his ability to fend for himself immediately when he is born) are celebrated as possibilities for fostering development in the community. The narratives transcend Nyerere's philosophy by being suspicious of a unitary *Ujamaa*, in which everyone follows the ideology of single-party rule.

Khamis's argument that the earlier nationalist Kiswahili novel cared little about technique is stressed by Wamitila (2001) in "Contextualization of Politics and the Politics of Contextualization." Freed from being the mouthpiece of the ruling elite, the literature has become more experimental. The banning of Kezilahabi's *Rosa Mistika* (1971) at the instigation of the church and the state because of its treatment of sexual and political freedoms more openly indicates that the censorship that Khamis sees as having dissipated with the collapse of socialist nationalism still exists. The writers have had to resort to fabulation to present sensitive issues without stepping on the toes of institutions, and Khamis is right when he comments that the novels appear like a "surface sign of something that ought not to be said directly" (2001, 120).

Wamitila observes that such novels as Katama Mkangi's *Walenisi* and *Mafuta* are written in a nonrealist way, veiling the political contexts they are thematizing, to elude censors in a politically intolerant Kenya, where the writer had been detained without trial for his criticism of Daniel Arap Moi's government. The novels were written at a time when Moi's paranoid government faced serious threats of being hounded out of power by popular opposition movements. In return, the government had sent the opposition underground, eroded the independence of the judiciary, and rendered itself notorious by detaining politically engaged intellectuals. To avoid repercussions from the government, the novels opted for "heavy symbolism, allegory, convoluted syntax, and opaque lexicon," even if the text was subterraneously calling for popular protest against an oppressive regime (Wamitila 2001, 138). From the varied emphases in Wamitila's and Khamis's accounts, I would urge us to see metafiction as complexly overdetermined by both political intolerance and political liberalism in the Africa of the 1980s.

There are novels that indicate to the reader that they adopt a nonrealist mode to avoid censorship that would easily happen in other mediums of expression. For instance, Chachage Seithy Loth Chachage's *Makuadi wa Soko Huria* (*Pimps of the Free Market*, 2002) thematizes the ironies of liberalism in 1990s Tanzania, where despite the freedom of expression that multiparty democracy is said to have heralded, the media are systematically gagged to protect capitalist projects. The playful narrator outlines in very vivid terms the genealogy of censorship in the Tanzanian press, including an instance in which an advocate of the socialist revolution in Zanzibar turns out to be the most repressive censor in the Tanzanian mainland. Sarcastically named Alhaji Seif Said, the registrar of newspapers gets rich serving the government during the 1990s and manages to go on a pilgrimage to Mecca. Also trained in Soviet Russia, Seif Said seems to have been fully converted from the firebrand revolutionist of the mid-1960s fighting against rich, racist Arabs in Zanzibar to one of the most cynical oppressors in mainland Tanzania and a protector of the rich exploiters. At one point he urges the narrator to stop agitating against environmental degradation and support *utandawazi* (globalization), while the narrator wants to expose globalization for what it is: *utandawizi* (stealing from all over the globe). By detailing his experiences as a writer at the hands of the censor Alhaji Seif Said, the narrator suggests that he has had to tell his story in a novelistic and fabulistic mode because he cannot tell it in objective, factual language after he has been denied the registration of his own newspaper by a government keen to shield foreign investors at the expense of the local population. The novel explains that even if many newspapers have been set up in the 1990s, the media owners collude with editors to make sure multinational interests are never endangered through exposés of capitalist excesses and malpractices.

Mocking the Dictators: Moses Isegawa

While dictatorship and its repression of the arts was a theme covered in the novels of the 1960s and 1970s, these novels were still fairly realist. Later novels tackling the theme, however, adopt a more hallucinatory mode. An excellent case in point is Ugandan Moses Isegawa's presentation of Milton

Obote's and Idi Amin's dictatorships in the 1970s. *Abyssinian Chronicles* (2001) and *Snakepit* (2004) present Uganda as a version of hell in which national priorities are turned upside down while the state invokes nationalism to repress its subjects. A *Bildungsroman* in which the life of its principal character, Mugezi, intersects with that of the nation (including sharing a birthday with his nation, as does Saalem in Salman Rushdie's *Midnight's Children*), *Abyssinian Chronicles* playfully confers upon its autobiographical narrator the omniscience to present events preceding his birth as a way of contesting a singular history.

Abyssinian Chronicles is the story of Mugezi, the narrator, as he grows up through Uganda's early days of independence, Idi Amin's military dictatorship in the 1970s, to the regimes that took over after Amin. He also relates his experiences in European ghettos. He symbolizes doomed freedom through his parents, Padlock and Serenity, whom he paints as dictatorial at every level. Padlock and Serenity experienced the heady days of independence in the 1960s, and they have watched the situation deteriorate to absolute chaos. The experiences "made them realize that the cancer was not all Amin's doing" (469). The novel indicates that the African belief in strong male leadership could well have led to the successive abuse of power both at the national and domestic levels. Through Mugezi the novel seems to be suspicious of all forms of authority and organized religion, irreverently equating misgovernance in Uganda with the Catholic doctrine. The despair is openly brought out in the way the novel puns in Wordsworthian manner the word *abyss* as a trope for the false bottom of African nations and the collapse of the nation-state under civilian and military dictatorships. *Abyssinian Chronicles* presents the corruption, religious hypocrisy, and violence that govern postcolonial Uganda.

The events in the novel are reconstructed by Mugezi from the vantage point of the present, imagining the characters that precede his biological life. Reading the past in sexually coded terms, Mugezi weaves a narrative in which sex is at the heart of the intersection between the national and the personal in a manner that would make the novel part of what Fredric Jameson calls a "national allegory" in the way the libidinal self and the national consciousness implicate each other. In "Third World Literature in the Era of Multinational Capitalism" (1986), Jameson contends that unlike Western realist and modernist novels, where the personal is radically split from the public, in "Third World" novels that binary—between sexuality and the unconscious on the one hand, and the public and the political on the other—is dissolved. Although Isegawa's novel cannot be described as parochial in the way Jameson wrongly regards political novels from the "Third World," in which the ideal reader is radically different from the actual Western reader, the novel demonstrates the conflation of the national and the libidinal.

In the novel's metaphors, the practice of Ugandan national politics is compared to what is taking place at the domestic and sexual levels in the lives of the story's individual characters. Nowhere is this metaphor better demonstrated than in the wedding of the narrator's parents, which is most probably reconstructed from his wild imagination or from the rumor-filled discourse that structures power in the postcolonial state. Ugandan society collectively copulates in tandem with the newlyweds, and the disappointments of the events are registered both by the two individuals and the society at large. At the moment when the first-person narrative changes to the third-person perspective of the narrator's mother, the narrative emphasizes the collectivity of the sexual act that is expressed through obscene dance and body movements:

> The newlyweds were installed on a wooden dais covered with white mats, and seated in sofas covered with white cloth not so much to disguise their diversity of design or ownership as to cater to the uniformity and a sense of conjugal purity . . . To the deep, hard beat of the big drum the dancers made the most profane, most horrifying, most beshaming pelvic thrusts she had ever seen. They had comically accentuated their waists with padded long-haired colobus monkey sashes, making their thrusts look disturbingly larger, bolder, and more obscene. . . . The crowd was fucking her, raping her, deflowering her, gobbling the rivers of blood that poured from her cavities. (Isegawa 2001, 40–41)

The fact that the bride is called "Virgin" at this point in the story, while she is the one gazing at the crowd, indicates that the focalization is not only from her center of consciousness; it could also be through her husband and the larger crowd who assume her to be a virgin. The mixture of voices accentuates the polyphony of the novel and the desire for a more representative political order, a desire later to be denied by the autocratic leaders who take over from the colonialists.

The extended description of the dances and the crowd's engagement with the aesthetics of vulgarity as the nation enters the cusp of independence signify that the crowd could well be deconstructing the colonial authority that had banned this kind of performance. This is a moment of the grotesque, which Bakhtin saw as the province of the ordinary people resisting authority. Bakhtin was more interested in realist fiction than in self-reflexive modernist and postmodernist aesthetics, but his observations on grotesqueness and playfulness in the novel as a genre are germane to the reading of metafiction as well, and especially to a novel such as *Absynnian Chronicles* that deliberately flaunts its own playfulness.

Later in the novel, we see politicians participating in similar grotesque and obscene acts, a fact that seems to conform to Mbembe's suggestion in *On the Postcolony* (2001a), that Bakhtin's typology be extended to include the African politicians who routinize the obscenity and excess as a confirmation of the state's legitimacy. Indeed, Isegawa seems to be as pessimistic as Mbembe about the possibility of the African nation being able to pull out of the morass into which its leadership has dragged it. For Isegawa, the only hope—as expressed in his *Snakepit* (2004), which echoes *Abyssinian Chronicles* in certain passages—is that the leadership is so obscene, cannibalistic, and selfish that it will annihilate itself without much effort from the already disillusioned and cynical public. The mention of Samuel Beckett's *Waiting for Godot* as one of the existentialist texts that Mugezi is reading accentuates the guarded optimism with which the novel regards the chances for positive change in Uganda.

At the same time, Isegawa's extended description of personal *jouissance* and collective euphoria in *Abyssinian Chronicles* helps intensify the irony in the sense that the bride (symbol of Uganda and many other things in the story) is not the virgin she is presumed to be. It is also suggested that marriage within a patriarchal society escorts a woman to collective violation of her body. Later, the narrator's father, Serenity, is presented as one with the crowd, and images derived from political functions at the onset of Ugandan independence are used to describe his feelings:

> Serenity was on the same wavelength with the crowd . . . The wave thrust him into the center of a hot political rally, with the loudspeakers booming, the politicians shouting, and the crowd intoxicated with promises of a better life. Independence was approaching, and something coming of the imaginary rally crowd told him that he could not miss out on this chance of a lifetime . . . They [the crowd at the wedding] thrust their *dancerly* pelvises at him, stimulating copulation at its hardest and most playful. He shook fluidly, as they grabbed his arms and quivered as if the earth were coming off its hinges. Then, raising their legs as if they were male dogs with cramped thigh muscles attempting to piss on a high section of a pole, they quivered their withdrawal . . . he was swallowed up by the crowd. (46–47, emphasis added)

The adjective *dancerly* echoes Barthes's theoretical term *readerly* to underline the playfulness, improvisation, and adventitiousness with which the grotesque dance is executed. At the same time, by using a term that echoes literary theory, the novel self-consciously acknowledges its artifice, enticing the reader to be not just a mere consumer but an active participant in the construction of the text. The text thus calls attention to the various rhetorical techniques it uses to produce an illusion of realism in order to shun a fixed, predetermined reading; this textual strategy incites the readers to reject the authoritarianism that the novel so vividly describes.

Yet the novel is not a passive reproduction of literary theory, however radical that theory may be. While Barthes coined the term *readerly* or *scriptible* to describe regenerative texts that violate the conventions of realism and compel the readers to work out multiple meanings in the text beyond the one intended by the author, Isegawa uses the term *dancerly* in a negative sense because the event is viewed from the perspective of Serenity and Padlock, who do not endorse the carnivalesque dancing. Here the crowd is different from the ones in the socialist realist novels by Sembene Ousmane that Jameson uses to describe the aesthetics of the African novel. While the crowds in the novels Jameson theorizes are used as symbols of the unity of struggle, and of the utopian hope for a better postcapitalist society, Isegawa uses the crowds to signify collective euphoria, delusion, and hopelessness. The events after the wedding are described with grotesque images of vomit and other bodily effluents to foreshadow the disillusionment with postindependence Uganda, or what Jameson in the essay calls the "poisoned gift of independence" (1986, 81). The marriage between Serenity and Virgin is doomed to be unhappy because of the intolerance of its patriarchal underpinnings, the puritanism of modern religion, and the violence of the state.

Further, through the protagonist's parents, Padlock and Serenity, the novel depicts the despair that has gripped the nation. The frustrations with nationhood are paralleled by tensions in their marital relations. The fact that Padlock—so-called because of her supposed sexual prudence—was not a virgin on her wedding night symbolizes a Uganda already flawed at independence. Feudalism, patriarchy, and colonial modernity had already contaminated the nation at independence. Serenity is no virgin either, but no one seems overly bothered by the fact, a development that indicates the existence of a double standard in sexual relations in society. Through his narrator's reconstruction of events, Isegawa's language is replete with sexual descriptions that capture the initial euphoria of independence and the disillusionment and despair that were to later envelop the whole nation. Scenes of rape and incest symbolize the pain that Ugandan leaders have visited upon their own nation. Through Mugezi's cynical lens, women are romanticized symbols of the nation that the male leadership has defiled. Yet none of these women emerges as the possible source of hope. The principal women characters are all killed in bizarre incidents to signal the abyss to which Uganda has been reduced. Mugezi also presents what he views as his sexual victimization by women as symbolic of the abuse of the nation by the local elites and the international donor community.

Through Serenity, the narrator's father, the novel reveals how the trauma of violence has eaten away at the remaining strands of hope in the country. Even when one dictatorship is ended by the physical death of the despot, little is likely to change on the ground. But even this gritty despair is narrated in a playful language that seems to be making fun of the victims of the governments:

> It was during the depth of suffering that Serenity came up with the only political statement he ever made. He said that Uganda was a land of false bottoms where under every abyss there was another one waiting to ensnare people, and the historians had made a mistake: Abyssinia was not the ancient land of Ethiopia, but modern Uganda. Buoyed by intermittent bouts of optimism, he would go over the statement, looking for ways to improve it and make it attractive enough for ambitious politicians to pick up, for he believed that the time had come to change the name of Uganda to Abyssinia. (2000, 469)

In mocking Serenity's discovery, while using it throughout the novel to depict the endless abyss in which African countries have found themselves, Isegawa seems to be alluding to a deluded character, Wamala, in John Ruganda's play *The Burdens* (1972), who, in the most satirical part of the drama, hopes to sell campaign slogans to the lewd and corrupt politician Kanagonago. Much like this play within a play, in which Ruganda dramatizes the delusions of the former government minister reduced to abject squalor and self-delusion after participating in a failed coup attempt, Isegawa's novel uses metafiction to indicate a level of degeneration where even glimmers of hope are shot through with absurdity.

Unlike earlier novels that are told mainly from a single perspective, *Abyssinian Chronicles* exaggerates its ironic heteroglossia (many-voiced-ness) not only through the self-deprecating humor that runs through it from beginning to end but also through the multiple focalization through which the characters relay the events to the reader. In the novel, a single character may have multiple names. The narrator's mother, Nakkazi, is called Virgin by her husband, and Padlock by Mugezi, her son (the narrator of the story). She calls herself Sister Peter. The multiple sobriquets for a single character, which change depending on who is naming her, and the ability of the narrator to fictionalize his own experiences, form a parallel, for the reader, with the contested nature of history itself. History here becomes what Hayden White provocatively saw as imaginary in the sense that the characters view events subjectively and fashion themselves and one another in contestatory terms that have not been settled when the last word in the narrative is uttered. In fact, although he is the character with whom we are most familiar, it is hard to believe that Mugezi's account is based on disinterested facts. We are supposed to critique him as much as he critiques the rest of the society.

In a New Historicist fashion, the novel indicates that Mugezi is creating his own history, even as he shows that the other characters invent the most basic facts about their own lives, just as fiction writers do. Though focusing on Uganda, *Abyssinian Chronicles* has a strong disregard for national boundaries or those people in society, like Mugezi's parents, who have essentialist and puritanical ideas of culture. Though the metafictional elements of Isegawa's novels are not intense, despite their use of literary terms as metaphors and their setting in an openly ambivalent and polyvalent border-space, the novels nevertheless reveal the influence that metafictional writers such as Rushdie have had on African writing.

Inscribing Human Rights Abuse: Habila's *Waiting for An Angel*

In the wake of human rights abuses and infringements upon free expression in postcolonial Africa through the 1970s and 1980s, it is perhaps not surprising that censorship, police harassment of artists, and detention of political writers are constant motifs in Africa literature of the 1980s and later. The metafictional thrust in these newer novels, conceived at the turn of the century, derives from the tribulations of earlier writers such as Ngũgĩ, Alex la Guma, and Soyinka at the hands of the state. The new writing refers to fiction, nonfiction, and poetry by older generation of writers to draw parallels between the current state of censorship and earlier forms of blatant human rights violations by successive regimes in African nations.

One of the most remarkable of these later novels is Helon Habila's *Waiting for an Angel* (2002) because of the way this "new generation" Nigerian novelist metafictionally weaves gender and sexuality into the narrative to present the theme of political censorship in African cultures. The novel is to a large extent realist and compounds its bent toward factuality with a structurally unnecessary afterword which, though as playful as the rest of the novel, helps anchor the fictional narrative in the real political developments in the Nigeria of the 1990s with reference to historical facts. However, Habila weaves a hallucinatory and nonlinear story that evokes the unstructured thoughts of an artist under duress. The novel tells the story of a journalist and poet, Lomba, who is incarcerated for more than two years without trial by the Nigerian government for reporting on a political meeting. Interweaving the past into the present, part of the story is in the form of the notes and poetry that Lomba wrote while in prison. Lomba tells the reader at the outset that he wrote the diary primarily to himself, "because here in prison there is no one to listen" (3). Then the inclusion of Lomba's prison notes as part of the novel not only attempts to recover for him the humanity that his jailers denied him, it is also a testimony to the power of narrative in helping the speaker cope with a traumatic past and memorialize his eventual freedom.

Habila experiments with self-reflexivity as a means of survival against the very government that it excoriates—the Abacha regime of the 1990s. The story is told in a congeries of voices, with some sections narrated from the perspective of the embedded novelist, who at one point meets a character bearing the name "Helon Habila." The appearance of Helon Habila as a minor character is a mischievous pretext that he is not the one satirizing the brutal military regime presented in the novel. The nonchronological plot accentuates the sense of chaos in Abacha's Nigeria without directly reproducing Nigeria in a referential sense. The voices of the silenced, like that of the graffiti artist, Nancy, are given prominence as a way of mocking a regime that has denied its subjects the basic right to express their thoughts. Above all, despite its mention of extratextual events and Nigerian cultural icons such as Fela Kuti and his politically charged Afro-beat (music of postindependence disillusionment), the novel is pervaded by a sense of placelessness. This does not just refer to its applicability in the different nations of Africa; rather, through the device of placelessness, it avoids direct confrontation with Abacha and repercussions from a brutal state.

Like all narratives of incarceration, Lomba's diary celebrates his triumph beyond prison walls. While the description of prison life is interesting in itself, exposing as it does the malaise that defines a military government, it is the description of censorship after physical imprisonment that reveals the victims' complicity in their own oppression. Before going to jail, the young writer is advised by a senior editor, James Fiki, against wasting his time writing a certain kind of fiction because the circumstances in the nation militate against such art. The editor underlines the futility of artistic production in a country gripped by dictatorship, brutal military juntas, censorship, poverty, low levels of literacy, and general apathy:

> You won't find a publisher in this country because it would be economically unwise for any publisher to waste his paper to publish a novel that nobody would buy, because the people are too poor, too illiterate, and too busy trying to stay out of the way of the police and the army to read. And of course paper is

> scarce and expensive—because of the economic sanctions placed on the country. (Habila 2002. 192)

James Fiki's pessimism is deconstructed by the circumstances of the novel itself in the extratextual world. Despite the editor's prophesy that a Nigerian novel would not win a major international award, *Waiting for an Angel*, self-published, won the Caine Prize in 2001 and the Commonwealth Prize for the Best First Novel, Africa Region, in 2003. Its central message is against pessimism among artists, editors, and publishers, even in the most adverse moments. The novel, giving itself as an example, uses the advice from the editor ironically to showcase the possibilities of transcending the pessimism that defines life in Africa. Lomba is a writer with a magazine specializing in art and culture in Nigeria. His position allows him to comment on the relationship between politics and literature, including his own writing. To Lomba, poetry becomes a safety valve that enables him to survive the trauma of prison life. Yet art, seen as politically innocuous, is at the same time used by the prison authorities as a tool of sexual seduction; in the novel, the prison superintendent plagiarizes the prisoner's poetry to impress his lover. The prison authorities do not recognize the subversive power of art.

In her *The Age of the World Target* (2006), Rey Chow has usefully recuperated the self-referentiality of non-Western cultural discourse from the esoterism of poststructural moves, indicating that nonreferentiality does not constitute an inward-turning linguistic prison-house in which literary signification is limited to a recursive exercise without extratextual agency. The radicalization of language in postmodernism and high modernism, as Chow notes in this context, is an attempt to rhetorically rebel against a repressive order. Without necessarily staging a rebellion against Western, postmodern, linguistic self-referentiality, most of the African novels that use metafictional devices insist on their agency in the real world. For instance, in Habila's and Mpe's self-conscious use of metafiction based on the fictionalization of writing and incarceration, the writers go to great lengths to illustrate, through choice passages in which the novels discuss their own projects, that their self-reflexivity is different from the apolitical esoterism associated with Western postmodenism.

Self-reflexivity does not amount to imprisonment in language because literary statements are produced and circulated in the society through a subjective lens. Habila's *Waiting for an Angel* presents a scene in which a dead metaphor, "save my soul, prisoner," chosen merely for its alliteration, is literalized to serve as a statement about the physical imprisonment of the poet. The poet produces one of the works bearing the line after witnessing the death of an inmate. Lomba, the embedded writer in the novel, repeats the line to secure intervention on his behalf from Janice, a woman with whom the prison superintendent has fallen in love and tries to impress her with plagiarized poems for Lomba's oeuvre:

> The first time I put down the words, in the third poem, it had been non-deliberate, I was just making alliteration. Then I began to repeat it in subsequent poems. But how could I tell her that the message wasn't really for her, or for someone else? It was for myself, perhaps, written by me to my own soul, to every other soul, the collective soul of the universe. (2002, 28)

Here the interiorized and inward-looking art, as long as it is articulated rather than completely silenced, has political significance. Even if the writer is not a writer in politics in the instance of this dead metaphor, his reader is. The line acquires political value because the female reader, a sophisticated connoisseur of the poetic form, is, unlike her lover, able to read the subtlely coded message when a poet deviates from the poetic norms to use the habitualized metaphors of everyday language and to imitate dead poets.

At the same, writers are shown as being vulnerable to cynicism about gender, even when they wax radical about national political themes. Habila seems to distance himself from his writer-character the way Achebe does in *A Man of the People* (1966), when Odili, the narrator and a student of literature in Achebe's novel, is criticized as part of the malaise affecting African political life, especially in the way he regards women. Like Achebe, Habila uses sexual desire and the fictional male author's misuse of metaphors of the feminine to signal a discomfort with a certain caliber of artists, even when they are antagonistic to a dictatorial regime. In Habila's novel, Lomba trivializes political conditions by using sexual metaphors in a way that does not distinguish him so distinctly from his coworker, Seun, whom he looks down upon for considering himself a comedian although he is not funny. In passages delivered to the reader verbatim from the writer's diary, imprisonment as an emblem of governmental abuse of civilian rights figures as denial of sex by this embedded artist: "What is left here is nothing but a mass of protruding bones, unkempt hair and tearful eyes; an asshole for shitting and farting, and a penis that in the morning grows turgid in vain" (Habila 2002, 23–24). The trailing paratactic clauses that make up this sentence signify Lomba's pain, abjection, and alterity. It also suggests a blurred gender vision in which freedom is seen in terms of subjecting women to male desire. The parataxis compares with the fragmented sentences in which the jailer speaks, as opposed to the fluent language of Janice. It is suggested that the embedded writer may not be completely different from the subjects that he criticizes. In fact, he draws the jailer more affectionately than he presents Janice, whom he mocks as "a little past her prime, past her sell-by date" (27). While the superintendent, Muftau, is seen as human (not beyond human passions and infatuation, despite his callous behavior as a jailer), Janice is presented eventually as a pitiable individual, despite her passion for poetry and sympathy for the prisoner.

It is useful to note that Lomba's thoughts, which link imprisonment to denial of sexual gratification, are triggered by Janice's presence. Janice becomes an object of Lacanian desire, a condensation of wish and drive for a pleasure-giving phenomenon that the poet longs for but cannot achieve in incarceration. Secretly desiring Janice, Lomba expresses in his diary his repressed lust for women prisoners: "Her perfume, mixed with her female smell, rose into my nostrils: flowery, musky. I had forgotten the last time a woman had stood so close to me. Sometimes, in our cells, when the wind blows from the female prison, we'll catch distant sounds of female screams and shouts and even laughter. That is the closest we ever come to women. Only when the wind blows, at the right time, in the right direction" (29). To Lomba, the women do not seem to have individual identities; they are more like sexual objects to satisfy his arrested desire. Indeed, when he is coincidentally released from prison after Sani Abacha dies, he is welcomed by Liberty, who though not overtly gender marked, suggests that freedom is a female awaiting him for a moment of *jouissance*. The narrator's choppy prose in this scene seems to be imitating Lomba's poetry: ". . . when he opened his eyes Liberty was standing over him, smiling kindly, extending an arm/And Liberty said softly, 'Come. It's time to go.'/And they left, arm in arm." The text, then, does not seem to see the liberation of women as likely in a culture where the most sensitive of writers such as Lomba continue to have gender stereotypes, even when expressing the loftiest political ideals about democracy and respect for human rights.

To think of a Nigeria free from poor governance is to enter a Kantian transcendental illusion—a conclusion that is not based on experience, and that is powered by its own steam, where a subjective position is claimed as objective in order to defy the limitations of the observer's knowledge. Through self-referencing, *Waiting for an Angel* indicates that although literary texts might be applauded at national and international forums, it is often for their signification of a hopeless situation. In the novel, hope is confined to figural signification that nevertheless helps sustain positive expectations as a safety mechanism against despair. Yet, as Lomba insists, in a situation of recurrent regime changes without any forward movement, one cannot risk exuberant optimism. This disenchantment with the state of the nation in *Waiting for an Angel* and the author's restrained optimism run parallel to the motif of sexual betrayal and frustration. At the end of the novel, Lomba is abandoned by his lover, a suggestion of unresolved crisis in the nation.

While Habila expresses the culpability of the ruled in their own enthrallment both through James's pessimism and the female lover's abandonment of the champion of democracy and rule of law, the novel's association of the woman figure with the collapse of the nation contains an uncomfortable tinge of masculinist ideology.

Distorted Priorities and Homegrown Solutions

If Isegawa's characters see Africa as an intractable abyss and a dangerous snakepit, then much of the metafiction is not an exercise in Afro-pessimism—that Eurocentric philosophy that foregrounds only the negative things that happen on the continent. Even in the most playful texts of the twenty-first century, metafiction in the African novel presents itself not as a distortion of the realities of Africa but as a representation of the vexed and fragmented "truths" in different forms. Evoking the spirit of the Bandung Conference, which emphasized the Global South's self-reliance from either Soviet communism or Western capitalism, novels such as Kezilahabi's *Nagona* (1990b) seek local strategies of apprehending a continually elusive "truth" while acknowledging the difficulties of such an attempt. The theme of self-reliance is explored in novels such as Nuruddin Farah's *Gifts* (1999), in which not only Western economic and humanitarian aid is criticized, but African society is shown to be capable of giving something to the rest of the world.

Zimbabwean Nozipo Maraire's *Zenzele: A Letter for My Daughter* (1996) follows a similar trajectory. Even when critical of the West, Maraire's novel makes powerful use of the epistolary mode to evoke a dialogue between a mother in Africa and her daughter in the African Diaspora instead of making an attack on the West. Though the novel tends to be tendentious, presenting too many glib pronouncements about Pan-Africanist struggles, like Gordimer's *The Lying Days* (1953), it suggests the unreliability of the narrator, especially in her naïve endorsement of heteronormative attitudes. The novel is extremely successful in veiling its nonrealism until we consider the status of its narration that it flaunts in a long series of letters by an ailing African mother in Harare, Zimbabwe, to her daughter studying at Harvard. Despite its obvious play on Mariama Bâ's *So Long a Letter* (1981) and Sindiwe Magona's *To My Children's Children* (1990), and its unsubtle critique of Eurocentric literary and history curriculum, *Zenzele* maintains an illusion of realism throughout the narration. In fact, like Chachage's *Makuadi wa Soko Huria* and Sello K. Duiker's *The Quiet Violence of Dreams*, *Zenzele* contains too many glib political pronouncements from its characters, even if the reader is likely to agree with these statements about Pan-Africanism and women's struggles in Africa.

Not even the narrator's references to storytelling and the subjective nature of truth and history are able to detract the reader from the apparently transparent realism of Maraire's novel. Neither does the bizarre scene toward the end of the novel, where the bodies of a dead couple buried separately are later, in defiance of the laws of science, found with their hands joined together in a different grave. *Zenzele* exploits this impression of realism and the homiletic statements of a mother to her daughter to not only expose the double standards in the treatment of African women vis-à-vis men but to showcase optimism in the possibility of self-liberation through virtuous behavior, respect for African cultures, and the embrace of modern education.

The novel's postrealism is best understood in relation to the texts it invokes regarding women's self-liberation. *Zenzele* is a narrative of female bonding in which the mother-daughter relationship is presented as a positive, nourishing element in women's empowerment, despite the intergenerational difference between Mai Zenzele and her daughter Zenzele. Unlike Mariama Bâ's *So Long a Letter,* which dwells on African women's involvement in their own mistreatment or in betraying their fellow women, *Zenzele* is unapologetically Pan-Africanist and focuses on the possibilities of a transnational and intergenerational community among women of African ancestry. The choice of an older woman to tell the story is because she is in possession of a rich trove of memory that her daughter can use to empower herself without repeating the mistakes of the past, such as women's subservience to a male order in the semifeudal African societies. The older woman also is able to criticize the younger generation in a way that might not be possible if the story were being told by the younger Zenzele.

One may, however, ask why we are not provided with Zenzele's response to her mother's letters. Zenzele's voice and that of important characters like her father are framed in the mother's narration. Is the novel flaunting the putative alterity of the modern young African woman as a subaltern who cannot speak, despite her education and exposure to the world? If we consider its playful relationship with other women's writing, then we see that, despite her silence, Zenzele can be said to be the novel's overall narrator. It is most probable that she, as the recipient of her mother's letters (assuming that her mother would not keep a copy of nonofficial communication with her daughter), is the one who has provided the correspondence to the reader. By keeping quiet and removed, Zenzele maintains an aesthetic distance and an impression of objectivity in a novel where the verbatim reproduction of tendentious political statements is the norm. The silent narrator, who provides her mother's letters to the reader without uttering a word, seems to understand that, despite the political points her mother's statements score, they compromise the artistic integrity of the novel by making its criticism of life too transparent.

At the same time, through the silence of the younger Zenzele, the novel suggests that the elderly Mai Zenzele is not the spokesperson of the novelist, Maraire. Mai Zenzele is at times prejudiced and therefore unreliable as a narrator, especially in her nationalistic essentialism and her naïve heteronormative attitude toward, for instance, single mothers in modern urban Zimbabwe, whose status she attributes to self-inflicted alienation and disrespect for African values. Through a mimicry of objective realism, the novel manages to cue the reader to not only take with a pinch of salt Mai Zenzele's lionizing of her husband as the source of all political wisdom and instrumentality but also to expose Mai Zenzele's inability to pay enough attention to the patriarchal conditions that would lead a girl to single motherhood. Both women are made to criticize themselves and each other as Mai Zenzele laughs at her fatalism vis-à-vis her husband's agency, and as Zenzele exposes, through her mother's letters, her earlier naïve belief in Western superiority.

The title of the novel foregrounds the female letter writer, Mai Zenzele ("Mother of Zenzele"), and the eponymous embedded reader (Zenzele herself) to suggest the novel's historically grounded investment in women's self-liberation. "Zenzele" is a Ndebele name that means "do it yourself." In the novel, a female Zenzele is both the narrator (Mai Zenzele) and the audience (Zenzele, the embedded "narratee"). By relocating both the narratorial and reading agency to specifically female subjects and subordinating male voices to Mai Zenzele's narration, the novel gives absolute agency to women as the carriers of memory and narratives of self-liberation. In doing so, the novel unsilences the voices of the poor and of women whom colonial and postcolonial history has tended to erase, even if these women are at times criticizing themselves and each other.

Connoting togetherness and self-reliance, the name "Zenzele" is also the term for the women's movements that sprang up in the 1920s to promote the welfare of rural women in southern Africa. The movements, made up mainly of educated, middle-class African women, were largely apolitical in the sense that they shied away from nationalist anticolonial activities. The novel, however, uses the memory of Zenzele's mother, probably already dead by the time we read her letters, to remind the modern girl about her political duties to uplift the welfare of her people. A key theme in the novel is women's involvement in the guerrilla fight for Zimbabwean independence and the trauma of racism and colonialism. However, on the whole, rather than a criticism of the West and its policies toward Africa, the novel calls for educated female Africans to give back to their communities (in the Zenzele spirit) and improve the welfare of underprivileged women. Like northern Nigeria's Zaynab Alkali (who through realism captures the dilemmas of women in Muslim African communities), Maraire portrays in *Zenzele* the liberating potential of modern education. However, this education should not mean either a wholesale embrace of the West or a total rejection of Western values. Modern education should have its roots in African beliefs and customs if attempts at transformation of the modern woman into a liberated self are not to result in girls being alienated from self and community.

For its part, Francis Imbuga's *Miracle of Remera* (2004) is a novel about the fight against HIV and the search for a local cure for AIDS that thematizes its own self-reflexivity to distinguish productive self-knowledge from obsession with one's self. It serves as another excellent case in point to show the social function that metafiction in African novels assigns itself. Portraying a stage in life when young people get carried away writing letters to people of the opposite sex as a way of sexual self-validation, the novel demonstrates its awareness of the process of reading and writing. It launches its narrative by laughing at an act of unproductive self-expression in which the culprit is sentenced in a mock judicial trial that introduces the metafictional impulses through which the novel handles the theme of AIDS in Africa. The one-time appearance of the character, who writes letters to himself in order to create the impression among his peers that he is popular with girls, is meant to qualify the self-referential novel as being different from the childish textual play enacted by the boys:

> One of the most frequently recounted stories at Mbitini High School was the story of a Form Three student who had not received mail for nearly two months. Mike Jondiko, better known as Honorable G. M. Jondiko, was so frustrated by the mail drought that he finally decided to do something about it. He decided to write himself. He sacrificed part of his pocket money to buy a few postage stamps. (2)

It is notable here that the boy is a minor character, appearing only once in a flashback, yet his narcissistic act has etched an indelible place for him in the lore of the school. The title "honourable" mocks the habit among African leaders to appropriate high-sounding titles that have no substantive meaning. The waste of resources in Africa, contrasted in the novel with the need to commit resources to the fight against AIDS, is metaphorized by Jondiko's use of his limited finances in an ego-boosting, narcissistic act. Jondiko is found out because he makes no attempt to disguise his handwriting and uses the same pen and ink to address the letters he writes to himself. He also uses the same type of envelope and postage stamp.

This jocular treatment of a serious postcolonial problem is further lightened by the playfulness with which Jondiko is punished. A "council of elders" is appointed to try the case and punish him if found guilty:

> The meeting of the council of elders was scheduled for the next day. They met for thirty minutes during the lunch break. Honourable Jondiko was *tried* and *found guilty* of cheating himself. He was fined two loaves of brown bread and warned not to repeat that sort of dishonorable conduct. Jondiko paid the fine, and members of the *elders'* council consumed *it;* and the matter ends there. (2, emphases in original)

Imbuga's narrator pokes fun not only at the political obsession of the self, but the self-serving judicial system and inquiry commissions set up regularly to investigate problems in the postcolony. The text uses italics to emphasize that some of the words are used in a jocular manner by boys role-playing in their daily interactions. The narrative uses the playful boys to deconstruct authority through mimicry in a self-reflexive gesture that criticizes the boys and the object of their mimicry, the judicial system. Jondiko's unproductive correspondence with himself is compared to the impressionability of the girl Brenda, who is swept off her feet by the artificial way in which an Ethiopian boy speaks English, so that "his tongue wrestled with every syllable as if the words did not come from his mouth" (22). This impresses Brenda so much that she accepts an invitation to his hotel, where she is drugged and raped, resulting in her infection with AIDS.

The main character in the novel is Ezra Maiyo, Brenda's boyfriend. He too contracts AIDS. Brenda is redeemed in the story, but not before the reader is warned against the sterile affectations of Englishness. Jondiko's and the Ethiopian youth's unproductive self-consciousness is contrasted metafictionally with the writing and art that benefit society. The novel presents a moment of suspense and humor in which the leading character, Maiyo, presents a performance about the fight against AIDS, which is the theme of the novel itself. He later contracts the virus and discovers its cure, underscoring the need for an indigenous search for the AIDS cure. The narrative also refers to itself when Maiyo's performance mentions a fictional play *I Wish I Knew*, and its author, a judge of the performance, offers first prize in the competition. The fictional cautionary play, like the novel itself, warns the audience against engaging in sexual activities that they would later regret. The myth that Imbuga constructs and locates in the fictional nation of Remera uses myths and drama to deconstruct such misrepresentations as "HIV and the resultant AIDS are due to witchcraft" (31). This is a myth that also has been deconstructed in Marjorie O. Macgoye's *Chira* (1997).[25]

Like Ngũgĩ's *Wizard of the Crow,* Imbuga's narrative shows that drama is not idle entertainment but an educational tool in the sense that in the novel it improves Maiyo's political skill appreciably. It is the actor, utilizing theatrical skills, who dramatically leads the community in debunking a myth created and circulated by an unscrupulous mortuary attendant who claims that people who die of AIDS-related ailments have to be buried in plastic bags. The mortuary attendant invokes "orders from the above" to give credence to a lie circulating in a society so confused by the prevalence of AIDS that they call the condition "the big one." It is Maiyo, a thespian, who dramatically seizes the moment and leads the mourners in viewing the body of his teacher:

> Even if *Mwalimu* died of the *big one* that is no reason to prevent people from viewing his body," Maiyo persisted. "And if anyone knows that, it is the government. I mean, you cannot catch AIDS merely viewing the body of a person who has died of the disease." (2004, 65, emphases in original)

The upgraded reporting clause ("Maiyo persisted") underlines the young actor's resolve to do what is right amid the myths circulating about AIDS. The scene also exposes the exploitation of people living with AIDS by the professionals in order to line their personal pockets. The mortuary attendant cashes in on the people's ignorance to sell plastic bags, presenting herself as the bearer of a government order that "no naked coffins were allowed to leave the morgue" (2004, 66). Imbuga's novel heightens its playfulness by referring to a real work of art, "Francis Imbuga's *The Successor*" (1979), which "had been receiving rave reviews in the local newspapers" (135). The reference is not developed, but it signals the need to focus on new issues such as the AIDS pandemic, to break from literature's obsession with political contestations.

This Realism That Is Not Dead Yet

To conclude this chapter, I would not want to create the impression either that all of the novels emerging from Africa since the 1980s are metafictional, or that I am giving aesthetic priority to metafictional texts over realist prose. Although Catherine Belsey (1980), Diana Brydon and Helen Tiffin (1993), Timothy Brennan (1990), and Peter Hulme (1986) variously suggest that classical realist fiction tends to interpellate its readers to the bourgeois status quo, it would be wrong to assume that self-reflexive novels are always liberating. Brennan (1997) and Neil Lazarus (2005) sound a warning that postmodern fiction from non-Western societies can itself be used to maintain the global capitalist machine. So far I have shown some of the pitfalls in the stylistic and linguistic choices in the nonmimetic novels, especially because the genre is dominated by male writers.

Further, the proliferation of metafiction does not amount to the death of realism. As a mode of narration, realism is still alive among certain important writers, with some individual writers moving back and forth between realist and postrealist modes in their sequential novels.[26] For example, Helon Habila and Chimamanda Ngozi Adichie have a stronger affinity for the realist fiction of Chinua Achebe than for the magical realist narratives of contemporaries such as Ben Okri, even if unlike the earlier Achebe they have a more fervent investment in showing the differences in women's experiences in postcolonial Nigeria. The experimental novels of the 1980s would then have to be read in the context of the earlier literature that they invoke and try to depart from. This is a point succinctly underlined by Deepika Bahri's reading of the new novels emerging from the postcolonial world. Following Herbert Marcuse, but emphasizing the conjunction between form, content, and reception, Bahri has shown how even the experimental forms that challenge traditional genres "are recognizable owing to certain considerations of form that are closely imbricated with content" (2003, 125). The examples I have given in this chapter are drawn mainly from recent postrealist novels in English, where metafictional play is more or less obvious. In the next chapter, I elaborate on claims made here about metafictional elements in novels written during the realist phase.

Chapter 2

(En)countering Sex in the Nationalist Canon

If colonialism involved a systematic emasculation of the colonial subject by the colonizer as Fanon emphasizes in *Black Skin, White Masks* (1967), then the project of decolonization is at times attended by an inspired reclamation of masculinity and protection of women from sexual and moral corruption by rapacious foreign tendencies. Postcolonial nationalism is therefore gender weighted. In the previous chapter, I presented a heuristic explanation of the development of metafiction. In this chapter, I turn to some texts written before the 1980s to demonstrate that the binary between realism and metafiction is not fixed. The realist novels of nationalism use metafiction in certain sections to suggest gender issues.

I seek to show the sexualized nature of canon formation that nationalist novels instantiated. With an interest in texts where the narrator discombobulates the reader with excursions into literature and interpretation, I focus on Gordimer's *The Lying Days* (1953), which discusses the effects of literature on a young black girl; Ngũgĩ's *Petals of Blood* (1977), which presents characters discussing the canons of African art and suggests multiplicities of readings and misreadings of the visual arts; Kibera's *Voices in the Dark* (1970), which presents an intellectual playwright's idea of the canon; and Bukenya's *The People's Bachelor* (1972), which portrays the training of critics and poets at an African university. These novels are critical of Western modes of expression without hesitating to critique some of the emerging trends in African popular expression. I call these novels "nationalist" because of their thematic investment in arguments for an aesthetic that departs from the colonial canon and their sympathetic portrayal of anticolonial endeavors.

In the heady days of postindependence nationalism mundane issues such as "sex" were to be removed from serious literature. As a result, texts that extolled sex were condemned by a foremost critic of African literature, Chris Wanjala, to "pavements and ladies' handbags" (Wanjala 1978, 48)—a statement that equated nonrefined sites of pulp readership with women's paraphernalia. Reading the literature from a Hegelian perspective, Wanjala's other fear about noncanonical literature was that women were imitating the bedroom techniques they had encountered in Western-style novels: "To a degree, popular literature impairs sexual morality (how many women we take to bed today want sex in the style of a heroine they have read about in Ian Fleming' thrillers?)" (Wanjala 1978, 18). He assumes here that women, like the nation, have to be protected from literature that corrupts their sexuality, and that they are incapable of reading with the required level of critical discrimination materials presented to them. Oblivious to Wanjala is that by quoting liberally from the texts at which he is scoffing, he is institutionalizing them. Maillu does not have copies of his own books that Wanjala criticizes because they are self-published and already out of print. But readers are able to get Maillu's mischievous ideas from Wanjala's criticism.

For his part, Bernth Lindfors, one of America's leading Africanists and the founding editor of the premier *Research in African Literatures*, is almost Platonic in the way he reads noncanonical works. In the variously anthologized "A Basic Anatomy of East African Literature in English," he views canonical literature as appealing to the mind and popular writers as paralleling nonintellectual parts of the body. In an anatomical analogy, he sees Ngũgĩ's fiction as representing the head, while Maillu's represents the groin (1994, 79). The popularization of the literature, he notes, is an indication of rising literacy.

Created and theorized mainly by male critics who could easily access publishing opportunities (not to mention men's easier access to general literacy), the realist novel is more interested in issues of nationalism. Women's rights and sexual issues are treated as secondary categories. Literature that deviates from nationalist rhetoric is equated with pornography because national liberation and the rejection of capitalism are regarded, rightly or wrongly, as urgent issues with which every artist must grapple. The realist novel of literary nationalism is, nevertheless, sexualized, and houses its sexual dimension in metafictional moments in which the artist-character demolishes the boundary between the canonical and the noncanonical. Even in the most political of novels, ordinarily mundane references to sex are incorporated in serious presentations of the nation in a way that disturbs the traditional high/low binary opposition.

The False Canon: Gordimer's *The Lying Days*

Much of Nadine Gordimer's fiction uses localized metafictional techniques in an attempt to present the tensions in canon formation while remaining on the whole realist. An excellent case in point is her first novel *The Lying Days* (1953), which examines the theme of literature's role in shaping the reader's perceptions of the world and in forging mature political positions about racial inequalities in South Africa. Compared to her later fiction, *The Lying Days* is not an especially accomplished work of art. It is idealistic in its liberal humanism. It follows the gradual transformation of its principal character, Helen Shaw, into a politically conscious young adult. The story is told by Helen Shaw herself in the first-person narrative mode. Given that it covers her life between ages seven and seventeen, it presents us with a narrator whose reliability is limited. In Helen, the reader encounters a narrator who presents more in her story than she realizes.

The novel's importance rests in the way it self-consciously uses a female character's perspective to address the political issues facing the nation, setting a trend to be followed and complicated by African women writers in the later decades of the twentieth century. Following the trend set by George Eliot and Olive Schreiner, *The Lying Days* traces the development of a young female character through ignorance and self-delusion toward what she considers a mature vision of society. The novel does not deal directly with issues of sexuality, but its choice of a female character to tell the story of the nation, as opposed to the traditional male hero of the *Bildungsroman* genre, is complemented by constant references to literature as a tool to develop self-awareness, to draw attention to the intersection of metafiction and gender in the novel. As the story presents the linear development of Helen Shaw from a naïve girl to an intellectual able to come to terms with the racial inequalities in South Africa, conventional realism is subverted, especially at the end of the story. This suggests that the story is about a fictional character telling us how stories should be told. Reading becomes a metaphor for appreciating life, and life becomes a way of appreciating art. Toward the end of the novel, *The Lying Days* ironically characterizes itself as a mere fictional creation by its deluded twenty-four-year-old narrator.

Born in a small mining town, Helen Shaw comes of age at a time when segregationist politics has consolidated itself as an official nationalist ideology in South Africa with the official establishment of the apartheid state in 1948. She is critical of the apartheid system that privileges her, but the reader is compelled to wonder whether she is living an illusion, even when she considers herself an adult who understands the apartheid situation. Helen uses metaphors of literary genres and reading in her attempt to understand apartheid; if the walls of the Native Affairs Department building look on the outside "like a diary," the documents in the office look like "stains in the wall" (282). There is an intricate link between literature and the mundane society that produces it.

Like Chinua Achebe in *Things Fall Apart*, Gordimer gets the title of her novel from Yeats, in this case from his "The Coming of Wisdom with Time":

> Though leaves are many, the root is one;
> Through all the lying days of my youth
> I swayed my leaves and flowers in the sun;
> Now I may wither into the truth. (1916, 102)

The persona in Yeats's poem suggests an essence that can be reached when superficial outer elements of identity inevitably fade away. To the persona, there is a truth to be discovered as one gets older and sheds the naïveté of youth. Like Yeats's poem, Gordimer's novel thematizes growing up, suggesting that as one ages one comes to better understand the superficiality of racial identities based on skin pigmentation.

The place of books in the creation of a politically conscious apprehension of the society is important in Helen's struggle to understand herself and her unfair society. Although she initially appears at ease with the system, from the very first paragraphs of the narrative we encounter a character ready to oppose the established order by refusing to join her parents who want her to carry along an escapist book about life in Europe, as opposed to the material conditions in South Africa. She is about seven years old at the time, but seeming to comment with the benefit of hindsight in the present time of narration, she links her parents' actions and demands of her to paranoid fear that she would be sexually assaulted by the black boys. She mixes the naïve perspective of the eight-year-old girl and the reflective adult to present her parents as racists. Although her mother is friendly to some Africans, she comes across as quite condescending in her attitude toward nonwhite people. The reader is aware that at the time Helen is speaking in the narrative, she is already a mature woman reconstructing her innocence as a child against the background of the brutalities of racial segregation. She attributes her naïveté to her upbringing as a member of a privileged race in a town where the performances she attends are limited to *Alice in the Wonderland*, from which black children are barred.

Helen's story vividly highlights the suppression of the African narrative in racist South Africa, even within the liberal humanist tradition. As a child, Helen seems to prefer literature that expresses her world in realist terms:

> Even when I was smaller, fairy tales had never interested me much. To me, brought up into the life of a South African mine, stories of children living the ordinary domestic adventures of the upper-middle-class English family—which was the only one that existed for children's books published in England in the thirties—were weird and exotic enough. Nannies in uniform, governesses and ponies, nurseries and playrooms and snow fights—all these commonplaces of European childhood were

> as unknown and therefore immediately enviable as the life of legendary castles to the English children for whom the books were written. (Gordimer 1953, 20)

In this passage, Helen theorizes that literature that appears realistic in the bourgeois aesthetics of the Western imperial center is ethereal and abstracted in the South African situation. This is a point to be later elaborated on by Ngũgĩ, especially in *Decolonising the Mind* (1986a), about the relevance of European children's literature in Africa. Helen in the novel would prefer to read "a book in which I myself was recognizable" (20). By telling her own story in *The Lying Days*, she makes a step in that direction, even if her political perspective at the time she experiences the events she describes is not as mature as she deludes herself. On the whole, Helen seems to be addressing a European audience who might doubt what she sees as the real and horrid consequences of apartheid.

Despite her heightened self-consciousness—the way in which she calls her auditors' attention to "this pen and this paper" with which she is scripting her life story (357)—Helen is condescending to the point of cynicism in her view of the educated indigenous Africans' enthusiasm about writing and discussing literature. Using metaphors borrowed from the arts to illustrate how far removed the natives are from standardized ways of reading, Helen pokes fun at the overzealous and long-winded Mr. Thabo's response to the canons of Western literature. Thabo is given no agency, despite the reproduction of the convoluted speeches and gestures he stages in the English tutorial class with the patronizing Dr. East. This black male character comes through as an obsequious clown, whose main interest is to pass exams:

> Sir, well, I should say—in my humble opinion that is—this bad habit of Thackeray's, it makes it very difficult for the student. It is hard for him to know what is in the story, if you know what I mean, and the examination it may be that you are asked a question about the story, and you know the book too well and put in what is not the story? He smiled round the class with a slowly widening gesture, as a conductor acknowledges applause by taking it for his whole orchestra. (129)

How can we empathize with a narrator who is so condescending, notwithsanding her stated chagrin at condescension? At age seventeen, Helen is not as politically mature as she thinks she is. Our empathy toward her is restored when we consider, without putting too fine a theoretical point on it, the well-known distinction that Franz K. Stanzel makes in *Narrative Situations in the Novel* (1971) and *A Theory of Narrative* (1984) between the narrating self from the experiencing self. Stanzel observes that the meaning of a first-person narrative derives from "the references and relationships between the fictional world and the figure of the authorial narrator and from the resulting tensions in values, judgments, and kinds of experience" (1971, 28). This helps the readers of an autobiographically presented narrative, such as Helen Shaw's in *The Lying Days*, see a probable difference between the character experiencing the events in the story and the character telling that very story, especially in terms of age. For Stanzel, in a quasi-autobiographical narrative there is a spatial, temporal, and even psychological difference between the narrating "I" who speaks to the reader in the text and the experiencing "I" who witnesses and assesses the events presented. Using Stanzel's insights, I would prefer, like Michael Wade (1978) and Dominic Head (1994), to read the narrating Helen as different from the Helen who experiences the event in the story. In other words, although not directly stated in the story, there is an older Helen describing her life up to the age of seventeen and probably mimicking her ignorance and prejudices when she thought of herself as having grown into a knowledgeable and liberal woman. Thus the Helen who is speaking to the reader is different from the adolescent who deludes herself to be a politically mature woman, despite her persistent adolescent naïveté and prejudice.

Helen's attitude toward her black college classmate Mary Seswayo is not just paternalistic. The white girl does not seem to see that the literature she studies at the university is racialized, sexualized, and gendered. At the time she is narrating the story she is perceptive enough to understand, probably in retrospect, her mother's sexual stereotypes toward black Africans, but in college she is not able to see through the masculinist nature of the canon. Even as the novel ends and she emerges from what she considers delusions of her youth (the days of lying to herself), she does not see how sex plays a part in canon formation, where the literature is male, its teachers are male, and its most vocal students are male—even when all of them are wrong in the way they teach and read literature. Her self-consciousness serves mainly to enhance the reader's sense of her authenticity as an eyewitness account of what goes on in South Africa. Not interested in writing back to the metropolitan center, but in appealing for a liberal humanist alliance against racial discrimination, Helen's narrative fails to see that the West from which she seeks support on behalf of the oppressed blacks could be experiencing similar forms of apartheid in the form of discrimination against women and women's exclusion from the canon as evidenced by the literature that the metropolitan colonial center has brought to its colonial outposts—literature written by men, to be taught by men, and discussed by men.

Country and the Canon: Ngũgĩ's *Petals of Blood*

The radical critique of the postindependence intellectual and ruling elites forms an orbiting constellation in Ngũgĩ's *Petals of Blood* (1977). The novel can be described as realist because it is primarily relayed by an omniscient narrator who presents the stories of different characters, ultimately suggesting a dialectical relationship between its fictional narrative and the reality beyond the text. The narration and the multiple focalizations of events as experienced by the characters give *Petals of Blood* an illusion of documentary verisimilitude while critiquing the betrayal of constitutional independence by postcolonial African leaders. The leadership, according to the novel, has mortgaged the nation to Western corporatism. Through its main characters and the array of narratives, Ngũgĩ depicts the neocolonialism as a condition threatening to destroy the country.

The novel revolves around its character Munira, a teacher, who is arrested by the police on suspicion that he has killed three prominent capitalists in a brothel owned by his friend Wanja, a prostitute. The narrator plunges us into the character's consciousness as the character reconstructs, probably as a statement to the police to exonerate himself, the past leading to his arrest. He explains his relationship to other characters in the novel, such as Karega, a young teacher in love with Wanja. Wanja, the prostitute symbolizes the abused nation, the tendency of the exploited to contribute to their own oppression by exploiting other people, as Wanja does with the young girls in her brothel, and the capacity of the oppressed to destroy the structures that would support them, including those (like Wanja's brothel) they have set up themselves.

As the novel comes to its end, Wanja sees that as a woman she is condemned to a subordinate status: "If you have a cunt—excuse my language, but it seems the curse of Adam's Eve on those who are born with it—if you are born with this hole, instead of it being a source of pride, you are doomed to either marrying someone or else being a whore. You eat, or you are eaten" (293). The demonstrative *this* to describe her genitalia further enhances the immediacy. Exiled from her rural home by her own parents for getting pregnant by a rich neocolonialist, Wanja does not see her complicity in compounding the exploitation of women when she opens a brothel or in denigrating her own body. It takes Munira to burn down the brothel, with three capitalists in it preying on innocent girls to make the point.

The plot is presented metafictionally to the reader unmediated from Munira's diary as "a mixture of autobiographical confessional and some kind of prison notes" (227). Although it is documented as a police statement in which Munira is "meant to tell the truth, the whole truth, and nothing but the truth" (41), his rendition of events is highly manipulated, and at one point he confesses to "mixing fact with fiction" (100). The characters whose narratives he frames confess to manipulating facts for effects—as is the case when Wanja, theorizing narrative to justify her own mode of rendition, says, "After all, a coherent narrative depended on knowing what details to tell and what to leave out" (322). Although there is a heterodiegetic narrator who frames Munira's diary, Ngũgĩ further enlists deliriums, drunken characters, and ideologically befogged individuals to sift the events in what Patrick Williams (1999) calls a "polyphonic" discourse, upgraded from the dialogism of Ngũgĩ's earlier work (95). The polyphony approximates the desire for self-reliance in which the indigenous voices are not silenced. The Bandung idea of development based on local initiatives as opposed to capitalist maneuvers is emphasized by this socialist realist magnum opus.

Plagued by the very sensational pulp novels it criticizes, *Petals of Blood's* central narrative revolves around investigations into the murders of three wealthy businessmen in a fire at a brothel in Ilmorog, a rural town.[1] The narrator depicts each of the main characters—Munira, Abdulla, Wanja, and Karega—being interrogated in connection to the murders and reflecting about their existence in the postcolonial nation. A canonical text in African letters, the novel stakes a claim for the African canon in African schools by equating the supposedly foreign Shakespearean canon with the sexually explicit pulp fiction of David Maillu and James Hadley Chase (172).[2] It equates the two sets of literatures through subtle rhetorical devices; Shakespeare is contrasted with the pulp writers by a mentally colonized African head teacher whose point of view the novel does not endorse. The teacher is mocked for his pride in quoting Shakespeare's work to justify the exclusion of African literature and the studies of African knowledge from the curriculum:

> The heavens themselves, the planets, and this centre
> Observe degree, priority, and place,
> Insisture, course, proportion, season, form,
> Office, and custom, in all line of order;
> And therefore is the glorious planet Sol
> In noble eminence enthron'd and spher'd
> Amidst the other, whose med'cinable eye
> Corrects the ill aspects of planets evil,
> And posts, like the commandment of a king,
> Sans check, to good and bad. But when the planets
> In evil mixture to disorder wander,
> What plagues and what portents, what mutiny,
> What raging of the sea, shaking of earth,
> Commotion in the winds! Frights, changes, horrors,

Divert and crack, rend and deracinate,
The unity and married calm of states
Quite from their fixture! O, when degree is shak'd,
Which is the ladder of all high designs,
The enterprise is sick! How could communities,
Degrees in schools, and brotherhoods in cities,
Peaceful commerce from dividable shores,
The primogenity and due of birth,
Prerogative of age, crowns, sceptres, laurels,
But by degree, stand in authentic place?
Take but degree away, untune that string,
And hark what discord follows! (Ngũgĩ 1977, 172)

This passage from Shakespeare's *Troilus and Cressida*, a play about the Trojan War, captures a moment when the Greek general Ulysses argues that for the stability of society, order must be maintained at all costs by making certain that each social category knows its place in the polis (1.3.103–120). Ulysses's statement is nationalistic in its justification of hierarchies that support the preservation of power in a defeated society. It is not unlike the society presented in *Petals of Blood*, where African society has been excluded from cultural studies in its own institutions. Within this context, the head teacher is arguing that African literature should not be allowed to disrupt the canon of the Great Tradition. For the teacher, "the school's traditions, which had stood the test of time, had to be maintained. He did not therefore want to hear any more nonsense about African teachers, African history, African literature, and African this and that: whoever heard of African, Chinese, or Greek mathematics and science . . . history was history, literature was literature" (172). Advancing a universalist aesthetics that the novel does not endorse, the teacher quotes a "great educator" (Matthew Arnold), that literature is "the best that had been thought and written in the world" (172). The teacher is presented as a misreader who quotes selectively and out of context to justify the status quo.

The character's misreading of the context in which Ulysses speaks underlines the hypocrisy behind the construction of the school canon. Ulysses' statement that "the enterprise is sick" parallels the postindependence state and reminds us that the title of the novel is borrowed from Caribbean writer Derek Walcott's *The Swamp*, a metafictional poem about the deformations of the environment and a poet's alienation from his own physical landscape. *The Swamp*, is an intense work of art that captures alienation and degeneration in a series of images based on tropical fauna and flora, which, despite proliferation, are defined by horrifying deformities. Ngũgĩ uses Walcott's poem to underline the sense of impotence that intellectuals such as Karega and

Munira feel in the overwhelming decadence that faces postindependence Kenya, a plight shared by the poet's persona in Walcott's *The Swamp*. The physical deformities that the novel recalls from Walcott's poem signal the entangled and problematic nature of human relationships. But the title of the novel and the development of the theme also profoundly recall William Blake's *The Sick Rose*, a poem that presents guilt and destruction through sexual allusions.[3] Like Blake's flower and Ulysses' Grecian society, the society in Ngũgĩ's novel is visibly sick and needs regeneration; this renaissance will not come about if the Western canon were to be retained.

The conservative neocolonial academy that Ngũgĩ mocks with this citation of Shakespeare and Arnold in *Petals of Blood* invokes the Western canon not because it admires the timeless values in Western texts but to deliberately distort the texts and justify the exclusion of African cultural and aesthetic texts from the canon. *Petals of Blood* assails the argument in support of the universalism of literature by making the teacher mouth the words of an unnamed "famous educator [who] described [literature] as the best that had been thought and written in the world" (172). The teacher uses Arnold's maxim to justify ignoring African studies, perhaps unaware that Arnold, a radical in the prevailing nationalism of his time, was himself in favor of the expansion of the English syllabus to include lesser-known writers. The fact that it does not fully explain the passage it quotes from Shakespeare, or even name Arnold, signals the text's position that Western canons are so ingrained in postindependence cultures that their invocations need no glossing. Ngũgĩ does not necessarily endorse all of the noncanonical writers the teacher invokes in contradistinction to Shakespeare, but the teacher's reference to Arnold reminds the reader of the need to question the canon by engaging literatures and languages that are traditionally disparaged.

Ngũgĩ clarifies his attitude toward Matthew Arnold in *Something Torn and New* (2009, 53–54). Citing Arnold's essay "The Study of Celtic Culture," Ngũgĩ shows his problem with Arnold is that (despite Arnold's inclusiveness), the latter did not mind the extinction of the Welsh and Celtic heritage to give way to the universal use of English. It is useful to remember that the essay was delivered as Oxford lectures, serialized in the premier Victorian London's *Cornhill Magazine* in 1866, and published the same year in New York in *The Eclectic Magazine of Foreign Literature, Science, and Art*. At the time of the lectures, Britain was under the threat of fragmentation, as confirmed by Fenian bombing activities in the fall of 1865. In Arnold's thinking, all non-mainstream cultures needed to be reigned in if the United Kingdom was not to be reduced to anarchy. For him, the "sooner the Welsh language disappears as instrument of practical, political, social life of Wales, the better; the better for England, the better for Wales itself" (quoted in Ngũgĩ 2009, 54). However, although Ngũgĩ was later to complete an epistemological break involving abandonment of writing in what he saw as a colonial language to writing in the equivalent of Arnold's Celtic languages, at the time of conceiving *Petals of Blood*, Ngũgĩ was not radically any different from Arnold (1866); in writing the novel, he used Gĩkũyũ indigenous traditions to express the African spiritual power but did it in the English language, just the way Arnold advocated for Celtism while promoting the English language. As already seen, Ngũgĩ seemed to have a low opinion of noncanonical African writers, such as Maillu, whose writings he mocks in *Devil on the Cross* (1982) as part of an escapist neocolonial culture. The only major difference between Ngũgĩ and Arnold is that Ngũgĩ did not wish African languages a quick death.

Ngũgĩ's deployment of the documentary style and the unmediated stream-of-consciousness technique, in which the characters could be recreating fictional selves in the realist fiction, gives *Petals of Blood* the rare quality of at once endorsing and undermining realism. Indeed, the novel appears to be the kind of text it criticizes within its own pages through the character Karega:

> Imaginative literature was not much different: the authors described the conditions correctly: they seemed able to reflect accurately the contemporary situation of fear, oppressions, and deprivation: but thereafter they led him down the paths of pessimism, obscurity, and mysticism: was there no way out except cynicism? Were people helpless victims? (200)

The novel articulately presents the fears and deprivations that many undergo at the hands of global oppressors and their local lackeys. It evokes the need to steer off cynicism in gendered metafictional ekphrasis, in which painting and drawing are presented as sites upon which subjectivity and desire are inscribed. Wanja is presented as a playful artist who at one point accepts Munira's advances with a "playful gratitude" (32), revealing herself as a performer who takes delight in being fought over by men.

Although most of Wanja's sketches are not fully described in the novel, it is suggested that they are nonrealistic, provoking debates because of their ambiguity and multiple possible interpretations. While serving as the manager at Abdullah's bar in the village, Wanja tries to catch the eye of customers through a signboard that indicates that she was giving a special offer of a "PERMANENT CLOSING DOWN SALE" (55). Though visually striking to the reader because it is capitalized to give the impression of its prominence in the extratextual world it describes, the signboard would be inaccessible to its target audience because of its low literacy rates. An innovative communicator, Wanja decides to accompany the verbal notice with "sketches of a shop and people running toward it in a hurry" (55). The children, as a result of low literacy and perhaps driven hunger in the drought-stricken village, misread the "little sketches of men" in Wanja's drawing to mean that the shop was closing down, and that the shopkeeper was giving things away. The drawings, even when accompanied by words, generate different interpretations because they are nonrealistic. In this instance of irony and misreading, *Petals of Blood*, a novel rendered largely in representational realism, recognizes the agency of nonrealist art. This agency is sexualized during the course of a similar attempt to interpret a representation in which a male freedom fighter, Kimathi, is depicted as having breasts. The visual representation provokes the characters to engage in a discussion of sexual hierarchies in society, with the novel using this instance of visual representation of Kimathi by a prominent sculptor, Wanjau (probably a reference to Kenya's pioneer sculptor Elimo Njau in a way that would also evoke Wanja's name), against the grain of prevailing logic to recognize women's contribution to the liberation of Africa from colonialism.

The innocent misreading by the kids and the interpretive engagement with Wanjau's carving of Kimathi provide moments of comic relief in grim and tense parts of the narrative. But misreadings by an adult can be quite irritating, as evidenced by Munira's misinterpretation of a sketch Wanja draws to capture the dilapidated condition of peasants in the scorched village. In pursuit of a cathartic experience to vent her frustrated desires, Wanja metaphorizes in sexual terms the brutal condition in which the villagers find themselves:

> One day, after a stream of invectives and careless complaints, she jumped from the counter, got an exercise book, and quickly drew sketches of a group of old women raising dust as they ran from a pursuing lusty young man sun toward thin old man rain with a tiny head and legs. (75)

Wanja's sexualized visual portrayal of the drought situation is not a mere purging of emotions or expression of erotic desire. The narrator has described her sexual longing, and the fact that she gives the portrait to Munira, whom she desires, might suggest seduction. Munira praises the peasants' resilience, but Wanja insists on a bleak interpretation of the situation she has presented.

What emerges from the sketch and its interpretation is the idea that art seeks to disturb the conscience of the contented. From his own misreading of the sketch, Munira realizes that he has accepted the situation as it is, while Wanja wants to urge him to wake up to new possibilities. As an artist, Wanja speaks openly about women's sexuality, especially the "curse" their sexuality has imposed upon them in postindependence nations.[4] However, the realist novel has to make Wanja a prostitute to justify her having the courage to articulate a taboo topic. Even so, her speech is punctuated with signs of hesitation, and she also uses periphrastic expressions such as "excuse my language but . . ." (293) to reduce the disgrace in her language.

Sex and Anomie of the Artist: Kibera and Bukenya

I have already shown that the literature of the late 1960s and the 1970s was marked by disillusionment with postindependence politics. Emmanuel Obiechina observes that, as a result of rising unemployment, the growth of slums, the spread of disease, and numerous military coups that saw twenty-five unconstitutional changes of government between 1960 and 1968, the African writer became alienated from the political and bureaucratic elites responsible for the social malfeasance in the new nations. There was also a growing sense of self-reproach among writers, who felt that they may have contributed to the national crisis. Obiechina points out that "faced with the new realities of power and politics in Africa, writers have had to reappraise their role in society. The preoccupation of the past had given way to concern with the pressing problems of the present" (1990, 122). The figure of the street beggar predominates in this literature that contains numerous references to crime and prostitution. What eludes Obiechina here is that the writers were addressing in their own novels the crisis facing them as producers of art, where they combined literary theorizing and creative production. The writers seem to be haunted by the question: Are artists in fact the very same educated castrates, whose testicles had been crushed by books, as described by the female persona in Okot p'Bitek's (1966) long narrative poem *Song of Lawino*? The result is a self-reflexive literary theorizing in novels that conflated imaginativeness with sexual potency.

The early 1970s witnessed the publication of novels that captured the end of the nationalistic euphoria of the 1960s but that inserted commentary on the role of the artist in the face of political and social crises. While the novels of the 1980s were marked, as Ngũgĩ points out in *Moving the Centre* (1993), by a sense of hope that the conditions facing the nation would be resolved through mass action, the earlier novels of the 1970s were marked by a critique of the intellectuals who, like the nationalist politicians, had failed the nation. One of the novels that express this critique is Leonard Kibera's *Voices in the Dark* (1970). Simatei is right when he argues that Kibera structures the stasis facing the independent nation using "the mode of the theatre of [the] absurd" (2001, 41), but I want to propose that the novel is also a critique of that mode of aesthetic presentation.

Before I discuss Kibera's novel, it may be appropriate to turn briefly to Ugandan poet, literary theorist, and dramatist Austin Bukenya's only novel *The People's Bachelor* (1972), which explicitly indicates, through its presentation of a budding member of the literary elite, the way in which writers and critics have betrayed their own society. A campus novel, Bukenya's *The People's Bachelor* engages the crisis of representation in postindependence East Africa by posing the following questions: Can African intellectuals, so steeped in Western modernity and an individualistic drive, adequately speak on behalf of the oppressed populations? Can critics and artists represent the hopes and aspirations of the people amid governmental abuse of power and the intellectuals' natural need for self-preservation? Can the artists avoid conscription as agents of the status quo? In the novel, Bukenya uses a literature student's experiences on campus and in the wider society to cast a disapproving gaze upon the postcolonial intellectual community for its waste of the nation's time and resources.

The People's Bachelor is not as accomplished as Bukenya's poetry and drama, but for all of the melodrama surrounding its depiction of the exploits of what it satirically termed the "Academic Anonymous" and "cap-and-gowned" (intellectuals) in the novel, it nevertheless illuminates how nationalism, race, and sexuality are intertwined in postindependence Africa and the role of the writer in advocating the interests of the indigenous populations. Conflating references to Uganda and Dar es Salaam, the novel satirizes socialist nationalism and the discrimination against blacks by whites and against Asians by blacks. Maalas, the name of the fictional campus where the action takes place, seems to be an anagram for Salaam, but at the same time it echoes Makerere, Uganda's premier university and East Africa's hub of intellectual life in the 1970s. The discrimination against Asians in the novel recalls the buildup to the expulsion of Asians from Uganda in 1972, the year the novel came out. By setting the novel in Dar es Salaam, where he took his degree in English, Bukenya hints at the failure of socialist nationalism in Tanzania.

Told mainly by an omniscient narrator, but from the perspectives of several students of literature on a college campus, *The People's Bachelor* is self-conscious in its language, occasionally playing on differences between Anglophone African "Engleesh" and the uppity English of the colonial "Britishers" (the term the characters use as a corrupted descriptor of the Britons). The primary aim of this form of abrogation is not to "write back" to Standard English in order to decolonize it; it is mainly deployed to satirize neocolonial institutions as is the case when a government minister is called a "mini-star," in mimicry of local mispronunciation (92). The novel humorously mixes high and low culture, combining poetic commentaries, descriptions of raw sex, political theorizing, and campus toilet graffiti to describe in bearable terms the malfeasance of the professors and the students.

The descriptions are peppered with sexual terms, and the language of literary theory gets enmeshed with sexual imagery. Take, for example, the opening paragraph of the sixth chapter, the same chapter in which Bukenya describes the rape of an Asian girl in order to characterize the xenophobia that culminated in the expulsion of Asians. The chapter is hoisted with a description of the nationalist liberation effort in a language borrowed from literary commentary:

> Imagine a Frelimo fighter, grenade in hand, squatting in the thick, dark-green bush of Mozambique, ambushing a Portuguese army convoy; or a rifle-armed government artist in any other part of Africa, kneeling in a banana, cassava, or rice garden some seven or eight kilometres outside the capital, rifle at the ready, eyes glued to the road, waiting for the arrival of the presidential motorcade, having decided, as it often becomes necessary on a continent where the ballot is bourgeois and reactionary, and does not project the African Image, that a too benevolent *Baba wa Taifa* would be eliminated. (104)

The narrator here presents a hypothetical scenario in which a hero or a heroine would be constructed in a narrative of liberation. Art is seen as a facet of anticolonial nationalism, with the line between the artist and the liberationist fully blurred. There seems to be a correspondence between artistic projects and the desire for liberation, a relationship that becomes strained after independence. Alongside the levity in the reference to artists and freedom fighters is the satirical invocation of the title *Baba wa Taifa* (father of the nation), the label most African dictators chose for themselves in the decades after independence, presenting themselves to the citizens as the principal fathers and the most virile individuals in the nation.

Perverse and extravagant copulative energy and state power are presented as mutually enhancing, but these are characteristics also to be found among those who claim liberatory and oppositional instrumentality. The Rabelaisian grotesque realism that Achille Mbembe sees as characteristic of postcolonial politics is not limited to perverse state machinery and its love for grandiose displays of power; in Bukenya's novel, this excessive corporeality is a common feature of intellectuals seeking to liberate the society from state abuses of power. In such a scenario, is there any hope for Africa? Is not the situation even grimmer than Mbembe sees it in *On the Postcolony* (2001a), in which the condition of the postcolonial nation is cast in radically pessimistic terms? Bukenya is not necessarily presenting the perversity of state power as irreversible; rather, he suggests that it is absurd to expect the intellectual elite to provide a panacea to the problems created by the political leadership because the latter at one point also espoused the intellectual idealism of those now seeking to remove it from power. While Mbembe seems to rule out the possibility of the society staging a successful resistance to the rulers, Bukenya's novel neither affirms nor rejects the community's agency. The aporia provides an illusion of utopia where state power can be deconstructed—if not by the intellectuals who are no different from the rulers, then by ordinary citizens.

Bukenya develops the metafictional imperative further with closer references to sex, nationalism, and literary production:

> This is heroism. Not the throwing of the grenade or the pulling of the trigger, but the physical inactivity of the waiting. And the examples of freedom fighters are perhaps unnecessary extremes. Any case of keeping still will do: from the second wife who sits listening to her husband making love to her co-wife in the next room, to the budding writer who checks his pen, despite a feeling of certainty that a new idea has blossomed in his mind, to the village shopkeeper who, outside the coffee and cotton seasons, may not get a customer for six hours on end, to the young graduate who stands thirty minutes at an office reception desk before the standard-seven girl behind it even asks him what she can do for him. If any of these characters *chooses* to remain still, arrest all physical activity, and concentrate on himself or herself, the character may be crowned a hero or a heroine. (104–105, emphasis in original)

Here Bukenya intertwines raw sexual pleasure with acts of nationalism and literary creation to comment on the euphoria following independence and to hint at the betrayal that followed. The narrator seems to be unaware of his own gender bias or that of Mutwe, from whose perspective the story is relayed to the reader. Notice that the graduates are seen as male (although the campus we have been presented with has females too). In the metaphor of a wife enduring a sexual act between her husband and a cowife, the novel presents women as submissive to the heteronormative order. In the same sentence, it is illiterate girls who become the bane of graduates in governmental offices. The above descriptions are followed by a scene in which an African male student rapes an Asian girl. The traumatic episode is reflexively presented to demonstrate that "we could have chosen to tell such tales, full of swing and flare, signifying life" (106). There is a hint here of the cynicism of the narrator and of the intellectuals who view the pains of the ordinary people as mere material for their creative writing. The intellectuals cannot represent meaningfully—in terms of advocacy and artistic portrayal—the plight of women and the oppressed in Uganda. What is apparent in the poet's hypothetical metaphors and in the embedded reality within the novel is that women are reduced to the role of phallic receptacles in scenes of both rape and consensual sexual orgies.

Moments later, the novel criticizes the obscurantist African poets, whom the Western literary fraternity holds in such high esteem, for their failure to effectively address local audiences. Focalized through a final-year literature student, Kale, the passage refers to a guest lecture by an African literary icon in a context that suggests that the fictional icon is a thinly disguised reference to Wole Soyinka:

> The speaker was a poet, perhaps Africa's leading poet after the dissolution of Senghor's *tigritude*. Kale, though, did not like the poet. He hated him in fact. But he was looking forward to meeting him. The boy wanted to ask the poet why he always wrote in what looked like incomprehensible telegraphic messages. That was Kale's own description. It was fairly accurate, for one of the achievements for the muse-inspired son of Africa could claim distinction was that he has never written a complete sentence in his career. But American and British connoisseurs said he was very good. (120–21)

It should be remembered that *tigritude* is a term Wole Soyinka coined at the 1962 African Writers' Conference at Makerere University to criticize the racialized polemics of negritude.[5] Soyinka saw as essentialist and reductionist the "negritudist" emphasis on skin color as a basis for self-affirmation. It was at the same conference that Christopher Okigbo, departing from mainstream negritude as practiced by Léopold Sédar Senghor, declared that he writes for fellow poets. The character Kale in Bukenya's novel presages the criticism that Soyinka and Okigbo were later to receive in some Afrocentric critical circles for betraying Africa by participating in obscurantist aesthetics.[6] The young poet in the novel would agree with the early Soyinka's critique of negritude, representing as he does a post-Senghorian aesthetics. Furthermore, the student of literature, from whose perspective the analysis of both the visiting poet and his critic is presented, deconstructs the poet's philosophy as ineffectual in solving African problems. But although he is vocal in criticizing inaccessible poetry that seems to be selling out Africa to the West, Kale himself later joins the ruling elites in trampling underfoot the rights and desires of his own people.

To heighten its sense of fictionality, the scene is followed by a comic episode. The focalizer (Kale), while rushing to the toilet because of a bout of diarrhea he is suffering after eating bad food in the college dining hall, mistakenly enters a room where fellow literature students are copulating. The bodily effluents and the bad food that causes Kale's diarrhea are symbolic of the rotten state of the postcolonial nation. The scene, exaggerated as it is, signals that as products of a dysfunctional society, the writer, the student of literature, and the critic in postcolonial Africa are a completely confused lot. Either wallowing in *jouissance* or too keen to please the powers that be, the artists are presented almost in the way Plato famously described them—as untrustworthy guardians of the interests of the polis.

Overall, despite its playfulness, *The People's Bachelor* veils its metafictionality under a strong illusion of realism. More sophisticated, if less readable, than Bukenya's novel is *Voices in the Dark* by Kenyan novelist, short story writer, and literary theorist Leonard Kibera (1942–1983). Using a passage from Fanon's *The Wretched of the Earth* (1963) as its preamble, *Voices in the Dark* (1970) treats the theme of disillusionment with the constitutional freedoms of the 1960s, which have not produced better economic opportunities for the local populations and the people who fought to dislodge colonialism. More importantly, it is narrated by an academic reflecting on the interimplication of activist politics and cultural production in Africa. Thus it explores the possible complicity of intellectuals in the crises facing the postindependence nations; like Gordimer's *The Lying Days* (1953), the novel is about the canon, agency, and self-interpretation. The narrative in *Voices in the Dark* is only moderately metafictional, but through its references to the nature and political function of artistic endeavors in modernist prose that mimics itself, the novel destabilizes its own positions on the nature and function of African literature. In the story, nationalists who liberated the country from colonialism are marginalized by the new ruling elite, and the society is defined by violence, alienation, and poverty. Enmeshed in gendered metafiction, the novel tells the story of Gerald Timundu, a playwright who professes anticapitalism, although he has befriended the daughter of a tycoon and lives a middle-class existence.

The novel advertises its own artificiality to mimic the estrangement and hypocrisy of its main character and to signal his alienation from the society in which he dwells. The playfulness of the novel resides in its attempt to create a congruency between writing and sexuality, where sexual lust is combined with poetic figural practices to capture the alienated state of the nation. The vocabulary of textuality is used to describe illicit sexuality. For example, a young editor goes to pick up a prostitute and, focalized through his center of consciousness, the event is relayed to us in editorial grammar:

> The boy worries of the crisis of the spirit for precisely three seconds in memorized poetry conveniently subedited and he says he feels denied. Then he agrees to pay the money as Njoki

> presses him possessively to herself so that the young editor might not escape. But the deal of the flesh thus made, he has forgotten his imported lines and is now aching with a more urgent editorial crisis. (14)

The novel's view of the canon is rendered in terms of sexual relations. The depravity of postindependence culture is symbolized by deviant or dysfunctional sexuality. In a city street scene, we encounter what is implied to be a lesbian relationship: "somewhere in the far corner two ladies are locked in each other's arms, while farther down one of two gentle beggars tries to find what peace he can amidst the noise of a man beating his wife upstairs" (14). The rendition of the beggar's condition is ensconced between a scene of deviant sexuality and domestic violence, drawing the reader's attention to the dysfunctional nature of the postindependence nation. Unwelcome possibilities of male homosexuality are jokingly referred to in *Voices in the Dark*, but the text shows such perversions to be above the male community. The pairing of men in private spaces such as the case of the boy and Timundu in the public toilet and the two beggars on the pavements is suggestive—but masculinity is underlined even in the toilet graffiti described in the novel. It is women's bodies that serve as the site upon which the narrator inscribes the supposedly perverted desires that symbolize a corrupt state.

The disillusionment with independence is symbolically signaled in *Voices in the Dark* not only through grammatically incomplete, fragmentary structures and loose, paratactic sentences but also through a narrative that problematizes its own completeness. Paradoxically, however, the author himself has been critical of novels that do not present the possible completion of the struggle for liberation against the rottenness that defines African nations. In his criticism of Armah's *The Beautyful Ones Are Not Yet Born* (1968), Kibera expresses his disappointment with the Ghanaian writer's failure to celebrate the human ability to change prevailing conditions.[7] As a critic of Armah, Kibera does not call for utopian optimism but for some indication that the artist sympathizes with the subject's conditions and hopes for change in the future, even if hope appears too unrealistic now:

> Satire and cynicism when not tempered with sympathy—and humility—refine into mere techniques. Techniques not as a discovery of a truth which is constantly eluding us as in Ngũgĩ's *A Grain of Wheat*, but as a justification of a pre-selected truth or idea. (70)

This statement prompts us to think twice about Kibera's project in *Voices in the Dark*, a representation of the world that seems to share Ayi Kwei Armah's vision of society. But the novel is framed by a pervasive absurdist vision. It is the kind of aesthetics that Timundu, the cynical and pessimistic writer, would espouse—and it is therefore modeled on the kind of work that Timundu would write, which is suggested in the story; first, other characters in the novel use expressions that we would associate with Timundu in a way that suggests he is the one who created them. For example, he "jokingly" calls his suburban dwelling the "anthill" (45) and, curiously enough, the beggars call the residential houses below which they sleep "decent anthills."

The metaphor suggests a confluence of voices through which the narrative is relayed to the reader. Timundu is better equipped theoretically to analyze the other characters; if they existed outside of his imagination at all, then they would be able to analyze him. Linguistically, we note that the bulk of the novel is articulated in the simple present tense. Chapters 2, 3, and 13 of the novel strike our attention because they are written in the past tense, suggesting a narrator who is presenting events in retrospect as opposed to the other narrating consciousness presenting the events as they unfold. Throughout, the narrative voice is heterodiegetic, telling the story from the perspective of the characters whose consciousness the narrator is able to penetrate. Against this background, the present-tense narration serves as the kind of stage directions that Timundu would write, or commentaries that he would enunciate in academic discourse. Timundu comes across as a psychologically disturbed person, and it would not be beyond him to imagine his own death, given the irrational way the text presents him as having died. His paranoia may have led him to imagine his own death as he drives to his rented house after dropping Wilma home. The supposed death is reported to us not in the past tense but in the present tense (and in a parenthetical statement). Its reportage belongs to the fictional sections of the narrative that Timundu conjures up. If Timundu is not physically dead as he imagines, then his death must be a realization that the community considers him as good as dead for not having intervened more meaningfully in the problems of the nation. We should not lose sight of the fact that his death appears to be focalized through the very beggars he has conjured into existence.

Reality and fiction reinforce each other in *Voices in the Dark* as the narrator foregrounds the fictionality of the narrative while at the same time recuperating the fictional events and personalities to real historical circumstances. For all of its stylistic experimentation, the novel is faithful to the Kenyan realities of the late sixties, buy through metafictional devices, the writer playfully advertises the novel's fictionality by aesthetically distancing the story from the rank and gritty reality that it projects. The main character is named Timundu, which is the Gĩkũyũ for "it is not a real person."

While the name also might be appropriate for a person like Timundu who is alienated to a level that he *ti* (is no longer) *mundu* (human), the name is particularly chosen for the artist among all of the other alienated characters in the novel. The story's denial of its own reality is enacted through a real Kenyan language, Kibera's own mother tongue. Probably to evade censorship, later Kenyan works, including novels and plays by Ngũgĩ wa Thiong'o, Rebeka Njau,[8] Francis Imbuga, Wahome Mutahi,[9] and David Karanja,[10] are set in spaces whose names are foregrounded as fictional and nonreferential. But the narratives contain words that signal their national setting, so the attempt to run away from reality anchors them even more firmly in an extratextual world.

Undermining Parochialism

This chapter has demonstrated that metafiction as a technique is not new to African literature. Even the earliest novels used it to address their own status as works of art and to suggest ways in which they would want to be read. The predisposition to see metafiction as fully divorced from earlier representational modes is overturned when we consider key moments in realist novels where metafictional gestures are deployed. My argument in this chapter can be summarized as follows: There are metafictional elements in the realist novel, especially the foundational texts that seek to examine the place of literature, literary studies, and artistic creation, circulation, and interpretation. These texts tried to theorize their own project at a time when African literary theory was not yet fully developed as a guide, as it would be to later fiction. The novels tend to frame the self-consciousness of their narrative within representational realist aesthetics. The realist canonical African novel uses metafictional moments to figure sexuality or to allegorize sex as a symptom of social conditions, especially the sexual exploitation of women in urban spaces. This representation of women as sexual victims has its own problems because it reduces female agency and treats the female body as a site of masculine wars between different ideologies.

Although we tend to see modern African literature as a remonstrance against Western aesthetics, the realist novel invokes canons of planetary literature, not the least Western literature, that engage in a similar project of shattering a quest for totality. This seems to vindicate Gikandi's view in *Writing in Limbo* (1992), that although postcolonial aesthetics may be opposed to European and colonial notions of culture, it is not necessarily opposed to European art (1992, 4–5).[11] The realist Anglophone African novel is especially adept at using metafictional elements to undermine parochialism among colonialists and powerful locals as well as to criticize the misuse of art in precolonial and postindependence Africa as a tool for brainwashing marginalized categories in the society. The canonical realist novel suppresses explicit presentations of sex, but it is gendered, and it deploys metafictional impulses to signify the marginalization of women in a society gripped by nationalistic fervor.

Chapter 3

Potentials and Pitfalls of National Language Literatures

The growth of local publishing and writing in indigenous languages in the 1980s largely accounts for the proliferation of defamiliarized fiction that moves away from the protocols of realism to a more mythopoetic signification that Ato Quayson observes in *Strategic Transformations* (1997). Although Quayson's argument focuses on African texts published in Western venues and written in English, such as the work of Ben Okri, Amos Tutuola, and Wole Soyinka, it is clear that indigenous publishers were producing work, regardless of the individual author's location, in similarly transformed aesthetics in African languages.[1] This chapter examines several nonmimetic Kiswahili novels to demonstrate their rootedness in extratextual realities. Careful not to romanticize African languages as the purveyor of freedom, as Ngũgĩ tends to do in his anticolonial polemics, I illustrate the potentials and pitfalls of works written in Africa's indigenous languages.

The puzzlement expressed by Gerald Gaylard as to whether self-reflexive fiction might be thought of as an imitation of Western aesthetics and therefore "a mere liberal cosmopolitanism, a dilution of the virulent anticolonial rhetoric of the previous generation" (2005, 6) is discounted by the proliferation of the technique within texts written in local languages, texts that are produced by small, indigenous firms that are politically combative in their criticism of dictatorship and unequal economic world order. This is a literature that shows little interest in being part of what Gaylard, using Timothy Brennan's term, fears might be regarded as "saleable 'Third Worldism.' "[2] Just because the metropolis has been drawn to this kind of literature, produced by imitative, aspiring novelists based in the West who are out to cash in on the Western audience's longing for an exotic Africa, it does not mean that such literature is not produced locally for indigenous readership, independent of Western aesthetics and market forces. The critique of colonialism and neocolonialism in Ngũgĩ's, Okri's, or Mahajoub's self-reflexive novels cannot be said to have been blunted by self-reflexivity or publication in Western venues. What marks these works is an inward gaze at the local community and its intelligentsia for their complicity in allowing colonial tendencies to thrive. Without any sympathies for colonialism and without any apologies for the violent way classical colonialism was dislodged from Africa, the novels focus on local subjects, sometimes uncharitably, to reveal the perpetuation of colonial subjection in postindependence Africa.

Contrary to the general belief in postcolonial theory that European colonialists imposed their languages on Africans to erode indigenous identities and to facilitate cultural domination by converting Africans into pseudo-Europeans, evidence offered by African linguists and historians, such as Ade Ajayi (1965), Moradewun Adejunmobi (2004), and Ngũgĩ wa Thiong'o (1986a), indicates that African indigenous languages received a major boost from colonial administrators and missionaries during the colonial era, even if the Europeans' support for local languages was not always in good faith. Although some African societies had a written literature before colonialism, much of literature in African languages was first nurtured by Christian missionaries who brought printing presses with them.

Articles published in *Journal of the Royal African Society* (later *African Affairs*) and *Africa: Journal of the International African Institute* from the late 1920s to around the 1950s display colonial administrators' and Christian missionaries' zeal for the development of literatures in local languages. For instance, Eric R. J. Hussey (1885–1958), a British colonial administrator who worked in various parts of Africa from as early as 1914, believed in the adaptation theory of education in which local cultures and languages would be given primacy in the learning process. For him, "it is the opinion of the majority of those who are qualified by experience to judge, that there is a preponderance of advantage in the use of a well-known African language in preference to a European tongue as the literary language of the masses of the people" (Hussey 1932, 171). Implicit in Hussey's argument is that African culture was to be conscripted in spreading European Enlightenment to the Africans. British linguist Ida Ward (1880–1949) also advocated the promotion of African languages among indigenous communities, arguing in 1944 that "too long has the European written for the African in the African's language. A literature cannot grow in this way, and if it is to be truly indigenous, the African himself must take a large, if not an exclusive, share in its development. The European's work, however, is not done: he cannot as yet just hand over to the African the task of writing books without help" (Ward 1941, 88).

As indicated by the debates on the promotion of African languages or not, the opinion of the Europeans was not uniform. In one of her studies of vernacular discourses, Adejunmobi lists a number of rationales for the colonial and missionary investments in African languages. These include the missionaries' need to provide biblical scriptures to the Africans through their own language. She also notes that some colonial administrators strongly distrusted Western-educated African nationalists, and the promotion of vernacular education would alienate the indigenous political elites from that majority. On the whole, the project also was teleological in the sense that the colonialists believed Africans belonged in the past and the vernacular languages would be a good avenue of transcribing that past and strengthening African traditions, which—in the colonialists' eyes—were not equal to Western modernity.

In *Decolonising the Mind*, Ngũgĩ notes that colonialists and missionaries did a commendable job of establishing presses that published in local languages. "But imperialism tried to control the content carried by those languages. Publications were censored directly through government licensing laws or indirectly through the editorial practices of those running the government and missionary presses. African languages were still meant to carry the message of the bible" (Ngũgĩ 1986a, 67). The renewed energy to write in African languages is a continuation of a long tradition, but the writers are now interested in liberating the literature from the shackles of missionaries and colonialism to provide a more complex picture of postindependence Africa.

Guarded Criticism of *Ujamaa* Socialism

The emergent metafictional novel in Kiswahili deserves a separate, book-length study because of its variety and the philosophical and stylistic adventures the writers engage in as they critique local complicities in the global neocolonial order. It is so inventive that it arguably surpasses the locally produced novels in English from East Africa in its approximation of what might be regarded as transnational, postmodernistic trends. One of the most vibrant indigenous languages spoken in the East African countries of Kenya, Uganda, Somalia, and Tanzania, not to mention its spread to central Africa, the Kiswahili language emerged from the contact between Middle Eastern traders and Bantu East Africans from, according to some accounts, as early as the first century AD. Alamin Mazrui (2004, 2007), Ali Mazrui and Alamin Mazrui (1995), Albert Gerard (1981, 1990), Cancel (1993), and Elena Bertoncini-Zúbková (1989) have offered useful genealogies of Kiswahili literature that need not be detailed here. These scholars trace the written literature to the seventeenth century, hinting that the writing tradition might have thrived long before the Portuguese came to the East African coast in the fifteenth century, and that the literature has been dynamic in reflecting and refracting a society in flux.

With its religious roots in Islam, the early Kiswahili literature in Arabic script tended to be homiletic. But by the time of the Berlin Conference of 1884–1885, there was a considerable body of secular and religious art in poetic and prose Kiswahili. The novel form, which developed in the 1930s after James Mbotela's slave narrative *Uhuru wa Watumua* (Freedom of the Slaves, 1934), also leaned toward religious themes and a skepticism toward Arabic and Islamic aristocracy because the literature was patronized by Christian missionaries. Tanzanian literature of the 1970s served the *Ujamaa* socialist policies of communal self-reliance that the Nyerere government formulated with the Arusha Declaration of 1967. The policies failed, but the literature is moderate in its criticism of Nyerere. It is largely driven by the Zanzibar revolution of January 1964 in which the constitutional monarchy of Sultan Jamshid bin Abdullah was overthrown, and the Indian Ocean Island declared a republic that was to soon join the mainland Tanganyika to form the Tanzanian nation. Kimani Njogu (1997), for instance, has astutely connected this class-based revolution to the burgeoning of a Kiswahili literature that leaned toward Marxist aesthetics. The Tanzanian university curriculum was changed in the late 1960s to reflect the socialist principles of the government. Grant Kamenju, a Kenyan Marxist critic teaching at the University of Dar es Salaam, saw the role of the African university to be to "actively assist in the struggle to make a complete and total break with the neocolonialist, capitalist, and Uncle Tom mentality" (quoted in Sicherman 1997, 124). At the risk of ignoring form, Kamenju focused on socialist ideals in his analysis of African literature.

I should point out here, however, that the general reluctance to critique "neo-colonial capitalism and dependency" that Alamin Mazrui (2004, 220; 2007, 41) observes in the Tanzanian socialist literature of the 1970s has been broken by the advent of metafictional art. Mazrui (2004) anticipates the possibility of the growth of a post-*Ujamaa* literature that would be critical of neocolonialism; he suggests the arrival of that moment in his *Swahili beyond Boundaries* (2007), where he notes an upsurge in nonrealist art by a diverse set of writers, including Euphrase Kezilahabi, Gabriel Ruhumbika, Emmanuel Mbogo, William Mkufya, and Said A. Mohamed. Even when critiquing globalization from thinly veiled socialist positions, novels by Mohamed, Kezilahabi, and Chachage point to the hypocrisy that led to the failure of Nyerere's *Ujamaa* socialist policies. While Chachage, for example, is far from endorsing post-Nyerere liberalism (which he tendentiously casts in images of crude male sexual urges and Western sex tourism), he indicates in *Makuadi wa Soko Huria* (Pimps of the Free Market) that the current rampant corruption and the existing gap between the rich and the poor in Tanzania have roots in *Ujamaa*, where "*wakati sisi tulidhani tunapigania usawa, wenzetu walikuwa wajilimbikizia mali. Hakuna hata mmoja kati ya viongozi waliokuwa wakihubiri Ujamaa ambaye ana hali mbaya leo. Wote wameukata*" [2002, 18; when we deluded ourselves that we were fighting for equity, our comrades were busy amassing wealth. Not a single one of those leaders who were preaching socialism to us is doing badly today. They are all living in clover].

Granted, the character who mouths this negative verdict against *Ujamaa* is a censorship bureaucrat sarcastically named Alhaj Said Seif. He is negatively portrayed as a turncoat who betrays both the ideals he fought for during the Zanzibar revolution in the 1960s and the Pan-Africanism he displayed in his journalism in the 1970s. Other characters who utter cynical statements against Nyerere, such as the Asian Tanzanian Alibhai, are presented negatively as supporters of global exploitation of indigenous populations. The novel seems hesitant to criticize Nyerere's socialism per se; rather, it criticizes corrupt and inefficient bureaucrats who made it impossible for Nyerere's policies to thrive. It stages what Peter Nazareth in *Literature and Society in Modern Africa* (1972b) proposes as one of the ways of criticizing socialism in a socialist novel, mainly, "to show, by presenting all the social, political, historical, and psychological facts, that socialism has not yet been achieved or has been side-tracked" (216). The other method that Nazareth identifies—presenting the criticism "subjectively through a bourgeois consciousness" (216)—is used in the novel to ridicule the characters who hold anti-Nyerere positions. The novel further expresses disenchantment with the liberal policies adopted by the governments after Nyerere's administration. What is clear from the novel is a strong skepticism toward blind nationalism or an unabashed adoption of Western liberal policies in Africa.

But we need to note that there is little evidence from the novel to deny Alhaj Said Seif's account, which echoes the disillusionment with *Ujamaa* voiced by personas in recent Tanzanian poetry in English by writers such as Richard S. Mabala, Jwani Mwaikusa, and Freddy Macha. Written by a sociology professor, the novel seems to seek co-relations between an individual's behavior and the larger society. Then, it may be argued that, as a product of his social environment, Alhaj Said Seif has been constructed into the cynic that he has become by his experiences in the 1970s where the *Ujamaa* government controlled the media and forced it to portray the government only in a positive light.

Humanistic Deconstruction

In a survey of Kiswahili literature from Kenya and Tanzania, Said A. M. Khamis comments on the emergence of self-reflexive narratives since the 1980s and their proliferation in 1990s, noting that these nonmimetic works are symptomatic of crises in the region; thematically, the new novel looks inward, showing East Africa, and perhaps Africa as a whole, as experiencing "real" and "psychological" wars.[3] These wars result primarily in frustration and desperation of the citizenry worried about declining economies, mounting corruption, rapid population growth, bloated and at times repressive states, the collapse of the basic infrastructure, gross infringement of human rights, the deterioration of physical and social life, cultural decay, and loss of political authority—hence anarchy, apathy, and the incorrigibility of the politician. In this double-edged socioeconomic relationship of power and oppression, a common thread is the anger of the writers of the new novel. It signals the highest level of frustration and desperation that the Kiswahili novel has ever registered (Khamis 2005, 95).

In Khamis's explanation of the new trends in the novel, there are unmistakable echoes of Erich Auerbach's and early Georg Lukács's Hegelian conceptualization of tragic realism and historical realism in which there is a preponderance of subjective narrations from the perspective of alienated, introspective characters in eighteenth- and nineteenty-century European fiction. Neither Auerbach nor Lukács would likely find much value in the self-conscious and modernistic nonrealist prose of the 1990s, but Khamis, in Hegelian fashion, aligns the new novel with the emerging social-economic disintegration in Tanzania, finding beyond the art's nonrealism, attempts to grasp the inner dynamics and dialectical contradictions in society. Without writing an elegy to realism, Khamis's nostalgia is not for the preindustrial society but, like most Tanzanian novelists in the 1990s, he has an almost idealistic longing for the *Ujamaa* era. His explanation is further reminiscent of Indian theorist Kumkum Sangari's observation that as a mode of self-description, the nonmimetic narration of minority discourse is contingent, discursively signaling the present and pointing to future possibilities in society. For Sangari, the nonmimetic novel of the "Third World," such as Gabriel García Márquez's *One Hundred Years of Solitude*, "answers an emergent society's need for renewed self-description and radical assessment, displaces the established categories through which the West has construed other cultures either in its own image or as alterity, questions the Western capitalist myth of modernization and progress, and asserts without nostalgia an indigenous preindustrial realm of possibility" (1987, 162). We may add that the African novel in the 1980s goes beyond questioning the West to question itself and indigenous practices that parallel colonial hegemony.

The writers—including Khamis himself writing as Said Mohamed, whom he cites frequently—use postrealism to explore the themes of fragmentation, alienation, and dissolution and to exploit the new freedom resulting from the fall of one-party states in East Africa, especially the *Ujamaa* policies. A case in point is the Tanzanian novelist and poet Euphrase Kezilahabi. Slipping between realism and hallucination, Kezilahabi's *Nagona* (1990b) tells the story of the birth of a mysterious female spirit, presented as both a gazelle and a beautiful woman, who promises hope for a world dominated by masculine philosophies. The philosophers are presented as comical figures whose creed is dramatically less meaningful than it is cracked up to be. Sarcastically dubbing Western philosophers Nietzsche, Plato, Marx, Hegel, Freud, and Darwin as "*askari wa mwanga*" (soldiers of the light), the novel portrays these philosophers as failing to comprehend their own souls, despite the reverence in which they are regarded by the rest of the world. When the philosophers are questioned about their creed in the African public square, they are unable to offer sensible answers. The relief they display when dismissed from further interrogation because of their failure to explain their own essences captures the world's tendency to rejoice in ignorance. Set against these so-called warriors of the Enlightenment and truth are African organic intellectuals, represented by old, uneducated, rural men who are shown to be more capable than the European philosophers in helping the society search for its identity, even if that identity is elusive. The elusiveness of a secure identity is signaled by the mysterious girl, Nagona, the search for whom is not fully realized by the end of the story.

From the novel, it is clear that male philosophers would not help the protagonist understand Africa, but there is hope of reaching "Nagona" (the mysterious symbol of insight and enlightenment) via consideration of vanishing indigenous knowledges. Yet harking back to a remote past in search of solutions for present-day problems would not be viable, as indicated by the novel's open-endedness, its refusal to deliver upon the great promise that precolonial African knowledges would offer the road map to "Nagona" (insight). The novel's composite meaning seems to be that truth is fragmentary, and insight requires endless thinking and probing. *Nagona's* open-ended, self-conscious narrative signifies the fragmentary nature of truth and identity, and calls for a more pragmatic strategy to resolve African problems without having to rely on absolutist positions.

While some novels, such as *Dunia Yao* (2006) (Their World/Their Globe), by Said A. Mohamed, offer a polemic against globalization in narratives marked by fluid structures, they are more critical of the local political leadership's and local intellectuals' collusion with external exploiters to silence local perspectives and plundering African societies. Kyallo Wamitila's *Bina-Adamu!* (2002), whose title loosely translates as "Son of Adam," "Human Being," or "The Oppressor of the Humans," is a mosaic of texts, including epics and foundational narratives from different parts of the world, that undermine nationalist projects in the societies from which they come, including the chauvinism of African societies. Unlike sociologists Katama Mkangi (1944–2004) and Seithy Chachage (1945–2006), whose experiments with postmodernism are much more spontaneous and unaware of postmodern theorizing, Wamitila is conscious of a global trend in which narratives stage self-consciousness to deconstruct totalized notions of truth and history. Like Said A. Mohamed, who has written criticism in which he describes his own work as postrealist,[4] Wamitila is undoubtedly aware of global metafiction, given that he has analyzed metafictional writing by Kezilahabi and is one of the critics who popularized the term *metabunilizi* (for *bunilizipiku*/metafiction). Critical of oppression that presents itself as "globalization," the novel stages internal heteroglossia and inserts African narratives and briefs that may appear absurd by the standards of Eurocentric logic in order to indicate the need for an expanded worldview, one that does not suppress multiple methods of self-representation. The novel engages the reader in the unreal, as the African child from whose perspective the story is told visits places where, for example, rivers flow backward.

As a literary theorist Wamitila has examined other self-reflexive novels such as Kezilahabi's *Nagona*. In *Bina-Adamu!* (2002), he uses in African modes of storytelling that self-consciously defy time-honored traditions of writing a novel. Despite intense experimentations with literary theories and artistic techniques, Wamitila ensures that the text is comprehensible to everyone with a basic understanding of Kiswahili. Yet the story is not simplistic in its structure; it is a complex mythopoetic narrative that critiques oppressive practices in the West and Africa. The reader is warned by the narrative to be particularly cautious about Wamitila's language which, though simple, engages in linguistic play and heavy punning. Even a simple punctuation mark is invested with shades of political meaning. For example, the title of the novel, in its unconventional spelling of *binadamu* (Kiswahili for "human being"), suggests many things at the same time. By spelling *Bina-Adamu* with a double "a" and a hyphen, the title seems to approximate the pronunciation of the word. Thus the spelling (complemented by the exclamation mark) emphasizes the orality of the novel. By referencing oral literature, the novel highlights indigenous modes of expression, even as it borrows from Western classics, the epic in particular.

More subtly, the title suggests the main theme of the novel. *Bina* (which is also spelled *binya*) means to suppress. This captures the repression of Adamu, the once-free man in the Garden of Eden (referred to repeatedly in the narrative). The hyphen could refer to the chain binding the world to the oppressor, a connection that must be broken. At the same time, the hyphen signifies the fragmentation of subjectivity in postindependence Africa. The title's exclamation mark relates to a series of protests, occurring in the narrative, against all forms of aggression against the powerless. The children's protests are of particularly significance. The narrator urges us to take them seriously if we are to learn anything from our experiences. The significance of the exclamation mark is emphasized when the children shout "*Beberu! Beberu!—Linanuka beberu!*" [The colonizer! The colonizer!]. Several words later, the narrative repeats it to punctuate the word "*Umero-Japa!*," an expression that suggests, to me, that the Bina (oppressor) of Adamu (humanity) is none other than an axis comprising Europe, America, and Japan.

Yet *Bina-Adamu!* is a protest against neither the West nor Western aesthetics. Making subtle references to ideas about time, death, and reincarnation, the lines of T. S. Eliot's poetry we find in the novel's preliminary pages demonstrate Wamitila's acquiescence to Eliot's view that "no poet can have his meaning alone." To this end, Wamitila resurrects dead poets not to exalt death, past poets, or tradition, but to protect the living by inscribing their own individual talent in the Kiswahili literary body. Written in a marginalized language, the novel employs myths from around the world to demonstrate the possibility of dialogue and discourse between cultures outside of the politics of exploitative globalization. The result is a layered narrative that exposes, with devastating precision, the oppression masked under what the dominant political and economic ideologies peddle around the world as freedom. The novel unmasks the hypocrisy behind catchphrases such as "global village" and "New World Order," which are employed by dominant nations to continue their oppression in the Global South. The novel is not against globalization when the concept is defined objectively as, to use Anthony Giddens's words, a dialectical "intensification of worldwide social relations which link distant localities in such a way that local happenings are shaped by events occurring many miles away, and vice versa" (Giddens 1990, 64). On the contrary, like Ngũgĩ and Achebe before him, Wamitila appears to become suspicious only when the buzzwords such as "globalization" are taken to mean the Westernization and suppression of local cultures. Recognizing language as the site on which identity is sculpted, Wamitila prioritizes Kiswahili against the background of dominant discourses. In so doing, he does not, however, ignore the need to appropriate liberating components that the Western cultures offer.

By telling the story from the perspective of a dead person, the writer dismantles the death/life dichotomy and at once demonstrates how deep in the political, social, and economic abyss we have been pushed by our leaders and their Western supporters. The narrator, in my opinion, is not literally dead. He is an embodiment of those parts of our being that have been repressed. The fact that the dead narrator can still communicate is symbolic of our resilience in the fight against social death. His voice indicates that we can be repressed but never fully destroyed, an indication that we have the incarnate power to identify spaces where we can narrate ourselves into being, even if we have been pushed to the margins. The novel loosens the distinction between creative writing and critical literary theory. Wamitila seems to be shrewdly engaging in critical polemics by problematizing literary practices that we associate with the West. He suggests that although postmodernism is seen as a Western phenomenon of the postindustrial societies mostly after the 1980s, its defining components form the everyday modes of expression in Africa. The novel's structural techniques suggest that our cultures became postmodern long before Western colonialism brought to Africa its metaphysics of rigidity and rationalism, which Western postmodernism has only now decided that it is fashionable to puncture.

In *Bina-Adamu!*, Wamitila assembles various genres to create a novel whose very form is political. In mixing genres and voices, the writer suggests the need to replace self-absorbed Western domination with a more democratic order that allows others to speak. Although mythological, taking the reader to the netherworld where the dead dwell, the story is full of references to real locations, famous brand names, world currencies, capitalist buzzwords, preexisting texts, and personalities. There is an allusion to the mythical *Ivya ya Nzambani* (the Nzambani Rock) in Kitui, Kenya, which is said to be capable of changing one's gender if one runs around it several times. What is most incisive is the way the novel, angry and playful by turns, satirizes the neocolonialist whom it figures as the ogre *mnuka beberu* (he who smells like the he-goat; *beberu* is the Kenyan denotation for the colonialist). Colonialism, slavery, and all forms of cultural domination are seen as manifestations of the evil nature of "*mnuka beberu*," thus signifying that colonialism has different manifestations even within contemporary African nations.

Khamis's humanistic recuperation of the nonmimetic novel is also by a Russian critic of East African culture, Mikhail Gromov, in the "Postmodernistic Elements in Recent Swahili Novels." Gromov notes that unlike the works of Western postmodernists, in which "all the values are devalued," African novels "re-evaluate anew the values of human society, to appeal to the initial basics of being, which, according to these authors, were lost to mankind in the process of self-destruction which was labeled as progress only by mistake" (2004, 35). His choice of the term *postmodernistic* indicates that he does not believe that the literature is postmodern; it merely displays characteristics that would easily be associated with postmodenist literature. Even if there is a subtext in Gromov that sees Western postmodernism as the yardstick against which other semblances of nonrealist modes are to be judged, he is correct that the Kiswahili writers display a sense of social responsibility in the presentation of global development and are critical of blind acceptance of discourses of development. As they present the momentous changes taking place in the last decades of the twentieth century, the novels are political in their refiguration of a destabilized world and in their treatment of new anxieties couched in utopian hopes.

Fat of the Land

Katama Mkangi's Kiswahili (1984) novel *Mafuta* (fats/ointments/oils/riches) obliquely addresses both the East African's obsession with the discovery of oil and the hidden histories of a people who would be exposed to blatant exploitation if such natural resources were to be discovered. Using the technique of *mise en abyme*, in which it replicates itself within the frame narrative, *Mafuta* is also the story of the gap between the rich and the poor in postindependence Kenya; in this society, only the rich can afford *mafuta* (fats/ointment), required for a good night's sleep in the bed of the "wateule" (the chosen few), while the majority are condemned to dehumanization, sleeplessness, or sleeping in the mud.

The *mafuta* (fats)/*matope* (mud) dichotomy corresponds allegorically with the rich/poor binary in the society. The novel disrupts binaries by placing a fictional manuscript, also entitled *Mafuta*, in the hands of the poor, as the rich have no use for it. Like M. G. Vassanji's *The Book of Secrets* (1996), Mkangi's *Mafuta* thematizes the centrality of texts in revealing to the general public their identity and the historical realities in their society. Creative literature, which the character who is the embodiment of the greedy capitalist in the story dismisses as an inedible sheave of papers, is recuperated as part of the cure of the social ills in Africa. The embedded manuscript is presented as possessing the key to ideological consciousness. Written, like other Mkangi novels, within a socialist perspective, *Mafuta* offers a case for the contextualized reading of fiction by presenting the theft and reading of a manuscript from an old rich man by truant kids who do not fully understand the manuscript's importance.

Framing the sociological novel within children's play, *Mafuta* creates a strong sense of fictionality that tends toward postmodern self-reflexivity. Before the children accidentally find the "mafuta" manuscript, they are engaged in a fictional game, gambling using bottle tops. The tops are used as symbols of money, and whoever loses bears a debt repaid by stealing fruit from an old man, the custodian of the text. The fictional money draws the actual reader's attention to the fact that the novel *Mafuta* and its internal manuscript of the same title signify the capitalistic greed in postindependence society, where the poor are reduced to empty fantasies of possessing any wealth. The novel signals that it is up to the poor to seize the coveted *mafuta* from the rich, and it suggests that unless there are more inward-looking strategies of economic revival, the gains and discoveries made will be taken away by other societies. At the same time, it signals a hope that wealth will be transferred from the rich minority to the powerless, symbolized here as poor kids. The presentation of the rich as old and the poor as young signifies the novel's hope that the greedy rich will be replaced by the suffering poor. It is only through access to the historical realities in the small manuscript that society can have any hope of gaining the self-awareness and agency necessary to disrupt the status quo.

At the beginning of the novel the majority is presented as a hoodwinked mass that threatens to kill an innocent man to protect their exploiter.

After a careful reading of the manuscript on the stark realities facing the nation, there is hope that young readers will mature into ideologically sophisticated individuals. The fictional text within the text is, starting in *Sura ya Kwanza* (Chapter 1), set off from the "real" life of the novel, which is largely relegated to the *utangulizi* (prologue). In other words, the framing story is demoted to a metatextual introduction. The fictional manuscript appears to be independent of the earlier section, linked to it by a description of the beginning of a secretive reading of the document, after which there is an ellipsis to indicate the transition from the reality of reading to the fictional text itself. The fictional text is presented to us as the children read it, as a verbatim reproduction of a text whose young readers do not fully understand.

The fictional, embedded manuscript, reproduced to the reader verbatim, ends in Chapter 9 of the novel, giving way to the metatext in which it is contained. However, instead of the next chapter being the epilogue, it is named Chapter 10, integrating the fictional *Mafuta* with the real *Mafuta*. The reality-fiction dichotomy suggested in the opening of the text is fully destroyed. We are told that it took the children a long time to read the text that we have already finished reading because of "various reasons," such as their tender age, the poor handwriting, and the children's other duties (89–90). Unlike the fictional child readers, the real readers do not take months to read the text because, in part, the text is short and in print. Mechanically produced, as opposed to the poorly handwritten manuscript, the frame *Mafuta* belongs to what Walter Benjamin ([1936] 1992) heralds as the use of new technologies to disrupt old hegemonic beliefs. But we are told that to interpret the text, the children had to ask questions, if only indirectly, about the data in the text.

The fictional writer of the embedded manuscript "Mafuta" fictionalizes fiction, prompting the young readers to historicize the fiction and physically participate in the transformation of their nation. Mkangi's novel, therefore, seems to emphasize the importance of sociological factors in its interpretation. Equally, we expect the reading of the metafictional *Mafuta* to reveal important information about the real society and to animate the search for self-knowledge. The *mafuta* (oils/fats/riches) theme is also explored in the context of globalization by Sudanese Jamal Mahjoub, who thematizes the politics of Sudanese oil and the exploitative tendencies of foreign oil companies that care nothing about the welfare of local populations. The theme also preoccupies the work of Ogoni writer Ken Saro-Wiwa, who abrogates the English language not primarily in resistance to Standard English as the norm but to resist the official practice of power in Nigeria, where minority societies are dehumanized by successive regimes in collaboration with foreign oil multinationals. What should be underlined here is that while writers excoriate the global exploitation of local populations, the main focus of their criticism is the local cartels and national leaderships that collude with global capitalism to plunder rural Africa.

Locals Pimping for the West

Although deemphasizing classical colonialism and focusing its critique on postindependence forms of oppression, the metafictional novel can at times be devastating in its criticism of the West, poking fun at locals who collaborate with neocolonists at the expense of their indigenous communities. Chachage's (2002) Kiswahili novel *Makuadi wa Soko Huria* (*Pimps of the Free Market*) is a fairly realist text, but its obtrusive narrator keeps holding up to the reader his status as a fictionalizing and fictional character by insisting, throughout the story, on his narrative's *ubunilifu* (fictionality). He calls himself Fidelis Mvumi Msakapanovu (Hehe-inflected Kiswahili for "the patient hunter/fisherman who catches the fattest game/fish"), but although he highlights the meaning of his baptismal name as connoting faithfulness when he introduces himself to the reader, Fidelis is not always reliable with facts. He embellishes his story with *uvumi* (gossip) and an ideologically one-sided presentation to hammer home his hatred for the capitalists ruining rural Tanzanian economy in the name of development.

Makuadi wa Soko Huria is based on the novelist's research on environmental degradation in Eastern Tanzania. It revolves around a corrupt fishing project in rural Tanzania sponsored by private investors in the Rufiji Delta of the Indian Ocean coast. The novelist gives a fictionalized account of the controversy that emerged from a project in which environments were pitted against the Tanzanian government and the private investors in the Rufiji Delta, the largest delta in Eastern Africa containing the world's biggest continuous mangrove forest that covers over 53,000 hectares and supports the delta's twenty islands and thirty-one villages. A private enterprise, the African Fishing Company (AFC) was granted permission in the mid-1990s to establish what has been described as the world's largest prawn plantation which exploits local population. The project caused an international outcry, especially because elements in the Tanzanian government had falsified reports to support the feasibility of the project (Gibbon 1997, 52; Martinez-Alier 2002, 90–91). In a fictionalized account reminiscent of Ken Saro-Wiwa's environmental efforts in the Ogoni Delta of Nigeria, the reader is presented with the repressed history of the Rufiji Delta from the 1840s, as the novel also covers in detail the later development of Tanzania from the heyday of anticolonial nationalism in the 1950s through the *Ujamaa* socialism of the 1960s and 1970s to the present neoliberal order of *soko huria* (free market).

Critical of the neoliberal privatization of the Tanzanian economy for exposing indigenous societies to rapacious global capitalism, the novel sets the metaphorical *makuadi* (pimps) against the indigenous environmentalists. Japhet Lupocho and Mwenerumango collide with foreign investors Paul Mooney and Balfour Beatty by providing falsified documents about the benefits of foreign investment to rationalize the displacement and exploitation of the local communities. The local member of parliament, Luhala, greedily supports the project because he receives kickbacks from the investors. Peasants and scholars also have been compromised to frustrate the efforts of the progressive environmentalists. On the other hand, journalists, eco-feminists, and peasants such as Binti Wenga successfully challenge the capitalist destruction of the region.

As John P. Mbonde notes, *Makuadi wa Soko Huria* is among the Tanzanian novels sensitive to gender issues in that it exposes ways in which women "*licha ya kunyanyaswa, kuonewa, kudhulimiwa na kuhujumiwa, [. . .] hunyimwa haki zao*" [besides being exploited, discriminated against, oppressed, and short-changed, are denied their fundamental rights" (Mbonde 2004, 218)]. Mbonde observes that the novel presents women characters at different levels of society, producing typical characters that represent different ideologies and practices in society. Sensitive to gender issues, the novel denounces domestic violence, the sexual objectification of Tanzanian women by local and international sexual tourism, the exclusion of women in important decision-making organs in the villages, and the failure to compensate women for land sold to multinational investors.

Beyond lamenting their exploitation and marginalization, the narrative gives voice to peasant women such as Binti Wenga, from whose perspective the most informative parts of the narrative are told. However, it unfortunately joins earlier nationalist realist literature in using woman as ahistorical symbols of the nation, especially in its deployment of the motif of rape in a way that presents women as passive victims of masculinist foreign penetration. In the novel, the nation is equated to woman, as in the nationalist discourses unmasked in Indian nationalism by Radhakrishnan (1993) and Partha Chatterjee (1993), in which nationalism uses rural women as ahistorical figures through whom the condition of the nation can be projected without focusing on the particulars of women's liberation. To project the political and economic violence of globalization done to the Tanzanian economy, Chachage uses rape as a metaphor for all that is bad in the new economic order. Like his earlier novel, *Almasi za Bandia* (Fake Diamonds), *Makuadi wa Soko Huria* opens with a description of a scene of attempted rape, in which neocolonialist "pimps" are implicated in an attempt to rape a positively drawn character, Sifuni Karanja, because she threatens their projects of plundering the nation through development projects that degrade the environment. African supporters of Western development paradigms are seen as inveterate rapists, they do not accomplish their mission in *Makuadi wa Soko Huria* as they do in Wamitila's novels.

Most notable in *Makuadi wa Soko Huria* is the highly dramatized and visual way the novel marks the first appearance of Westerners. The scene is set in an exclusive nightclub, of the kind that sprang up after independence, "*kutokana na kupigwa marufuku kwa klabu zenye misingi ya ubaguzi za Wazungu au Wahindi peke yao*" [when whites-only and Asian clubs based on racial discrimination were banned" (2002, 83)]. The narrator, an investigative journalist, reveals that "*mwanzoni mwa miaka ya 1980*" [at the beginning of the 1980s], similar exclusive clubs reemerged in Tanzania to cater to Western development experts and diplomats. The purpose of these clubs is to shield Westerners from the commodity shortages that their policies toward Africa have created. Non-Africans are drawn in sexual terms, as flat characters with no redeeming value. To underscore their perversity, the narrative immediately takes the reader inside the club and onto a stage where three girls (most likely Africans) are entertaining the guests. The novel has already established theatre as an important trope by naming its prologue *kifungua pasia* (the curtain opener) and by using various modes of oral narration, including intrusive direct address to *msomaji wangu mwema* (my good reader).

The narrator dwells in detail on the girls' provocative sexual on-stage gestures to suggest the perpetuation of voyeuristic tendencies:

> *Bendi ya Muziki ilikuwepo, ikipiga nyimbo za kuigiza za kutoka nje. Wanamuziki hawa walipiga kwa ufundi hasa, na waliokuwepo walichangamka kwelikweli kwa kucheza na kushangilia. Wasichana watatu waliokuwa pale mbele, wakiwa wamevaa nguo ambazo zilisitiri matiti na sehemu ngogo tu za maungo ya uzazi, walikuwa wakicheza. Nao walishangiliwa kwa nguvu sana kadri walivyochezesha nyonga zao na kubinua viuno vya kwa ufundi ulisoshirisha vitendo vya ngono. Lilikuwa ni tamasha lilitia fora. Hapa na pale palikuwa na watu waliokumbatiana na wale wasichana waliohudhuria pale au na wake zao. Wengine walikuwa wakipigana mabusu, na baadhi walikuwa wakitoka pale na kuvutana hadi vyumbani, au nyuma ya miti ya vivuli vya pale uwanjani kwenda kukidhi myoto ya ashiki za mili yao. Kwa wenye kumbukumbu za misahafu ya ndini, mengi yamatendo yalioyipanza Sodoma na Gomora hadi kutiwa kiberiti na Mwenyezi Mungu yalikuwa yakifanyika hapa.* (Chachage 2002, 85)
>
> [The music band was playing, imitating foreign tunes. The musicians played with great expertise, and the members of the audience were really entertained, dancing and cheering. Three girls took to the front stage, wearing costumes that only hid

> their tits and only a small portion of their genitalia. And they were cheered vigorously because of the way they expertly swung their bellies and thrust their waists forward in imitation of having sex. It was a great show, indeed! Here and there, people danced, holding girls they met at the club or their wives. Others were kissing loudly, while yet others pulled one another to small rooms or just behind the trees to satisfy their bodily urges. For those of you that know your Bible well, it was like the Sodom and Gomorrah before the Almighty God grabbed his matchbox and decided to set those cities on fire!]

This instance in the novel demonstrates what Said's *Orientalism* sees as the West's voyeuristic relationship to non-Western societies, whereby the Orient is associated with sex, a non-Western woman. In orientalist discourse, a non-Western woman is stereotyped as a symbol of the whole culture. She is seen as "less a woman than a display of impressive verbally inexpressive femininity" (Said [1978] 1994, 187). Chachage presents Africa as so completely intertwined in sexual fantasy with the feminine in the Western imaginary that the depiction of the shortcomings of neo-colonialism seems possible only through the presentation of foreigners and their indigenous lackeys as sexual predators and voyeurs partaking of the generative energy, raw sensuality, and coital delicacy of African girls. The hypocrisy of the West is exposed through the novel's depiction of Westerners as not interested in the ideals of development and democracy they like mouthing, but in sexual gratification and adventure. True to the neocolonial set-up, the local male elites have joined the West in sexual tourism at the expense of indigenous women. Indeed, the derivative foreign tunes played at the club are emblematic of the continued economic and cultural domination of Africa by the West. The figures of the dancing women symbolize the systematic mortgaging of the nation and its ideals to the West; the narrator duels on the graphic description of the female dancers to foreground them as the ultimate symbols of (s)exploitation of the continent. Untiring in their sensuous gyrations, the girls are no more than machines. Their raw sensuousness suggests that they are prostitutes as well. The songs they perform are, to use Gerald Prince's (1988) term, "disnarrated," only implied to have been sung in the "real" world portrayed without being reproduced in the narrative. Suggested by this omission is that the song is unoriginal and probably vulgar, unworthy of verbatim reproduction in the narration. The possibility of using their body movements, facial expressions, and tone variation in the carnivalesque theatrical space to subvert the powerful members of the audience is completely foreclosed by disnarration of the music. As is the case in Said's *Orientalism*, this presentation of women vis-à-vis the European male is problematic in the sense that it reduces the agency of African women, who are presented as silent sexual vassals of Western men and as complicit in their own oppression.

This socialist-leaning novel vilifies Salama by contrasting her to an equally assertive feminist character, Sifuni Karanja, whom the novel, based on metafictional playfulness, does not develop beyond stating that she is one of the people allied to the narrator in fighting environmental degradation through journalism. Salama has made it hard for Mjuba, her sympathetically drawn husband, to divorce her and marry the progressive journalist Sifuni Karanja. To make matters worse, Salama has been converted by "*walokole*" (evangelists) into a fundamentalist Christian who now tacitly supports "*mauaji ya halaiki*" (genocide) in Rwanda. Her husband Mjuba (Kiswahili for cheerful/boisterous) and, by extension, the narrator and the reader cannot believe their ears when she contaminates the Pan-Africanist spirit of her kids' names, Nkrumah and Bob Marley (named for Pan-African liberationists), by renaming them Bill Graham and Abrahamu.

While the narrator presents Binti Wenga as a one-sided unreliable narrator, even using the term *payuka* (rant aimlessly) to describe her discourse, his own earlier observation of the politicians is in complete agreement with Binti Wenga's view. Here the politicians are described as spending valuable time in exclusive clubs "*kwa mazungumzo ya utani wa kila aina—ikiwa ni pamoja na ule wa matusi ya nguoni, huku wengine wakitupa ndoana zao huku na kule wakijaribu kuwanasa waliofika kule mnadani kuwarubuni hawa wabunge wenye fedha za posho chekwachekwa*" (43) [in abusive talk of all kinds—including hate speech and taboo language, while others were busy casting their fishing rods here and there, trying to catch the girls in that open-air market who had come to sell themselves to these cash-loaded parliamentarians]. Prominent women leaders are completely excluded from the picture, and ordinary women are presented either as evil prostitutes or as gullible victims of politicians, who, with little effort, get them pregnant, then dump them. By excluding women politicians and suppressing Binti Wenga's oral testimony as too dirty to reproduce verbatim, the self-righteous narrator is unwittingly performing the function of the censors he is complaining about for refusing to register his newspaper. It is only by viewing him as either an unreliable or self-indicting narrator that his story would read as a fair representation of the world.

By and large, Binti Wenga fits the category of the rural woman Chatterjee (1993) and Radhakrishnan (1993) see as the representative of the nation in nationalist discourse. She is the repository of the nation's memory and past. We are told she is the latter-day version of such historical figures as Binti Titi Mohamed (1926–2000), a woman politician and one of the founding members of the Tanzanian African National Union (TANU), who played a major role in fighting for Tanzania's independence. The narrator emphasizes that Binti Titi Mohamed, despite her recruitment of thousands of women into the liberation movement, was betrayed by the male nationalists after independence (Chachage 2002, 212). Through his narrator, the novelist laments the continued exclusion of women from national public affairs, but the fictional Binti Wenga seems to parallel Ngũgĩ's mythological Nyakinyua and other romanticized presentations of women by nationalist male writers as the quintessential figure of "Mother Africa." Florence Stratton (1994), Elleke Boehmer ([1992] 2005b) and Mineke Schipper (1987, 1996) have independently shown this presentation of "Mother Africa" to be a masculinist move in African literature to rhetorically elevate women in discourse by romanticizing the continent as a nurturing woman while eliding women's material problems in the new nations.

Like Ngũgĩ, Chachage disrupts that ahistorical and ancient rural "Mother Africa" figure a bit by accompanying that foundational image with the figure of an equally nurturing modern urban woman who symbolizes Tanzania's sexual travails at the hands of the present-day neoliberal capitalists, including the denial of conjugal rights by her unfaithful husband. Sifuni Karanja, a journalist and an eco-feminist, is a positively drawn character who echoes Wanja in Ngũgĩ's *Petals of Blood*. Through Sifuni Karanja, Chachage indicates progression from the old rural "Mother Africa" represented by Binti Wenga and Ngũgĩ's Nyakinyua to the combative urban female intellectual. Although her name seems Kenyan, suggesting the desired transnational nature of the struggle against global capital in Africa, Sifuni Karanja is no doubt a symbol of Tanzania that her personal suffering as a victim of rape attempts and betrayal by her sexual partner parallels the problems of the modern nation. By naming her Karanja and having her contribute her articles to an English journal while other fictional journalists write for Kiswahili publications, Chachage is not only underlying Sifuni Karanja's transnationalism, but the problems of the Tanzanian nation she represents are shared by the wider East African region.

As a symbol of the nation Sifuni Karanja, like Binti Wenga, is presented as a stereotype. Most of the accusations by the men whose sexual advances she has turned down are not deconstructed in the novel. The male narrator seems to relish the rumors circulated by dejected men about her body being sexually dysfunctional because she has not had sex for years on end. Though male sexual predators in the novel (symbols of local and foreign exploiters) do not manage to rape Sifuni Karanja, despite several attempts (unlike in Chachage's other novel, *Almasi za Bandia*, in which Patricia, a woman from the Global South, is raped by a smuggler in metropolitan Europe), it is not the character's own efforts that save her from the predators. Rather, every time there is a rape attempt, Sifuni is saved either by a coincidence or by some masculine intervention outside of the story. In a word, as a strategy of narration, metafiction allows the novels to discuss taboo topics and to reject any form of teleological hegemony.

Masculinist Stereotypes of Women

To conclude this chapter, I need to reiterate that while we welcome the growth of the novel in African languages, we should note that the field is dominated by male writers, with only a few already established female novelists such as Grace Ogot and Asenath Bole Odaga having had their works published in indigenous languages—mostly by their own publishing companies.[5] Even if major firms publish works in Kiswahili, most of the novels are by male writers. The female equivalents of Kyallo Wamitila, Gabriel Ruhumbika, Said A. K. Mohamed, and Euphrase Kezilahabi have not yet emerged in the publication of self-reflexive Kiswahili fiction, even in Tanzania, where Kiswahili is widely spoken. One still finds in these novels by men uncomfortable echoes of the continuation of the realist nationalist narrative, especially in the way the writers present the wronged nation in terms of women being raped. Following the exploits of male characters and focalized by male narrators, even when women's stories are being narrated, the narratives suppress the individuality of female characters, subordinating them to masculinist nationalist fears and desires. Except for a few novels, such as Ngũgĩ's *Mũrogi wa Kagogo*, novels in Gĩkũyũ and Kiswahili use the motif of rape, in which women are presented as passive victims at the hands of foreigners or locals serving multinational interests.

The newer metafictional texts are, like the earlier novels, critical of any form of repression of individuals, or the community as a whole. But the lack of depth in the metafictional novels' characterization in some instances produces an intensified risk of stereotyping women characters, especially because most of the metafictional novels in African languages are written by men and are narrated by male characters who present a one-sided picture of women's experiences.

Judging by the output in Gĩkũyũ and Kiswahili, the new-style writers in indigenous languages tend to be predominantly men—with women breaking into the literary scene with novels in English, the best of which are published abroad. Is it that women are not crafting experimental novels in local languages? It seems that one has to be male or an established female writer to get local venues to publish new fiction in local languages. We should remember that even Ngũgĩ wa Thiong'o, Gabriel Ruhumbika, and Grace Ogot started their careers with works in English, producing realist fiction in the 1960s before embarking on experimental prose in the 1980s and after. Said Mohamed, too, began his career in the 1970s with socialist realist fiction and poetry. Only a few writers, among them Kyallo Wadi Wamitila, have launched their creative careers with postrealist novels in an African language.[6] The fact that new women writers seem to be doing better in experimental fiction in English published by transnational outlets could be an indicator of gender imbalance in the indigenous publishing industry.

I must add that this gender imbalance is not limited to novels in African languages. I have already shown uncomfortable subtexts in Habila's (2002) *Waiting for an Angel*, where the image of Mother Africa is evoked in a way that stereotypes women. We will see similar images in English-language novels by Ngũgĩ and K. Sello Duiker. Another caveat should be introduced here regarding indigenous languages and nonrealist discourse: the choice of language in itself cannot account for the texts' self-reflexivity in the sense that not all novels in African languages are self-reflexive; African languages such as Kiswahili have produced realist and nationalistic novels and poetry. The facility of the language, its adaptability to indigenous orality, allows the author to employ factors already mentioned to signify the fragmentation of self and the absurdities of the world. The next chapter analyzes the ways in which African novels utilize oral literature to depart from some of the ideological positions it stands for. While invoking precolonial and autochthonous forms, the texts disavow nativist affiliations and use the antirealist elements in folkloric genres to deconstruct essentialist notions of gender and nationalism.

Chapter 4

Orature and Deconstructed Folklore

In the following pages, I attempt a disruptive response to Africa's indigenous interpretive landscape by using metafictional texts to argue against the trend in African literary criticism and theory to yoke the Africanness of African literature to oral literature. Although most critics who see an affinitive relationship between oral literature and literacy in Africa admit that modern writers are not servile imitators of indigenous orature, the general subtext is nevertheless that modern literature forms an unbroken continuum with precolonial oral literature. I focus on the tensive relationship between oral literature and modern literature as more productive than dwelling on continuities in explaining the gender dynamics in postcolonial Africa. I submit that in spite of modern art's affinitive use of oral literary techniques and materials, contemporary writers deploy metafictional devices to illuminate a deep skepticism toward the fixed African past evoked by folkloric texts, especially in their representation of gender. This skepticism, so strong in moments of metafiction, is rarely studied, with much of the focus being on the celebration of orality as an anticolonial gesture.[1]

My argument is based on the conviction that the dichotomy between literacy and orality is disrupted by texts across cultures and epochs, and that there is nothing so peculiarly African about a novel borrowing from oral methods of communication and aesthetics that it warrants linking Africanness to orality. More crucial is how particular elements of orality are deconstructed and redeployed in specific texts to unmask the power relations in the texts cited or suggested. Needless to say, African identities and arts are multiple and dynamic; despite the negative impact of colonialism and the need to recover that which colonialism sought to destroy, African novelists are not fixated on recovering and reinstating the precolonial past. Therefore I see the power of African novels as residing in the way their writers run against the grain of even Africa's autochthonous arts, especially in portraying gender and sexuality.

I am apprehensive about my own position. By indicating contemporary Africans' skepticism toward the very past that colonialism sought to destroy in order to justify its mission, isn't there a major risk here of aiding the neocolonial denigration of African traditions and the endorsement of colonial incursion and the global domination of local cultures? This concern is readily dispensed with when we consider that it is only through a binary logic that reservations about African precolonial practices could be viewed as an affirmation of the colonial hegemony that devalued, and sometimes decimated, important cultural practices in Africa. I argue that even when running counter to some precolonial ideologies, the modern novels I study here do not sanction colonialism in any form. They evoke oral modes of self-fashioning as an anticolonial move while using orality to contest the very idea of the nation as a stable construct and to instantiate a shift toward cosmopolitanism. I further show that the novels rely on a gendered grammar in which orality, in addition to being deployed as a counterdiscourse in relation to colonial aesthetics, is used to deconstruct precolonial art forms, thus addressing issues of gender inequality and provoking thought about the empowerment of women. To use Helen Mugambi's observation in a different but related context, rather than passively propagating oral literature, the novels dialogize folklore and further use the site of intersection offered by orature to interrogate one another.[2]

The Oral-Written Continuum and the Negative Habitus

The view that conflates the Africanness of literature with orality is articulated most influentially by Chinweizu and colleagues in their controversial treatise *Toward the Decolonization of African Literature*. Identifying African literature as "an autonomous entity separate and apart from all other literatures" (Chinweizu et al. 1980, 4), they advance the view that African art adheres to folklore in opposition to Western forms, which they view as lifeless by comparison with oral literature. In effect, they freeze oral literature as equally static and unaffected by colonial modernity. If the negritude aesthetics of the 1940s and 1950s seized Western stereotypes and invested them with value as expressions of Africa's comparative advantage over other cultures, Chinweizu and colleagues have, in their conjoining of orality and Africanness, turned on its head the tendency to equate underdeveloped parts of the world with primary orality and the advanced societies with literacy; they have succeeded in valorizing orality as more immediate in expressing African realities than writing, which approximates scripted poetics.

To hold such an exclusionist position is not only to assume that oral literature exists only in Africa, but also to be blind to the presence of oral communication in technologically advanced stages of development both in Africa and the rest of the world, which Chinweizu and colleagues seem to define Africa against. I will demonstrate that contemporary novelists use orature not so much to differ from the Western canon but to deconstruct local oral and literate texts and to invent a new Africa that dialogues with itself and other cultures of the world. Acknowledging orature's dynamic and nonreplicable nature in either writing or performance, this chapter shows that African novels rework orature to address issues that the traditional African societies from which folklore originates would have taken as a given.[3]

Furthermore, to yoke the Africanness of a text to orality is to assume that only African texts display an affinitive link to verbal communication, whereas seminal studies of the interface between orality and literacy by scholars such as Walter Ong are in fact based on non-African cultures. This means that orality is not the distinguishing characteristic of African literature. Literatures from other cultures (some seen to be diametrically opposite in the colonizer/colonized and developed/undeveloped axes) display an interface between oral communication and written discourse as well.[4] It is the way in which orality is deployed in a particular set of texts that should concern us. Furthermore, the binary opposition between orality and literacy is not, in itself, a central concern in African literature. Major theorists such as Isidore Okpewho, Chinweizu and colleagues, Abiola Irele, and Harold Scheub have seen Africa's contemporary art as a continuation of precolonial modes of articulation. This is in recognition of the fact that modern African literatures have spun off from centuries of oral literary traditions.[5] In *The Slave's Rebellion: Literature, History, Orature* (2005), Adélékè Adéèkó observes that an emphasis on the axioms of oral communication, especially the immediacy and dynamic nature of orality, "enables African critics to produce sophisticated explanations of what distinguishes African cultures from others, especially modern European traditions" (2005, 121). Though he reverses the diffusion theory (flow of influence from the powerful center to the marginalized periphery), Adéèkó sees orality the way Pascale Casanova, in *The World Republic of Letters* (2004), views its presence in modern writing: namely, as a productive site for rejecting the dominance of another cultural aesthetics.[6] Adéèkó regards orality here as the expression of a "native consciousness." For him, a critic will account for the "Africanness" of texts by assessing "the relationships they share with oral traditional practices" (2005, 121). In focusing on the traces of orality in modern writing, Adéèkó develops in a deconstructive context Abiola Irele's argument that oral literature is an organic part of what Irele calls "the African imagination." According to Irele, the modern written tradition has had to integrate aspects of orality to ground itself in a distinctively African perception of self:

> Despite the undoubted impact of print culture on African experience and its role in the determination of new cultural modes, the tradition of orality remains predominant, serving as a central paradigm for various kinds of expression on the continent. The literary component of this tradition, in both its expressive modes and with respect to its social significance, provides the formal and normative background for imaginative expression. In this primary sense, orality functions as the matrix of an African mode of discourse, and where literature is concerned, the griot is its embodiment in every sense of the word. Oral literature thus represents the basic intertext of the African imagination. (Irele 2001, 11)

Here, Irele links modern and diasporic African imaginative expression to oral cultures and finds an affinity between the two modes of self-realization, but he qualifies that the use of oral traditions involves modification.[7] The modification of earlier texts would offer a site of engagement between old ideologies and a cosmopolitan way of thinking. Adéèkó should be read in a similar context. While he notes the importance of orature in modern African literature, he emphasizes that oral communication is dynamic and difficult to reproduce in a different time or context.

Writing earlier, Scheub contends that "there is an unbroken continuity in African verbal arts forms, from interacting oral genres to such literary productions as the novel and poetry" (1985, 1).[8] In *African Oral Literature: Backgrounds, Character, and Continuity* (1992), Okpewho notes that modern African writers call on oral literary material "as a basis for writing original works that reflect, from a more or less modern perspective, some of the major concerns of today to demonstrate that traditional African culture is not obsolete but relevant for the articulation of contemporary needs and goals" (1992, 294). To be sure, although some African societies had an alphabet that predates colonialism, the writing tradition as we know it today began after colonial and missionary incursions into Africa in the late nineteenth century.[9] But despite the sequential relationship between oral and written traditions, it is not fair to see the two modes of transmission of culture in evolutionary, positivist terms, or to view modern writers as using oral materials without problematizing some of the perspectives in folkloric art. It is pertinent, then, to heed Mark C. Amodio's warning against a positivist view of the sequential evolutionary development from orality to literacy because such a view "can lead, and often has led, to the creation of [a] false dichotomy between orality and literacy, a dichotomy that reinforces the tendency of literate cultures to see them not as mutually dependent and enriching cultural components" (Amodio 2004, 2). The two means of expression and cultural creation complement each other in fundamental ways. Even with the rise of literacy and digital technology, oral traditions inform scriptural and electronic communication.[10] For Amodio, despite the tendency to see literacy as emblematic of a more developed and superior order, texts use the two means of artistic transmission to create a hybrid discourse that is at once oral and literate.

Gender theorists of African literatures, such as Ode Ogede, Mary E. Modupe Kolawole, Carole Boyce-Davis, and Molara Ogundipe-Leslie, have remarked on the use of oral literature to highlight women's issues and recover the agency for women in Africa. Apart from being used to decolonize African literature by signaling a break between it and European colonial forms, oral literary techniques are deployed in specific circumstances to portray gender issues in society. Kolawole notes that "women use oral literature and exclusive female genres to condemn social problems, immorality, unfaithfulness, and idleness—and make demands" (1997, 77). But rather than harking back to an authentic precolonial past that is untouched by colonial modernity, the use of orature has been dynamic, illuminating the changing situations in Africa, and sometimes criticizing the very precolonial order from which the materials are borrowed.

Nationalist-nativist views of the incorporation of orature into modern writing tend to romanticize this precolonial mode of aesthetic production and transmission, as though it were free of negative cultural practices. However, oral literature also participates in the negative habitus of its creators—to such an extent that some scholars, while careful not to dismiss all folklore as malignant, have seen it as having played a key role in the genocides and ethnic polarization in Africa.[11] If we may use Pierre Bourdieu's term in an oral literary context, then we would be able to name those subjective and ingrained social attitudes as a "habitus" in which oral artists operate. Like any other folk literature, African oral literature is not innocent in its handling of gender issues. It is because of their awareness of the power of oral literature (orature) to entrench oppression that feminists who have analyzed the art call for a gendered transformation. While insisting that orature is an important element of cultural heritage, feminist readings of the art have revealed embedded stereotypes in the artists' presentations of women. For instance, in her reading of Kalenjin and Maasai oral literature from Kenya, Ciarunji Chesaina has noted that the literature presents women as voiceless victims and victimizers of men:

> The images that come through are those of women as voiceless individuals who have little intelligence and therefore have to be totally dependent on men. They are portrayed as careless, vain, and idle beings who cannot be relied upon for seriousness in

> handling life's experiences. Women are also depicted as dishonest schemers whose jealousy and malice can be a real threat to the welfare of other people. (1994, 87)

Far from calling for the abandonment of oral art, Chesaina recommends changes to it that remove stereotypes and produce "images which are in line with our developmental aspirations" (1994, 91). Wanjiku Mukabi Kabira, another perceptive student of gender and orature, has systematically unmasked gender stereotypes circulated in Gĩkũyũ oral literature: "In the Gĩkũyũ oral narratives, wives are generally portrayed among other things as: unreliable, disobedient, irresponsible, disloyal, disagreeable, adulterous, cunning, senseless, easily cheated, forgetful, not dependable, evil, tricksters, lazy, etc. There is hardly any story among the Agĩkũyũ that describes wives positively. As co-wives, they are ogres, cruel and malicious" (Kabira 1994, 79–80). It is unlikely that a modern feminist text would want to reproduce these stereotypes.

Though her analysis is based on sociology and national politics, Sylvia Tamale has shown in *When Hens Begin to Crow* (1999) how vernacular folklore, popular theatre, and traditional literature are invoked to exclude women from public offices and bolster the heteronormative matrix. Echoing Judith Butler's concept of performativity, Tamale has pointed to the ways in which oral literature is used as a vehicle for the subordination of women by entrenching itself in the minds of individuals through repetition. Micere Githae Mugo, a strong proponent for further study of oral forms, which she uses heavily in her poetry and drama, admits that some oral literature is used to enhance male dominance: "Orature that celebrates patriarchal values of domination, all forms of injustice and the silencing of the powerless in any society, is negative" (Mugo 1998, 47).[12] In a word, Chesaina, Kabira, Mugo, and Tamale demonstrate that indigenous folklore can be, and usually is, misogynistic. Nevertheless, these critics show the possibilities of women using oral forms to cultivate solidarity and political self-determination among African women or, to use Kolawole's words, "as channels for enunciating women's self-healing and self-assertion" (1997, 77).[13]

Contrary to the nativist view, which emphasizes a continuum between oral literature and modern writing, feminist perspectives seem unanimous in calling for a transformation of oral literature so that it can shed its gender stereotypes and still recuperate indigenous cultural memory and survival modes that colonialism has suppressed. Contemporary African writers, while using oral literature in their texts, are not beholden to traditions. As Eileen Julien notes in her study of orality in the African novel, the writers are "thinking architects rather than prisoners of a cultural heritage" (1992, ix). Rather than reproducing oral literature in written texts for nationalist purposes as Chinweizu and colleagues demand of them, contemporary writers have exploited the dynamic nature of oral literature and reworked folk materials to present the politics of gender and to undermine ideas of a unitary nation counterpoised to Western identities.[14]

One aspect of metafiction relevant to a discussion of orature is the novels' thematization of the place of the arts in modern African writing. This theme is treated in Ngũgĩ's *Devil on the Cross* (1982) and Achebe's *Anthills of the Savannah* (1988), in which the relationship of oral performance to modern music and nation formation is constantly addressed. Achebe's *A Man of the People* (1966), and Ngũgĩ's *The River Between* (1965) and *A Grain of Wheat* (1967) particularly indicate the possibilities of the abuse of oral literature by modern states and the traditional patriarchy. Written in realist mode, these novels criticize the abuse of orature from the perspective of a narrator watching the naïve artists from a distance. In contrast, metafictional novels refer to oral literature in moments of a character's self-criticism. For instance, in Chachage's Kiswahili novel *Makuadi wa Soko Huria* (*Pimps of the Free Market*, 2002, 44), it is Binti Wenga, a participant in the abuse of oral literature during election campaigns, who laughs at how in political rallies young people danced themselves lame with obscene gyrations while "*sisi akina mama tukajaribu kuwapiku na ngoma yetu ya* chomanga" [we women tried to outdo them with our *chomanga* dance]. Note that in the word *kuwapiku* (outdo), the suffix *piku* (equivalent of the prefix *meta*) is used to accentuate the exaggerated dancing in honor of the politician and heighten the speaker's irony at her own expense. It is a meta-dance, a dance that outdoes even a most exaggerated dance by young people. Drawing attention to her own self-consciousness, the oral performer in the novel has realized that she has been misused by the elite leadership to boost its hold on power, while it does not represent her wishes and fears in national politics. The moment serves as a juncture of self-criticism for previous follies.

In the introductory section of the novel where the narrator indicates to *Ewe Msomaji Mwema* [You Dear Good Reader] that he is both writing (*kuandika*) and orally narrating (*kusimulia*) the story, he underscores that oral literature has been selectively used in the past to suppress diversity of opinion under the pretext of promoting national unity, progress, and global capital investment. Although a proverb would always have a counterpoint, one of the proverbs is suppressed to justify the status quo. Then, to justify telling the scandalous story that is about to unfold before the reader/listener, the narrator argues that as uniquely human attributes, oral literature and memory are weapons that enable the society to forgive without forgetting events of the past so that history would not repeat itself "*kwa sababu kutataa kuvinjari yale yaliopita*" (12; because of not taking seriously past events). Thus memory and orature become a means of *kujikosoa* (self-critique) that society exploits to avoid past mistakes. It is in a similar context that oral literature is used in the metafictional novels—not to reproduce an ontological fixed past or to rail at foreign domination but to criticize what is going wrong in the present and to criticize the society for allowing itself to repeat its earlier mistakes. In *Makuadi wa Soko Huria*, the narrator is not so much angered by the foreigners who have dispossessed the local populations under the guise of globalization and development; rather, through oral techniques, the novel directs its most pointed criticism at local intellectuals who, seemingly having forgotten the colonial past, have allowed this new form of colonialism to reemerge.

Anti-Oral Orality: Coetzee's *Elizabeth Costello*

The most withering criticism of the view of modern African literature as oral comes from J. M. Coetzee's metafictional *Elizabeth Costello* (2003), in which the eponymous character wages a searing diatribe against the notion that the African novel is primarily verbal. The novel's metafictional impulse emanates from its descriptions of the performances of a series of fictionalized lectures that touch on the nature and function of art. We know that the novel is set in 1994 because we are told that Elizabeth Costello was born in 1928 and is sixty-six years old when the novel opens. This is the year minority white rule in South Africa came to an end and Nelson Mandela was elected the first black president of the South African republic. Elizabeth is a writer who engages directly in metafictional gestures. At the beginning of the narrative we are informed that she achieved fame because of her 1969 novel that presents the life and times of Marion Bloom, the wife of Leopold Bloom, who is himself a principal character in James Joyce's *Ulysses* (1922).

It is through Elizabeth's view of the character Emmanuel Egudu, an African lecturer and literary critic who advances the theory of the intersection of orality and textuality, that the criticism of orality is delivered. African literature belongs to the subaltern order of the peasants that Spivak discusses in "Can the Subaltern Speak?" (1985), those who have been disarticulated by hegemonic conditions to such an extent that they would have to be spoken for by intellectuals. As an intellectual, Egudu claims to be speaking on behalf of contemporary African literature to international audiences, but his views only serve to bolster stereotypes. Debunking his views as self-contradictory, Elizabeth sees Emmanuel as an intellectual charlatan who survives in the Western academy and tourist industry by lying about African cultures:

> In her opinion, all of Emmanuel's talk of an oral novel, a novel that has kept in touch with the human voice and hence with the human body, a novel that is not disembodied like the Western

> novel but speaks the body and the body's truth, is just another way of propping up the mystique of the African as the last repository of primal human energies. (2003, 53)

Egudu's representation, though ostensibly radical, is racist in the sense that it denies contemporary Africa its modernity by insisting on the primacy of the primeval in African aesthetics. Readers might be tempted to see Elizabeth as Coetzee's mouthpiece on the issue because, unlike Negroid African novelists, Coetzee and other white writers rarely deploy orature in their works.[15] But it is critical to note here that, like all of Coetzee's central characters, both Elizabeth Costello and Emmanuel Egudu are webs of contradiction, and the novel is at once empathetic and critical toward both characters without privileging either. Egudu is the winner of a Commonwealth Award for his fiction, a development that contradicts his polemical view of the African novel being dichotomously opposed to the Western novel when we consider that literatures from Britain and its former colonies are equally eligible for the award.

One notices that Egudu excludes gender from his discussion of the African novel because the people he is addressing are not interested in the internal differences in Africa but in an invention of an authentic Africa radically different from supposedly more developed cultures. Elizabeth herself eschews the question of gender, even when expressing skepticism about Egudu's agency and sincerity. Despite his arguments for the complete autonomy of African literature, Egudu's award-winning work is part of a commonwealth of literature, in which art from different parts of the world congregates. Egudu then emerges as part of what Appiah calls the "comprador intelligentsia" who form the basis of postcolonial studies by constructing Africa as a cultural commodity to sell to Western audiences. Despite his espousal of radical politics to a liberal bourgeois audience, Emmanuel Egudu inhabits what Ali Behdad calls "comfortable and depoliticized sites of alterity" (2000, 84). The culture on whose behalf he claims to be speaking is excluded from metropolitan spaces through what Behdad terms "tokenized inclusion" (2000, 84). Through Emmanuel Egudu, Coetzee offers an explanation for the intellectuals' attempts to invent an authentic Africa that they know does not exist in reality; Egudu creates that Africa to conform to the intellectual taste of Europeans who flatten out other societies by seeing them as Europe's polar opposite. Here Egudu, though occupying a diasporic space that is inevitably contaminated by other cultures, conforms to the essentializing notion of authenticity claimed by institutions that seek to reify Africa as culturally stagnant. Thus Elizabeth Costello's critique of Egudu, despite the fact that she belongs to that category of Europeans, might indicate to the reader that the perception of Africa as Europe's "other" is an illusion.

Coetzee gives Egudu credit for understanding that the institutional environment in which he works has shaped his contradictory self. His subaltern identity is politically constituted into a network of contradictions with which we identify even though we wish he would grow out of it. Uprooted from his Nigerian homeland, where academic freedoms are trampled underfoot, Egudu enjoys no liberty in the West because his host society expects him to conform to its desires:

> How easy do you think it is, ladies and gentlemen, for this fellow to be true to his essence as a writer when there are all these strangers to please, month after month—publishers, readers, critics, students, all of them armed not only with their own ideas about what writing should be, what the novel should be, what Africa should be, but what being pleased should be? Do you think it is possible for this fellow to remain unaffected by all the pressure on him to please others, to be for them what they think he should be, to produce for them what they think he should produce? (Coetzee 2003, 43)

Egudu is circumscribed by the hegemonic discourses in which his own actions and statements circulate. In *The Invention of Africa*, Mudimbe (1988) has ably shown how the construction of Africa is complicated by the interactions of the continent's cultures with Western practices. For Mudimbe, the trends and preoccupations of even the most essentialist anti-Western movements in African philosophy and arts are structured by the insights of European thinkers. Through Egudu in *Elizabeth Costello*, Coetzee shows the dilemma of the African intellectual operating under the gaze of Western thinkers and artists. Egudu, though willing to initiate changes in the way Africa is viewed and produces its discourses, is compelled to produce what the West will buy and consume. Through metafictional devices, Coetzee subtly urges Western consumers of African literature and the comprador intelligentsia that circulates "Africa" as a cultural commodity in the West to consider allowing African art to demonstrate its autonomy, rather than binding it to Western expectations and tastes.

Egudu's position further reminds us of Spivak's subject in "Can the Subaltern Speak?" in which Spivak presents the former subjects of colonialism as so overwhelmed by the hegemonic situation before and after colonialism that they cannot articulate themselves outside of colonial and patriarchal paradigms. Egudu is not just a part of the masses that Spivak describes as unrepresentable by intellectuals; in fact, in a Eurocentric space like the ship where Egudu gives his lectures, the intellectual/subaltern dichotomy is disrupted by the fact that he occupies both spaces, claiming to speak for the underrepresented African cultures as an intellectual authority in a space that does not allow him any agency. In a global order that puts Egudu at a disadvantaged position both at home and in exile, he cannot entirely separate himself from the oppressive and dominant Western discourses that have shaped and literally fed him.

Egudu has been appropriated by the West and capitalistic commerce to offer images of Africa that the dominant discourses expect to see coming out of Africa. Always on the defensive and excessively sensitive to criticism, Egudu leads himself to convoluted self-contradiction. The "Third World" intellectual and the people he represents in his discussion of African art are elided into pitiable figures, both subjects of higher analyses by Westerners. Although an intellectual and analyst, Egudu develops into a character similar to the "native informant" in Spivak's chapter on history in *A Critique of Postcolonial Reason* (1999) who is complicit with the very imperial structures he claims to be deconstructing. Instead of engaging his audiences in a transnational discourse that reveals the interconnectedness of texts from across cultures, he tries to trap his audience in the narrow-mindedness to which he feels they may be susceptible.

Equally self-contradicting, the Western cultural and academic venues seek authenticity by hiring Egudu to lecture about African culture "in the same way an elephant is an expert of elephants" (Coetzee 2003, 43). Such a view is essentialist, but his audiences are at the same time uncomfortable when he defends the authenticity of that culture. Coetzee's novel criticizes Egudu for the same reason Spivak excoriates the diasporic native informant in *A Critique of Postcolonial Reason*—for giving in to these forces. At the same time, the novel criticizes the West for compelling a marginalized figure like Egudu to willfully articulate inaccuracies and to further marginalize his culture. While earlier versions of the postcolonial subject in Spivak's writing were seen as incapable of acquiring agency in the context of repressive colonialism and patriarchy, *A Critique of Postcolonial Reason* contains mild optimism for the subaltern; here the subaltern can enter a transnational network that would enable her strategic agency to oppose hegemonic forces in both the West and at home. Similarly, Coetzee seems to see some hope for the subaltern diasporic intellectual.

That Egudu is able to voice his contradiction to his bourgeois audience is indicative of his potential for agency; nevertheless, he operates in the periphery of a cultural world that has little room for the margins, despite the inclusion of marginalized discourses in academic and leisure events. Elizabeth's cynicism is the subject of the novel's criticism, but her view of Egudu, and those with whom he interacts, reveals her attitude toward Africa to be framed by racism as well. Egudu voices a negritudist position on "the essential substratum that binds all Africans together and makes them uniquely African" (Coetzee 2003, 43) because he knows an exotic Africa shorn of all diversity is much more saleable to Western audiences. Although Egudu identifies the dates of these statements through icons of the negritude movement, he does not bother to update his position; he ignores the fact that Africa has changed to embrace a less essentialist and more realistic position regarding other cultures.[16] As articulate as he is, Egudu displays more emotional defensiveness than intellectual objectivity. He wants to market an emotional, irrational, and oversexed Africa to retain his position in bourgeois academic and tourist venues. It is little wonder that Elizabeth, herself a subject of Coetzee's ruthless critique, sexually gazes at his body in a way that suggests that the African intellectual is an object of erotic exploitation. To the reader, Egudu is no different from the likes of Modin in Armah's *Why Are We So Blest?* (1972).

The metafictional gestures that *Elizabeth Costello* stages through a figural representation of a writer and a theorist of African literature are enacted in oratorical terms that cancel out Elizabeth Costello's arguments against orality. Although a good writer, she is an ineffective speaker because she lacks the kind of oratorical skills Egudu displays. We are left in great doubt about whether Elizabeth is able to love the animals whose rights she advocates in tedious lectures, since she seems incapable of loving human beings or communicating with them in life or even in a live performance. Her return in Coetzee's later (2005) novel, *Slow Man*, intensifies her portrait as a manipulative and heartless writer who is as degenerate as the subjects she criticizes. *Elizabeth Costello* is not a statement against orality, especially because the novel is set in oral situations and criticizes subjects without oratorical skills. Rather, it pokes fun at the treatment of orality as a formulaic mechanical reproduction that we should demand of every African novel we read.

The Deconstructed Epic: Margaret Ogola

More interesting is the way writers use oral traditions to undermine the nationalist and ethnic impulses that those traditions would ordinarily be used to reinforce. Feminist studies have variously shown how African women writers deploy orature in a reinvented way to give voice to women whom traditional and modern societies have reduced to silence. Such studies include Juliana Makuchi Nfah-Abbenyi's *Gender in African Women's Writing* (1997), an extensive study of identity, sexuality, and difference, which transcends European linguistic barriers to explain the ways African women reclaim their doubly silenced identities. Cynthia Ward has also ably shown in "Bound to Matter: The Father's Pen and Mother Tongues" (1997) how women novelists have used the fluidity of orature and vernacular to deconstruct both colonialism and patriarchy. It is critical to note here that writers do not slavishly reproduce traditional orature; they sometimes have to rework the materials radically.

Nuruddin Farah's *Maps* (1986) set in motion an interesting trend in which the epic genre would be subverted to criticize the masculinist military exploits that have left many African nations in deep crises. A benchmark in literary craft and gender sensitivity by one of the very few male African writers who, from the very beginning of his career, exposed the parochial underpinnings of patriarchy and nationalism, *Maps* deploys the traditional oral epic to undermine the genre's patriarchal tendencies.[17] Since *Maps* has received a fair amount of perceptive criticism, I turn to Margaret Ogola's *The River and the Source* (1994) to show how, like Farah's *Maps*, the author uses and at once undermines the epic conventions to present women's issues. Unlike Farah, who is self-conscious in his use of the epic—he acknowledges the use of Isidore Okpewho's *The Epic in Africa* (1975) in the preliminary pages of the novel—Ogola is tapping more directly from orature. *The River and the Source* uses the epic genre spontaneously to undermine the nationalistic and masculinist tendencies of the traditional epic. The novel draws on Luo mythology and published literature to destabilize the reader's perception of reality in precolonial and contemporary Africa. It successfully creates an illusion of objectivity while debunking notions of objective comprehension of reality. Where Eileen Julien, in *African Novels and the Question of Orality* (1992), sees a general disinclination among women writers to use the epic because the genre's "hierarchic form is tied to nationalistic agendas and military might" (1992, 47), Ogola uses the epic in a feminist-inflected mode to deconstruct its originary obsession with nationalistic and military conquest and to highlight the epic battles Kenyan women have waged against patriarchal and sexist practices. Julien's observation is germane here. Ogola's feminist intervention demands a rupture from the Luo epic, which, though overlooked by Ruth Finnegan, who argues there are no epics in Africa, remains a vibrant genre in this East African community living near Lake Victoria.[18]

The uniqueness of the novel lies in the way it uses the epic to subvert the masculinism typically associated with the genre. The novel's encyclopedic scope, its temporal setting, and the construction of its principal character evoke the very epic tradition that it consistently undermines in inscribing its deconstruction of sexism in precolonial and contemporary Africa.[19] Describing itself as an "epic" in its paratexts, the novel stations the word "epic" at strategic points in its narrative to emphasize the enormity of women's struggle in precolonial and postcolonial exile. In the narrative, the traditional epic's focus on the male warrior is replaced with a consideration of the struggles of a woman, Akoko, to shape her destiny. The characteristic qualities of the epic hero—a prophesied and spectacular birth during a time of crisis, a royal background, a precocious development, a display of courage and determination, and a life in exile, triumph, and betrayal—are strategically used to underline the marginalization of women and their resilience against the patriarchal order. These conditions that the epic character has to undergo in the traditional epic are, in *The River and the Source,* motivated by specifically gendered activities; for example, Akoko's exile from her home is a result of the brutalities of her misogynistic and jealous brother-in-law. The invocation of the society's military heroes contains names of female Luo soldiers and is juxtaposed with contemporary struggles to acknowledge women as being among the important personalities that have shaped the destiny of the Luo nation.

Certain structural characteristics of the epic—digressions, rhetorical questions, and authorial intrusions—are employed to give a commentary on the conditions of women in Africa. Through its epic heroine, the novel undermines the nationalistic exclusivity of the epic in the sense that she encourages and participates in cross-border marriages, despite society's derogatory references to non-Luos. Influenced by the Opus Dei teachings and first published by a Catholic venue, the novel is markedly heteronormative and seems to suggest that it would condone European colonialism and modernity if this would liberate women from precolonial patriarchy. At the same time, it discourages blind acceptance of marriage and Westernization. One of the successful women characters in the novel is contrasted to her twin sister who dies of AIDS. The successful character, Vera, takes her education seriously and studies electrical engineering at the university, a male domain. In contrast, her more beautiful sister, Beckie, is only good at literature and is described as having "flunked in all the other subjects" (197).

The narrative seems to institute a Cartesian mind-body dichotomy, in which good brains are rewarded and good bodies punished as embodiments of immorality, but it succeeds in unmasking the dangers of unbridled border crossing and postmodernity. Beckie is not only using her job as an air hostess to move from one city to the other, but she also marries a Canadian. Her death from HIV/AIDS signals the novel's doubts about any form of multiculturalism in which a woman does not improve her intellectual capacities but uses her bodily endowments to subject herself to Western male, sexual domination. Although suspicious of the usefulness of the study of literature as an academic subject vis-à-vis engagement with the sciences and technologically oriented subjects, the novel invokes stories from the West and from Africa to underline the value of engaging creatively with the arts, as well as the epic genre. The structure of *The River and the Source* accords with Bakhtin's qualification in *The Dialogic Imagination*

(1981), that sometimes the epic can fit into the "yet uncompleted" framework of the novelistic discourse. The novel avoids the kind of closure that Quint, in *Epic and Empire* (1993), sees to be characteristic of the imperial genre. The novel not only ends in ellipses to signal the continuation of struggle, but it also uses an internally heteroglossic structure to underline the need to incorporate marginalized voices into mainstream society. While Lukács sees the epic as lacking in subjectivity, Ogola uses female subjectivity to subvert phallocentric nationalism and to arouse further struggles against sexism.

The novel's open-endedness seems to have inspired a sequel, *I Swear by Apollo* (2002), in which Ogola self-consciously writes back to the earlier novel whose story the sequel seems to continue. Before reverting to the realist mode, *I Swear by Apollo* launches its narrative in a gaudy utopian atmosphere, whereby the country has had its first female president. Deconstructing reality in Kenya, where forty years of Kanu rule was ended in 2002 by a coalition of parties, the novel refers to this momentous political development but makes the presidential victor female.[20] The earlier novel seemed to see women's leadership only in terms of claiming spaces in a professional field, but *I Swear by Apollo*, a novel about corruption even in the medical field, expands women's possibilities to the field of competitive politics. While *The River and the Source* appears antimale in its elimination of male characters in freak accidents, *I Swear by Apollo* places male characters in more visible spaces in the narrative, celebrating their role in the empowerment of women. In *I Swear by Apollo*, the virile female, or what Ifi Amadiume calls the "male daughter" in the Igbo context, does not require the death of the actual "male son" to realize her potential, as is the case in *The River and the Source*, where aggressive girls achieve power through the death of their male equivalent. In eliminating this trope, the writer indicates women's ability to compete with men on a level playing field, rather than relying on accidents coming to the aid of the woman.

Furthermore, the negative attitude toward the arts and their connoisseurs, such as Beckie in *The River and the Source*, is dropped. The opening paragraphs are told from the perspective of a musician who holds the reader's attention through her perceptive reading of architecture and her knowledge of artistic institutions in East Africa. The arts-sciences dichotomy that *The River and the Source* creates, despite the intertextual webs that inform its narrative, is demolished in *I Swear by Apollo*. Further, unlike in *The River and the Source*, terminal conditions such as HIV/AIDS are presented in a sympathetic light, not as conditions that sexually loose characters willingly court. The same attitude is seen in Ogola's *Place of Destiny* (2005), in which she creates a formidable female character fighting cancer and passing the mantle of leadership to a younger and highly motivated woman. *I Swear by*

Apollo playfully invokes Emecheta's *The Joys of Motherhood* (1979) but ignores the irony of Emecheta's title. By overlooking the irony in the source text, Ogola displays an affinity with the concept of "motherism" championed by Catherine Acholonu as an alternative to what is viewed by most African women writers as radical Western feminism. However, while Acholonu conceives of the rural as the ideal place for the African woman, Ogola sees redemptive value in modernity and urbanization.

Like Ifi Amadiume in her anthropological analysis of the Igbo, Ogola underlines through fiction the centrality of motherhood in a woman's self-realization in African societies. Unlike Amadiume, who views the precolonial woman as possessing agency against male dispossession, Ogola is highly skeptical about the notion that precolonial societies were more observant of gender equality. Ogola seems to eliminate gender parity from precolonial practices and to welcome Christian reforms in Africa. The alienation produced by Western formal education that we see in the works of Ngũgĩ and Okot p'Bitek becomes, with Ogola, an enthusiastic endorsement of formal education for men and women in Africa, hence, her deconstruction of the very traditional oral techniques and genres she uses in her fiction.

Myth of Origin/Origin of Myth: Grace Ogot's *Miaha*

Margaret Ogola's fellow Kenyan Luo woman writer Grace Ogot reworks, especially in *The Strange Bride* (1989), the traditional Luo folklore to express the discrimination against African woman in the feudalistic, colonial, and postcolonial African societies. Ogola's and Ogot's use of folk narratives is far from a passive recording of the past; rather, it is a devastating deconstruction of the patriarchal view of women as objects to be exploited and denigrated for the survival of the patriarchy. The metafictional subversiveness of *The Strange Bride* resides not in the use of the mise-en-abyme technique, as in her *Promised Land* (1966), or the treatment of the theme of prejudiced and patronizing male criticism of women's writing, as in the short story "The Middle Door" (1976), or in the experimental use of the diary form to resurrect a suicide victim of male oppression, as in the short story "Elizabeth" (1968); in the novel, Ogot self-consciously uses an Adamic myth from her native Luo culture to deconstruct both the patriarchy and its use of mythology to sustain its exploitation and marginalization of women.

Composed in Dholuo language as *Miaha* (1983a), the novel draws on Luo orature to rework a foundational myth that criticizes women as the source of suffering in the world.[21] The foundational myth is etiological in that it tries to explain why the Luo people have to work to earn a living, while in the primordial past work was not necessary. Stuart Hall, in the essay "Ethnicity, Identity, and Difference" (1991), has demonstrated how discursive strategies are summoned to consolidate national and ethnic identities. Narratives of the nation are told and retold in continuous and primordial myths that would be sacrilegious to challenge because they ostensibly present the divine view of the origins of the nation. In *Miaha*, Grace Ogot demonstrates her awareness that myths constitute an invention of the past to legitimize present power relations. She selects myths and turns them on their head to disrupt patriarchal privileges. Departing from the foundational myth that condemns women as villains who provoked God to force people to labor for a living, *The Strange Bride* (1989) portrays the power of a woman to transform Got Owaga from a low-productivity village, highly dependent on preternatural powers, to an agricultural and fishing entity, where people shape and control their destinies. Similarly, the narrative celebrates women's ability not only to determine their own destinies in a male-dominated society but to transform the nation's economy and politics. The story revolves around Nyawir (the "strange bride" of the title) who angers God by working on the farm against the convention. While Nyawir would be criticized for condemning the society to work rather than to sit back as the farmlands till themselves, the narrative seems to be celebrating her rebellious nature, which leads her to steal the magic hoe and to work on the farm. Her activity leads to a revolutionary change in which people start farming more aggressively for their betterment.

The Strange Bride opens with a folkloric story structure, signaling a story told by a communal narrator. Focalization is shared between male and female characters, and as the story progresses, the collective, plural narrator gradually fades away. The narrative focuses on Nyawir, who constitutes the narrative's internal consciousness. Take, for example, the description of her response when her in-laws assail her:

> They started to trot towards Were Ochak's home. Within no time there was a big crowd in front of his gate. At that same time Were Ochak left home, hurrying, with his sons behind him.
>
> Suddenly Nyawir felt unable to walk properly. Her knees were knocking against each other because she was perplexed by the state of affairs. She wondered how Lwak had found out so soon. And what should she do? Should she run away and disappear completely?
>
> But before she decided on what she ought to do, Lwak came out of the open field, ululating, and running towards where Were Ochak was. Were Ochak started to trot, going to meet Lwak, with the clansmen behind him. (1989, 95)

This passage demonstrates how the narrator speaks through Nyawir's consciousness. The questions "And what should she do? Should she run away and disappear completely?" are uttered by the narrator but express Nyawir's dilemma.

The mixture of voices is more audible in the Dholuo text. The passage in the English text is made up of three paragraphs, while in the original, the section is narrated in a single paragraph, expressing a single thought, fully collapsing the narrator's description of Were Ochak's acts and Nyawir's response. Further, in the Dholuo text, the sentence beginning "She wondered how Lwak . . ." uses, quite unconventionally, an exclamation point as the terminal punctuation mark, indicating that the sense of amazement is articulated by both the character and the narrator. The translated text also silences some deictic elements that locate the narrative within Nyawir's frame of reference. In the Dholuo original, the narrator begins the sentence "They started to trot . . ." with the word *koro*, which translates into the connector *so*, or the deictic element of time *now*. The same word is left at the beginning of the sentence "Were Ochak started to trot . . ." The use of the deictic element *koro* instead of the conventional indicator of the past, *eka*, denotes that the narrator is collapsing the past into the present and signals the fact that the narrative is being sifted by the character, Nyawir, as she experiences her present circumstances. While some elements of Nyawir's consciousness are lost in the translation process, the text at least retains indicators that the narrative is largely focalized through her.

The space Nyawir is given in *The Strange Bride* prioritizes her as the most important character in the text. She is the "bride" of the title, but she is initially kept away as the narrator opens the story, not only to create a sense of expectation and suspense in the narration but also to give the background of the world she is set to change through her agricultural and industrial interventions. Our entry point into the narrated world is a panoramic view of the society, its belief system, and its economic activities. The society is at one with nature, and everybody appears settled in their roles. For example, the other bride in the family into which Nyawir marries is smug in her domestic role:

> Achola was a hard working-woman [*sic*] and grinding grains (on a grindstone) [*sic*] was nothing to her. She, therefore, did not allow her mother-in-law to tire herself by grinding. She did all the grinding herself, both to make food for the birds and get the flour that the family used for making ugali and porridge. She had a good voice and she sang sweetly as she ground her grains. (5–6)

Achola is introduced early in the story to serve as a point of reference when the narrative contrasts her contentment with the revolutionary spirit that Nyawir brings into the community.

Through her mother-in-law, Lwak, the narrative praises Achola as a hard-working, obedient woman. The mother-in-law uses the adjective *wonderful* to describe Achola's character, and the elder woman instructs her to teach Nyawir good behavior when the latter joins the homestead. She comes out as a modest woman who knows that she cannot teach Nyawir as if the new bride were an empty vessel; the two would need to "teach each other" (49), for Achola has no intention of acting as a bank-clerk teacher doling out knowledge to the young wife. On the whole, she is a sensible, ideal daughter-in-law, who is described by Lwak as closer to her than a real daughter (48–49). The narrative uses her to foreshadow Nyawir's difficult disposition. It is Achola who warns the reader that Nyawir might not listen to anyone (49). Furthermore, she serves as a contrast to Nyawir because the latter possesses the opposite of those qualities for which Achola is praised.

To read the silenced part of Achola as a way of voicing Nyawir's character, it is appropriate to remember what Roland Barthes says about the unstable nature of characterization:

> To read is to struggle to name, to subject the sentences of a text to a semantic transformation. This transformation is erratic; it consists in hesitating among several names; if we are told that Sarraine *had "one of those strong wills that know no obstacle,"* what are we to read? *Will, energy, obstinacy, stubbornness* etc.? (1974, 92, emphases in original)

Although Achola's character traits are directly described with approving adjectives, and her actions and the praise she enjoys would portray her as a good person, the narrative undercuts her stature by contrasting her with Nyawir. The narrator does not show the reader the negative part of her character but consistently hints at it. She is pragmatic, but only in a narrow sense compared to Nyawir, who revolutionizes the society.

A similar method is used to construct Lwak, the mother-in-law. She is the major force countering Nyawir's revolutionary curiosity. Ordinarily she would be a negative character because she is acting against the interests of the main character. However, she is depicted as a pragmatic woman who has the gift of foresight. From the outset, she is the only person who can see elements of Nyawir's character that her husband is blind to:

> That beauty of hers even I have noticed and agree that she is very beautiful. But this beauty of my daughter-in-law does not seem to be for nothing; it's rather unusual. What kind of girl is this whose eyes do not seem to fear anything; and who appears to be seeing the deep secrets of your heart when she looks at you? (Ogot 1989, 60)

From her reaction to Nyawir, it appears that a woman would understand another woman better than a man because of an individual's socialization to see women as innocent beings who have no depth beyond physical beauty. Ochieng', a boy who has not gone through this social programming can innocently see that Nyawir is strange. He tells Lwak:

> Grandmother, I really like my younger mother. But sometimes when her eyes and mine meet, I feel frightened. Why does that happen? . . . Each time I'm near her, when our eyes meet, I always feel a sudden rush of cold blood in my body. I'm frightened. (Ogot 1989, 63)

To think through the boy's fear of Nyawir, one would need to return to Cixous's "The Laugh of the Medusa." Following Freud, who calls women the "dark continent," Cixous expands the Freudian metaphor to show that a similar binary system is used to structure power relations. To Cixous, women are associated with strangeness and otherness, while men are aligned with selfhood and normality. It is for a similar reason that Nyawir is seen as a strange creature in Got Owaga—because she threatens the social order. Lwak and Achola are conniving with the male-dominated society to align her with strangeness and otherness.

In the myth of the Medusa, the woman is feared because instead of hair she has many writhing penises that challenge the male order. Society fears Nyawir because she keeps her plaited hair long, while society wants it short for fear that other girls might follow her example. Beth Newmann has linked the hair of the Medusa with Medusa's gaze, seeing the gaze as castrating. The fact that the gaze is most enervating to the boy is peculiar. Ochieng' embodies the future center of power in the Got Owaga state, but when his eyes meet her gaze, "there is a sudden rush of cold blood in [his] body." The boy, who is the future of the nation, fears Nyawir's gaze because it threatens him with castration. The boy reports his fear to his grandmother to signify that the older woman serves as a custodian of male privilege; she is more efficient than men in maintaining the phallocentric order. She too fears Nyawir's gaze because it threatens the male power for which she is a high priestess. Her intention is to bestow her authority upon Achola, who is a good handmaid of the system. Nyawir threatens the perpetuation of order and thus is seen as a Medusa out to castrate men and to neutralize male power.

The narrative silences Ochieng' immediately after he notes that his younger mother is strange; his role in the story is to underline the castrating potential Nyawir holds in relation to male hegemony. Although on the surface the narrative seems to be giving credit to Ochieng' and Lwak for their foresight, it is more fundamentally critical of them, and especially her, for their failure to see the positive side of Nyawir's disruption of the social order. The elderly woman uses her power and respect to hold back the society, particularly its female members. Her praise of Achola as the guardian of order and peace after her death (49) exposes her short-sightedness because, the narrative seems to maintain, it is Nyawir she should be supporting for securing future prosperity.

When Nyawir is introduced into the narrative, the others are pushed to the background. The narrative shows her to be a curious child who will flout the rules quite easily. When she is told by her father to wait for her mother at home, she chooses to go outside the homestead to look for her. The narrative suggests a mother-daughter union in the sense that she could have stayed with her father at home. The father's inner thoughts are revealed to us so that we realize what he does not. The man does not "realize" that the girl does "not want to be alone." The narrative signifies, though not in so many words, that Nyawir would be one with him spiritually, despite her father's physical presence.

After she bends the metal-headed hoe while working with it, Nyawir is banished from the community for acting against the will of God, Were Nyakalaga. At this point, her husband Owiny emerges as the ideal man who gives his wife unqualified support. Initially, he is depicted as a naïve boy who loves Nyawir because of her beauty even before he has seen her. Rumors and gossip about her looks lure him to her before he knows her background. As the narrative progresses to its dénouement, he becomes a resolute character who will not abandon his wife simply because society has declared her persona non grata. Nyawir's appreciation of his gesture (120) augments his stature in the reader's mind.

Before strategically silencing Nyawir to empower her through the speech of others, the narrative allows her to underline the story's main theme, the inevitability of change. She agrees that she has done wrong but argues that what she did was necessary for society's advancement:

> The muscular-armed one, I agree that I sinned and now I have brought a big problem for Were Ochak, my father-in-law, and Lwak, my mother-in-law. But look, Owiny, the people of Got Owaga have a saying that generations replace one another in the enjoyment of the pleasures of life. In my own mind, that saying means there must be change in the world. Meaning that when our elders' days are finished and they die, then those who are born after them become elders and take their place; and the youth also go through the various stages of growth until they become adults and assume leadership. (Ogot 1989, 121)

The positive side of Owiny's character is called into question when he speaks out against Nyawir's philosophy of change. He is shown to be as conservative as the rest of the society, which has exiled them for challenging its complacency.

He turns out to be fatalistic in comparison to Nyawir's trust in the human capacity to change for the better. He says:

> Now, if our generation begins to change the customary laws with which our forefathers established the world, it will look as if we are rejecting our forefathers. It will appear we are belittling all the good deeds which our forefathers performed here in Got Owaga, so that our children may forget them. (121)

The narrative silences Owiny's philosophy of pessimism by giving it voice using Nyawir as the focalizer. Against Owiny's fatalism, Nyawir comes through as the dynamic philosopher who sees the need for people to use their intelligence to change their lives instead of waiting for some supernatural power to rescue them:

> *Ayaye* Owiny, why don't you realize that if a man is not willing to use his intelligence which Were Nyakalaga gave him, one day Were Nyakalaga may take that intelligence from him? Personally, I think it is when we help ourselves, instead of waiting for Were Nyakalaga to do everything for us, that we also help him; and that is when knowledge can increase in the world. (122)

Nyawir couples knowledge with power and sees technological development to be possible only if people stop their blind worship of supernatural beings. The narrative says that Owiny "marvelled" when she says this, but the narrative muffles his illogic to privilege Nyawir's thinking. She stands her ground, and Owiny is presented as illogical in his failure to see her point. The narrator uses the words *argumentative* and *unyielding* to describe her character (123). The adjectives refer to negative attributes and are used not to reflect but to constitute a dubious aspect in Nyawir's character. However, disapproval of Nyawir is not warranted. The descriptions are focalized through Owiny, whose perspective the reader has been encouraged to see as suspect. From the focalization and the words Owiny uses to describe Nyawir, the reader is expected to disregard Owiny's view of Nyawir and infer from the narrative that she is incredulous toward any knowledge that treats everything as a given.

After underlining the narrative's philosophical mission, Nyawir becomes silent, but the voice given to an unconscious Owiny, buttresses Nyawir's perspective. In a sense, Owiny speaks only to undercut his agency. When he visits the king in the netherworld and attempts to blame Nyawir, he is ordered to keep quiet because "quarrelling or noise is not permitted here." Further, he is warned against "quarrelling and discrimination" (131). People are allowed to speak only when they are advancing the interest of a better world, one in which female voices are listened to. Even the voice of the male king in a preternatural world where only men dwell is silenced. This only enhances Nyawir's view that people should not entrust their destiny to God without working to achieve their goals. Whatever agency Owiny has toward the end of the story—teaching the community how to make canoes, cut trees, fish in the Mihoo River, and farm—is all predicated on Nyawir, thus entrenching her agency and making her philosophy the enduring wisdom of the narrative.

Play on the Play of *Pakruk*: Grace Ogot's *The Promised Land*

If Maillu's *No!* (1976) and *Broken Drum* (1991) replicate themselves in a mise-en-scene, Grace Ogot's *Promised Land* (1966) uses orality deconstructively and praises itself for the effort. It is useful to study the mise-en-scene in some detail in *Promised Land*, one of the earliest novels written by an African woman author, because of the way the narrative uses the technique to subtly dismantle patriarchy through folkloric self-praise. The inclination of *Promised Land* toward carnivalesque discourse in its use of communal songs performed in an open-air theater reveals the gender imperatives implicit in the ways in which the text is created by its narrator and consumed by its ideal audience.

Bakhtin has discussed the carnivalesque as a mark of the novel in detail in his *Problems of Dostoyevsky's Poetics* (1984a) and *Rabelais and His World* (1984b). The thrust of Bakhtin's argument is that the carnivalesque is a counterhegemonic strategy that exploits grotesque realism, turning realism and the traditional order on its head in order to question the power relations in a particular society. The carnivalesque is heterogeneous, oxymoronic and miscegenated in its choice of situations and mixture of genres. In *Problems of Dostoyevsky's Poetics*, Bakhtin speaks of the "Menippea," a genre linked to the carnivalesque that involves oxymoronic, characters, a multiplicity of styles, and violations of etiquette and the social order. According to Bakhtin, the carnival is a site of struggle in which a new order is articulated, and the inhibitions engendered by the prevailing archaic social situation are lamented and subverted:

> Carnival is the place for working out, in a concretely sensuous, half-real and half-play-acted form, a *new mode of interrelationship between individuals*, counterpoised to the all-powerful

> socio-hierarchical relationships of noncarnival life. The behavior, gesture, and discourse of a person are freed from the authority of all hierarchical positions (social, estate, rank, age, property) defining them totally in noncarnival life, and thus from the vantage point of noncarnival life become eccentric and inappropriate. (Bakhtin 1984a, 123, emphasis in original)

While *Promised Land* as a whole rejects a monological structure and incorporates dialogue not only between characters but also with other genres and texts, it is in the dance at the party Ochola and Nyapol host in their new Tanganyika home that the characteristics of the carnival, with all of its eccentricities, are manifested.

Of interest is the novel's engagement in the art of *pakruok*, a complex, indigenous performance in the Luo culture, the parallels to which Peter Amuka has observed in different African societies. As an open-ended literary genre, *pakruok* involves self-praise in a playful way that allows its performer to stage different identities in different contexts to construct a sense of self in relation to others in society. David Parkin (1978) has noted the political significance of *pakruok* as self-fashioning in public spaces, whereby performers compete with each other openly to claim the highest social status for themselves. Noting its tendency to elude classificatory logic, Amuka observes that the genre is a stylistic play on words that has implications for naming and political self-fashioning in a social context. *Pakruok* is brief, but it is an encapsulation of multiple longer narratives, anecdotes, and myths that "predate and succeed" its utterance (1978, 90). The interpretation of *pakruok*, then, would of necessity be contextual because the five-word utterance unpacks contingent narratives about the individual in relation to others in the verbal contest.

In *Promised Land*, the use of the *pakruok* mode of self-praise is gendered in that it reveals the sexual relations of power in society while alluding to a traditional art form that claims a distinct identity for the African subject in modern Kenya. The *pakruok* entertainment that the novel presents involves songs by a harpist that are interrupted by the audience, members of which interject their praise names. The carnivalesque interruptions resonate with gendered commentary that, to use Amuka's term, would precede and succeed the linguistic utterance. For instance, when Okech, the son of Sipul, stands to address the harpist, he gives himself a gendered praise name: "I am the carrier of a bicycle. I am the back of the bicycle where you carry ugly, shy girls who don't know how to keep a conversation going with the gentlemen" (1966, 106). Okech's praise name is oxymoronic. While pretending to elevate himself, he insults himself as the seat for the ugly. The praise name advertises its eccentricity in order to entertain but at the same time comment on the noncarnival situation. The name at once articulates, and criticizes the male view that women are dependent on men. This is the view Ochola holds when he insists that Nyapol should accompany him to Tanganyika. The praise name is double-edged; it praises men and insults women, but both groups appear entertained: "The men roared with laughter, looking at women, while the women giggled in agreement with the son of Sipul" (106).

The men "roar with laughter" because they do not seem to comprehend the irony loaded in the praise name. In praising himself, Okech is also criticizing himself and men in general for their unkind view of women. It is imperative to remember Achille Mbembe's statement that the grotesque and the obscene may be used as a "means of erecting, ratifying, or deconstructing particular regimes of violence and domination" (2001a, 105). In the scene portrayed in *Promised Land*, Okech uses the obscene and grotesque in the hope of ratifying an already-established domination of women. However, the text as a body of diverse ideas secretes other meanings, in which Okech's words deconstruct the very power relations he seeks to ratify.

When another man stands to praise himself, his name is also gender marked: " 'Listen to me,' he said. 'I am the female mosquito, a female mosquito which lands on the skin first before biting' " (107). The man is given eccentric qualities, and his praise name is both equivocal and ambivalent. He is made to qualify the mosquito as female to draw the reader's attention to the gender politics involved in his praise name. He compares women with cunning creatures which have a clever strategy of attacking their victims. Little wonder that someone in the audience remarks: "Yes, you are right, these female things are so cunning, you know them" (107).

Nyapol uses a similar strategy in criticizing the male order that her husband has inherited from the society. As Stratton has noted, she plays carefully with gender politics, thus gaining the confidence of her relatives in trying to rein in her husband. The novel, too, is careful not to criticize patriarchy blatantly; it does so subtly while posturing as if it were calling for its retention. In a sense, *Promised Land* is a female mosquito that lands discretely before biting the patriarchy. Even when the text suggests that women are fetishes that encourage men to fight vigorously for the nation and to make them laugh and cheer "hysterically" as a girl declares herself the "castor oil that is given to cause diarrhea to girls who lack a slim waistline" (110), the reader is made to feel that the narrator is playing with the psychology of the male audience to make it accept the criticism of the patriarchy encapsulated in the litany of praise names.

The use of the carnival spirit to restructure power relations forms an excellent point of reference to compare *Promised Land* to Ngũgĩ's fiction, especially to *Petals of Blood*, in which Ngũgĩ creates a carefree atmosphere where the text interacts with genres such as popular song and dance. Ngũgĩ (1998) sees this form of generic interaction in African narratives to be a mark of indigenous African democracy:

> The audience could participate as critics and performers. In the stories, for instance, a choral phrase or song or response was often taken up by the listeners, who, in so doing, became part of the unfolding of the action. (1998, 110)

This seems to tally with Bakhtin's sense of the carnivalesque, in which "everyone is an active participant, everyone communes in the carnival act" (1981, 122). The *gitiro* dance in which Nyakinyua leads the other characters during the Theng'eta drinking ceremony in Ngũgĩ's *Petals of Blood* is one instance of the carnival presented in the novel. The dance is marked by what the narrator calls "erotic abuse," in which the characters engage in an "opera of eros" (207). While Ngũgĩ uses this obscene opera to stage a protest against colonialism and the privileged classes, Ogot uses *pakruok* to unmask embedded stereotypes.

The Interrupted Continuum

To conclude this chapter, I want to refer briefly to a concept Ngũgĩ wa Thiong'o borrows from his Gĩkũyũ culture to analogize generational changes and the relationship between the state and the artist. In the chapter "Enactments of Power," Ngũgĩ (1998) describes performance art in terms of the indigenous Gĩkũyũ revolution, celebrated every twenty-five years or so, to commemorate the juncture in the community's history when a centralized monarchical system of government was replaced with an egalitarian system based on family as the most important social unit. This moment is called *ituĩka,* meaning "a break, a complete break with what has gone before" (Ngũgĩ 1998, 38). Ngũgĩ, following Kenyatta's (1938) account in *Facing Mount Kenya,* observes that until the British banned the *ituĩka* ceremony, it "marked the passing of power from one generation to the next" (38). Ngũgĩ suggests that the primary role of the artist is to participate and inspire an *ituĩka*-type performances in which the power of a hegemonic state is subverted and replaced with a decentralized and nonhierarchized arrangement through arts performed in open-air theaters, where the actor/audience binary is replaced with participatory community theater that exploits performance arts in local languages.

Ngũgĩ names his writer-character in *Wizard of the Crow* (2006) Karamu-Mbu-ya-Ituĩka (the pen that screams during *ituĩka*) not only to yoke writing (pen) and oral articulation (screams) with revolution (*itũika*) but also to indicate the possibility of the misuse of indigenous concepts such as *itũika* to maintain the status quo. In the novel, Karamu-Mbu-ya-Itũika, a former revolutionary, has been co-opted by the retrogressive government to distort history and the national memory. While in the essay Ngũgĩ concentrates on the *itũika* phenomenon as a marker of the break with the colonial and neocolonial state, I have suggested that similar revolutionary breaks with the past can be enacted regarding gender hierarchies. The novelists I have discussed here seem to be using oral literature to enact an *itũika*-like break with traditional folklore. I have suggested that folklore contains attitudes that need to be changed. I should reiterate that oral literature, even in the precolonial era, was not static. By its very nature, orature is a dynamic phenomenon—always breaking with the past to such an extent that no performance can duplicate another. Novelists utilize orature's malleability to undermine settled notions of gender roles and power hierarchies. In other words, oral literature is a double-edged tool that can be used to either entrench or disrupt gender stereotypes. This is because orature is a versatile mode of performance deployed in contemporary novels to challenge the very attitudes it traditionally helped legitimate.

The epic has undergone various changes in the contemporary novel. Like Nuruddin Farah in *Maps*, Euphrase Kezilahabi seems aware of the theoretical arguments about the epic hero when constructing his character Kakulu in the Kiswahili novel *Mzingile* (Labyrinth). Kakulu (the diminutive old one) is so named because "*alizaliwa akiwa na ndevu tayari*" [he was born with a beard already] (1990a, 8). Kakulu, like most archetypal epic heroes, was born in extraordinary circumstances; in his case, he was born with a full set of teeth and thus does not suck his mother's breasts. Even at a tender age, he expected to solve the problems facing his society, but unlike the traditional hero who is held in high esteem in the grand poetic narration, Kakulu is ridiculed most of the time in *Mzingile* and is portrayed as an anti-hero like most of Africa's nationalists, whose policies did not improve the welfare of the citizens. Rejecting the nationalism of the epic and producing what might be called epic anti-heroes, Kezilahabi criticizes the nationalism of Senghor and Nyerere, among other founders of the African nations. He uses the epic genre to undermine the very nationalist project that the genre traditionally praises and to challenge the very nationalistic attitudes the epic traditionally helped to legitimize.

Kyallo Wamitila, too, is aware of epics and their characteristics as evidenced in *Bina-Adamu!* (2002) and its sequel that draw parallels between epic traditions across the globe. He is even more self-conscious in his use of the oral epic in *Dharau ya Ini* (2007, The Mischief of the Liver), whose title highlights irreverence and slipperiness. Invoking canonical epics such as

Paradise Lost, but boisterously drawing attention to its status as a performed work of oral literature that is as elusive to grasp as a piece of liver, *Dharau ya Ini* declares that its main character's story "*kilifanana na mugani wa fasihi simulizi*" [was like a piece of creation in orature] (10). The use of the literary terms *fasihi simulizi* (oral literature/orature) and *mugani* (narrator) in the novel draws the reader's attention to the playfulness, as the narrative urges the reader not to despair while listening to its narrator and not to take its narrative for granted like the proverbial *mwewe* (kite), who out of pride and impatience, could not fully grasp a piece of liver. The kite symbolizes those with power in the society; *ini* (liver) stands for those preyed upon by powerful protagonists such as Munene (Bantu for "Big Man" or "the Leader"). The novel subverts the power structures by portraying the powerless as elusive, beyond the grasp of the powerful. In close proximity to references to *fasihi simulizi* (orature), protagonist Munene's story is compared to "*shujaa wa tendi na migani*" [hero in epics and legends] because of the extraordinary circumstances of his birth to a mother who dies soon after.

Like Fidelis, the intrusive narrator in Seithy Chachage's *Makuadi wa Soko Huria* (*Pimps of the Free Market*), who was born at the cusp of party nationalism in Tanzania in 1954, Wamitila's Munene is born in 1950, around the time Kenyan nationalists began guerrilla warfare against the British. But despite his epic birth, Munene is an anti-hero who betrays the dreams of nationalism in Africa. Like Kezilahabi's Kakulu in *Mzingile*, Munene is born with teeth in his mouth. That typical characertistic of an epic hero is not given the positive quality of precocity; the narrator delights in foregrounding the dramatic irony as Munene bares his teeth wondering where the adults are taking the body of his dead mother. Munene's precocity, beyond being born with teeth, and whose mother dies moments after his birth, involves developing an early sadistic taste for violence, as we see him beating up laborers on his father's farm at a very tender age. As the story develops, we learn that Munene is a rapist, and he becomes one of the most oppressive postindependence leaders. Wamitila's novel marks yet another instance in which the traditional epic is used to examine the ironies of nationalism rather than to endorse the nationalist projects of African leaders.

In a word, this chapter has examined the use of oral literature in contemporary novels in a way that seeks to challenge the view of modern African literature as an unbroken continuation of traditional oral literature. While students of "magical realism" have emphasized the affinity of nonrealist modes of narration for oral literature as a discursive means of countering Western discourse, I have focused on departures from orature in order to reveal the ideological reconfigurations of Africa's patriarchal traditions. The novels evoke the fantastical world of folktales not to uphold the tenets of traditional oral culture; rather, most of the narratives invoke orature to foreground their departures from traditional forms of expression. Therefore, contrary to conventional arguments that the modern African novel should be treated as an offshoot of oral literature, it would be more germane to study how particular texts contest the folkloric forms to which they refer. We have seen that writers deconstruct the patriarchal assumptions of folklore in a way that contests the West-versus-Africa Manichean dichotomies, but the novels focus more on the deconstruction of local assumptions that entrench hegemony.

It is worth emphasizing that African literatures mark local identities through orality. The texts try to excavate Africans' suppressed subjectivities through recourse to precolonial modes of expression. In a way, an African nation owes its consolidation into an "imagined community" more to oral communication than to print capitalism because the expressive economy of modern Africa is defined by a pervasive sense of orality. The intimacy that Benedict Anderson's *Imagined Communities* (1991) observes between nationalism and print capitalism in Western nations does not apply neatly to African nations that were created by imperial powers in the late nineteenth century and that, still seeking autonomy from the European cultural and aesthetic conditions that created them, depend on verbal and other informal ways of producing, circulating, and exchanging art.[22] It is perhaps for this reason that in a metafictional novel such as Ngũgĩ's *Wizard of the Crow* (2006) revolution is engendered by oral theatrical performances by intellectuals like Nyawira rather than from reading written classics. The contribution of printed texts to nationalism, though important in the long run, is practically minimal in cultural spaces where literacy is in some countries as low as 19 percent[23]; where official and national languages are spoken only by a minority; where there is a markedly low rate of book purchasing; and where the few books that officially circulate do so mainly in the sanitized laboratory-like environment of the classroom.[24]

The use of folklore in written forms gives the novels a rich, internal heteroglossia that signifies the desire for freedom and the need to look at phenomena from different perspectives. It serves to deconstruct the positivist view of the world while rejecting some precolonial practices and discourses that justified oppression. This process of deconstructing preexisting texts does not end with the rewriting of old folklore; the novels rewrite older ones to emphasize a similar desire for a more liberated Africa. I suggested earlier that Margaret Ogola has rewritten not only Luo epics but also her earlier narratives to make them more gender-conscious. The next chapter examines the writers' deconstruction of earlier texts. I am particularly interested in examining how writers overwrite their earlier novels and the gendered implications of these revisions.

Chapter 5

Politicized Palimpsests and Gendered Intertexts

The previous chapter examined the orality/written interface, itself a form of reinscription and excavation of cultural texts overwritten by colonial discourse. This chapter examines the gendered dimensions of the ways in which African novels are palimpsests rewriting earlier written literature from the continent. By a palimpsest, I mean the deconstructionist survival of an early text in the current one in a way that we can hear echoes and see traces of the earlier text in the current narrative. I am mainly concerned with the textual layering produced by effacing or modifying preexisting writing to provide a new impression that does not fully expunge the earlier text.[1] I proceed from the premise that literary texts display gendered voices and silences in their treatment of themes and development of characters regardless of whether gender is a central thematic concern. As Pierre Macherey notes in *A Theory of Literary Production* (1978), a text is subtended by a certain determinative silencing; what it does not say or tries to erase under a more dominant voice could be more decisive than the voiced message (1978, 87). This chapter reads the palimpsests in African metafiction, these being traces of erased or obscured older texts that the novel invokes but tends to conceal under the current imprint, or what Derrida sees as the inevitably contradictory logic of a text written atop another which it seeks to simulate and dissimulate at once.[2] Some of the novels discussed, such as Ngũgĩ's (1986b) *A Grain of Wheat,* are realist, but they acquire metafictional status when we consider their rewriting of previous texts and previous editions of the same story.

Sites of Infinite References

If we accept the argument by major poststructuralist theorists (such as Barthes and Kristeva) that a text is a mosaic of multiple other texts, then we would see all literature as reinscriptions and the canceling out of previous texts. In metafiction, the reinscription can be so intense that the novel serves as a palimpsest of its own narrative, canceling out its own positions and arguments, engaging in what Derrida's "Living On: Border Lines" calls "an apocalyptic superimprinting of texts . . . Only relationships of cryptic haunting from mark to mark. No palimpsest" (1979, 133). The text would thus demand that we read the traces or obscured traces of its own narrative as an old text being replaced by a new but an impermanent text.

It is no accident that even mimetic African literatures present cultures as layered palimpsests. European colonialism in the late nineteenth century imposed Western values on traditional African cultures without effacing the practices of the local populations. This is especially true of Anglophone Africa, where the British pursued "indirect rule," a practice involving indigenization of the colonial state.[3] Major texts have commented on attempts by the British to efface African texts and values and replace them with colonial modernity. We have already seen how Ngũgĩ's use of Shakespeare and Blake in *Petals of Blood* (1977) hints at the abuse of the Western canon by neocolonial educationists and to figure the despoliation of Africa by modern capitalism. In a similar criticism of the abuse of the Western canon, Ben Okri's *Infinite Riches* (1998) presents a colonial officer trying to erase the subjectivity of the community by denying Africans the possibilities of culture.[4] Abdulrazak Gurnah's *By the Sea* (2001) also presents the attempts by the British to flood Zanzibar with colonial texts and atlases as a strategy of erasing local texts. Hassan, the narrator's brother, is forced to mechanically memorize a scene from Shakespeare's *Julius Caesar* but thinks the word "dagger" that he mouths in a reenactment before the narrator means some kind of wine. The scene deconstructs blind colonial education and the belief in the supremacy of the Western canon, whose texts the African student is coerced to reproduce uncritically.

The literatures mix local values with global desires and anxieties to signal what Bhabha has called "interstitial spaces," locations in which precolonial practices are not separated from colonial modernity but are mediated through mutual exchange. European metropolitan culture is also a palimpsest in its composition. As a refugee in London, Gurnah's narrator in *By the Sea*, Saleh Omar, observes that the British culture itself is layered with past experiences that recall outdated movies and medieval texts. Through an invocation of visual texts, Saleh suggests that his host culture is as palimpsestuous as his "native" culture back home, an intercultural layering that has been intensified by the inevitable forces of globalization. Thus to examine colonial and postcolonial literatures is to experience layers of interrelated practices because the texts reconstitute cultures that are themselves layered in a complex way.

The borrowings between texts are infinite. Here we only focus on a few to demonstrate the gendered implications of a writer revisioning an older text.

Rosemary Marangoly George has pertinently reminded us that colonialism and the emergent nationalism are not the only issues that preoccupy African societies, as Western postcolonial theorizing might have us believe. She notes that feminists in the postcolonial field have described how anticolonial nationalism has exploited women as symbols without empowering them in the material world. Women's writing is therefore not primarily a "writing back" to the colonial center; it writes back to local male writers. Indeed, Florence Stratton, a leading critic and one of the most energetic readers of African literature, uses the tools of postcolonial and feminist theories to point out that two key components of African women's writing are dialogue and the deconstruction of African male writers (1994, 18).

Though operating outside of feminism, Gikandi is right to underscore the necessity of studying intertexts to appreciate the ideological layeredness of the economy of African texts. In "Reading the Referent: Postcolonialism and the Writing of Modernity," Gikandi underscores that "postcolonial literature is intertextual in nature" (2000, 94) and notes that although more emphasis is placed on how the postcolonial texts subvert metropolitan discourses of power as represented in colonialist fiction, postcolonial literature is not a monolithic body. To Gikandi, there are texts within the postcolonial body of writing that interrogate and subvert the positions of others within the same canon: "The canonical texts of African nationalism, which emerged initially to counter colonial images of Africa and to call into question the politics of imperialism, were notorious for repressing the experiences of women, or for turning women into icons of male desires and power struggles" (Gikandi 2000, 94). Women writers attempt to transform the grammar of nationalism in male texts into a politicized intertextual deconstruction of images of women in masculine discourses of nationalist liberation. The study of the intertextual, as noted by such theorists as Riffaterre, is inevitable in any composite reading of a text, be it postcolonial or not.[5] I should point out here that the intertextuality in African novels is not necessarily insurrectionary. Nana Wilson-Tagoe emphasizes that texts by an African woman writer are "not merely the obverse of the male tradition or simply an imitation or revision of the writing of her male predecessors but a multidimensional discourse embedded in both male and female traditions" (1997, 27). This is to say that they are not primarily a negation of male discourse; they mine different traditions to express phenomena in a comprehensive way.

Affecting Deconstruction: King-Aribisala's *Kicking Tongues*

The uniqueness of Karen King-Aribisala's *Kicking Tongues* (1998) lies not so much in its readability or deconstruction of Western literature as in the way it provokes the reader with sometimes trivial references to texts across cultures. The novel does not seem to pursue stylistic accomplishment; most of its references are awkward and not particularly subtle. Its publication in Heinemann's African Writers Series is a departure from the series' earlier focus on realist novels for educational purposes.[6] It combines these themes with a self-conscious theorizing of literature and society in an equally nonrealist and nonnationalist manner. King-Aribisala collapses the binaries between prose and poetry, between African oral literature and Western folklore, between oral performance and scripted texts, and between tragedy and comedy to capture the amorphousness of a society at the intersection of democratic struggles and military dictatorship and between rural existence and urban growth.

Defying generic categorization, the novel does not belong to the magical realist tradition, but it exhibits what Brenda Cooper, in theorizing magical realism, calls "sensuous irreverence of carnival, reveling in the riotous imagination, in the truths of mysteries and imponderables" (1998, 25). In the subversive attitude it takes toward canonical texts, national leadership, feminist theorizing, and cultural nationalism, the novel exhibits the utmost irreverence toward established notions about identity and its politics. It is as unanticipated and capricious as the social and political conditions that it describes through a compendium of voices framed by an imperious, highly unpredictable narrator. While African novels have always made references to Western texts, *Kicking Tongues* forms the apex of bold and overt transfigurations of texts in the way the narrative extravagantly and self-referentially claims to transpose Geoffrey Chaucer's *Canterbury Tales* to an African context, despite the fact that its links to Chaucer might not go much farther than mentioning him and his *Canterbury Tales*. Ben Halm is correct to note that the novel "has that staple of postmodern writing and representation, that which I call 'magpie-ism,' in that it is a shameless appropriation of other stories and literary works" (2003, 168). Through her learned characters, the novelist invokes texts from across cultures—but she sometimes does so to satirize the characters that mouth titles of artistic works without much depth of reflection. Although located in global spaces of underdevelopment, the intellectuals are portrayed as wallowing in the depthlessness that Frederic Jameson (1991, 12) sees to characterize the postmodern world. The depthless, one-dimensional, affectionless nature of modern African life is signified by multiple references to rich works of art whose relationships are not deeply explored. The fleeting references can be irritating, but through their depthlessness, the novel manages to question the integrity and relevance of modern intellectual life in Africa.

Indeed, the extravagant claims mimic the obsession with the Western canon among the educated elites that Ngũgĩ articulately criticizes in

Decolonising the Mind (1986a). King-Aribisala also cautions the reader against nationalism and dogma. If earlier African texts have configured older texts to give way to new texts, then *Kicking Tongues* "kicks" texts about without a sense of self-effacement. Rather than leave its references open to speculation, as Coetzee's fiction does, King-Aribisala's narrative flaunts its sources, even when those references are irrelevant to the novel's interpretation. In this sense, *Kicking Tongues* compares to Okurut's *The Invisible Weevil* (1998), whose mention of Milton's *Paradise Lost* and *Paradise Regained* is not a reengagement with those texts but a playful reference to the destruction of Uganda by Idi Amin's military dictatorship in the 1970s and the possible reconstruction of the nation, a theme picked up in Moses Isegawa's satirical *Snakepit* (2004). The discussion of these texts by the literature students Nkwanzi and her boyfriend Genesis in Okurut's novel parallels the state of their romantic affair, which has been disrupted by the ruling elites who succeed in sleeping with Nkwanzi, a chaste girl, although, unlike her boyfriend, the elites are intellectually degenerate. Like *Kicking Tongues*, *Invisible Weevil* would achieve the same effects without the European texts. Alternatively, perhaps these hyperreflexive texts want us to argue that their erasure of European texts is so complete that Chaucer and Milton are heard as distant echoes.

Although the narrator's hyperreflexivity in the invocation of literary texts and debates borders on quackery, *Kicking Tongues* provokes us to read an absent Chaucer in the story. Like Chaucer, King-Aribisala uses fabliaux that are scatological and obscene to figure the condition of the Nigerian postcolony. The novel mixes prose with poetry, creative writing with commentary, and the serious with the macabre to signify the contradictions in modern Nigeria. Through its "melancholy" narrator, who frames myriad other narratives, the novel deliberately attempts to irritate the reader with excessive digression, references to titles of other works, and obsession with its own narration as an artistic project. Thus the central aim of the novel is not to deconstruct the English text but to use its structure to address contemporary issues in Africa.

The indulgent narrator makes extravagant claims and portraitures that point to convergences with, and divergences from, the European mode of discourse. Though dedicated to God, the novel rejects all forms of unitary authority—including the authority of its own initially aggressive female narrator, whom it deflates toward the end. It covers religious themes about penance and self-imposed punishment for political ills in the society, but on the whole, *Kicking Tongues* embraces a multiplicity of perspectives and loyalties, dissociating itself from the bossy nature of African politics to such a degree it can be said to be irreverent. Further, King-Aribisala's authorial disguises, revealed by the repetition of part of her name in the title, work to reveal the self-conscious conjunction of the actual and putative voice in the story. At the same time, the play signals a rejection of the authoritarian "king" mentality that has bred dictatorships that close themselves off to alternative voices.

Like Chaucer's text, the story is a journey of penance, in which individuals narrate their contribution to the state of the emerging Nigerian nation which, even four decades after independence in 1960, is still plagued by crisis after crisis. Important to all the pilgrims is the fact that the Nigerian nation has been straying in the wilderness for forty years in the way Jesus wandered for forty days in the desert. King-Aribisala bases the narrative on a journey from Lagos to Abuja, the Nigerian federal capital. Before embarking on their journey, forty travelers gather at an inn, where a frame narrator who calls herself "a melancholy hostess" but is also coyly named "The Black Lady The" selects and introduces them to the reader and the audience in the narrative. Each of the chosen travelers tells the story of his or her life. "The Black Lady The" uses poetic forms to garnish the narratives that are presented as a series of public oral performances with the profuse narrator serving as the master of ceremonies.

The narrator's propensity to theatricality and narcissism is seen at the very beginning of the novel, where she gives decrees in the same fashion as the dictatorial regimes that the novel satirizes. As the novel develops, her grip on the story is scuttled to signify a rupture with the authoritarian monotony of military and civilian dictatorships in Nigeria. Coming from a younger generation of Anglophone writers, King-Aribisala draws on texts from across the world to portray the postcolonial condition in her country, thus creating a dialogue that transcends the linguistic boundaries that colonialism put into place. The novel, then, engenders a conviviality of texts—local and global—to deconstruct the traditional monolithic African novel. *Kicking Tongues* plays not only on Amos Tutuola's orally presented and phantasmagoric *The Palm-Wine Drinkard* (1952) and *My Life in the Bush of Ghosts* (1954), which it gives a feminist interpretation, but also on contemporary women's work, such as Mariama Bâ's *So Long a Letter* (1981) and Buchi Emecheta's*The Joys of Motherhood* (1979). The women it presents are stronger in their resolve against patriarchy than are Ba's and Emecheta's female characters. Their feminist resolve in fact anticipates Sefi Atta's *Everything Good Will Come* (2005), which subversively echoes the title of Achebe's *Things Fall Apart* (1958) in celebrating endless possibilities for women in Africa. This position deconstructs not only Achebe's modernist apocalyptic view of Africa at the onset of colonialism but the depiction of women in Emecheta's *The Joys of Motherhood*, which gloomily presents in an equally apocalyptic tone the fate of women in Africa.

While King-Aribisala deconstructs both Achebe's *Things Fall Apart* and Flora Nwapa's *Efuru* (1966) by giving women more agency and undermining the earlier novels' obsession with the supposed happiness in motherhood, Atta's *Everything Good Will Come* conjures up more utopian happiness for African women without recuperating the traditional institutions of marriage and motherhood from Emecheta's skepticism. The title of the novel comes from a declaration made by the principal character, Enitan, after her father is released from detention and after she has been released from domesticity. Although the wider society continues to suffer strife and political instability, the novel celebrates the freedom of the individuals and reveals the need, unlike in *Things Fall Apart* or its feminist counterpart *The Joys of Motherhood*, to see the future through an optimist's lens.[7]

Unlike Tutuola, who uses nonrealistic settings and fabulistic details but who also tries to explain the logic behind the events, *Kicking Tongues* does not bother to explain the contexts; some of the references appear completely out of context.[8] Thus while offering the reader the agency to work through the meanings that it evokes, the novel can be quite frustrating. The pseudo-feminism with which the narrator pretends to attack Tutuola's texts is a call for a nuanced reading of male writers, as opposed to the rushed dismissal of texts on the basis of the sex of the author. The male student of African literature in the novel is shown as being capable of changing to more gender-sensitive positions. The novel uses references to many other works to undermine any form of essentialism, which it seems to see as the main cause of problems in African politics, where the leadership is unwilling to listen to alternative perspectives.

Writers and Politics: Gordimer's *My Son's Story*

If in *The Lying Days* (1953) Nadine Gordimer uses realism to examine a canon produced through interaction with hegemonic texts and ways of reading, her *My Son's Story* (1990) is a more layered and self-conscious fictionalization of the processes of writing and interpretation. In this novel, Gordimer productively employs metaphors of painting to present issues of canonization and emerging identities in South Africa. The story thematizes not only the story it references in its title but various characters' self-fashioning from books and art. Critical to Gordimer's metafictional project in *My Son's Story*, then, is the place of books, art, and interpretation in the politics of apartheid South Africa. Published in 1990, toward the end of the apartheid system, the novel is an evaluation of the intervention of art in the struggle against racial injustices. It is remarkable not only because of its self-reflexivity but also because it is the first novel in which Gordimer situates agency in nonwhite characters and narrators. Sonny, the implied speaker in the novel's title, is a mixed-race father who has been radicalized by the politics of apartheid South Africa. Fearing that his son might grow up into a frivolous person, he names him Will, after William Shakespeare, and expects him to be a conscientious and politically engaged writer. This indicates a clear difference between clowning and political engagement. Greenstein aptly reads the novel to be about the "mystery of becoming a writer, and the construction of a myth of authoring" (1993, 201), a point affirmed by Gordimer in an interview with the *New York Times Book Review* (Graeber 1990, 20). Although it appears didactic and openly political in its view of the purpose of writing, the narrative is at odds with itself in a way that seems to poke fun at its own liberal ideas and its avoidance of more African-centered political imperatives. The novel lays bare the exigencies that force one into activist writing and shows how concrete socioeconomic conditions shape the interpretation of art, and thus shape political and aesthetic practice.

My Son's Story follows the experiences of Sonny, a "Coloured" (mixed-race) schoolteacher and an avid reader, as he gets into activist politics. It appears Sonny is interpreted and recreated by the other characters he has interacted with, mainly his son Will and his girlfriend Hannah Plowman. Linda Weinhouse's Lacanian interpretation associates the title of the novel with "ventriloquism" and sees the narrative as "composed by the father in the voice he imagines for his son" (Weinhouse 1993, 69). Greenstein reads the first-person voice in the title, *My Son's Story*, as Sonny's articulation referring to Will's writing. But the novel is ambivalent about the speaking voice in the title. It could well be Sonny imagining how his own son would write about him, or it could be one of the other characters who serve as the centers of consciousness in the narrative speaking in Sonny's voice as they observe him evolving into an activist writer and imagine his son's judgment of him. I read the story as Will's reading of his father as his father is read by, and as he reads, other characters, including Will himself.

In the initial stages of the story, told through Sonny's center of consciousness and framed by his writer-son, the novel depicts the complicity of the oppressed in the apartheid system. As a nonwhite, Sonny belongs to the category of people who cannot visit certain parts of the beach, eat in certain hotels, or visit certain libraries set aside for whites. It is through his reflections on ideas, books, and libraries that Sonny—as interpreted by his son—comes to terms with the world that circumscribes and limits his being. The apartheid system has managed to present concrete reality as an intellectual abstraction. Some of Sonny's contemporaries do not want to struggle against segregation: "What did it matter that the seaside hotels, the beaches, pleasure grounds with swimming pools were not for us? We couldn't afford hotels, anyway . . ." (1990, 21). Sonny himself is complacent, impassively reading about trials in the newspapers and nonchalantly reflecting on the black community's clamor for equality. This political impassivity does not last long when the "Coloured" people realize that they are no better off than the blacks, and that their security and privileges under apartheid are no longer assured. It is to be remembered that, according to apartheid racial taxonomies, the "Coloureds" (mainly people of mixed-race, especially of white and black ancestry, but including non-black, non-white communities such as the Asians and Arabs) were considered superior to blacks but inferior to whites. In the nineteenth century Africa, "Coloureds" had equal rights with whites but the National Party stripped them of some of those rights when it instituted apartheid in 1948. With laws such as the Prohibition of Mixed Marriages Act of 1949, the Immorality Amendment Act of 1950, the Group Areas Act of 1950, the Population Registration Act of 1950, and the Separate Representation of Voters Act of 1951, the apartheid regime stripped "Coloureds" of their basic rights despite the fact that they would also be regarded as superior to blacks. Although most of the anti-apartheid activists were "Coloureds," some middle class liberal humanists among this ethnic group, such as Sonny in Gordimer's story, would either by cynical to the plight of black people or very mild in their opposition to apartheid. Without mocking them, Gordimer captures the irony defining a group of people marginalized by apartheid but who are reluctant to fight alongside the majority black populations because of the privileges the government offers them over black people. In the novel, it takes a tragic and traumatizing event to jolt Sonny from his complacency. When he witnesses the killing of his pupils by the apartheid government, he is impulsively drawn into activism, which he thought he would never get involved in, even though his cousins were a part of the country's military struggle for self-determination.

Sonny's reading of literature helps him interpret the situation a little better than his cynical contemporaries. He contrasts Kafka with Shakespeare but rejects the apparent despondency that Kafka's texts seem to apologize for. Suggested in Sonny's interpretation of art is a Marxian position that artists should not just portray the society objectively but should attempt to transform it. Kafka's fiction seems to express the pathetic situation in South Africa more realistically than the living human beings, but the people lack the will to change that Sonny finds in Shakespeare:

> Kafka named what he had no names for. The town whose walls were wandered around the Saturday people was the Castle; the library whose doors he stood before were the gates of the law at which K. sat, year after year, always to be told he must wait for entry. The sin for which the schoolteacher's kind were banished to be a prescribed area, proscribed in everything they did, procreating,

> being born, dying, at work or at play was the sin Joseph K. was summoned to answer for to an immanent power, not knowing what the charge was, knowing only that if that power said he was guilty of something, then he was decreed so. (17)

The invocation of Kafka's 1922 *The Castle*, a modernist text about totalitarian and dehumanizing bureaucracy in which personal struggles yield minor results, indicates Sonny's reading of the apartheid system as a powerful, castrating regime against which one cannot meaningfully struggle. The reference is mainly to give the reader a sense of not only the oppression and alienation that the majority suffers under apartheid but also the hopelessness the regime has systematically constructed in the people.

Sonny knows his cousins have joined the military struggle, but he seems to accept that Kafkaesque presentation of society as an unfathomable labyrinth of bureaucratic arrangements. Yet he rejects the defeatism he reads in Kafka when gritty reality faces him: "And although Kafka explained the context of the schoolteacher's life better than Shakespeare, Sonny did not go so far as to believe, with Kafka, that the power in which people are held powerless exists only in their own submission" (1990, 17). The bitter irony is that confrontation with the system breeds more despondency and a reliance on his white girlfriend, Hannah, with whom he is having an affair behind the back of his wife, Aila.

Literature offers Sonny some aesthetic agency because in his speeches he clinches his arguments with vigor and he is straight to the point by avoiding the beaten track:

> If he used the vocabulary of politics because certain words and phrases were codes everybody understood—no interpreter necessary, even in the English in which they were formulated they expanded in each individual's hearing to carry the meaning of his own frustrations, demands, and desire—Sonny did not adopt the usual mannerisms the vocabulary produces. He did not have a calculated way of standing or using his hands, when the eyes of the crowd were on him. (1990, 112)

Underlined here is the idea that sophisticated ideological language has been rendered mundane by constant use in the political struggle. He appears to be spontaneous and in full command of language. What is remarkable is that this agency is framed by Hannah, a priggish connoisseur of art who seems to view herself as radical despite her multiple contradictions. Although she leaves her husband when he, clinically depressed, abandons South Africa for London and remarries, she befriends a married man and seems to look down upon the family in a way that dispossesses it of its agency. Her struggle to free South Africa from apartheid is itself a romantic project that dispossesses Aila and emasculates Sonny in the long run. Although she helps the reader understand that the community apprehends the mental breakdown suffered by whites like her husband under the apartheid regime, she herself is a contradictory product of a political system that disadvantages the very racial category it seeks to privilege.

Even if the text does not seem to question her commitment to her husband, whom she should have accompanied in his recovery from what she characterizes as "clinical depression" (1990, 88), it is suggested that she is an intellectually dubious person. At the moment she leaves her lawyer husband, Hannah ships everything to her husband except a mattress and the drawing by a "follower of Jackson Pollock" (88–89). Jackson Pollock (1912–1956) is an American painter in the abstract expressionist movement, but it is peculiar that Hannah's painting is not by Pollock himself but by a follower, a derivation of abstract-expressionist art.

There is an air of falseness about Hannah. She chooses a particular mattress because it would grant her the flexibility to sleep anywhere in the subversive struggle against apartheid. At the same time, the mattress becomes a symbol of her perverse sexuality which, although transgressive against apartheid's racialized control of the body, leaves a lot to be desired. She reads the apartheid situation in libidinous terms, and her interest is more sexual than political. Like the "all-over-the-place" paintings of Pollock that are unconsciously created to have a life of their own, Hannah displays some kind of polymorphous perversity that suggests that her love for Sonny arises from an unconscious desire for the art lover, who only turns out to be political. It is not incidental that we discover her by accident when Will meets her and Sonny at the movie theater. For her, life under apartheid is just another movie to be enjoyed, an adventure as an activist without any specific program. She admirably sees in Sonny the psychic automatism of expressionist art, a form of spontaneous expression: "Words came flying to his tongue from the roosts of his private pleasures. When he was told he was good, he laughed and said embarrassedly that he was a teacher, a public speaker in the classroom every day of his working life" (33). Her presentation could itself be a spontaneous misreading because it appears to be from Will, who starts the section of the narrative about her with the question "Who is Hannah Plowman?", a question that he proceeds to answer through what appears as a fictional construction.

If Hannah is a connoisseur of the surreal, in which parts do not relate to the whole, then, Sonny too reads Hannah sexually, in abstract, libidinous terms, as a painting that expresses raw desire. But while Hannah dismembers social texts to conform to her surrealist schemes, Sonny organizes her into a subject with organic unity, which she lacks in reality:

> The face of a woman who uses no makeup has unity with her body. Seeing Hannah's fair eyelashes catching the morning sun and the shine of the few little cat's whiskers that were revealed, in this innocent early clarity, at the upper corners of her mouth, he was seeing the whole of her; he understood why, in the reproductions of paintings he had puzzled over in the days of his self-education, Picasso represented frontally all the features of a woman—head, breasts, eyes, vagina, nose, buttocks, mouth—as if all were always present even to the casual glance. What would he have known, without Hannah! (1990, 102)

A Freudian consideration of the latent material in Picasso's painting reveals a form of sexual and/or aggressive wish-fulfilling content, organized according to primary-process form involving condensation, displacement, and symbolization. Sonny's gaze at Hannah connotes sexual longing, underlined by phallic references to her body. But in this instance, Sonny organizes the crude reality of Hannah's polymorphous existence into a sublime artistic expression that could itself be a reflection of an amorous reality.

Readers will note Sonny's dependence on Hannah expressed in the last sentence that is punctuated with an exclamation mark to underline Sonny's amazement. He sees her as a miracle because under apartheid he has been conditioned to aspire to whiteness. In *Black Skin, White Masks* (1969), Fanon notes the "psycho-existential complex" wrought by the juxtaposition of white and black. As a mixed-race character, Gordimer's character Sonny is an embodiment of this complex, but he chooses to pursue whiteness and the white canon. He does not break out of the limitations of the canon by befriending and marveling at Hannah, who seems to be impressed that in his library he has more than "Marx, Lenin, Fanon, Gandhi and Nkrumah, Mandela and Biko always to be found as a sign of political self-education" (Gordimer 1990, 91). She takes note of Kafka and D. H. Lawrence who, from the context, she seems to view as writers of texts better than the confrontational polemics a black intellectual would be expected to stock in a library. For her, Sonny is admirable because he has aspired to white tastes, which she equates with being a complete person. Although he has radical Afrocentric books in his study, he does not refer to them, preferring to create metaphors out of Shakespeare, Kafka, and Picasso. On the other hand, Hannah seems to look down upon African theories in favor of the liberal humanist canon of Western art.

When the apartheid government catches up with Sonny for inciting boycotts, the narrator uses a center of consciousness somewhere between Hannah's and Will's to underline the centrality of writing and language in Sonny's life. We are shown Sonny "preoccupied with writing notes for the lawyers to use in his defense" (54). Writing becomes an important activity to link him to his wife Aila and to underscore his loss of basic freedom in the cell. But within this description of the place of writing in his past, present, and future is a suggestion of his romanticization of the source of texts. For example, Sonny is less interested in the meaning than in the form and the possible source of Hannah's expression "happy for battle";

> The phrase filled, for a few days, the hours that were so hard to fill, left over from the disciplined programme he had set himself in his cell—deep-breathing exercises, running on the spot, study, reading . . . happy for battle. He lay on his bed in the dark and sounded over his mind that phrase, so simple, so loaded, audacious, such shocking, wild glorious juxtaposition of menace and elation, flowers and blood, people sitting in the sun and bodies dismembered by car bombs; the harmonized singing and coming from somewhere in the cells, and the snarl of a police dog leaping at his face, once, in a crowd. (1990, 56–57)

There is nothing particularly remarkable about the expression or its source, but underlined in Sonny's self-conscious response to Hannah's language are the limitations of prison life where he will not be allowed to read and write—as he is forced to "keep the bed-time of chickens and children" (56)—and cannot dig out the source of the phrase because he is away from his library books at home. He is marked by the same contradictions that shape his society, where opposites revoltingly commingle to represent what he views as the romance and ugliness of South Africa under apartheid.

The self-consciousness of African novels could itself be a product of the limitations imposed on it by the political and economic situation, as it tries to come to grips with its potentials and limitations. As a teacher of English, a lover of classics, and a political speechwriter, Sonny is meticulous in his choice of words, but ideas and linguistic virtuosity unaccompanied by public visibility make him much more vulnerable to the apartheid state than the firebrand activists for whom he crafts radical speeches. The novel suggests the need to participate in radical politics rather than merely to articulate self-conscious programs. While the harassment of activists would draw the ire of human rights groups whose discourse Sonny seems to view suspiciously, despite his articulation of a similar liberatory mantra, the denial of Sonny's basic rights would make little difference because he is not well known, "a backroom boy, useful for writing statements that appeared or were spoken under the names of the venerable, or for tidying the vocabulary of the rising stars to give them more weight" (236).

The writer must possess the will to live a public existence of unlimited visibility, as opposed to launching underground volleys at the state using an arsenal of words. It is Will who closes the narrative and indicates that the foregoing is his fictionalized recreation of his father, his predicament, and his relations with different members of the family and society. He suggests that the political stance he takes might witness the suppression of his work:

> What he did—my father—made me a writer. Do I have to thank him for that? Why couldn't I be something else? I am a writer, and this is my first book—that I can never publish. (1990, 277)

Probably he feels he has been too harsh in his criticism of his father, who introduced him to writing, but Will has the will to create history and free writing and reading from the liberal humanist ideology he identifies in his father and his girlfriend Hannah. Ironically, it is this identification with a radical political aesthetic, as opposed to the hypocritical self-fashioning of the predecessors, that might limit the publication of his book in a world still controlled by bourgeois tastes and where a subaltern like him or his father cannot yet speak but has to be spoken for by the dominant race.

Writing against One's Own Grain: Ngũgĩ's Revisions of *A Grain of Wheat*

Ngũgĩ's *A Grain of Wheat*, arguably his most stylistically accomplished novel, involves not only a rewriting of earlier texts but a revision of its own narrative. First published in 1967 and revised in a 1986 edition, it is one of the African novels that reveals what Ogude calls the "historical farce" of the post-independence euphoria gripping African nations in the first decade of independence. In spite of its use of modernist techniques such as fragmentary narratives, multiple narrative voices, and stream of consciousness, the novel is largely realist. The revisions and the resultant palimpsests reveal Ngũgĩ's gendered nationalist message. The revised edition blunts the earlier portrayal of elements of possible atavism among African freedom fighters. Indeed, most of the revisions revolve around an incident in the first edition in which Koinandu, a freedom fighter, rapes his European employer, Dr. Lynd. A novel of political disillusionment, it contrasts the past struggles for independence with the current outcome to underscore the betrayal that the new nations have suffered at the hands of their ruling elites. It is condensed, focusing on a few days before and after Kenya's independence, but through flashbacks it illuminates the colonial relations in the country. Among the white characters is Thompson, a colonial administrator, and his wife Margery. Dr. Lynd, a scientist and an associate of Thompson's, hates Africans because she was betrayed by one of her black workers during the war of independence in the 1950s. In the earlier edition, the character Koinandu raped Dr. Lynd; in the later text, the character (revised as Koina) does not sexually assault the employer, Dr. Lynd, but he kills her dog.

The novel's commentary on another earlier text sometimes connotes a critique of the values the referred text stands for. For instance, the colonial District Commissioner in *A Grain of Wheat* is presented writing a book entitled *Prospero in Africa*. This echoes the effort by a similar colonial officer in Chinua Achebe's *Things Fall Apart* (1958) to write a text entitled *The Pacification of the Primitive Tribes of the Lower Niger*, a report Tony Clark in Achebe's *Arrow of God* (1964) is shown reading. Both authors are engaged in nationalist and realist projects in which they are countering the possible misrepresentation of the postcolonial subject by the colonizer before it happens again, as it used to at the onset of the colonial era. As James Snead notes in his brief commentary on intertextuality in Achebe's novels, the project, in which fictional colonial texts are created and mocked, preempts Western writers from writing such denigrating narratives (1990, 243). They are, indeed, writing back to the Western canon by conjuring up titles of fictional texts and forestalling the racism of these texts before they can be written by colonial officers. Ngũgĩ, by creating and mocking *Prospero in Africa*, preempts the white discourse that would conflict with his sense of history.

Although in the novel Ngũgĩ rewrites colonial narratives about Africa, inserting them into his novel in the form of fictional narratives of jaded colonial officers who need to be stymied before they circulate to reentrench stereotypes that rationalize colonialism, the novelist also calls Western narratives to his aid. In *A Grain of Wheat*, he faithfully follows the structure of Conrad's *Under Western Eyes*, with his character, Mugo, echoing Conrad's Razumov.[9] Ngũgĩ's text has a little bit more faith in military interventions against the colonial establishment while, like Conrad, Ngũgĩ is suspicious of the nationalist euphoria. Furthermore, as noted by Ponnuthurai Sarvan (1977), Ngũgĩ presents women much more realistically and celebrates their participation in armed struggle against colonialism in Kenya. Besides its nationalistic subterfuge of Western texts that are not necessarily gender marked, the novel contains a gendered abrogation of racialized texts. A case in point is the narrative about Queen Elizabeth that it parodies and critiques. This information is presented as a summary of a narrative told by a white missionary. Ngũgĩ shows that the missionary's audiences are not a passive lot; they are not duped into accepting dominant ideological values.

The community to which the missionary relates his story about the queen also traffics in narratives. In renarrating the missionary's story, the novel is populated with voices of the audience interpreting the story, as well as that of the missionary who originates it:

> The whiteman told of another country beyond the sea where a powerful woman sat on a throne while men and women danced under the shadow of her authority and benevolence. She was ready to spread the shadow to cover the Agĩkũyũ. They laughed at this eccentric man whose skin had been so scalded that the black outside had peeled off. The hot water must have gone to his head. (1967, 13; 1986b, 10)[10]

Throughout the novel's various editions and reprints, Ngũgĩ uses the unconventional compound noun *whiteman* to signify the Kenyan speech, where the colonizer would invariably be seen as male and white, regardless of gender. In the novel, there seems to be no difference between white women and the male European colonizers. African women who take on traditionally male roles are seen as men. Their activities portend doom for the community, reminding the patriarchal society of the traumatic events they have suffered in the past allegedly because of women's poor leadership skills. In this instance in the narrative, the missionaries' story about Queen Victoria is translated selectively to discredit women's leadership by conflating it with colonial oppression.

To comprehend the notion of a woman leader, the community refers to other social texts available prior to the new narrative. The story is nativized, and expressions such as "men and women danced under the shadow of her [the queen's] shadow" appear as the audiences' interpretation of the original narrative. The contamination of the objective account with the audiences' prejudiced view of the foreign narrative is registered by the community's view of the complexion of the missionary. The Africans assume that white people are white because their skins have been burnt with hot liquids. The reader knows that the missionary has not been scalded until "the black outside had peeled off," as Africans believe. This is the community's interpretation of the "unnatural" skin color because they belong to another culture. At the same time, the text laughs at the colonialists. The benign ignorance of the native observer is allowed to pass, while the missionary's hypocrisy, which he covers behind his evangelism, is foregrounded.

Furthermore, the fact that the colonial government is headed by a woman evokes a different quasihistorical mythical text that has a female Gĩkũyũ leader as its main character. The two texts are conjoined to explain the parallels of injustice informing the colonial administration and the indigenous women-led government:

> Nevertheless, his words about a woman on the throne echoed something in the heart, deep down in their history. It was many years ago. Then women ruled the land of the Agĩkũyũ. Men had no property, they were only there to serve the needs of the women. Those were hard days. So they waited for women to go to war, they plotted a revolt, taking an oath of secrecy to keep them bound each to each in the common pursuit of freedom. They would sleep with all the women at once, for didn't they know the heroines would return hungry for love and relaxation? Fate did the rest; women were pregnant; the takeover met little resistance. (1967, 14; 1986b, 10–11)

In the myth, fate that goes against biological facts is invoked to create a situation in which all of the women become pregnant at once.

In Wangu's case, she is made to overreach herself in a way that would justify her dethronement:

> Came a night when, no doubt goaded by the admiration she aroused, or maybe wanting to gratify their shameless longing, Wangu wa Makeri overreached herself. Removing all her clothes, she danced naked in the moonlight. For a moment, men were moved by the power of the woman's naked body. The moon played on her: an ecstasy, a mixture of agony and joy, hovered on the woman's face. Perhaps she too knew this was the end: a woman never walked or danced naked in public. Wangu Makeri, the last of the great Gĩkũyũ women, was removed from the throne. (1967, 14–15; 1986b, 11)

The elliptical syntactical structures, such as the one comprising the first sentence in the quote, are meant to create the impression of a colloquial conversational discourse in which the narrator is reproducing the text as it was supposed to have been articulated from the source. The colloquialisms help create reader-writer rapprochement. They make the story informal, as though the text is actually speaking to the reader.

Critics have noted, however, that embedded in the friendly discourse is a hostility toward women.[11] Mumbi is equated with Wangu: "some people called her Wangu Makeri because of her looks" (1967, 15; 1986b, 14). The same name is given to her when she appropriates traditional male roles of building a house when her husband is in detention. The women like Mumbi, who put on trousers to do male duties, are viewed as a threatening embodiment of the spirit of colonialism, in which "a woman—a new Wangu—in England had been crowned" (1967, 160; 1986b; 141). While her partner, Karanja, cannot be entrusted with the future of the nation because he is a traitor, she cannot lead the nation because she is a "Wangu." By virtue of being a woman she embodies misrule. Little wonder that the leadership of the desired nation is left in the hands of Gikonyo. Similarly, in *Petals of Blood*, Njuguna teases Nyakinyua about antelopes, which are "supposed to have been women's goats which had run wild because the women could not look after them" (Ngũgĩ 1977, 139). Ngũgĩ appears suspicious of the views expressed by the oral narratives but does not offer a rebuttal to them.

While as a nationalist and realist text *A Grain of Wheat* "writes back" to colonial texts, its gendered force can be traced in a reading of how it wrote back to itself in the 1980s. Reading the revised edition of *A Grain of Wheat* against the original version allows us to appreciate the gendered revisions Ngũgĩ introduces in the new narrative that then becomes an excellent reference point for the use of intertextuality in structuring gender politics.[12] For the writer, the new version is a better expression of his vision. In struggling toward the artistic ideal he had visualized but could not achieve in the earlier text, however, Ngũgĩ reduces the role that gender plays in the revision; the "artistic logic" he speaks of points more toward a nationalistic theme than gender issues.

In the new edition, Koinandu changes to Koina. The old name means the "one who breaks people"; the dropping of *andu* (people) in the revised narrative purges some of Koinandu's misdeeds, especially his rape of a settler woman, Dr. Lynd. It appears that the narrative's project is to represent Koinandu as a person who would not deign to rape colonialists. So even though the colonialists are shown raping the country, the empire does not stoop to raping the woman who represents the metropolis and its evils. In the earlier text, Koinandu and the other freedom fighters jointly rape Dr. Lynd:

> On opening the door, two men rushed at her and dragged her to the sitting room, the houseboy following. She looked to him for help, but he was smiling. She waited for them to kill her, for after the initial shock she resigned herself to death. But when she saw what was happening to her, she felt suddenly cold all over. People say women faint on such occasions or else struggle. She wished she could faint there and then. But that was the terrible part, she saw *everything*, was fully conscious. (1967, 53, emphasis added)

The description of the rape is repeated later as an anticipated fantasy in cruder terms that echo Koinandu's name's linkage to sexual penetration, the euphemism which is homonymous in Gĩkũyũ with the word for "break." The scene is focalized through Koinandu as he expresses to his colleagues his obsession with raping the white woman: "Man, I'll break her in. I'll swim in that hole" (1967, 242). By portraying Koinandu as part of violence against the West, the earlier *A Grain of Wheat* runs the risk of endorsing Western texts that play up the stereotype of the African male obsessed with having sex with white women. In the new text, the African is restored from the stereotype of an oversexed beast in the sense that Koina is neither obsessed with raping the white woman nor does he seize the opportunity to do so when the freedom fighters raid Dr. Lynd's home—despite the fact that they are described tying "her hands and legs together" (1986b, 45). While in the earlier text, the fighters' actions shock the reader as much as the victim, in the later text the attack seems less brutal, even though it is told from the perspective of the traumatized woman:

> She waited for them to kill her, for after the initial shock she resigned herself to death. But what followed was no less cruel and barbaric than if they had killed her. Her dog had barked at the two men. But on seeing the houseboy it wagged its tail and held back its attack. But the houseboy hacked it to pieces. Blood splashed her clothes. She wished she could faint there and then. But what was the terrible part, she saw *everything*, was fully conscious. (1986b, 45, emphasis added)

The expression "no less cruel and barbaric" is from Dr. Lynd's point of view, but to the reader what they do to her is a lesser evil. The action connoted by "everything" in the earlier text is rape, while in the later text "everything" refers to the killing of a dog. The ideal audience does not value a dog the way Dr. Lynd does, and it would appear rather petty on her part to be traumatized over such a minor thing. While the earlier text is at least neutral in its description of the action as "everything," the later edition has Dr. Lynd use a hyperbolic locution, a pronoun that would mean in the context "the gravest thing" to mock her worldview. So while the earlier text is hardly generous in its depiction of Dr. Lynd, the later is even more detached from her; it does not seek to elicit much sympathy toward her from the reader.

In the 1967 edition, Koinandu is ravaged by guilt for the corporeal engagement he has had with a representative of the exploiter race. The text tries to justify the rape by showing the suffering that Koinandu has gone through at the hands of the colonial government. He served in World War II, but he has been repaid only with frustration and unemployment. Because the colonized nation is shown as being raped, there is a sense in which Koinandu is himself a victim of abuse:

> His strength had left him. He felt himself like a corpse. The feeling had been with him for two days. He could not understand

> this. He had surely gone through worse experiences during the second whiteman's war and in the forest. He was glad of being a whiteman's cook in those campaigns. After the war, he proudly talked about it, until constant unemployment frustrated him and half-opened his eyes. Koinandu was one of those people who ran into trouble with employers because he was constantly complaining. (1967, 242)

In contrast, the 1986 edition says:

> He felt low. He had been like that for two days now. He could not understand it. He had surely gone through worse experiences during the second white man's war and in the War for Independence. These should have taught him to expect the unexpected in life. He had for instance been quite proud of having been a cook in the Second World War. After the war, he proudly talked about it, until constant unemployment frustrated him and half-opened his eyes. Koina was to become one of those people who ran into trouble with employers because he was forever demanding his rights. (1986b, 212–13)

The shift in emphasis is brought about by the change of the expression "whiteman's war and in the forest" into "whiteman's war and in the War for Independence." The narrator intends to locate the "war" in historical time; he is not talking about a vague white man's war but World War II. Here, Koinandu is a "whiteman's cook in the campaigns," but in the later text, Koina is a "cook in the Second World War." Again, the new text emphasizes the particularity of the period. While Koinandu "was one of those people who ran into trouble with employers because he was constantly complaining," in the later text, the narrator insists that "Koina was to become" a thorn in the flesh of the employers. There is emphasis on his "becoming" to show that his character has evolved from the social circumstances surrounding him. While Thompson's conduct is explained as a result of his colonial service, before which he was a good student with a poetic sense, Dr. Lynd's eccentricity is not explained. The text is silent about which of Rudyard Kipling's poems Thompson admires (whether they are the ones that speak passionately of the empire), but on the whole he is an empathetically drawn character before colonialism contaminates him (1967, 62; 1986b, 53).

The 1986 text tries to clear Koina(ndu) from blame by making him repent his own misdeed. The replay of his thoughts and words before the rape is meant to show the guilt he is suffering in the present:

> What now worried him was this: in the forest he had fought and killed so ruthlessly. But not one of the bloody scenes in which he had taken part had broken into his sleep. On the contrary the fight for freedom had given him a purpose. It had made him a man. Why then should her ghost shake him so? Many years had passed since he left her service . . . he had liked her dog and this seemed to please her and she gave her presents. Every Christmas. Then suddenly his thoughts started working again: she had no husband; she owned a big house: why? Why should he, a man, live in one-roomed shack? He found his tongue and revealed his thoughts to other people: she was alone; it was not right for a woman to live alone. Man, I'll break her in. I'll swim in that hole. The others laughed at Koinandu's delightful tongue. But what started as joke became an obsession. The opportunity came during the emergency. He and two men laid her to the ground. (1967, 242)

The revised version develops Koina(ndu) into a more rounded character by showing his past to the reader. He is presented more empathetically as a person who loves dogs but has been led to be violent to Dr. Lynd's pet because she values it more than human beings:

> He had liked her dog. As a boy he owned a pack of dogs which he used for hunting antelopes. How he would have liked to take her well-fed dog for a real chase of hare and antelopes in the forest. It seemed to please her that he and her dog got on so well. She gave her presents. Every Christmas. Then he started thinking. The amount of steak the dog ate could have fed a whole family. The amount of money spent on that dog was more than the total wage of ten Kenyans. The dog had its own room in the house, with a bed and seats and a blanket. And what about the woman? She had no husband, no children, no extended family. Yet her house could easily have sheltered many families. How could this be? Why should he live in a shack while this woman and her dog lived in such opulence and luxury? He became restless. How glad he was when he took the oath to join the Kenya Land and Freedom Army! He had seen the way. Independence when finally won, would right all the wrongs, would drive the likes of Dr. Lynd and her dogs from the country. Kenya after all was a black man's country. (1986b, 213)

While Koina(ndu)'s motives are developed, Dr. Lynd's extravagance is further emphasized, both by the more detailed description of the luxury she lavishes upon her dog, even as African families suffer abject poverty, and by the reminder that she is unmarried. There is no irony in Ngũgĩ's view of Koina's attitude toward Dr. Lynd: she is a symbol of the exploitation of the black man's country.

The new text also celebrates Koina's maturity in deciding to join the fight for independence against Dr. Lynd and her exploiter race and class. It is not interested in balancing the gender issues that, as demonstrated, betray a bias against female categories. The revisions tend to reflect nationalistic concerns, and little attention is paid to the splintering differences within the nation and in the settler community. Indeed, aside from the more developed depiction of Koinandu's motives, some of the more substantive revisions are statistical, such as the number of people killed while protesting the arrest of nationalist Harry Thuku, which is changed from 15 to 150. The "Party" in the new text also becomes the "Movement," to register what Williams (1999) and Sicherman (1989) see as the writer's skepticism about the political party that ruled Kenya after independence. Ironically, the "movements" that came to power around the time the revised edition came out, such as Ugandan President Yoweri Museveni's National Resistance Movement, eventually turned as undemocratic as the parties they sought to oust.

Because the main agenda of the revised text is to cleanse the freedom fighter of the crime of rape, there is a celebratory atmosphere as it narrates how Koina leads the men into Dr. Lynd's "house and they took her two guns and a pistol" (1986b, 213) without raping her, as in the earlier narrative. The elided rape structures the heroic actions that the fighters stage. Analyzing the earlier text, David Maughan-Brown (1985) is right to argue that Koinandu's obscene act gives the text an aura of seriousness by creating balance, showing as it does that even the European could in a way be seen as a wronged category in the liberation war.[13] But Ngũgĩ sacrifices this balance by tendentiously siding with the nationalist cause and the abuse of white women in the colony.

Dr. Lynd's story as told to Thompson in the novel's fifth chapter forms a story within the story. Here Dr. Lynd subtly gives the rationale for her hatred toward Africans. Her narrative gains more self-reflexive power when it is referred to as a story told earlier in her conversation with Thompson. The earlier narrative portrays Dr. Lynd as a pestering person, telling Thompson a story he does not want to hear. When it is retold, it expresses her desperation because the freedom fighters still loom large in postindependence Kenya:

> "Remember the incident I told you about yesterday?"
>
> "The dog?"
>
> "No, no-The-the-my story."

"Yes."

"You remember I told you about the houseboy."

"Yes."

"He was never caught."

"Yes, I believe you told me so."

"I'm frightened. I don't know what to do."

"Yes."

"Why, what happened?"

"Because-because, I saw him again—"

"When?"

"Yesterday." (1986b, 143)

Thompson is unwilling to speak to her; the narrator uses the word "compelled," which gives the impression that he gives her an audience because he is forced to. The conversation is elliptically stopped, but it appears that it goes on in the narrated time. This is contrasted with the portrayal of the conversation in the revised edition. The male and female whites appear to be united in their campaign to keep a stranglehold on the postcolony. In the narrating time, Thompson is not reluctant to listen to Dr. Lynd:

"You remember the incident I told you about yesterday?"

"The dog?"

"Yes . . . the murder of my dog!"

"Yes."

"You remember I told you about the houseboy."

"Yes."

"He was never caught."

"Yes, I believe you told me so."

"I am frightened. I don't know what to do."

"Why what's happened?"

"Because—because, I saw him again—"

> "When?"
>
> "Yesterday . . . Do you think it is going to be safe for us who remain?" she asked him. But before he could answer, she added defiantly, "No, safe or not, I'll not leave this place. I'll not leave my property to them."
>
> "Then you'll have to get better homeguards!" he said, rather savagely. But Dr. Lynd did not get the irony. She clung to the idea. "Yes . . . many more mbwa kalis to protect our lives and property," she said, and started talking about the qualities of the most loyal and the most ferocious guard dogs. (1986b, 165)

The negative portrayal of Dr. Lynd, relative to Thompson's image, is removed from the new text. In the earlier text, she opposes Thompson's relatively better conduct, suggesting that a colonial man is better than a colonial woman. In the later edition, they both connive to retain their power in Africa, and it is Thompson who proposes a way of guarding white property. Both are unsympathetic characters, but while Dr. Lynd is shown to be a naïve coward, Thompson is a pragmatic strategist who knows what to do in a time of crisis. The text is ironical in the perceptiveness it gives Thompson because he stands for what the narrator is against. However, he is better off than Dr. Lynd, who wants to remain in Africa but does not know what to do in case of attack from the landowners.

In creating and revising Dr. Lynd, especially with reference to Koinandu, the narrative in the new text is so concerned with nationalist rhetoric that it contradicts itself. We have already been shown, in two flashbacks—one from Dr. Lynd's point of view and the other from Koina's—that the freedom fighters have killed Dr. Lynd's dog. But because the dog is a symbol of exploitation of postcolonial Kenya by the West, it reappears in the revised *A Grain of Wheat*:

> And there in front of him was Dr. Lynd and her dog. She stood there as if she was mocking him: See me, I have still got the big house, and my property has even multiplied. (1986b, 214)

It should be noted that the dog does not appear with Dr. Lynd in the original narrative (1967, 202). In the revised edition, the narrator does not say how Dr. Lynd acquired the dog (if it is a different one from the one the freedom fighters killed), and there is the temptation to see it as the old dog that we have already encountered in an earlier version of the story, especially because it stands for the same political dispensation as the earlier pet. Its resurrection symbolically indicates the postcolonial control of the country by Westerners like Dr. Lynd, but its reappearance causes a structural flaw in the story because the narrator is obsessed in exonerating Koina(ndu) and incriminating Dr. Lynd.

In the later edition, General R, too, is nearly exonerated from the violence in which Reverend Kigondu is killed. Kigondu is a preacher who exhorts the people to join the colonialists and, with his religious blinkers on, back-peddles from the liberation efforts. In the earlier text there is a detailed description, through General R's recollection, of the evening he and his colleagues hacked the clergyman to death. In a scene reminiscent of Okonkwo's guilt after the killing of Ikemefuna, a child who called him father in Achebe's *Things Fall Apart*, General R feels guilty in a way because Reverend Kigondu is like his father:

> Now it was the face of the Rev. Jackson Kigondu which stood before him, accusing him. "He looked like my father," General R had once, in a moment of weakness, confessed to Lt. Koinandu, soon after they had killed the man of God. Jackson had consistently preached against Mau Mau in churches and public meetings convened by Tom Robson. He called on Christians to fight side by side with the white man, their brother in Christ, to restore order and the rule of the spirit. Now, every detail of the scene as they surrounded the preacher's house and hacked him to pieces glowed before General R. Jackson never showed fear. He knelt down and, as the pangas whacked him dead, prayed for his enemies. This act had almost unnerved General R. He called on his followers to dip their pangas in the man's body that all might share the guilt. Why did the man's face now suddenly appear before him? You had to die, he addressed the face, but the words did not leave his throat. He clutched the microphone to steady himself. (1967, 280)

The revised text is ambivalent about the brutality of the killing. It uses the euphemism "he had to be silenced" and the gory description of the killing that almost martyrs him in the earlier text is removed, and the religious man reappears in the form of a ghost:

> Now it was the face of the Rev. Kigondu that stood before him: Jackson had consistently preached against Mau Mau in churches and public meetings convened by Tom Robson. He had called on Christians to fight side by side with the white man, their brother in Christ, to restore order and rule of the spirit. Three times had Jackson been warned to stop his activities against the

> people. "In the name of Jesus, who stood against the Roman colonialists and Pharisee homeguards, we ask you to stop siding with British colonialism!" But Jackson became even more defiant. He had to be silenced. It was the same Jackson who now stood before him, mocking him, "We still are here. We whom you called traitors and collaborators will never die!" And suddenly General R recalled Lt. Koina's recent misgivings. Koina talked of seeing the ghosts of the colonial past still haunting independent Kenya. And it was true that those now marching in the streets of Nairobi were not the soldiers of the Kenya Land and Freedom Army but the King's African Rifles, the very colonial forces who had been doing on the battlefield what Jackson was doing in the churches. Kigondu's face was now transformed into that of Karanja and all the other traitors in all the communities in Kenya. The sensation of imminent betrayal was so strong that General R trembled in his moment of triumph. He clutched the microphone to steady himself. (220–21)

Through Koina(ndu), again, the narrator reverts to nationalist politics. The reappearance of Kigondu's ghost is an expression of the continuity of the colonial order in postindependence Kenya. After colonialism, symbolized by Thompson, has ended, neocolonialism, symbolized by Dr. Lynd and Kigondu, sets in. The latter two are worse than Thompson who has left Africa; the institution and authority they represent are seen as worse than colonialism itself. In the aggregate, the revision seems to have been conceived with a nationalist agenda in mind. There are direct announcements—sometimes without subtlety or structural motivation—of authorial positions to the effect that the country is still in the hands of the colonialists and their cronies. Gender representation is marginalized, and Dr. Lynd, the only female character in revised sections, comes through as a worse and weaker person than in the earlier text.[14]

Against Superficial Textual Boundaries

To conclude this chapter, we need to underscore our observation that the palimpsestuous nature of African texts signifies the inevitably hybrid nature of African postcolonial societies and aesthetics. The texts intersect not only with European texts but with each other. At the same time, the need to insert new ideas, especially about gender, has required the texts to rewrite earlier African texts. Even when a text extravagantly mentions Western texts, it is far from a confrontational rewriting. The works rewrite themselves much more intensely than they rewrite texts from the Western canon, and they can be read by a population that may not have prior knowledge of the Western texts invoked. There is also a filiation between gendered European texts and African ones, as evinced by the relationship between such texts as Thomas Hardy's *Jude the Obscure* (1993) and later African novels such as Phaswane Mpe's *Welcome to Our Hillbrow* (2001). Mpe reincarnates Hardy's novel in different locations, including a pub near Oxford University Press, to address the hypocrisy eating at the vitals of the South African nation. *Welcome to Our Hillbrow*, a text that opposes traditional purism and calls for the cosmopolitan abandonment of superficial boundaries, commingles writing and oral literature, the dead and the living, and the published and the unpublished to undermine any ontological essence. I discuss this text in more detail later, but it is pertinent to note here that its relation to Western literature is far from adversarial; in his references to *Jude the Obscure*, Mpe portrays the existence of a single text in varied forms to deconstruct essentialist and gender-insensitive attitudes in rural South Africa.

I have read Ngũgĩ wa Thiong'o's *A Grain of Wheat* in detail because it instantiates a writer's revision of his own novel in a way that is strongly gendered. Despite his skepticism toward nationalism, Ngũgĩ's rewriting of *A Grain of Wheat* in 1986 seems to be more invested in nationalistic matters. A study of the departures he makes from the earlier text reveals logical contradictions in his portrayal of gender. Ngũgĩ has rewritten the narrative of *A Grain of Wheat* in later texts, in which he gives more urgency to considerations of women's involvement in the liberation war. His later works are less interested in belittling white women caught up in the colonizing machine than in celebrating the role of African women in liberating their nations from colonial and neocolonial forces. Some of the novels we have discussed so far refer not only to other novels and to orature but also to visual modes of aesthetic production. Gordimer's *My Son's Story* (1990) signifies Hannah's ideology through references to Jackson Pollock's paintings. In the next chapter, I focus on the use of motif of visual arts in contesting dominant views of the society and relocating agency to the ordinary people.

Chapter 6

Painted Metaphors

The Gendered Deployment of Visual Arts

The palimpsests of African texts come in different forms. So far we have examined the use of oral literary materials and the echoes of other written texts in modern novels. Related to these forms of intertextuality is the deployment of visual artistic media as a figural terrain through which the metafictional novel subverts established gender norms. In the narratives, the division between visual and verbal genres is collapsed as the art draws attention to its vexed relationship with the real world it evokes. Although Dele Jegede claims that contemporary African visual arts are "individualistic and elitist" and "art for art's sake" (1990, 34), in metafictional novels, at least, they are deployed in political contexts.[1] More immediate than other arts, visual culture becomes what Rey Chow calls "the place where battles are fought and the strategies of resistance negotiated" (1995, 29).

By using visual arts and their interpretation, the novels signify these contestations and negotiations while remaining alive to the myriad problems facing African societies. Some of the novels provide what Chow further calls an "image-site" by offering "alternative ways of watching *that would change the image*" (1995, 29, emphasis in original). What follows in this chapter is a discussion of the trope of visual arts and the represented art's relationship to gender politics. I read the novels as using visual artistic references as cultural codes to signal the politics in the society presented. The African novels' presentation of visual representation is a means of stationing the authority of artistic enterprise in the desires of marginalized and peripheral subjects. The very invocation of these arts is a strategy to retrieve them from the matrix of elision they have been consigned to by students of African art and to reuse them to refigure gender in various societies.

I examine how the novels use indigenous arts from an angle different from the anthropological viewpoint by giving the images a gendered interpretation that also privileges aesthetics. I also want to follow Cornelius Adepegba's preference for a reading of African visual cultures that does not sideline contemporary production. In "The 'Otherness' Syndrome and the

Study of African Visual Art" (2000), Adepegba argues that African art does not end with traditional art objects. The art is not fixed to a single time frame; it has changed to reflect the effects of intercultural engagements in African societies. But why would scholarship want to stereotype African art as the authentic precolonial art and exclude contemporary visual forms as non-African? Homi Bhabha and Stuart Hall have variously pointed out that if domination of a culture is to be rationalized, then the dominated culture must be stereotyped as incapable of change. The art is stereotyped through simplifications into what Bhabha calls "an arrested, fixated form of representation" (1994, 75). The indigenous art is invested with aberrant characteristics and then privileged as the quintessential expression of the only possible form of African subjectivity in order "to make us see and experience *ourselves* as 'Other' " (Hall 1990, 225, emphasis in original).

Olu Oguibe (2004) explains in clear terms the tendency of colonial education to elide aesthetic capabilities of Africans by both denying Africans access to colonial modern art education and suppressing the indigenous art forms as barbaric. Oguibe notes that "while the colonial curriculum ignored art education and discouraged teaching art to the colonized so as to preclude the emergence of new forms affined to the European tradition, the Christian missions equally engaged in the deprecation and destruction of existing art traditions in the colonies" (Oguibe 2004, 49). Metafictional novelists attempt to use the traditional arts erased by colonialism and the modern arts denied Africans by missionary education as a way of contesting the marginal status assigned by the West and criticizing new forms of oppression in postcolonial nations.

In focusing not only on precolonial art but also on modern visual forms as used in contemporary novels, I am following Wole Soyinka's view that the visual arts are part and parcel of African modernity, as opposed to the widely held belief that such artistic enterprises as painting are exclusionary Western practices. Soyinka disagrees with the notion circulated in Eurocentric art history and criticism, that painting, for example, is "an alien form to [an] African artist" that can be understood as "an expression of the artist's alienation from his roots" (1990, 7).[2] Dele Jegede (1990) explains succinctly that the tendency to elide modern arts from contemporary African culture is a symbolic way for the Eurocentric art historian and critic to insist on the authenticity of a gory Africa:

> The notion is that authentic African art subsists in sculpture, predominantly in wood, and within the parent culture. In this regard, ugliness becomes an aspect of beauty, as pieces that display streaks of animal blood or encrustations arising from continuous

> sacrificial offerings are more likely to be favored above new and unused ones. (1990, 30–31)[3]

While contemporary African novels make references to the precolonial visual arts, they are more inclined to contemporary visual art, which Jegede notes is an "art that glorifies itself—self-conscious, fiercely independent, and certainly uninterested in illustrating or remaining subservient to a socioreligious consensus" (1990, 34). I argue here that references to such self-reflexive arts in an equally self-reflexive language disrupt the received opinions about gender in contemporary Africa.

Furthermore, following Edward Said, Oguibe exposes the tendency in the West to associate African art with antiquity in order to claim for the Western society civilized modernity and postmodernity.[4] For Oguibe, the mode of Eurocentric thinking that creates a singular, unique Africa to ignore internal differences in African culture and justify the Western sense of superiority relies primarily on ignoring indigenous historical perceptions. The European view of African art is authentic only to the degree that it is premodern or "savage," only to the degree that it is *less than* European art. Then we can argue that African novels' use of indigenous art forms in particular counters the Eurocentric view of the arts as essentially savage and authentic. The writers emphasize the modernistic aspects of precolonial art, signaling that Africans, if I may paraphrase Achebe, did not hear about modernism for the first time from Europeans. Yet as Oguibe rightly notes, "to perpetually counter a center is to recognize it" (2004, 4). African novels that prioritize contemporary and precolonial visual art try to transcend the imperial center by reclaiming indigenous subjectivity without wasting too much time and space negating the West.

Tradition and the Playing with the "Tribal" Darkness

While most modern novelists ground their metaphors in modern modes of visual representation, Yvonne Vera's *The Stone Virgins* (2002), Zakes Mda's *She Plays with the Darkness* (2003b), and Henrietta Rose-Innes's *The Rock Alphabet* (2004) all go back to indigenous visual artistic production as a repository of ethnic and gender consciousness. Sidney Kasfir has termed this harkening back to traditional forms "One Tribe, One Style" (1984) to suggest that the talent of individuals is subordinated to the collective and functionalist view of art as just ethnic craft without a specific author. The question, then, is: Does the use of traditional forms in metafiction amount to defamiliarization through a prioritization of "tribal art"? As in the use of oral literatures, the deployment of indigenous visual art is a symbolic strategy of recovering erased subjectivities and countering the colonist agenda of silencing African art. This is expressed succinctly by Olu Oguibe when he argues that by giving priority to traditional arts, the postcolonial artist is countering the textual erasure and vandalism executed by the colonial powers that sought to obliterate Africans' claim to culture:

> To persist with traditional forms was to repudiate European insistence that these forms were heathen and that the cultures and worldviews that produced them were inferior. To retain them and remain faithful to the social and cultural institutions for which they were made, in spite of demonization by the Europeans, was to seriously reject and defy that imposition. (Oguibe 2004, 49)

Such cultural moves by the natives would be considered an affront to the colonial authorities. However, the modern writer does not use these arts as an affront to the colonizer but primarily to legitimate local aesthetics. Furthermore, when the arts are used to counteract colonist practices, they tend to take on uncomfortable gendered subtexts.

A case in point is Mda's two novels that use indigenous visual culture, *She Plays with the Darkness* (2003b) and *The Heart of Redness* (2000). Mda cut his teeth as a literary icon through political community theater; visual elements are important in his theme and technique, especially when he wants to debunk Western modes of mass communication and ideas of development. In these two novels, which thematize rural community development vis-à-vis globalization and Westernization, Mda tends to romanticize rural Southern Africa in what may appear to be a neoprimitivist turn that critiques modernity by privileging that which modernity would dismiss as primitive. In the stories, it is the woman who is seen as the custodian of quintessentially uncorrupted values. The male, like Camagu in *The Heart of Redness* and Radisene in *She Plays with the Darkness*, is regarded as aggressively alienated and in need of reintegration. The urbanized female invites a more critical examination for abandoning rural values, as does the female teacher Xoliwa Ximiya in *The Heart of Redness*, whose "quite tall and well-proportioned" bone structure is described as "good if you want to be a model in Johannesburg, but works against you in a village where men prefer their women plump and juicy" (Mda 2000, 11). Pitted against the traditional and the antimodernity of Qukezwa and her magic voice, the modern woman is bound to lose out. Thus Mda's critique of the diffusionist model of development in which Western technology and the service industry are seen as superior to African values tends to romanticize the rural woman as the epitome of resistance against modernity and to vilify women who adopt modern values in stronger terms than it criticizes men.

The association of the rural with women is not a particularly original artistic gesture, although it captures the continued marginalization of women from the benefits of modernity, idealized as they are as the symbols of all that is good with precolonial African culture. However, even if the woman is presented as the site of cultural interiority, ethnic artistic sensibility, and authentic heritage, there is a radical departure in the metafictional novels' presentation of what colonial anthropologists would view as "tribal art." The novels portray much more sensitively the characters interpreting and constructing this art. The characters are given more agency as individuals than colonial anthropological and historical accounts would have yielded to the African. Vera's *The Stone Virgins*, a novel about women's contributions in the war of liberation in Zimbabwe and their subsequent discrimination in the postindependence dispensation, uses secret drawings on the rocks of Gulati to show the oppressed community's use of folk art as a source of inspiration to fight for political self-determination. It is the drawings of women in combat that drive the women to fight against colonialism and the patriarchy that has silenced and mutilated them into nonbeings. The description of the "stone virgins" is graphic and told from the perspective of a man in postindependence Zimbabwe, Sibaso, who has already raped and mutilated the women alongside whom he fought: "The female figures painted on this rock, the virgins, form a circle near the burial site, waiting for the ceremony of their own burial. Here, the rock is almost pure" (95). The figures that the novel invokes are originally what Walter Benjamin calls "ceremonial objects destined to serve in a cult" (1992, 224). Although the individual painters are unknown, Vera's novel, a modern means of artistic production, reproduces the visual images in dematerialized figurative form rather than in the veridical, mechanical manner Benjamin fears characterizes fascist art. The novel uses visual art in a more secular context to contest official history that silences women's perspectives. The anterior and mysterious origins of the visual images are destabilized to undermine the authority of a current fascist regime that distorts history to suppress certain ethnic and gender categories in the nation. The palpable trace of the cultic images in modernity is employed in the novel neither for its own sake nor for the veneration of an exotic, originary past; rather, Vera invokes the vague outlines of the folk images to address contemporary issues in postindependence Zimbabwe.

The novel deploys the faded images that the observer's imagination would have to reconstruct as a sign that history is a mosaic of accounts reconstructed from memory. Folk art gives the novel an aura of the strange, especially because the abstract paintings are sifted to the reader through a confused character's observation. Sibaso's remembrance of the stone virgins, the later-day reincarnations he has defiled, lacerated, and silenced, indicates his guilt and suggests art as an avenue of repentance and conciliation. Projecting itself in the painting of the women in the cave, the novel successfully executes an equally wondrous painting of a precolonial, colonial, and postcolonial Zimbabwe nearly ruined by Mugabe's dictatorship, which had sanctioned a nationalistic silencing of the powerless. The novel's jerky plot recalls the tumult and trauma of anticolonial violence and the equally traumatizing violence that Mugabe has visited upon Matabeleland in a bid to consolidate his dominion in the 1980s, the first years of Zimbabwean independence. The fact that the novel came out in 2003, over two decades after independence, signals its use of history to comment on the present; just as the precolonial paintings in Gulati comment on the experiences in the colonial situation, the novel uses precolonial and colonial experiences to expose the compounded silence of women and to express the need for women to unite in the struggle against a repressive and sexist nationalism. The intersecting of different stories that form the novel indicates the need for oppressed minorities to seek completion in each other, as do male and female characters as the narrative comes to an end.

Like Vera, Mda uses indigenous paintings as figural sites where characters reorient themselves with history. In *She Plays with the Darkness*, Mda presents the desecration of the society—a subject pursued in the equally self-reflexive and cinematic *The Heart of Redness*—through its portrayal of folk cave paintings that are as entrancing as the narrative itself. They reaffirm Dikosha's belief in maintaining her traditional values in the face of encroaching modernity. The paintings are presented through her center of consciousness as a source of charismatic power:

> They left a legacy of caves with wonderful paintings on the walls, and black paintings of big-buttocked people chasing deer with bows and arrows, or dancing in a trancelike state. Dikosha was spellbound by one painting especially, which showed a dancer with the body of a woman and the head of a beast . . . Dikosha saw herself as the monster-woman-dancer, ready to devour all the dancers of the world, imbuing herself with the strength and stamina, and then dancing forever and ever, until the end of time. (2003b, 16)

Denied education by the male-centered society, Dikosha resorts to the magic of her community, unlike her educated brother, Radisene, who goes to Maseru and becomes an expert ambulance chaser. He ends up losing all of his property to a Nigerian conman, while Dikosha is poised, in the magical order conjured up in the novel, to live eternally. Without idealizing the mountain community vis-à-vis the modernity of the lowlands, the novel intertwines customs, legends, and historical events to capture the absurdities of modern South Africa.

The polyphony of this novel derives from its alignment with traditional Sotho modes of expression, which it invokes to show the past as a contested terrain and the present as a mosaic of different cultures that the rich and the powerful work to destroy. Like its character Dikosha, the novel nourishes itself with narratives and poetry from the past to question the possibilities of social equality in a modern South Africa tainted with greed and self-aggrandizement. The self-reflexivity of the novel signals not despair or entrapment in a hall of mirrors but a rejection of monolithic power structures encouraging dictatorships and the unequal development of local communities.

Magical Realist Art and Silent Subversion: Bessie Head's *Maru*

While the visual arts trope is much more pronounced in the metafictional novels of the 1980s and onward, especially the fiction of the 1990s, earlier realist novels try to shore up an illusion of actuality and authenticity by graphically reproducing the phenomena presented as a photograph in words. For example, the opening paragraphs in Chinua Achebe's *Things Fall Apart* (1958) and Ngũgĩ wa Thiong'o's *The River Between* (1965) are attempts at photographic verbal representations of the society, in which actions and topographies are described in an intense attempt to reproduce them on the printed page as verbal pictures. In Ngũgĩ's novel, the verbally painted ridges of Kameno and Makuyu facing each other menacingly foreshadow the deep conflict between Christianity and indigenous cultural practices in the central Kenya of the 1920s and 1930s. In Achebe's classic, the conviviality attending the graphically presented wrestling match between Okonkwo and Amalize the cat contrasts with the brutality of the contests between Umuofia and European colonialists.

Head's *Maru* (1971) is one of the African novels that serve as a precursor to feminist metafiction. The novel is influenced by the indigenous art forms of the San people of Botswana, but it is about modern painters and their role in fighting injustices in society. It uses a fairly realist mode of discourse but evokes a metafictional form at various levels in its deployment of the painting trope. *Maru* is an ekphrastic novel that can be read as a painting to problematize some of the conclusions reached about it as a pessimistic text because of its cyclic plot. Overall, the novel and the subjectivity of its main female character, the painter Margaret Cadmore, are as fluid and ungraspable as the paintings the narrative invokes. The agency of silenced groups and individuals lies in the silence and uncanny multiplicity of meanings of the visual representations that the novel verbally signifies.

Maru is a novel about the arbitrary discrimination of the minority Masarwa ethnic community by the Batswana majority. It focuses this theme, however, through the story of Margaret Cadmore, an artist and a teacher who succeeds against all odds in a society that treats her as a second-class person because she is a woman and a Masarwa. Her paintings usher in a new era in which the subracial hierarchies are disrupted by her marriage to Maru, the most powerful man in Dilepe. The plot ends with indications of dissolution of the Batswana-Masarwa binary opposition, although events that take place in the society at the beginning of the plot (but later in the narrated world of the story) suggest that this liberation is far from complete. Margaret's interactions with Maru and other members of the community are rendered using the stream-of-consciousness technique that makes the narrative hallucinatory in a way that Arthur Ravenscroft describes as a protean process that "involves simultaneously progression, introgression, and circumgression" (1976, 175). Intersubjective communication between the characters who help Margaret create images that other characters will recognize disrupts the fixed and independent stability of subjectivities. It is through the use of paintings as metafictional devices that the novel signals the intersection of identities beyond the superficial differences constructed by a racist society.

The Masarwa woman's birth inaugurates an artistic moment as her mother dies at childbirth and her condition is rendered through a drawing by an artist who also serves as the orphaned baby's foster mother. The novel shows the difference between the two artists, privileging the subaltern orphan vis-à-vis her privileged white foster mother. The older artist's drawings are described to the reader as motivated by a desire for "revenge" against the privileged Batswana people, whom she knows would most likely assault her because of her support for the Masarwa community. As she waited for her "orders" to be carried out she would sketch the image of "her victim" (13). The relationship is defined by definite power hierarchies. The European Margaret is presented as a powerful person who exploits her position to represent the indignities of the local community and its unfair practices. If we take into account the fact that her own drawings and her view of the local community are relayed to the reader in narrative segments told from her center of consciousness, then it should be clear that she is happy in her role as a victimizer of the local victimizer.

The white woman takes pleasure in tormenting the Batswana, forcing them to treat with respect a community they hate. She contributes to the dismantling of local hierarchies by attempting to reverse the arrogance of the Batswana vis-à-vis the Masarwa. But, overall, she displays a similarly disturbing attitude in the way she views the Batswana—a sneering condescension toward the dominant native community. It can be argued that the Batswana's denigration of the Masarwa only serves as Margaret's rationalization of her abhorrence of the Batswana. This is why she sees them as "victims" of her gaze, and her representation of them is more of an insult than a celebration of any values they may have. Drawing merely "prevented her from hurling out a continuous stream of abuse at her objects of representation" (13). However, her art serves as testimony to the injustices meted out to a marginalized community because it elevates the victim of Batswana racism to the status of a goddess and condemns the dominant community:

> Margaret Cadmore was not the kind of woman to speculate on how any artistic observation of human suffering arouses infinite compassion. She put the notes down on her sketch pad. One sketch captured the expressions of disgust on the faces of the Batswana nurses as they washed the dead woman's body for burial. She scrawled a note under the sketch: "These are not decent people." (14)

Her foster child, also named Margaret Cadmore, is more cautious in her criticism of the community in the paintings she will produce, but through the stream-of-consciousness device, the novel gives voice to the thoughts that she does not verbalize. Thus although the author uses the older Margaret Cadmore to make authorial statements, the narratorial agency is invested in the subaltern Margaret Cadmore.

The senior Margaret Cadmore is blindly optimistic, but the novel is only cautiously sanguine about the role of art in changing the society. The narrative enacts a disjunction between the *sujet* and the *fabula* by beginning its plot at a moment when most of the events narrated in the story have already taken place. This disjunction signals the blurred vision of the revolutionaries who have ended discrimination against the Masarwa community while the structures of domination by patriarchy are still in place. The younger Margaret Cadmore's art, though not imposed on her by the dominant group that serves as her patron, is haunted by their expectations. Yet her silence and the stillness of her paintings inspire change in the society.

Juliana Makuchi Nfah-Abbenyi is therefore right when she argues that the silence of the artist before the referential world augments the silence of the paintings "as the most subversive and the most revealing elements of her subjectivity" (1997, 141). Through the stream-of-consciousness device, the reader is made privy to the action and feelings taking place in the mind of the silent artist. Although the silence is enigmatic, it is more puzzling to the male characters in the novels. She and the reader are given the agency to read what is unarticulated. As a marginalized subject, she uses this unique agency to read the expectations of the oppressive majority and to produce art that provokes the powers that be to abandon their oppressive practices.

Margaret's art is subversive, but the dominant people read it as an expression of their desires. Her marriage to Maru is consummated in exile, outside of the conservative society that threatens to destroy both characters, to signify that the desired achievements of an avant-garde art would be realized only in utopia.

However, that is not reason enough for the oppressed and the artist to give up hope of changing the status quo. Alternatively, we can read the text as a painting by the younger Margaret Cadmore. Named for Maru, her lover, the narrative is focalized through Margaret's center of consciousness. She is able to conjure up powerful images constructed from other characters' thoughts. Although the novel begins and ends with what appears to be a heterodiegetic, third-person narrative voice (articulated by a narrator who is not part of the action), there are enough deictic elements in the story to indicate the mixing of the narrator's voice with that of a character with access to the main character's center of consciousness. The suggestive language the novel uses to describe Maru in the framing sections of the narrative is reminiscent of the sophisticated mode of presentation we associate with Margaret's arts. She could well be the one imagining Maru and painting him in words to the reader.

Modernist Art and the Reconstruction of Somali: Farah's *Links*

Nuruddin Farah's *Links* (2003) uses visual tropes in its reference to modern painting to contest the identity of modern Somalia as rooted in clannish claims that it sees as the cause of civil wars in the now nonfunctioning state. Although its focus is on the return of an English professor to his Somali homeland after twenty years in exile, a choice that would offer immense possibilities for metafictional representation, *Links* uses metafiction in a less pronounced manner than Farah's earlier novels, such as *Maps* (1986). But the physical Somalia that Jeebleh, who received his doctorate for writing a book on Dante's *Inferno* and refers to the Russian symbolist Osip Mandelstam, encounters in the war-torn country is a surreal Dantean hell that shocks all the more because it is not a piece of existentialist fiction for an intellectual to write an academic treatise on. Rather, it is the concrete reality of a city taken over by terror groups that Jeeblen is, in some sense, related to, despite their current adversarial stances toward each other. For Jeebleh, his homeland is "a fragmented land without a unifying theme," marked by the absence of the mythic pre-Islamic "hero worthy of being elevated to solar eminence" (40). The text's immediate background is the Somalia of the 1990s where, by the time of the novel's release in 2003, over 300,000 people had died in fourteen years of anarchy in interclan and subclan conflicts. The novel ironically recommends that once it becomes a functioning state again, Somalia should use the vulture as its national symbol in insignia and flags (65). This indicates the novel's recognition of visual art in representing the problematic and ironic history of a nation so intent on destroying itself that a scavenger becomes its savior.

In its examination of the connection between the past, present, and future, *Links* represents the prospects of the Somali society in visual terms. One instance of this is a sepulcher for Jeebleh's mother, whom he came from his adopted home in New York to rebury. Although unbelievable to Jeebleh, the chaotic state of things in the Mogadiscio of the novel is neither coincidental nor accidental. When Siad Barre was overthrown in 1991 after a thirty-year divide-and-rule reign and the ruthless slaughter and suppression of oppositional clans, Somalia reverted to its precolonial clan divisions without the restoration of the indigenous conflict management configured by British and Italian colonialism. But *Links* elides the colonial roots of the conflicts, only referring occasionally to the American peacekeeping "invasion" of Somalia in 1993 that ended with eighteen Americans dead and two Blackhawks down. It describes the scene in which the body of one of the eighteen rangers killed by militiamen is dragged through the dusty streets of Mogadiscio (66). It tries to reproduce the picture of the lynching as it was beamed by media outlets across the world, and it explains why the Somali people celebrated this brutality, blaming it on American disrespect for Somali culture. This is despite the fact that the narrative itself, through the visual symbol it ends with, and through Jeebleh throughout the narrative, is critical of the patriarchal and parochial attitudes of the Somali communities.

The novel silences the colonial roots of the Somali anarchy mainly to avoid what Farah (2000, 188) has called "blamocracy," the practice of holding outsiders responsible for the problems in Africa without accepting the local contributions to the collapse of civility on the continent. But through metafictional devices, the novel captures the divisions, whatever their roots, in modern Somalia, and it expresses the unattainability of a centralized government. The fissures in the novel, as in other works by Farah, are symptomatic of the deep-seated structural issues behind the current fragmentation of Somalia. The realism with which the fallen city of Mogadiscio is visually rendered is so haunting and tangled that the depiction tends toward the surreal, revealing the fluid and arbitrary nature of clan politics. The few metafictional instances in the novel pronouncedly underline its vision of a new Somalia that is linked by a humanity that transcends the chaos of clan-based war. The dreamlike moments of the novel, then, have strong allegorical dimensions that hold the novel together while simulating the fragmentation of a nonfunctioning state. The narrative tries to resolve all of the conflicts through the sepulcher as a visual symbol of regeneration.

Despite the conviviality evoked by the celebration of Jeebleh's mother's reburial and the annihilation of hedonistic warlord Caloosha, the narrative is cautious in striking an optimistic note—ending with Jeebleh still dazed, but with the expectation of comprehending more clearly the realities of his homeland. The novel mediates its optimism through the foreign artist who conceives the silent visual icon. The description of the sepulcher that Seamus, an Irish artist, designs, evokes the allegorical status of Jebleeh's mother as the symbol of the nation and the possibilities of her resurrection, and thus the possible regeneration of the fragmented Somalia:

> Seamus had spent much of the morning drawing *his* women, everyone of one of these Matisse look-alike, babies suckling at the singularly massive breasts; the women's features Madonna-like . . . Seamus had to be there, offering any help he could, because the illiterate mason could not work from his sketches, which he found most intimidating. (288)

Seamus is a symbol of hope not only because of his involvement in creating this artistic work that signals abundance and rebirth but also because the narrative uses him to recuperate Somali dignity beyond the hellish world that it has described in such visually graphic terms. He has fled Belfast for Mogadiscio, and the novel uses him to suggest that there are places in the world that are more insecure than Somalia. The invocation of Henri Matisse's painting suggests that the future of Somalia lies not in the illiterate masses or in the pre-Islamic mythical world of a hegemonic solar deity but in the educated few who are able to rise above clan politics and embrace a new humanism based on shared beliefs rather than blood ties. Yet it is the ordinary people, represented by the mason working on the piece of art, who are to realize and restore the dream of preserving Somalia, a country mutilated and destroyed by the warlords.

The person who perceives the visual images, the embedded connoisseur of the images is central in the narrative. The positions change from novel to novel, but they point to the need to deconstruct dominant paradigms. If Gordimer's (1990) *My Son's Story* signifies unconscious racism in Hannah by making references to her love for Jackson Pollock's painting, then Margaret Ogola's *I Swear by Apollo* (2002) conscripts the enjoyment of good art in the fight against corruption in Kenya, and Mpe's *Welcome to Our Hillbrow* (2001) uses a woman character's interaction with Thomas Hardy to expose South African sexual hypocrisy. In Ogola's *I Swear by Apollo*, the narrator launches the story with a fairly ekphrastic description of the main female character interpreting the art of an established male artist, Elimo Njau.[5] Infused by the character's reflections on historical facts involving Njau's work, the novel takes us into a utopia in which her country has had a first woman president who has put in prison perpetrators of corruption in the nation. References to the fire that destroyed Njau's Paa ya Paa, along with visual descriptions of Njau's art, reincarnate the destroyed art through a celebration of Njau's architectural work in the construction of the University of Nairobi.

Tied to this is the depiction of women in institutions of higher learning, where a woman architect who judges the efficacy of Njau's work in the contemporary world, rather than being an object of the male artist's gaze. Published in 2002, the novel's presentation of a fictional event in which a new woman president takes over the reins of power recalls the situation in Kenya, the setting of the novel, where a coalition of political parties pushed Daniel arap Moi out of power in 2002. But Ogola feminizes the triumph by making the winner female and completely devoted to fighting corruption. The optimism is almost delusional because the novel seems unaware that the end of the regime of what Caribbean economist and Economics Nobel Laureate William Arthur Lewis would call a "demagogue who, aided by a loud voice and a bunch of hooligans, captures the state and suppresses his rivals" (1965, 89) does not result in substantive freedoms or the end of corruption. But the novel is able to anchor its optimism in what appears to be reality through its references to the seemingly objective, visually verifiable art of a master sculptor and painter.

A similar strategy is used in postcolonial narratives that deploy the power of the visual arts to support the underprivileged in a given society. Although visual artistic expressions are sometimes portrayed as not particularly interesting or intellectually valuable if viewed from certain dogmatic positions, the novels point to the importance of art and its interpretation to indicate why African arts, their creators, and interpreters should be seen as constitutive subjects rather than objects of anthropological colonial gaze. Evoking the precolonial cave paintings in various parts of Africa, some contemporary novels attempt to reinstate the indigenous values facing the threat of erasure by modern lifestyles and a cynical tourism industry. They are able to do so, furthermore, without insisting upon isolation from modernity, which the novels seem to view as being necessary to free the society from certain forms of feudalistic hegemony.

The Métis as Art: Mda's *The Madonna of Excelsior*

Mda's *The Madonna of Excelsior* (2003a) is unique in that it is reluctant to endorse art presented from certain ideological perspectives, calling for a mode of interpretation that would problematize the images presented. It is the first major African novel to structure its themes around the idea of producing and interpreting paintings and to sustain its discourse around the theme of a painter and his work. The novel, through its character Popi, is critical of the art of Father Frans Claerhout, the real-life artist the work is dedicated to; this indicates the narrative's subversive project of investing agency in the reader as opposed to the painter. Mda, a professional beekeeper, activist, dramatist, professor of creative writing, composer, musician, and communication-for-development theorist, creates in *The Madonna of Excelsior* a multilayered text in which each chapter opens with a verbal representation either of visual art as perceived in the reality represented, or of reality appearing as a painting to the characters from whose perspectives the scene is narrated. This narrative technique makes the novel a hybrid text stationed between verbal and visual media. Suggested in this trope is the complex interaction between art and reality, and between experience and interpretation.

As the title of the novel suggests, *The Madonna of Excelsior* makes use of a Western and predominantly Christian tradition of representing the Virgin Mary and Jesus Christ in visual media. This is a trajectory that Giulio Carlo Argan sees to have "made a long voyage whose stations certainly cannot be reduced to the interpretations which the theme has received from the great masters," because the variations are culturally and politically motivated (1974, 19). To some extent, Mda can be seen as "writing back" to the Western center in the sense that his use of the Madonna-and-child trope serves as an energetic deposition of Western achievements replaced by the multiplicity of African ways of telling that have been elided by apartheid. But the novel finally amounts to a critique of the postapartheid dispensation rather than a deconstruction of Western politics and aesthetics. *The Madonna of Excelsior* is a fictional rendering of a historical event in apartheid South Africa in the early 1970s in which prominent white farmers in a small farming community were arrested alongside nineteen black women (the "madonnas") for contravening the Immorality Act. Seeking to sustain racial segregation and the marginalization of nonwhite populations through the notion of racial purity, the government enacted the law in 1927 to make sexual intercourse between whites and blacks a criminal offense. The National Party was to later pursue this policy to its logical conclusion by prohibiting interracial marriage in 1949. In 1950, the Immorality Act was amended to make the already-illicit sex between whites and nonwhites criminal.

Ann Laura Stoler (1997) has felicitously explained how miscegenation posed a threat to white supremacy in colonized regions. In "Sexual Affronts and Racial Frontiers," she observes that the interracial subject is, to the colonizer, a potential source of subversion and "an embodiment of European degradation" (1997, 199). Though theorizing Asia, Stoler's argument is applicable in Africa, where the colonial government had to keep the populations from mixing across racial lines. In South Africa, the racist regime feared the contamination of whiteness and created what Stoler, following Etienne Balibar, calls an "internal frontier," in which racial categories within the same nation have to be kept apart to ensure that white nationalistic essence is secured. Although ordinarily transgressive nonwhite males have to be put at bay to ensure that the pure white women are not contaminated with the sexual impurities of another race, we see in the South African case aggressive white males breaking from the "internal frontiers" and undermining the very regime that privileges them both as male and white. In *The Madonna of Excelsior*, as in the real-life event represented, the state produces the mixed-race children both as proof of contravention of racial rules and to shame the white men for the indiscipline of sleeping with supposedly inferior black women.

The fictional miner's wife Niki ("the Madonna of Excelsior") is one of the nineteen women brought to task for having had sex with a white man, Stephanus Cronje, who commits suicide to avoid the looming scandal. Popi, whose consciousness largely frames the story years later as the country enters a postapartheid order, is the product of Niki's sexual encounter with Stephanus Cronje. Unaware that Niki was raped by the white man, Pule abandons his wife Niki and immerses himself in religion. The irony is that she conceals the details from her husband to protect him from impulsively taking the law into his own hands and getting shot by the all-powerful white farmer. Their son Viliki suffers paternal abandonment, and Niki is internally scarred by the trauma of rape.

Popi, the child of miscegenation, is the equivalent of the *métis*, the interracial figure Stoler observes to be recurrent in postcolonial nationalism. But Popi is not only a threat to white supremacy, she is also seen as aberrant by the black community that prefers racial purity. As a child, she is an object of ridicule because in a segregated township she is neither white nor black. When she confronts her marginalization, however, she becomes the center of consciousness through which the narrative is framed. Her activities, such as her attendance of funerals of HIV/AIDS victims, are preceded by descriptions of paintings depicting a similar theme—in this instance, coffins. Although it uses an omniscient narrator, the novel indicates that its actions are sifted to the reader through Popi's memory. She comments intensely on the prevailing conditions in postapartheid South Africa as she studies the paintings of her and her mother (as Madonna and child) and other works by Father Frans Martin Claerhout. The painter, already retired by the time Popi's narrative begins, is playfully called "the trinity" because he is a priest, a painter, and a human being. Considered in the context of his career as a priest and his vocation as a painter, "the trinity" suggests Father Claerhout's power to create and his Godlike status in the eyes of ordinary people. Because the framing of the story by Popi happens decades after 1971, after the 1994 demise of apartheid, the story can be read as a commentary on the anxieties of postapartheid South Africa. Integrating visual commentaries on apartheid with humor, flashbacks, memory, and self-referentiality, the novel indicts both apartheid's irrational laws and the nepotism and corruption creeping out of the woods in the postapartheid state.

To highlight the interpretation of a new nation, Mda deploys art interpretation as the dominant trope in the narrative. Popi's interpretation and misinterpretation of Father Claerhout's drawings form her understanding of the society as it evolves from a past of racial discrimination most intensely felt in sexual racial segregation. I seek to illuminate here the political implications of this hermeneutics because the paintings represented verbally in *The Madonna of Excelsior* are embodiments of the silent "otherness" noted by W. J. T. Mitchell (1994) as the characteristic of visual representation. In the novel, otherness is transferred to the powerless people whom the "painter-God" makes into artistic objects—the marginalized women who pose nude for the priest to earn a living. The painter transforms the women's sordid materiality into occasions of aesthetic reverie in a fashion reminiscent of the occidental scholars and artists who, as unmasked in Edward Said's *Orientalism* ([1978] 1994, 184–90), used the orient to satisfy their sexual desires. The Eurocentric discourse presented by Said exoticizes Eastern cultures as fecund and female, seeing itself as the penetrating male. In Mda's novel, the white painter is obsessed with nonwhite females, who seem to fulfill his desires in a paradigmatic example of the mechanism of orientalist fantasy.

But the ultimate otherness is found in the child who, unlike her mother, consciously poses for the painter, unaware of her commodification by her mother and the priest. Popi's otherness is underlined by her critique of the paintings as unrealistic because of their portrayal of skewed subjects; she is not aware that in their deviation from prevailing realism, the paintings express of the absurdities that govern her society. The novel makes it clear that the reading of the paintings it presents is Popi's; one of the most repressed objects of Father Claerhout's paintings thus later gains agency to interpret the paintings for the community:

> Popi tells us that it all began when the trinity was nourished by Flemish expressionists. Theirs were ordinary subjects: sympathetic men and women living ordinary lives and performing ordinary rituals. Popi knows all these things, and shares them with all those who care to listen. We suspect that there are many other things that she knows, but keeps to herself. And there are others that she has decided not to remember. (Mda 2003a, 5)

The novel uses the collective narrative voice "we" to ground the agency of interpretation in Popi. She is given a level of omniscience similar to the narrative's own authority through the collective narrator's claim that Popi knows more than she registers in her statements as a child. However, unlike earlier postcolonial novels like, say, Ngũgĩ wa Thiong'o's *Petals of Blood* (1977), *The Madonna of Excelsior* does not invest authority in the collectivity of speaking voices. The narrative indicates distance from its own collective narrator when the communal "we" criticizes Niki for not participating in nepotism when her children gain power after the collapse of apartheid, and when the collective "we" regales the reader with the tricks they use to take advantage of Niki and get her honey for free (2003a, 229).

I turn briefly to Popi's reading of images produced by the authoritative painter because her (mis)reading contradicts the silence expected of an objectified native. Mda subjectivizes the mixed-race child in order to allow her to reject her silencing by the postapartheid political order. Roland Barthes, proclaiming the death of the author and of ways of reading enamored of rigid and fixed interpretations, reminds us that a text does not transmit a single intended meaning. Singular authority subverts itself through a multiplicity of contesting meanings. Barthes declares in an oft-quoted passage: "We know that a text is not a line of words releasing a single 'theological' meaning (the 'message of the Author-God') but a multidimensional space in which a variety of writings, none of them original, blend and clash. The text is a tissue of quotations drawn from the innumerable centers of culture" (Barthes 1977, 146). If for Barthes a graphic representation is more of a "message without a code" because it expresses reality in a way that is analogical but that nevertheless has connotative meanings (1977, 16), then a creative enterprise like painting engenders a reinscription of reality in ways that are even more socially fraught. The "trinity" who creates the paintings that Popi reads must be "dead"—at least in Barthesian terms—because his interpretations of apartheid and the motivations behind his representations do not yield a single meaning that can be taken as the gospel truth.

Popi's reading is subversive in the sense that she complicates the priest's portrayal of humanity to produce an interpretation of her subjective experiences. She thinks the priest is unrealistic in his artistic production. Her reading is vindicated when the priest later admits that he participates in the dominant ideologies that structure experience. To be sure, there is an element of masculinism in his paintings because, according to the narrative as relayed to us from Popi's perspective, "even the trinity's was a clearly male gaze. We do not forget that one of his threeness is a man" (13). The portrayal of the African women and their children, then, is not neutral; it is conterminous with the gender and ideology of the artist. Mitchell observes that in ekphrastic moments, there is a sense of gendered exploitation with overtones of "pornographic writing and masturbatory fantasy" (1994, 168). The painter is producing female bodies for an audience that is assumed to be male. But Popi seizes the masculinist art, which tends toward the pornographic, and critiques its representation of volatile subject positions in a South Africa in transition. In the process, she uses her agency as an interpreter of art to struggle out of the alterity to which she has been consigned by apartheid and the masculinist discourses structuring memory.

In the conjectural world Mda constructs in the novel, the authority invested in the marginalized populations is far from absolute. Although largely told using Popi's center of consciousness, the novel embraces omniscience at moments when Popi would not know what is happening to her. A case in point is when her mother treats her like an object of art that literally needs painting to mask and obliterate the child's mixed ancestry. Niki thinks she can erase the mixed-race signs in Popi by exposing the child's body to smoke. The narrator depicts with searing irony the mother's naïve attempts at "smoking the pinkness out of her" (66). To enhance the irony, the narrator presents the purpose of the act through Niki's perspective:

> Both heat and smoke would surely brown her and no one would say she was a light-skinned again. The baby whooped, then yelled, as the heat of the brazier roasted her little body and the smoke stung her eyes and nostrils. Cow-dung smoke is gentle in reasonable doses. But this was an overdose. There was so much that it made even Niki's eyes stream. She assured the baby that it was for her own good. She sang a lullaby as she swung her over the fire. Rocking her from side to side. Turning her round and round so that she would be browned on all sides. Evenly. (66)

The incident could be a fictional reconstruction from Popi's memory as an adult, yet it is Niki who doubts the scientific tests carried out by a doctor from Bloemfontein "to confirm that the blood [of the babies] was indeed mixed," as she wonders "How it was possible for the doctors to tell if the blood was mixed or not. Mixed with what? Was it not all red?" (64). This moment provides readers with an opening to reexamine the notions of essentialist and constructed realities. The apartheid regime has created its own criteria that it claims to be scientific in order to punish and discipline those who transgress apartheid laws. The novel claims agency for the naïve woman who wants to "paint" her child black by using her to dismantle apartheid's "scientific" claims. The narrative indicates that race is a social construction when, through Niki, it observes that all blood is red. Indeed, the more Niki tries to erase Popi's whiteness, the more it becomes manifest. Her failure to "paint" her child a different color illustrates the narrative's belief that racial markers need not be changed to suit an irrational political practice.

As already seen, the focalizers through whom the visual images are presented are crucial because they indicate the location of agency among the characters. Popi's seemingly naïve misreading of established artists is important because it not only generates dramatic irony but also situates her as the focalizer through whom the new South Africa can be understod. Popi reads a postcard painting by Father Claerhout with an unwittingly subversive gaze. In the visual portrayal of "Mother Mary with brown Baby Jesus" at a crossroads (226), the text presents a parallel between Popi and Christ. She is the child in the most prominent of the Madonna-and-child paintings by the Trinity, and she is currently experiencing the deepest dilemma in her life. As a mixed-race South African, Popi is not accepted by the black ruling elites who now thinks she is not black enough, although she fought together with them against the apartheid regime that thought her not white enough. The Messiah in the painting is given a brown body to signify his relocation from foreign and mystical mythology to the gritty reality of the South African situation. Unbeknownst to Popi, it is people like her, though marginalized by both apartheid and the postapartheid regimes, who would be the saviors of the new republic.

Significantly, Popi reads the picture as a distortion and harps on the misspelling of the painter's name:

> Popi read the bottom of the postcard and laughed. She had never noticed before that they had misspelt the trinity's name. They had added an extra u, which served him right, as he had mastered the art of distorting everything. It was poetic justice that the printer had distorted his name too. A man who could be possessed by such beautiful madness that he placed road signs in the middle of a sunflower field deserved to have his name distorted. (226–27)

As male and white, the Trinity is largely seen in the society as a figure of incontestable authority. Thus when Popi gives his painting a subversive interpretation, she is claiming some of the authority from traditional symbols of power. Ironically, in its supposed misinterpretation of reality (as Popi perceives it), the postcard presents a more profoundly authentic South African situation. The sunflower field in the postcard painting is the site where miscegenation first took place in the narrative. The scene is symbolically reproduced throughout the narrative to underline its current political significance, for it was in the sunflower field that gestures of protest against racial purity and sexual policing started. Yet the products of miscegenation are now the victims of postapartheid discrimination. The misspelling of the painter's name, noted by Popi, indicates a displacement of his own control to give agency to marginalized voices like Popi's. However, although much of the agency in the story is invested in Popi, it is suggested that she should not have absolute power that would transform her into a dictator like those of the white apartheid or the black postapartheid regimes.

Toward the end of the story, the painter is transformed and undermines the authority of the great masters:

> She had tried hard to identify the Flemish expressionist influence that she had read about in the oversized books in the library. The trinity had clearly strayed away from that early influence. All for the better. His work had the robustness that escaped the Flemish expressionists. (236)

Coming at the end of the narrative, the observation is significant in transferring the power of healing from art to a cosmological experience. Prior to this description, Popi is described ekphrastically from the image of herself that she sees in the mirror: "She enjoyed her own beauty and celebrated it" (266). It is suggested in this depiction that the therapeutic power of art derives from self-worth and self-determination. Niki, the beekeeper, and her daughter Popi reject the nepotism, greed, and corruption that their friends and family had reduced themselves to. Instead, they live a humble life. Niki is no longer the Madonna, but the Bee Woman, the name the collective narrator uses as the narrative nears its close. While the use of foreign modes of representation can be transformed to articulate the conditions of postindependence Africa, the full transformative power comes from the people naming themselves and rejecting the corrupting lucre they might be invited to share. Thus Popi's transformation from a self-hating "Coloured" girl to a self-determined, twenty-first century post-apartheid South African derives from her association with her humble mother and the collectivity of the bees that protect her. At the same time, this signals that creative self-determination is not provided by a painter-God (Trinity) but by the masses of the new South Africa.

Sighting Textuality

I conclude this survey by reiterating that the trope of visual arts is gaining increased prominence in the contemporary African novel. But it is in the novels of the 1990s and after that the visual arts trope is deployed to signal the texts' awareness of their own textuality. Earlier realist novels such as Ngũgĩ's *The River Between* (1965) and Achebe's *Things Fall Apart* (1958) try to reconcile the fictionality of the visual art to the realist project that preoccupies them, but recent texts are more interested in disrupting the idea of a unitary identity to which everyone should subscribe. In the novels by Mda, Vera, Head, and Rose-Innes, the subjectivities of Africa's indigenous orate and visual cultures, which did not have the facility of modern writing, are reinscribed through the meticulous evocation of folk art, which the texts proceed to simulate in self-reflexive strokes that draw attention to their textuality.

The texts highlight multiplicity and contradictions. Mpe's *Welcome to Our Hillbrow* (2001) presents the contradictions of postindependence South Africa and undermines xenophobia and homophobia. Although it is a narrative based on extravagant use of fantasy and addresses dead listeners, it creates visually vivid scenes in its invocation of an oral performance in which the narrator dramatizes a story using gestures, body movements, facial expressions, and décor to render the events and characters as spectacularly as possible. Invested in visuality, the novel refers to a film version of Thomas Hardy's novel *Jude the Obscure*, which gives the novel more immediacy. Refilwe, the dead literature student through whose consciousness *Jude the Obscure* is reincarnated in Mpe's *Welcome to Our Hillbrow*, reads Hardy's text in a way that addresses the problems in Africa and her personal desire for a foreigner whom her own society despises. Yet the novel suggests that if accepted blindly, visual arts can be a bane to the society, as has happened in poor neighborhoods in postapartheid Johannesburg, where crime rates have risen dramatically, because "crime was glamorized on screens and robbers were presented as if they were movie stars. Heroes of grimy courage and exceptionally vicious greed were followed by the voracious camera lenses of modern technology, and the little boys of Tiralong emulated their TV heroes" (2001, 5). Mpe's argument, then, is that we should not be passive audiences for visual culture; rather, we should tease out meanings and reject its fetishization of violence.

Like *Welcome to Our Hillbrow*, most of the novels that theorize visual arts observe that visual artistic production and its interpretation and enjoyment are grounded in particular ethnic assumptions within a specific indigenous African society. But the embedded artistic processes are used to undermine notions of ontological essence and promote a cosmopolitan view of different African nations in relation to one another and to the rest of the world. For example, thematizing the visual form as a strategy of recovering the past, Ben Okri's *In Arcadia* (2002) presents the contested and fictional nature of origins to underscore the provisional status of identity and to locate Africa within a wider global and postindustrial milieu. The novel does not deal directly with Africa; instead, it uses as its setting Virgil's Arcadia, a supposedly real historical site that six characters visit to come up with a TV program aimed at capturing, in documentary form, humanity's lost innocence. Viewing itself ironically, *In Arcadia* playfully links the "self-conscious" with "strange, phoney . . . greedy, egoistical, and childish people" (Okri 2002, 19). But it proceeds to demonstrate the productive ways in which self-awareness, especially in visual forms, can be used to help the world achieve a semblance of harmony. Dreamily theorizing the nature and function of painting, the novel's first-person narrator seems to have no words to describe the enchantment of the visual representation that he presents to the readers through the contemplative gaze of one of the characters. He utters a series of abstract, authorial ruminations whose coherence is secured only by the repetition of the word "painting" to express the subject matter. Removed from the narrative, and presenting the section in the third person, like someone viewing a painting from a distance yet drawn into the puzzling life of art, the narrator expresses the poetry and mystery of painting as a mode of self-presentation and self-inquiry: "Painting is the tentative deciphering of destiny, the visual haiku of human history, musing of life deep in dimensions. Painting is the illusion impacting on the real, becoming the real, insisting on its ability to be the real that has vanished" (Okri 2002, 188).

The poetic language with which Okri's narrator paints Arcadia, to which the novel's characters have traveled, signifies his wish to express even the mythical in concrete language. In the same breath, the novel articulates in philosophical, authorial statements its open support for the global underprivileged:

> The homeless all across the globe. Tribal peoples deprived of their land. Invisible imperialism spreading the cancer all over the earth. Diseases ravaging unloved millions. Poverty multiplying like bacilli . . . Human freedoms eroded by giant powers. Injustices and inequalities raging across the globe, but concentrated in the vast continents that are also the poorest and most exploited. (Okri 2002, 219)

In speaking for the Global South, the novel counters the hegemonic desires of the metropolitan center through the use of a fragmentary and hallucinatory narrative, using the myths and settings of Western culture. Although locating itself in the Western visual arts, the novel, like other of Okri's novels set in the netherworld, invokes Yoruba superstitions and the abiku myth, regrounding it in an indigenous, African, philosophical realm.[6] It recognizes the West as not a continuous, single whole but as fragmented and multiple. Some of its artistic creations can be used for liberatory purposes in other parts of the globe. In the novel, the primitive and distant past, symbolized by Arcadia, and the technologized global present are brought together to lend support to the cause against poverty.

Cinema is referred to in the novels, especially those with the city as their setting, but the works do not imitate the cinematic mode of representation. They seem to prefer lively imitations of movement in more static forms. Some of the novels, such as Mda's *The Heart of Redness* (2000), are cinematic, even while they criticize cinema. The cinematic qualities of the novels seem to come from either local folk art, such as cave paintings, or local interpretations of international art. Several contemporary novelists such as Gordimer, Mda, Okri, and Farah reference modern visual art to underline their belief in subjectivities in motion, as opposed to a return to a past that has created an unfair distribution of power. In most of the works that use this trope, visual art, and its interpretation, is seen as a crucial part of the struggle against dominant monolithic power structures. This is certainly true of Chris Abani's *The Virgin of Flames* (2007) and K. Sello Duiker's *The Quiet Violence of Dreams* (2001). I discuss Duiker in the next chapter. As we shall see, his novels use visual culture to address the subject of homosexuality.

Chapter 7

Refiguring (Out) Queer Sexualities

In African discourse, queer is unspoken, hidden. Homosexuality is figured in metafictional conceits that signify it as both a practice haunted by fear and a lifestyle that can only be apprehended through formal experimentalism. This is lost on many critics who want to argue that homosexuality does not exist in Africa. Global developments have not aided in freeing Africa from the label of sexual simplicity. The fact that conservative former American Episcopalian bishops recently went to Africa to be consecrated in protest against the American church's acceptance of openly gay clerics might give the impression that the whole of Africa is against gay lifestyles in contradistinction to the more liberal West.[1] By such a highly publicized move, the West is likely to be seen as the repository of sexual decadence and liberty, and Africa as the site of sexual naïveté and oppression.

Throughout this discussion, I have expressed my skepticism toward Western critics' supposed benevolence of depicting Africa as perfect, innocent, and uncontaminated by global modernity. Beneath these accolades for the continent is a subtext of racism that wants to see Africa as trapped in the past, as a cultural and geographical space where oppressed groups are passive victims with no means of undermining dominant practices. I want to disrupt the association of Africa with sexual conservatism and purity by using several novels from the continent to argue that homosexuality is not as rare in African societies as might be suggested by the West/African dichotomy, which claims the West as the site of sexual experimentation and decadence and Africa as the space of Edenic heterosexual purity. I am not claiming universalism of homosexual practice and desire; rather, homosexual identity in Africa is situated and localized, even when it gropes for transethnic and transnational cosmopolitanism.

Nevertheless, it remains a fact that in most African societies, homosexuality is a practice without a name. Students of the queer discourse have had to grapple with intense debates about whether some of the African words regarded to designate homosexuality, such as the Zulu *hlabonga* or

Kiswahili *ushoga*, actually specify same-sex eroticism or different types of relationships.[2] The supposed nonexistence of a signifier in Africa's indigenous languages is taken to mean that the signified does not exist, occluding possibilities of the borrowing of words from different languages to name new modes of self-fashioning. Ifi Amadiume's *Male Daughters, Female Husbands* even sees lesbianism as a sexual orientation imposed on African societies by Western-based lesbians (1987, 8). Furthermore, as noted by Brenna Munro, since the 1990s, heads of state from Zimbabwe, Uganda, Namibia, Zambia, Swaziland, and Kenya have made public pronouncements "denigrating homosexuals as both un-Christian and un-African" (2007, 753). Some African countries have antigay laws; for instance, in 2004, the Zanzibar parliament declared homosexuality illegal, un-African, and un-Islamic.[3] While it is true that Western queer theory and advocacy groups use Africa to advance their own politics of sexuality in the West, local texts seem to disagree with the nativist rhetoric that homosexuality is non-African.

Silencing of the queer in Africa has been compounded by the fact that metropolitan postcolonial studies silence homosexuality in favor of national and imperial contestations, while queer criticism largely ignores postcolonial cultures.[4] Even in the revised edition of the seminal *The Empire Writes Back* by Bill Ashcroft and colleagues (2002), homosexuality does not feature as one of the ways of positioning oneself in the postcolonial world. Scholars have only very recently attempted to critique the occlusion of gay practices from postcolonial studies or to expose the Eurocentric focus of queer theory.[5]

In the face of this elision and self-effacement of the queer in scholarship and everyday discourse, it is imperative to make clear at the outset not only what this chapter is about but also, and perhaps more importantly, what it is not about. I am not trying to "queer" the African postcolonial novel. Neither am I trying to position homosexuality in Foucaultian terms as a desirable alternative to heterosexuality, an activity and a lifestyle of self-creation that everyone should aspire to, as Foucault suggests in "Friendship as a Way of Life" (1989). In this interview, Foucault contends that "homosexuality is not a form of desire but something desirable. Therefore, we have to work at becoming homosexuals and not be obstinate in recognizing that we are" (1989, 308). Foucault here insists that society will be opposed to same-sex relationships, but that such relationships will continue to exist. It is hard not to see Foucault projecting homosexuality as the ideal form of sexual expression and praxis, even if his argument is for the diversification of pleasure and desire from heteronormative constraints.[6] I have no interest in claiming that homosexuality is universally advantageous just because it is found in African societies. Such a project—dominant in Western studies of African homosexuality—assumes, beneath the veneer of sexual liberalism, that alternative Western sexual identities are perverse and can only be justified within Western culture by insisting that they are also performed in non-Western societies, including Africa.

Within Africa, self-identification as a gay person is rare because discussion of homosexuality has for some time been taboo. If homosexuality features in early African novels, then it is only to serve as a sign of degeneration, especially in prisons and other sexually segregated situations, or as an unwelcome import from the West.[7] Even the most insightful theorist of the African psyche, Frantz Fanon, in his classical study on race, *Black Skin, White Masks* (1967), argues that there are no genuine homosexuals in the Global South, equating homosexual practices with white racism.[8] Fanon, it should be noted, qualifies his opinion as subjective, saying that he had not encountered personally any "overt presence of homosexuality," and speculating that those people who displayed seemingly deviant practices such as cross-dressing "lead normal sex lives" (1967, 180). The practice of homosexuality is repressed even in negrophobic men, and in *Black Skin, White Masks*, Fanon only speculates about African homosexual practice in a footnote explaining the equation of pederasty and anti-Semitism in a quote from another text. What emerges from Fanon's explanation is that homosexuality is something to be abhorred on equal terms with racism and psychopathology; Fanon's ideal homeland has to be cleansed of homosexuality if local, racial, and national identities are to triumph against colonialism.

But the claim Fanon makes about homosexuality's nonexistence in non-Western societies is based on his nonexperience of it. We do not need Paul de Man's deconstructive rigor in *Allegories of Reading* (1979) to literalize the metaphor in which Fanon refers to homosexuality when denying its existence. The context in which the denial appears signals that homosexuality is more common than his anticolonial statement would have us believe. If we accept I. A. Richards's division of a metaphor into a tenor (an abstract subject of discussion) and vehicle (the concrete and more familiar object with which the tenor is compared), we see that Fanon assumes that his readers understand homosexuality much better than colonial racism. He clarifies abstract colonial practices by using homosexuality as a vehicle that concretizes racial hatred. From the components of this metaphor, Fanon affirms what he disavows: that homosexuality exists in the postcolonial world, even if it is abhorred by the mainstream community.

In what follows, I show that a sizeable number of contemporary African novels use metafiction to claim that homosexuality is part of African postcolonial lifestyles and emergent identities. Others celebrate the practice but reveal (a la Foucault) its oppressive potential in both the material and the discursive world. It is clear that in contemporary novels, there is a deliberate attempt to desilence alternative sexualities, but is there a correlation between the figuring of homosexuality and the mode of fictional representation? Is the figuring of homosexuality a postrealist phenomenon? If homosexuality is a practice not expressed using existing linguistic signs, then how would a writer represent it without recourse to antirealist modes? I argue that because homosexual desire is presented in the interstices of the narratives, as opposed to explicit description, postrealism offers a potent site for the explication of homosexuality in a nonhomophobic context. I premise my reading on Eve Kosofosky Sedgwick's observation in *Epistemology of the Closet* (1990), that homosexuality does not only affect the minority that practices it. African novels seem to indicate that the practice may be gaining visibility, as African cities embrace cosmopolitanism. Without marking homosexuality as a universal desire that affects not just those who openly practice it, as Sigmund Freud did in showing homosexual longing to be extant in active heterosexuals, the novelists reveal that homosexuality is much more widespread than acknowledged.

"Homographesis" and Evacuation of Homosexuality from African Lifestyles

Despite the vibrancy of queer studies in the Western academy, homosexuality is one of the practices that many theorists, especially those from Africa, seem to erase from readings of African novels. Juliana Makuchi Nfah-Abbenyi narrates how, at the 17th Annual African Literature Association Conference in 1991, intellectuals claimed that lesbianism is not an issue in Africa: "African literary critics are not concerned with lesbian or gay issues because this topic is very sensitive and often controversial, or because they view other issues as more pressing" (1997, 29–30). Osita Ezeliora also has remarked that black critics of South African literature eschew commentary on K. Sello Duiker's novels "to avoid getting involved in the ethical problematic of sodomy and the politics of sodomistic narratives that largely fascinate Sello Duiker" (Ezeliora 2005, 164). Steeped in denial, critics seem to be in a rush to the conclusion that homosexuality does not exist in Africa, or that it is not an important issue.[9] This is a reflection of the attitude of the wider society toward nonheterosexual relationships. Sylvia Tamale (2003) gives a moving account of how she was vilified in the Ugandan media and by her friends for advocating gay rights. It is assumed that a university professor like her should be concerned with more important political issues: "I had previously been aware of the intolerance towards and prejudice against homosexuals in Uganda. I must confess, however, that the degree and extent of this bias came as a nasty shock to me; such bigotry and injustice I had read about only in history books on slavery and apartheid. That society could vilify the harmless, private, victimless acts of consenting adults defies logic" (Tamale

2003, 42). It was assumed that Tamale was advocating gay rights only because she was interested in getting funding from Western donor agencies.

Under surveillance from dominant sexual groups, sexual minorities express themselves in heavily coded terms, and the African novel uses metafictional devices to offer narratives that are formidable sites where suppressed erotic practices are staged.[10] While much of the nationalist literature of the 1960s and 1970s presented male homosexuality as an inexcusable, Western-imposed practice, Wole Soyinka's *The Interpreters* (1965) treats the issue as a complex expression of identity that may not be easily understood in an intolerant society. Notable are the novel's references to James Baldwin's *Another Country* (1962) in its depictions of the homosexuality of Joe Golder, an African American character. As shown in Desai's reading of the novel, references to Baldwin help us sympathize with Golder's alienation both in America and on his home continent, Africa.[11] Because the events take place at the time of the novel's release in the early 1960s, the mention of Baldwin's novel helps the reader not only to locate the temporal setting of the narrative, but also to see more clearly the plight of Golder at the hands of homophobes. Sagoe, Golder's Nigerian friend, is aware of Baldwin's sexuality because he crudely puns on the word "country" to suggest Baldwin's novel to be about alternative male sexuality. The novel does not endorse Sagoe's vulgar misinterpretation of Baldwin. Toward the end of the narrative, Noah, a student, dies when he jumps out of the window for fear that Golder would rape him. Sagoe, a homophobe, is wrong in his views of homosexuality; he views homosexuality exclusively as a practice of noncontinental Africans. Through this generalizing tendency, Soyinka enables the reader to distrust Sagoe's attitude toward Golder as a nationalistic vendetta against foreigners, including diasporic Africans.

Sagoe's pun on the title of Baldwin's novel—crude as it is—indicates that the conceptualization of homosexuality in society can only be read via what Lee Edelman (1994) proposes as "homographesis." A "homograph" is a word that has the same spelling as another but differs from the other word in meaning, pronunciation, or origin. By invoking the homograph, Edelman underlines the ambiguity that defines the construction of homosexuality, whereby otherwise physically identical men are seen as different, although the sexual activities upon which the difference is based are unverbalized. Edelman argues that the construction of homosexuality as a subject of discourse coincides "with the process whereby the homosexual subject is represented as being, even more than inhabiting, a body that always demands to be read, a body on which his 'sexuality' is always inscribed" (Edelman 1994, 10). Homosexuality is thus a construct grounded in assigning an identity to an individual in order to bolster notions of an equally elusive heterosexuality. Edelman proposes that homographesis involves the simulation of the mainstream sexuality which it further displaces. For him, homographesis

> can be unpacked as a compulsory marking or cultural articulation of homosexual legibility that proceeds from a concern that the homosexual might be inscribed, as I would put it, in the purview of the homograph. As an explicitly graphemic structure, the homograph provides a useful point of reference for the consideration of a gay graphesis. A homograph, after all, refers to a "word of the same written form as another but of different origin and meaning"; it posits, therefore, the necessity of reading difference within graphemes that appear to be the same. (1994, 12–13)

As a cultural process, homographesis presents the identical bodies of heterosexual and homosexual males as the same without having to prove its position by presenting the homosexual man in a sexual act. In Soyinka's novel, as in others that we discuss later, the sexual activity that would make Golder homosexual is suppressed in the sense that even his suspected rape of Noah is intended or suspected but never executed. Sagoe's heterosexuality in the novel is based on his homophobic utterances and never substantiated by the text.[12]

Disability and the Lesbian Neurotic: Rebeka Njau's *Ripples in the Pool*

From the beginning, Rebeka Njau has been a strong feminist writer, examining the precolonial and postcolonial oppression of women and signaling ways women can combat their marginalization.[13] In her writing, even when woman-woman bonding is not sexual, as is the case in *The Sacred Seed* (2003), women are sheltered from heterosexual aggression. The theme of lesbian desire as a supposed perversion that colonial modernity brought into Africa is suggested and subverted in her *Ripples in the Pool* (1975). The story revolves around Selina, a rich city beauty who marries Gikere and who joins him in the village of Kamukwa to start a dispensary and possibly depose the corrupt local parliamentarian, Kefa Munene. Like the rest of the village, Gikere's mother does not like her son's Westernized wife. As a modern woman, Selina epitomizes to the villagers the moral decadence of the city and modernity itself. Bitter fights take a toll on the relationship between Gikere and Selina. Selina turns to Gikere's sister Gaciru for affection and warns her against heterosexual relationships. But Gaciru falls in love with

Karuga, a male relative of Selina's. The psychologically disturbed Selina kills the young lovers by strangling Gaciru and stabbing Karuga.

In its *dénouement*, the novel relies on Selina's mental disability—which is introduced in the last quarter of the plot—but it does not present the cause of her pathology; rather, homosexuality is shown to be the formative consequence of Selina's madness. It is suggested that the mental condition may either have been hereditary or caused by childhood abuse by her father or by miscarriages (Gikere constantly beat her when she was pregnant). The novel does not explicitly connect the mental illness to its possible causes. In fact, as Celeste Fraser Delgado notes, this is a novel that constructs its narrative by undermining narration. It ends in dystopia, dissolving into "indeterminacy after a series of catastrophic climaxes undercut every attempt to establish a pure origin or true self" (Delgado 1997, 145). At the heart of this self-deconstructive efficacy and desire for a nonoppressive utopia is Selina's mental disability and homosexuality. This, and not Selina's childlessness, as Delgado argues, is the main issue of contention in the novel in the sense that her mentally disturbed relative, Karuga's mother, is equally stigmatized, possibly for threatening the heterosexual hierarchy.

Ripples in the Pool does not rely on overt metafictional conceits to generate the postrealist sensibility that structures its presentation of themes and characters. Here we do not encounter artists, the thematization of writing, or the presentation of the processes of decoding texts. The principal characters are moderately literate. Published in 1975 by a small press that soon went out of business, *Ripples in the Pool* is one of the early African novels that exploit a nonrealist mode by relying on folk narrative art and, in this case, a neurotic woman's focalization. Its publication was interrupted even when it was adopted by the multinational African Writers Series in 1978. But this is a novel that makes unique use of language and technique in its treatment of its theme, raising the question of why it is not given much critical attention. Most likely it is because homosexuality and neurosis are key motifs, in a way that generates what Ato Quayson (2007) calls "aesthetic nervousness." This happens, according to Quayson's reading of disability in literature, "when the dominant protocols of representation in the literary text are short-circuited in relation to disability" (Quayson 2007, 15). The principal character in the novel, Selina, is easily dismissed by readers as a monster because of her lesbian desire and the neurosis that leads her to murder two admirable characters in the novel. Readers fail to understand why Selina behaves the way she does because the novel also short-circuits the reasons behind her behavior in the plot.

The novel is caught up in the crisis of representing madness as a disability and homosexuality as a sexual option in a heteronormative culture. It resorts to narrative techniques in which logic is suspended. As noted by

M. Keith Booker (1998), *Ripples in the Pool* is one of the African novels that evoke magical realism in its presentation of postcolonial conditions in Africa. Thematizing witchcraft, neurosis, and folk beliefs from its various characters' point of view, the novel is permeated by hallucinatory, antirealist descriptions which, however, link it to the realities of the society depicted in the story.[14] Magical realism is used in the novel to signify, if we may use Gerald Gaylard's expression in his discussion of otherness in postcolonialism, "both the desire for escape from entrapment and the playful and dangerous desire for the new and strange" (2005, 300). The traditional society presented in the novel teems with men and women resisting change. It is shown as sexually enslaving, while the city is viewed as a dangerous space where perversion is the order of the day. Through magical realist prose that parodies village perspectives, the novel registers a yearning for escape from this premodern world. Yet the same technique is used to distance the reader from the political vulgarities of the modern world, while the urban space is seen to have the potential to liberate women from the oppressive forces of patriarchy.

Although conventionally read as presenting female-female passion "very negatively,"[15] the novel uses metafiction to critique heteronormativity by indicating the failure of realism in representing the nervous condition implicated in the principal female character's lesbian desire. By and large, the story comprises a nationalistic narrative about the conflict between Western urbanization and African traditions and attributes the failures of the postcolonial state to its nonobservance of traditional structures of leadership. There is a crisis in representation at a nationalistic level because the postindependence leadership does not advocate for the rights and privileges of the majority. The novel captures the tension between rural and urban values in postcolonial Africa, where homosexuality is seen as an urban pathology. But, as we will see presently, even the city seems to be uncomfortable with homosexuality. Homosexuality is seen as unrepresentable, talked about only in rumors. But through nonrealistic techniques of narration, Njau makes the lesbian speak for herself, signaling possible agency for the disempowerment of women who seek sexual options outside centralized heterosexual norms.

Through moments of postrealist presentation, Njau affirms Wendy Faris's argument in *Ordinary Enchantments* (2004), that magical realism is primarily a feminine mode of expression. Before it came into prominence in the 1980s, African women writers had been deploying magical realism to express their desires and fears in a male-dominated society. Although Faris urges us to pay attention to the splintering differences between texts and authors, she contends that magical realism coincides with Luce Irigaray's theory of *ecriture feminine*:

> Because of its general narrative properties, that it is a hybrid mode, combining realism and the fantastic, magical realism can

> be seen to embody (largely French) feminist ideas about women's discourse as reflecting women's experience of belonging to a sex that is, in Lucy Irigaray's words, "not one," and to begin to erode a dualistic mode of thinking that draws clear boundaries between self and others, an erosion that has been associated with strains of female writing. (Faris 2004, 170–71)

Using phantasmagoric imagery, early novels such as *Ripples in the Pool* have subtly suggested the possibility of sex outside of the heterosexual norm.[16] If we heed Faris's call to disengage the text from the actual author, we see that it is inaccurate to argue that only female African writers deploy magical realism; male writers such as Ben Okri have used the technique to good effect. What should be emphasized is that antirealist techniques allow for the presentation and voicing of the marginalized, whom realism has not been able to faithfully represent or give enough agency. It is a solution to the crisis of representation faced by a marginalized writer articulating the desires of a marginalized group in a world that is at times bizarre.

In *Ripples in the Pool*, the sections describing heterosexual relationships are presented predominantly in realist prose. For example, the novel begins in an objective mode, describing Selina's alienation as an urban woman as seen from the villagers' perspective at a distance. Although some of the descriptions are from the communal focalization of rumor-mongers who disapprove of her Western affectations and predatory gold-digging escapades in her love affairs with the city's rich and powerful men, there is an attempt to provide rational and causal relationships in her behavior and in the behavior of those with whom she interacts. What is most striking is that Gikere's heterosexuality is described in objective prose, despite his homosexual inclinations, even if this presentation is from Selina's subjective consciousness when they meet at the pub called the Star:

> She had seen Gikere many times around the Nurses Hostel, but had never felt any wish to talk to him. He did not look masculine enough, and it was rumored he had no interest in women. He had been very religious and narrow-minded and considered it sinful to have a girlfriend. But he was good at his job. At Mbagathi Hospital, everyone talked of his devotion to his work and, though recently he had started to frequent the Star, he was not interested in chasing girls. He was still naïve in matters connected with love-making but strangely enough this was the man Selina was determined to possess, a man no other ever touched, a man six years younger than she was. (4)

At this point Gikere is a positively drawn character, seen in opposition to the morally corrupt Selina. The point made by the narrator is that, despite apparent suspicions, Gikere is not gay. The emphasis indicates that Selina, through whose perspective Gikere is being analyzed, is aware that there are gay men in the city; Gikere happens not to be one of them. The reasons he behaves the way he does are presented in a way that grounds his behavior as logically explicable. He may have no women in his life, but this is because he is a religious fanatic, a virgin, and a prude. We are not told why he comes to the pub if he is "more or less" a teetotaler and a poor dancer, but the narrator suppresses the illogicality of Gikere's choice with a subordinate clause ("though recently he had started to frequent the Star").

There is some irony when we consider the meaning of Gikere's name. The word *gikere* means "leg muscles,"[17] but Selina does not find him "muscular enough." This is to emphasize that in her heterosexual relationships she has been seeing men who are more macho than Gikere (the muscle man). She only chooses him because she wants to settle down. It is notable that the orientation of the third-person narrative is distal. Except for the proximal deictic "this" toward the end of the description of Gikere and the adverb "strangely" (apparently uttered by a focalizer other than Selina because her name appears immediately to remind us that this is a third-person narrative), the words used to describe Gikere's nonhomosexuality represent Selina's speculation as opposed to Gikere's perception of himself. Indeed, the subjective description focuses on his timid nature rather than the fact that he is not gay. To enhance the realist objectivity of this segment of the narrative, the narrator uses the past tense and no contracted verbs to signal distance, although Gikere is presented to the reader through Selina's gaze.

In contrast, the scenes presenting Selina's homosexual desire and neurosis are presented using erratic, fragmentary, and choppy sentences and paratactic structures that indicate both her mental pain and possibilities of freedom. Moments before Selina kills the female object of her desire, Gaciru, in a bout of sexual jealousy and paranoia, the narrative focalizes the event from her perspective:

> She went back again to Gaciru's room. And when she set her eyes on Gaciru's innocent and peaceful face, her madness seemed to rise. Was it possible that another person would possess that innocence? And she decided to kill herself that night. She moved all over the place looking for a rope to hang herself with. . . . *Yes*, there it was, under the kitchen table. Her thoughts were now vicious when she remembered Gaciru lying side by side with Karuga making love in the vegetable garden. Could *this* really be possible? *This* thought was too painful to bear. She would rather die than let someone else take Gaciru away. She could not wait to see *this* happen. (152–53, emphasis added)

The rhetorical questions, the proximal deictic element "this," and the informal and conversational adverbial "yes" indicate that the segment of the narrative is sifted through the hysterical woman's perspective. The narrator has told us that Gaciru and her boyfriend met secretly in the vegetable garden when Selina was in the hospital. The lovers meet several times before this event. We do not know how Selina came to discover the rendezvous etched in her mind and mentioned in an unedited stream of consciousness. Perhaps she has been stalking Gaciru, the object of her romantic obsession. But while we are made to expect Selina to kill herself, she abruptly turns her anger on Gaciru and kills her instead. The explanation is probable but insufficiently supported "she was no longer a master of herself" (153). Similar stylistic choices are made in the description of the pool, the symbol of the newly disrupted social order. The pool is mainly presented to the reader through Karuga's consciousness but as focused on her transgressive mother and on Selina.

The novel contains a subtext insinuating that the liberatory potential of alternative sexuality would undermine the nationalist posturing that hinders development in Kamukwa village (Gĩkũyũ language for a dry strap or a tendon too tough to eat, connoting underdevelopment and food-deprived conditions). While critiquing the disruptive force of modernity, *Ripples in the Pool* subtly endorses changes from traditional lifestyles that hinder sexual liberty and modernization. The "pool" of the title serves as a symbol of the state of the society; at the pool's most serene, society suffers no anxieties; the expression "ripples in the pool" symbolizes the instabilities that modernity has brought in its wake. While most African novels of the 1950s and 1960s bemoan the crisis of the loss of rural innocence, *Ripples in the Pool* seems to embrace the disruptive "ripples" of sexuality, because the changes provide an avenue for the liberation of women, despite the wider decadence that modernity brings. Even the criticism of Selina's conduct in the city early in the story is deconstructed as a figment of the villagers' imagination when we consider the rural community's proclivity for unrealistic rumors. The village discourse cannot adequately represent a modern woman like Selina.

The local society's entry into the nexus of money has enabled unethical politicians to thrive and to subvert expectations and priorities in the impoverished rural areas. Critical of the disruptive aspects of modernity, the novel portrays the moneyed as malevolent and decadent. These include women who abuse resources under their control to cultivate social practices that curtail development. Wickedness is conflated with misogyny to portray the hopelessness that defines a collapsing postcolonial nation where a leader, Kefa Munene, arranges the death of his own wife and reduces heroes of the war of liberation to destitution. The politician's name, "Munene," connotes the Gĩkũyũ word for "Big Man"; the novel thus exemplifies the rejection of the masculinist Big Man syndrome in African politics. It is people like Selina who are to form a formidable opposition to Munene's cynicism. Gikere, though having ideals similar to Selina's in dislodging Munene from power, fails, but there appears to be a stronger possibility of Selina's method succeeding. In his opposition to Munene's politics, Gikere is more interested in the nationalistic, but Selina goes beyond nationalism to incorporate gender; her intervention is driven by the brutal way Munene treats his wife and ends up killing her in a road "accident."

Gĩkũyũ anthropologist Jomo Kenyatta (who later became independent Kenya's first head of state in 1963) contends in *Facing Mount Kenya* (1938) that "the practice of homosexuality is unknown among the Gĩkũyũ. The freedom of intercourse allowed between young people of the opposite sex makes it unnecessary and encourages them to acquire experience that was useful in married life" (1938, 197). Yet according to feminist research, female-female friendships are not unheard of in the community that forms the geographical setting of *Ripples in the Pool*. Njambi and O'Brien have discussed in detail "woman-woman" marriage in Gĩkũyũland, where the action of Njau's *Ripples in the Pool* takes place. They contest the mainstream feminist view that indigenous African women are silenced and disempowered subjects, showing that the institution of woman-woman marriage signifies a long history of women's liberation and resistance because the practice radically disrupts the patriarchal privilege and the domination of women. Njambi and O'Brien have asserted that, contrary to popular opinion that these marriages are only socioeconomic, the relationship between the female couple is not without an erotic component: "In our Gĩkũyũ locale, women in these relationships did not talk about sexual involvement with one another, although some did indicate sharing the same bed at night" (Njambi and O'Brien 2005, 148). Their argument is that although there is no overt indication that the relationships are erotic, "we can't simply dismiss the possibility" (149). For Njambi and O'Brien, the nature of the relationships is ambiguous and complex. We cannot rigidly compartmentalize the relationships as either sexual or socioeconomic.

If woman-woman relationships have existed at an erotic level in Gĩkũyũ culture, then why is the society presented in Njau's *Ripples in the Pool* so scandalized by Selina's desire for another woman? Selina, a woman who develops a sexual passion for a fellow woman, is aligned with the axis of negative practices threatening the vitality of the nation. Her lesbian desire is also associated with undesirable urban practices.[18] Njambi and O'Brien have questioned the notion of "female husband" used by anthropologist Louis Leakey to characterize the woman-woman marriage in the sense that this typology is masculinist and assumes a heterosexual hierarchy in which one of the women assmes the role of a man. In Njau's *Ripples in the Pool*,

Selina seems to stake a claim to be the "female husband" in the relationship because she is older and more socially and economically powerful. She comes across as an authoritarian sexual predator who subjects Gaciru to her perverted sexual desires.

Perhaps the greatest contribution that *Ripples in the Pool* makes to the East African postcolonial novel is to remind us that female-female desires are not new in Africa. Even if she tends to conflate lesbianism with neurosis in the classical Freudian sense, if we consider Selina's nervous condition a disability, then we would be able to recuperate the character from the marginalization she undergoes even at the hands of gay literary critics such as Murray and Roscoe (1998), who seem to stigmatize her as a disgrace to disruptive sexual options. When we place Selina in relation to similar characters in the novel, the narrative suggests lesbianism as just one sexual possibility among others. This sexual orientation could, indeed, be liberating. The weaknesses in Selina's personality are neither necessarily a result of her homosexual impulses—other nonhomosexual characters have these weaknesses—nor are they the cause of her sexual desires.

Indeed, the novel suggests that the liberation of women might manifest itself in those who fearlessly engage in activities considered perverse by the mainstream leaders. Without endorsing Selina's jealousy and violence, the story locates its tragic pathos in the failure of the society to recognize Selina's passion. Before she met Gikere, Selina had heterosexual relations in the city, but none of them satisfied her. The novel suggests that she is attracted by Gikere's passivity and nonmasculinity. She becomes domineering and jealous, but she is not the only character suffering these weaknesses. Gikere's mother, a homophobe who fears Selina will pervert her daughter Gaciru, is described by her own daughter as "too possessive" (20). Although she frames the threat as nonsexual when describing it to her son, there is a possibility that Gikere's mother senses that Selina is lesbian but does not want to voice her fears. Even though Selina has committed murder in a moment of emotional derangement, other characters have also killed, including the heterosexual area parliamentarian, Munene, who kills his wife.

Disillusionment and the Crisis of Representing the Disabled

There is a difference between homosexuality and disability because, as Lennard J. Davis (1998) notes, "disability is an identity divorced from family, nation, ethnicity, or gender. It is not a discrete but rather a porous category. Anyone can become disabled, and it is also possible for a person with disabilities to be 'cured' and thus become 'normal' " (Davis 1998, 321). Homosexuality is not an abnormality in need of a cure. But one cannot fully appreciate the attitude of *Ripples in the Pool* toward homosexuality on a personal and social level without considering the way the narrative projects disability in the realm of public affairs or Njau's invocation of the crisis of representation through metafictional devices. As in Kibera's (1970) *Voices in the Dark*, disillusionment with the postcolonial order in Njau's *Ripples in the Pool* is conflated with the author's unhappiness about the treatment of the disabled in society. In both novels, the physically disabled have fought for the nation's independence, but they have now been sidelined by the national leadership.

The eighth chapter of *Ripples in the Pool* offers insights into the mistreatment of the disabled. To express the crisis in representation, the chapter opens with a description of a phantasmagoric dream that Gikere experiences before he takes us with him to an institution of the disabled war veterans who fought for Kenya's independence.

> He saw himself among the marshes in a small lake. Suddenly, there appeared in front of him a young woman holding a lamb. She stared at him for a while, and called him by name in a familiar manner. Then with a cloth full of blood, she covered the little lamb and handed it to him, whispering some strange words as she did so. The blood in the cloth dripped all over him, and when the woman saw it, she burst out laughing. She laughed hysterically, staring at him till her eyes began to water. After that, she moved away quickly, and he saw her walk into the lake and float over water. Within a short while she disappeared, and was standing on the bank at the other side of the lake. (48)

The dream with which the narrator launches the chapter suggests many things at once, as it simultaneously displaces and condenses events into metonyms and metaphors with heavy sexual coding. The fact that the woman knows the dreamer by name suggests that the dream is about familiar circumstances cast in a strange metaphysical language to express the incommensurability between real-life experience and language.

Condensed in the dream in Lacanian terms is the idea of a mirage. The woman is an elusive fantasy who slips out of Gikere's comprehension. She becomes a metaphor for that which has escaped his grip. From the context, this young woman is a metaphor for Selina and other physically and sexually abused women in society, especially because the dream repeats the idea of the pool (a small lake in the dream). Once she crosses the pool, Gikere will never get her again for further abuse. Selina is disappearing from the heteronormative patriarchal order that Gikere duels in into hysteria and neurosis, where she can live in much more freedom than the physical abuse she suffers under him as he tries to assert his manhood, which is in a crisis. The blood is a metonym for the succession of the miscarriages Gikere's wife has gone through after the beatings she has endured at his hands. It also suggests his guilt, and that he is responsible for her condition. The lamb and the miscarriages also signify the new political independence that is not yet secure because of the corrupt politics of men like Munene.

The crisis of representation suggested by the dream is literalized when the chapter describes Munene's conduct of public affairs. Although he is an elected official, he only thinks about his welfare and political survival: "How often have people of Kamukwa sent delegations to Kefa Munene, who is their MP, asking him to help them and build them a hospital? But has [he] ever done anything about it? Empty slogans year after year, that is his game. Empty promises" (50). The asylum he has set up for the disabled is intended only to disempower them further and to help him retain his office:

> Men who were crippled by the bullets of the white man and now they have been reduced to such a state that they have become impotent and can no longer feel the pain that drove our people into fighting for freedom. They have been made to feel completely helpless. They do nothing here but eat, drink, and play cards all day. The brain they had has gone to sleep because of too much beer and spirits. The only good thing they are good at is casting their vote during elections. They are loyal to the MP. (51)

The suggestion here is that a progressive leader should start self-help projects like the ones we see in Njau's later novel, *The Sacred Seed*. The disabled should also fight for their rights the way Selina does in *Ripples in the Pool*. The reader is drawn into this ethical position. Rather than condemn the people out of hand, we should assist them, the way Maria and Gikere try to do, to come out of the enslavement they have been reduced to by the ruling elite. Individuals like Gikere also should be aware of similarly disabled people in their own domestic spaces if their public efforts are to win the reader's empathy.

A few moments later the notion of the mirage is reintroduced when we are told that the MP has hung goodies at the top of a post. Those with disabilities are supposed somehow to get them:

> The cripples can never reach the top . . . It is painful to see them hanging around watching the presents, free gifts at the top of the post. Then they hobble on their sticks in a pathetic manner. Some fall and collapse on top of others as they hungrily move towards scattered presents. To Kefa Munene, human beings are dolls to play with. (52)

The anger here is nationalistic in the sense that Munene and the ruling elites have failed to meet the people's expectations. In traditional folk tales, the cripple is a respected individual. He is the one who wins the most beautiful girl in the society, beating princes and the rich in contexts that sometimes involves dangerous activities such as climbing poles, as in the story dramatized in John Ruganda's (1972) play *The Burdens*. The cripple is gifted with remarkable foresight. But in postcolonial Africa, the people who got severely crippled in the fight for independence are reduced to insignificance by the new leadership. However, more fundamental is the call to the readers to distance themselves from the kind of conduct seen in Munene and his henchmen. Disability is something neither to be laughed at nor condemned. It should be treated with sensitivity and empathy.

Therefore, before we yield to the temptation to pathologize Selina's condition and demonize her, we should heed Nigerian feminist and psychologist Amina Mama's warning that multiple identities among African women need not be seen as a negative attribute. Being multiple, as are Selina in *Ripples in the Pool* and Margaret in Bessie Head's (1971) *Maru*, would be treated as pathological in conventional psychology. Mama urges us to reconceptualize the juggling of different identities as significations of a subjectivity that is "multiple and dynamic" (1995, 121). Selina represents a subjectivity negotiating for a space where alternative sexualities are seen as deviant. Those who pathologize her need to adapt to alternatives that have existed within the culture in a suppressed form. Indeed, in the story, Selina is not the first woman society has destroyed for appearing to be aberrant and for challenging the social order. Selina reveals to Karuga, the boy who marries the girl Selina is interested in, that his mother committed suicide because she could not understand why society could not accept her the way she was (121). The specificity of her aberration is not revealed to us, but the fact that Selina identifies with her suggests similar desires, an interpretation that gives credence to possibilities of Gaciru's mother coming to understand that female homosexuality exists, and that her daughter could easily be enticed into it by Selina.

The society presented in the novel tries to control Selina and other women like her by condemning any liberatory activities they pursue, although it is not able to provide them with alternatives. Through Gikere, the novel underlines that society's view of the relationship between Selina and Gaciru as "shameful to talk about" (64). But it is only in a relationship with another woman that Selina finds fulfillment, and she is confident enough to declare that her erotic love for a fellow woman is normal:

> It is no use talking to me about my behaviour towards Gaciru. I've done nothing wrong. My conscience is clear. It's not a crime

> to love her. She gives me joy. Peace . . . I cheated myself that I loved you. I wanted something precious. Something beautiful to look at, to touch and feel. During these years of our marriage I've been trying to pursue that thing and make it mine, but all I see is its shadow disappearing in front of my eyes. (68)

Her view of heterosexuality parallels the novel's view of the expectations of independence and nationalism. The new leadership, represented by Munene, is exploitative, repressive, and murderous. In conflating political disillusionment with Selina's sexual disappointment with heterosexuality, the novel subtly registers its repudiation of compulsory heterosexuality and euphoric nationalism.

Delgado is right when she observes that the marriage between Karuga and Selina is symbolic of "the system of compulsory heterosexuality that insures manhood only through a violent imposition of womanhood" (Delgado 1997, 144). The murder of the young heterosexual couple, Gaciru and Karuga, by the lesbian Selina suggests her role in ending the kind of naïve heterosexuality that Gaciru and Karuga represent. The novel uses nonrealist prose to express her aberrant and neurotic condition and also to suggest the end of unproblematized heteronormativity. Selina's fate parallels that of other women who have disrupted the social order but who die because, according to her assessment of one of them, they "gave up the battle halfway" (121). That Selina's assessment comes after failed suicide attempts signals that she is not going to give up the fight. Unlike the cripples in Munene's asylum, Selina has fully rejected the status quo.

Furthermore, by basing its tragic ending on Selina's compulsive obsession and her eventual madness, the novel advocates a society that would view homosexuality as a possible legitimate alternative to heteronormativity. Rather than condemn her, the reader is compelled to empathize with her plight; the novel champions a society where the lesbian would not be driven mad by social constraints. By making Selina's desire for Gaciru sexual, as opposed to socioeconomic, Njau seems set on desilencing the erotic part of the woman-woman relationship that anthropologists have buried under functionalist conceptualizations of such unions as being primarily for economic and social reasons.

The novel ends with an evocation of a new social order that underlines hope in the midst of a succession of catastrophes. This society is focalized by a male character, Maina, who has been marginal to the narrative, as he and Muthee gaze at Karuga's body:

> He looked at the old man who was whispering quietly, kneeling beside the body. Suddenly a light shone upon his face as he stared

> at it, and he realized that the fig tree would survive the generations and generations to come like the light, spirit, and truth that live on forever. Suddenly, there was a heavy downpour of rain, and the small crowd that had followed them dispersed, leaving him and the old man kneeling beneath the fig tree. (162)

These are the last three sentences of the novel. Even in pre-Christian Gĩkũyũ culture, *mugumo* (the fig tree) is, as in the biblical Eden, a symbol of fertility. It is the site of sacrifice and worship, continuity and purification. According to the Gĩkũyũ myth of origin, it is at a *mugumo* that the nine men who are to marry the daughters of the ethnic group's initial couple (who had given birth to girls only) miraculously appear. The novel invokes the tree to express solidarity with indigenous culture and mythology and to emphasize its optimism. The last time the tree appears in the story is in a scene where the villagers come to Muthee for the healing of their child (90). According to Gĩkũyũ mythology, the gesture the worshippers execute—going around the tree seven times (90)—would change one's gender from male to female, and vice versa.[19] Thus in the novel healing, worship, and sacrifice are conjoined with the myth of gender change to underscore the need for acceptance of new modes of self-fashioning.

The novel about disintegration, alienation, and death seems to end on a happy note. Syntactic parallelism (signaled by the use of the adverb "suddenly" to begin successive sentences and the loose subordinate clause in each sentence) emphasizes the connection between the universal symbols of hope, light, and water, and the more culturally specific fig tree. The utopia of absolute peace and healing we are presented with here is masculine, but we are aware that Selina's conflict is not fully resolved. The fact that she does not die indicates possibilities of her participation in the events of that utopia. But the narrative does not cure her because it does not see homosexuality as a disability; rather, it exposes the cynicism of a patriarchal society that abandons a deranged woman, although it is implicated in her mental condition. At the syntactical level, the novel's last three sentences are paratactic. They constitute an independent clause followed by a subordinate clause joined to the main clause loosely, without any overt conjunction. It is a structure that expresses loss, alienation, and lack of focus. From the context, the male custodians of the society's wisdom speak in a grammar similar to the one spoken by the deranged Selina. Though lesbian and mad, Selina is very much a part of the utopia that Maina and the old man forecast.

Although it does not portray lesbian sexuality as directly as *Ripples in the Pool* (1975), Njau's later novel, *The Sacred Seed* (2003), indicates through metafictional impulses a similar disillusionment with heterosexuality and patriarchal nationalism. Unlike *Ripples in the Pool*, which focuses on the putative alienation of women who do not conform to the heteronormative order, *The Sacred Seed* seems to heed the suggestion given by Ato Quayson in a study of feminism and modernity. Quayson sees the most essential contribution by male and female students of gender to lie not "just in the critique of patriarchy and of traditionalism, but in the careful construction of better structures by which women can express and fulfill their deepest aspirations, whether these are within marriage or outside it" (2000, 131). Njau's *The Sacred Seed* goes beyond "writing back" to patriarchy and Western top-down models of development to celebrate participatory strategies of self-liberation staged by women in collaboration with gender-sensitized men.

The Sacred Seed tells the story of mysterious women working collectively to preserve the natural environment against encroachment by the national leadership and other institutions such as the church that the state has co-opted to oppress the masses. Chinusi, the nation's president, and pastor Jonah are both rapists. Borrowed from Kiswahili literature, Chinusi's name suggests a mythical monster with a pimply skin.[20] Chinusi and Jonah and their collaborators suffer a mysterious skin disease for trying to steal the women's property and for sexually harassing the women. At the center of the story is Mumbi, whose name (creator) recalls the mystical mother of the Gĩkũyũ ethnic group. She is an artist who has brought women together via the indigenous art of pot-making. Nature is presented literally as an artist as well. Women are able to grow gourds with beautiful patterns on them. The modern artist Tesa can only fulfill her role in society by her integration into the indigenous women's group, where she teaches modern arts. She is able to draw gender-sensitive male artists like Muturi into the group to join women in fighting patriarchal abuse of the nation.

An African American woman is also integrated into the group after her failed collaboration with the male leadership. She contracts an ailment that afflicts the males who try to take away the women's property, especially their land and gourds. She eventually realizes that she should not have cavorted with the national elite at the expense of poor women:

> Since this unfortunate incident occurred, I have been questioning myself almost every day, and I have concluded that the ugly, blood-sucking worms have penetrated my skin because of my evil deed. As an outsider, I followed Jonah's direction in matters of religion and people's beliefs . . . I was misled as soon as I set foot in this country. (160)

It is suggested that modern and diasporic Africans must respect indigenous cultures if they are to be effective in any way in developing the continent. The metafictional appeal of the novel lies only partly in its use of artists and art as its central reference point. More interesting is its invocation of rural mysteries in which leaders who violate the will of the women suffer strange illnesses. The female characters are enigmatic, and they press the preternatural world into service in their artistic and economic projects.

The novel signifies in graphic terms the venality of male leadership in Africa in oppressing not only women but the rest of the nation. As McFadden (1990) argues in the context of the abuse of power in southern Africa, it is women who bear the brunt of oppression. Unlike in *Ripples in the Pool*, in *The Sacred Seed* Njau foresees better ways to intervene than a collective nervous breakdown. Her female characters in the novel emerge not as the passive beasts of burden that Ama Ata Aidoo criticizes Western feminists for foregrounding in discussions of African gender relations. As a new generation of women whose mission is to use intrinsically feminine creative power to liberate the continent from the shackles of patriarchy and dictatorship, the characters seem to heed Aidoo's words that women's survival "lies only in collective strength. When pressed, they rise to the occasion with awesome courage, strength, and clarity" (1998, 19–20). The novel demonstrates, through metafictional gestures conflating the creation of art with feminine agency, the power of women to collectively confront both patriarchy and dictatorship.

The theme of art runs through the novel. The female victims of the national dictatorship are artists who are able to weave better texts of emancipation from patriarchy and authoritarianism. The positively drawn male characters in the novel are artists too. The modern female artist Tesa is not only raped by the nation's leader, but the masculinist figures in the novel are diseased and suffer from an incurable ailment that reminds the reader of AIDS. The cause of the scourge facing the men is located at the intersection of the sexual and material abuse of women in the postcolonial nation. Drawing attention to its status as a work of art and to its compositional processes, *The Sacred Seed* weaves into its plot the theme of the possibilities offered by arts and culture in resolving the political and economic crises facing Africa. It invokes the female black diaspora, as do Ayi Armah's *Osiris Rising* (1995)[21] and Ngũgĩ's *The Wizard of the Crow* (2006),[22] as a possible source of regenerative power in the ailing continent. But in Njau's novel, the sexual union between the continent and the diaspora is not heterosexual.

Tesa, the contemporary artist in *The Sacred Seed*, finds fulfillment in bonding with other women, especially indigenous female artists, as opposed to accepting the positions of privilege offered by the masculine state. To heal emotionally after the trauma of attempted rape by the authoritarian head of state, Tesa is made to descend from the elitism of modern institutions to collaborate with grassroots women artists in the village. Ellen, the African American woman who returns to the continent as a missionary, is rewarded for her efforts with an attempted rape by the male pastor of the local church that hosts her. The leaders of this church have deep connections to the male head of state. The church's ingratitude and greed are underlined in the pastor's lecherous attempt, which parallels other acts of violence against women by the patriarchal society and the male-dominated postcolonial state. Indeed, the parallels between Tesa's and Ellen's experiences at the hands of the head of state and the pastor, respectively, underline the similarity of patriarchal institutions. There is very little difference between the church and the state because work to oppress the majority, especially women.

More sensitively than any other novel, *The Sacred Seed* demonstrates ways of bridging the gap between elite and grassroots women in Africa. This gap has been noted by Nigerian feminist Olabisi Aina, who points out that not only do grassroots women lack conceptual frameworks to confront oppression and improve their economic status, but there is also "a general lack of trust between rural grassroots women and the elite women who are mostly from the cities" (1998, 82). Aina observes that grassroots women view the educated female elite as privileged and opportunistic. Njau's novel calls to its aid the figure of artists to show that the immutable elite/grassroots binary opposition plaguing feminism in Africa can be demolished. The elite female artists in the novel—Tesa and Ellen—abandon their privileged status to join the rural artists. They do not dictate terms to the community; rather, they agree to be taught by this group of artists, and in the processes both groups are able to transform each other.

Evoking the language of metafiction, the novel signals that healing is only possible through an intertextual collaboration between the elite and grassroots artistic forms. Ellen's moment of self-realization comes when she abandons the elite church and joins women in a traditional shrine threatened by the state:

> Ellen felt gratified to have had the opportunity to be around the women who knew how to use their power calmly. She was fascinated by Tesa's music and was moved by her ability to relate to people at all levels. She admired her talent and skill in training the young village boys and girls. Within a short time they had learned to sing and create pictures which expressed their feelings, and told stories of joy and sorrow. (174)

Underscored here is the need for direct grassroots development, but it is stressed through references to participation in artistic production. Considering Njau's presentation of the contemporary female artist in relation to the grassroots women artist, we may argue that Selina's tragedy in *Ripples in the Pool* stems from her attempt to impose her homosexual desire on the village of Kamukwa, oblivious of the fact that disruptive practices are not completely unheard of in the village, as suggested through the figure of Karuga's mother.

Pursuing its anti-elitism theme farther, *The Scared Seed* signals that African Americans who go to Africa (metropolitan and elite in relation to the majority of Africans) are likely to interact with the Westernized, masculinist, and power-wielding elites, as Ellen previously did. They will be recognized by the church and state authorities, who want to exploit the diasporic Africans' Western connection to get donations and business opportunities, as the pastor in the novel tries to do with Ellen in order to export stolen gourds to America. The novel underscores that the diasporic African has a duty to deconstruct the formal structure put into place to oppress the ordinary African by the state and its organs. The creative potentials learned in Africa and taken to America in traumatic circumstances during transatlantic enslavement can be reinvented to assist the African continent:

> Her mother, she recalled, had been a skillful craftswoman. She had made fabrics and rugs using fiber plants which had grown in her backyard. Ellen had learnt the craft and she decided to pass the knowledge to the women before she left for the USA. (174)

In intertextual echoes of Njau's earlier novel, the figure of the pool recurs in *The Sacred Seed*, but now it is serene because women have discovered the secret of their joy in transnational bonding. The novel suggests that female bonding does not necessarily involve sexual activities. Tesa, the artist, cannot marry a man because she has a birthmark that signals death for any man who engages with her sexually. In spite of her desire for fellow artist Muturi, they cannot consummate their union. Thus heterosexuality is ruled out, even if lesbianism is not mentioned in the novel. It is not lost on the reader that the equivalent of Gikere (the man who moves from the city to the rural village to set up a clinic and to whom the women are close) is named Dr. Kim Mwera. *Mwera* means "a hen" in Gĩkũyũ, with connotations of virginity.[23] Most likely the women love Mwera because of the female aspects of his character. The bond has homoerotic resonances.

Homophobia as Misreading: Gurnah's *By the Sea*

Abdulrazak Gurnah's *By the Sea* (2001) provides an instance in which homographesis can help us understand the construction of homosexual desire in the postcolonial society. Like Wole Soyinka's (1965) *The Interpreters*, which refers to Baldwin's work to complicate conventional views of black gays, Gurnah's *By the Sea* offers a treatment of homosexuality by making references to Whitman's poetry. The novel is told from the perspective of Latif Mahmud, a Tanzanian immigrant teacher of English in southern England. It explores the theme of African migration to the Western metropolis, as refugees and homosexuality are only secondary issues here. Through irony, the novel demonstrates the widespread existence of homosexuality in the Zanzibari town where its narrator grew up. Although the narrator is cynical in his view of his homosexual brother, he self-consciously reveals that his cynicism is staged.

In Gurnah's *Admiring Silence* (1996), the unnamed narrator irrationally links homosexuality to such practices as miscegenation, which a rational person would not condemn. Therefore, when the gay issue crops up again in *By the Sea*, we are bound to see the contradiction in the characters who condemn it. In the novel, the narrator's older brother has a homosexual relationship with his father's friend, Hussein. The friend cons the family out of their house after sleeping with both the host's son and wife. The novel sees Hussein's sexual acts as an expression of moral depravity. Especially because his lust is expended on an innocent boy, it would be hard to forgive him. But the tone with which the narrator tells of his brother's homosexuality manifests his homophobia. He laughs at his own father, who cannot understand that his son was a victim of the homosexual visitor. Although the narrator does not fully comprehend the desires circulating in the society, he registers the latent gay lust pervading the town. What is especially striking is the town's response to the relationship between the boy and the man:

> The rumours started very quickly, and I was taunted about them by the boys at school. They said our guest had eaten Hassan, had eaten honey there. It was a way of saying something cruder, and they said it crudely too. One of Hassan's secondary schoolmates, who had been a former friend, chased after me in the street as I was walking home to Koran school to ask me if it was true that I had a new father. When I passed a group of adults lounging at street corners, which they seemed forever to be doing, I thought they smirked behind me, I feared they did. (Gurnah 2001, 95)

The narrative does not indicate how the wider society came to know of the relationship. He himself discovered it serendipitously, an indication that it has been going on for some time. It is probable that Hassan had a relationship with other boys, with whom he had talked about his relationship with Uncle Hussein.

The community teases Hassan for having been "eaten," but we are shown that they also desire both him and the narrator:

> They never left Hassan alone after that, the plunderers of flesh. There was nothing gay in what they did or sought to do. They coveted his grace and his effortless, supple beauty, and muttered to him as he strolled by, offering him money and gifts and transparent predatory smiles. (95)

They are not "gay" (either in the sense of happy or homoerotic), but there is something latently homosexual in the way they stalk Hassan. The ambivalence of the society is further expressed by the way the people stalk the boy: "They never left him alone, the looks, the comments, the casual touch, all were suggestive, something between cruel game and calculated stalking exercise" (95). One of the results of that callous ambivalence forces the boy to mask his sexuality.

Homosexuality becomes a burden to the boy because the society secretly desires him but publicly abhors his sexual orientation. The society punishes Hassan and not the grown-up man because it is itself predatory and would not mind being in the position of the latter. Hassan could well be a representative of many boys like him. This is revealed in the narrative voice that Gurnah uses to render in the critique of Hassan's sexuality. The story is told in a first-person narrative by Hassan's brother, who does not have access to other homesteads. His limited knowledge denies the reader access not only to other hidden practices of homosexual love but even to communication between Hassan and Uncle Hussein because the communication is in English, which the narrator does not understand at the time the communication happens. The limitations of the narrator's perspective register that Hassan's sexual experiences could be widespread among other boys and adults the narrator knows.

It is through a study of the language with which the narrative establishes an intertextual connection with others that the reader comes to understand that the narrator's homophobia is staged:

> He preferred the uncompromising tones of Whitman and of Iqbal. I knew Whitman from the USIS library days, and probably pretended to have an opinion on the matter, though I had reeled from *Leaves of Grass* with fastidious disapproval." (118)

Ironically, the narrator captures society's staged homophobia and unconsciously registers his own pretenses through the language he deploys. The reader detects some level of self-deprecation in the narrator's irrational hatred of gay literature. Whitman was homosexual, and his *Leaves of Grass* contains homoerotic poems. The narrator, just like the novelist Gurnah himself, is a professor of English who understands the politics of sexuality, although he does not openly state his position in his own narrative. Why is Latif Mahmud's disapproval of Whitman "fastidious"? Left unexplained, the disfavor of Whitman is likely a result of the fact that the poet was a homosexual, and the collection of poetry mentioned contains homoerotic verse. Is it not likely that his disapproval of his own brother's homosexuality is a "fastidious" act, equally staged like his society's homophobia? Through the silence, the novel suggests that articulations of bland homophobic statements could be a way to mask one's own homoeroticism. The narrator is defined by homosexual desire that he does not want to acknowledge.

Minorities and HIV/AIDS: Mpe's *Welcome to Our Hillbrow*

In *African Intimacies*, Neville Hoad (2007) presents an exemplary analysis of the South African novella *Welcome to Our Hillbrow* (2001) by Phaswane Mpe (1970–2004). This makes the discussion of this novella easy for me, especially the way he discusses Mpe's treatment of sexuality and cosmopolitanism in postapartheid South Africa. I will therefore focus on a few moments in the short novel where metafiction refigures sexuality and contests received opinion. This is a melodramatic novella whose complexity lies in its affectations to high literariness, to literary criticism and theorizing, and to polemics on the representation of the underprivileged. Telling the story in the second-person narrative voice, the narrating consciousness shifts from one position to another, rhetorically drawing the reader into the narration meant for dead characters, all of whom are associated with literature, publishing, reading, and aesthetics. In the opening chapter, the unnamed narrator addresses a dead writer (Refentse), an immigrant from the rural Tiragalong.

The novella's metafictionality resides only partly in the story it tells about a writer, Refentse, who has read the equally metafictional works of J. M. Coetzee[24] and has written fiction about a character who died of AIDS. More meaningful is the self-reflexivity the narrator instantiates by mimicking himself and the communities that he describes. Addressing Refentse in the second-person narrative voice about the relevance of his story to AIDS in a postapartheid South Africa, the novella dissolves the boundaries between the reader and the writer, between different racial, gender, ethnic, and sexual communities, between literary genres, and between different narrative positions. The mimicry is not so much directed at the colonial West that

Bhabha identifies as central to postcolonial discourse but rather at the local society's parochialism against outsiders and people who do not conform to mainstream practices.

From the very beginning, the novel frames itself as a self-conscious hybrid discourse, invoking the orature of the Limpopo region and addressing the reader, as well as its narrator's addressee, in the second person.[25] Carrol Clarkson, in "Locating Identity in Phaswane Mpe's *Welcome to Our Hillbrow*" (2005), notes that even if the second-person narration is disorienting and distancing, it draws the reader into the addressed collectivity. Since the addressee is dead, the narrative must be a performance in which the reader is expected to assume the role of the addressed author. Through the use of the second-person narrative voice, *Welcome to Our Hillbrow* simultaneously addresses the narrator's embedded audience and the reader to compel us to identify more closely with the addressed dead author.[26] As Clarkson further observes, there is a sense of community evoked by the novel's use of the collective "our" in its address; the novel makes us part of its "community of readers" (2005, 457). We are to empathize with the characters, especially those unnamed people in the margins that the new South Africa continues to oppress, despite its experience of the pains of discrimination under apartheid.

Strikingly, the dead writer has experimented with both realism and metafiction, and the realist story based on his real-life, unfaithful girlfriend turns out to be gender-insensitive, cynical about HIV infections among the poor, and xenophobic. In the mimetic story, the embedded writer seems blind to his own unfaithfulness with a friend's girlfriend. It is only when Refentse turns to metafiction that he is able to find his voice and correct the prejudices in his earlier story:

> Your story was in English, since unlike you're the naïve and hopeful woman of your fiction, you knew the limitations of writing in Sepedi. But, like your heroine, you wrote your story in order to find sanctuary in the worlds of fiction that are never what we label them. You wrote in order to steady yourself against grief and prejudice, against the painful and compel realities of humanness. (59)

The plot of the frame story of *Welcome to Our Hillbrow* is simple. The embedded heterosexual writer and his lover Lerato cheat on each other with their friends Bohlale and Sammy, respectively. Refentse commits suicide, and when Lerato fans rumors in rural areas that Refentse was bewitched by his own mother, the mother is accused of witchcraft and murdered.

The nameless narrator addresses the dead writer, showing to the reader the movies that Refentse is watching in heaven. One of these reveals the genealogy of Lerato, whose father, according to the film screened in heaven, is also accused of witchcraft and killed. The theme of cosmopolitanism is explored through Refentse's former girlfriend, Refilwe, who pursues her education at Oxford and falls in love with a Nigerian who resembles Refentse. She discovers she has HIV and returns to South Africa to die. Underlying this simple story is the question whether marginalized communities such as the people of Hillbrow, foreigners in Europe and South Africa, and homosexuals can be represented in literature or meaningfully advocated for in a society governed by stereotypes. The story is told in an oral mode by what appears to be a theoretically naïve narrator who relies on rumors. He calls the origins of the rumors "reliable sources" to mockingly avow veracity and highlight their fictionality. The novel indicates the difficulties of speaking on behalf of subalterns or of realistically portraying them in art. The oppressed can only be spoken for and artistically represented in circuitous discourse with a unique temporality that gives the work an aesthetic complexity but speaks to the inability of the subaltern to enunciate their own condition or to be spoken for by someone else.

Like Habila's *Waiting for an Angel* (2002), Mpe's *Welcome to Our Hillbrow* has dehisced into disillusionment with a postindependence nationalism based on the exclusion of the powerless. However, it uses metafiction to capture a similar scenario of disillusionment with what it views as xenophobic and homophobic nationalism in postapartheid South Africa through the figure of censorship. Mpe's novel treats censorship, xenophobia, and homophobia as mutually enhancing defects in the emergent postapartheid South Africa:

> In 1995, despite the so-called new dispensation, nothing had really changed. The legacy of Apartheid censors still shackled those who dreamed of writing freely in an African language. Publishers scared of being found on the financially dangerous side of the censorship border still rejected manuscripts that too realistically called things by their real names—names that people of Tiragalong and Hillbrow and everywhere in the world used every day. (57)

The novel, whose story revolves around the life of an embedded female artist, indicates the inability of the female writer (the fictional Refentse) to articulate the problems of postapartheid South Africa, although she "was writing in 1995, one year after the overthrow of the political and cultural censorship, and the damaging and dishonest indiscrimination system which had been aimed at forcing South Africans to believe that life's realities lay exclusively in euphemisms" (57). The writer is silenced when the "publishers in turn exercised their right to reject her literary contribution to Sepedi literature" (57–58). Here we see the subaltern as unable to articulate and practice her radicalism in a society defined by hegemonic control.

By telling her story and that of its writer, who serves as the embedded audience in the larger novel, *Welcome to Our Hillbrow* tries to restore the agency of both the female writer and the embedded male novelist who tells her story, despite the fact that both are dead. But are Mpe and the male writer who portrays Refentse, the unpublished female writer, able to transcend this hegemony that the novel talks about in its metafictional moments? For one, *Welcome to Our Hillbrow*, like the story embedded in it, is in English as opposed to the native Sepedi language.[27] It seems to offer an apology for being in a colonial language instead of the native tongue, despite the suggestion that the novel, through its embedded literary works, would be translated into Sepedi. The work has to resort to metafictional and nonrealist gestures to be effective in a postapartheid situation. It does not "too realistically call things by their real names," but it manages, through metafictional devices, to tell the story of Hillbrow that publishers and authors have suppressed, while excoriating the hegemony that informs the publishing industry in the new nation.

The novella presents the problems facing postapartheid South Africa in a fiction that sees the reality in the society as stranger than fiction.[28] It is through the commingling of fable and reality that the narrative sustains a sense of irony with which it presents the disjunction between expectations and reality in the newly independent nation. Less directly autobiographical than K. Sello Duiker's novels, Mpe's *Welcome to Our Hillbrow*'s investment in its author-character's life experiences foreshadows Mpe's own death—for the novelist-character in *Welcome to Our Hillbrow* dies, like Mpe "of what precisely, no one knew."[29] In using a narrator who stages himself as a writer and a literary theorist writing to another writer about yet a different writer and agonizing over vital debates such as the language he should be writing in, Mpe indicates the desire to give voice to identities that antiapartheid discourses have silenced, even if this means using English, a colonial language.[30] Hoad is right when he argues that the narrator's self-consciousness as an embedded writer in his own right and a reader of J. M. Coetzee, Herman Charles Bosman, Nadine Gordimer, and Zakes Mda is a strategy of "explicitly inserting his narrative into the history of South Africa letters, reanimating a range of living and dead writers" (118). Mpe is speaking to the power of narrative and memory in constructing a more cosmopolitan and tolerant society.

Like its character Refilwe, who is a mixture of rural Tiragalong, urbanized Hillbrow, and metropolitan Oxford, *Welcome to Our Hillbrow* is an assortment of texts and techniques, and the characters interpret the texts in terms of their own personal experiences. The novel's deconstructive efficacy rests in its self-mimicry and its ruthless mockery of Africans who exclude others from positions of privilege. Though sympathetic to the African consciousness, especially a Pan-African spirit that abolishes boundaries between different African nationalities, the novel does not spare those citizens who, out of ignorance, "turned diseases into crimes" (116). The novel questions the nationalist euphoria in the postapartheid era by indicating how unquestioning patriotism will inevitably produce xenophobia and violence. A story about xenophobia, AIDS, witchcraft, and urban problems, the novel tackles the theme of homosexuality in a narrative addressed by turns to a dead character. It destabilizes the dichotomies between the dead and living, between the urban and the rural, and between male and female and in so doing indicates the problems of a new South Africa, where the dichotomy between apartheid and postapartheid is problematized by continued discrimination against a certain sector of society.

With references to nineteenth-century British writer Thomas Hardy's *Jude the Obscure* (1895) as experienced by Refilwe—a subversive female character and an Oxford literature student dying of AIDS—the novel equates the moral malaise facing South Africa with the sexual hypocrisy that Hardy presents in *Jude the Obscure*. Although the South African constitution was hailed as the first in the world to recognize gay rights, the novel critiques the lack of material freedoms in the society itself. In their lived experiences, gay South Africans are discriminated against. Malignant myths circulate about their practice:

> Those who claimed to be informed—although none could admit to having seen or practiced it personally—said such sex was done anally. They also explained how it was done—dog style—to the disgust of most of the people of Tiragalong, who insisted that filth and sex should be two separate things. (4)

It would be wrong to argue that homosexual activities can be exempt from blame for the spread of HIV, but the text mocks the use of unsubstantiated myths about gay practices. The narrator distances himself from these popular myths by showing (as in the parenthetical element in the quotation above) that they are far from authoritative.

Later in the story, the narrator portrays a society that is aware of the fictionality of its claims and would wish certain factors were different to justify its conclusions: "Ah! This AIDS nonsense! I wish those girls and boys had more respect for their genitalia and did not leave them to do careless business in Hillbrow, only so that we can attribute the source of our dirges to Nigeria and Zaire and . . ." (20). Invoking writing and translation as figures of speech, the novel presents a society that combines xenophobia and homophobia to stereotype minorities and create myths about a condition threatening the population with decimation:

> But strange illnesses courted in Hillbrow, as Tiragalong knew only too well, could only translate into AIDS. This AIDS, *according to popular understanding*, was caused by foreign germs that travelled down from the central and Western parts of Africa. More specifically, certain newspaper articles attributed the source of the virus that caused AIDS to a species called the Green Monkey, which people in some parts of West Africa were said to eat as meat, thereby contracting the disease. . . . There were others [who] went further, saying that AIDS was caused by [the] bizarre sexual behaviour of the Hillbrowans . . . How could any man have sex with another man? They demanded to know. (4, emphasis added)

Here, Mpe sarcastically signals the ignorance of the community not only through the use of language associated with scholarship (for example, the use of the term *translate*) but also in his use of reporting clauses in sentences without direct speech and quotation marks. We are shown that even important institutions of knowledge production such as the media are complicit in spreading myths and fictions about AIDS. The narrator, confident that the addressee and the reader will agree with him, deconstructs the myths that society has created about foreigners and HIV. His voice and those of parochial members of society intersect to heighten the story's mockery of that group of people.

By parodying mainstream society without marking its words as different from his own in a sentence without direct speech, the narrator distances himself from the myths enunciated here by inserting the parenthetical clause "according to popular understanding," which attributes the AIDS myths to the ignorant community. The upgraded reporting clause "they demanded to know" heightens the mockery and conveys the narrator's outrage at the ignorance of a group of people who have made conclusions before considering any evidence. In showing how the society produces fictions to avoid the reality of AIDS, Mpe holds parochial identification up to ridicule. At the same time, the narrative is skeptical about the constructionist notions of identity that dominate postmodernism, which theorists of sexuality, from

Eve Kosofosky Sedgwick (1990) to David Halperin (2002) to Ross Chambers (2002), have criticized as obsolete and unproductive. Mpe's argument seems to be that while identities can be socially constructed, narrative should be used to consolidate identities in a way that liberates society, rather than to compound myths that fuel hatred and violence.

Pornography of the Oppressed?: K. Sello Duiker's Novels

Before he committed suicide at age thirty, South African journalist and screenwriter K. Sello Duiker (1974–2005) left behind two award-winning novels and a manuscript that would be published posthumously a year later.[31] The three novels are informed by a self-conscious mode of narration that disrupts traditional realism to address issues having to do with gender, sexuality, and cosmopolitanism in new South Africa. These novels reveal and awareness of other postrealist novels, especially the writing of Nigerian Ben Okri, which they recall in moments of oblique intertextuality or direct reference. The posthumous *The Hidden Star* (2006) is a more stylistically accomplished text in the way it uses myth and folklore to explore a transclass friendship between two girls in a South African township. But I would like to focus on his *thirteen cents* (2000) and *The Quiet Violence of Dreams* (2001) because of the different ways these two novels use metafictional devices to depict homosexuality in urban South Africa.

Although the principal character in *The Quiet Violence of Dreams*, Tshepo, claims that homophobia is a product of colonial modernity because homosexuality, to him, was a widely accepted practice in precolonial Africa, the novel as a whole seems to view homosexuality as an embodiment of a desired cosmopolitanism in postapartheid South Africa. For Tshepo, "it's stupid to even suggest that homosexuality and lesbianism are foreign to black culture" (Duiker 2001, 250), but his polemical stand is undermined by the overwhelmingly activist and unsubstantiated claims he makes throughout and the danger that he exposes himself to as a gay prostitute. The novel, while sympathetic to the gay plight, seems to satirize slapdash activism such as the one Tshepo stages. Nevertheless, the satirical tone of the novel does not fully rescue it from the unsubstantiated political and theoretical statements that Tshepo makes. At the end, it endorses the very masculinist ideology that it seeks to debunk, especially in Tshepo's attitude toward women and lesbianism. On the other hand, *thirteen cents* depicts the sexual abuse of a child at the hands of sodomites but indicates subtly that the victim might have to eventually accept homosexuality as his sexual orientation. A contrast of the two novels indicates that the metafictionality of the text is not in itself liberatory for all of the marginalized categories it presents, especially when the metafictional novel reverts to realist representation when voicing political opinions, as does *The Quiet Violence of Dreams* through its brash literature student from whose perspective the bulk of the story is told.

Although Mpe's *Welcome to Our Hillbrow* contains a few explicit descriptions of sex, it is usually through the consciousness of characters from whom it nudges us to disassociate, as they are being parodied by the unnamed narrator. Though not speaking directly to the readers, the characters are the ones who supposedly have made crude remarks about the assumed perverse sexuality of foreigners. For all the lyricism of some of the sentences, the scenes in which the main characters' sexual engagements are explicitly described are marked by irony because the narrator does not endorse the sexual philandering of these characters. Mpe's novel does not degrade the characters it describes in sexual entanglements; it seeks to signify their self-degradation in participating in sexual acts or stereotyping foreigners as the perverse Other. Not so Duiker's novels, in which pornographic reproduction is used as a textual means of political protest against both the Western canon and a parochial and homophobic nationalism.

While the novels we discussed in a previous chapter seize visual arts from the Western gaze that exoticizes African art as the Other, Duiker's novels, especially *The Quiet Violence of Dreams*, are projects in the "decolonization" of pornography. In the Western orientalist interpretation, Africa is a sexual object, and texts have been produced for a group of Westerners that Bernth Lindfors describes in "The Rise of African Pornography" as "jaded pornophiles who like a little exoticism with their eroticism" (67). This kind of fiction, Lindfors argues, "is interesting to us only as an imaginative projection, a phallic fantasy, a voyeur's voyage into the groin of Africa via the lubricious daydreams generated by the perverted muse of the Western world" (Lindfors 1973, 67). The Eurocentric perspective is subverted by African writers such as Dilibe Onyeama in *Sex Is a Nigger's Game* (1976), in which the diasporic African is not the victim of Western sexual aggression but the phallic conqueror of white women in Europe.[32] Duiker follows a similar route in wresting pornography from Westerners' gazing at Africa. But while earlier pornographic texts focused on the heterosexual exploits of the virile African male or the sly female prostitute, Duiker examines homosexuality as a subversive lifestyle in urban South Africa. My questions are these: Can pornography serve as a liberatory gesture, especially when the scenes marking it stand out because they are presented in representational language in a novel that is largely metafictional? And, does uttering a radical, sexually subversive message in metafictional conceits signify a welcome contribution to sexual liberation in postapartheid South Africa?

In the two novels I discuss here, Duiker treats taboo themes with varying degrees of postrealism to chaff at the moral hypocrisy of modern South

Africa and to signal emergent sexual identities in urban spaces. In discussing a taboo topic, Duiker challenges the traditional gender hierarchies, although he does not fully transcend the categorizations that he so acutely exposes for deconstruction. The first novel, *thirteen cents*, is simpler to read but subtler and more effective in its presentation of homosexual desire. In contrast, *The Quiet Violence of Dreams* is more dense in its prose, intertextuality, and learned references. A more difficult and defamiliarizing read, the novel has the basic characteristics of metafiction. In its spiral plotting, the text rejects chronological and developmental linearity to suggest that the shift from apartheid to majority rule in South Africa does not necessarily translate into liberation for certain individuals and minorities within the nation. Through the coiled textuality, the novel seems to be at once signifying its characters' foggy vision and groping for elusive liberation of sexually transgressive individuals and groupings. But it disappointingly presents homosexuality in bland, political statements that reduce its thematic impact.

On the whole, Duiker's fiction seems to echo the sentiment enunciated by Ugandan feminist Sylvia Tamale's "Out of the Closet: Unveiling Sexuality Discourses in Uganda" (2003), in which she shows how patriarchy exploits cultural traditions and modern laws to sustain gender hierarchy in African societies by enshrouding sexuality in secrecy and taboos. Tamale contends that issues such as homosexuality are prohibited in decent conversation for fear that the discussion of those issues would disrupt heterosexist privileges. While novels coming out of respected presses since the 1980s have covered taboo topics avoided by earlier novels or even revised them in later editions,[33] Duiker extends the metaphors of sexual violence to cover male same-sex rape and exploitation in narratives that will deconstruct traditional national essences. The city space he presents in surrealist prose celebrates the commingling of the national with the foreign, even as it recuperates the foreign that has been denigrated as an expression of all that is bad in new South Africa.

In *The Quiet Violence of Dreams*, Cape Town is seen as the ideal space where, despite poverty, gangsterism, and violence, Tshepo lives "with foreigners, illegal and legal immigrants, what black South Africans call makwerekwere with derogatory and defiant arrogance" (424). Like Mpe's narrative, Duiker's stories are impatient with nationalistic intolerance among black South Africans and go farther to reject transnational black associations, such as the Rasta movement, for their essentialist perspectives on race. The novel indicates that cultural essence and purity in the postcolonial era is an illusion that can only be performed at tourist venues; through the character Tshepo, Duiker's *The Quiet Violence of Dreams* suggests that this performance of cultural purism is itself an enactment of a fictional script because it involves an assemblage of cultural practices that tourists would consider authentic. More directly than Mpe, Duiker, paticularly in *The Quiet Violence of Dreams*, seems to be taking a position similar to Appiah's, that hybridity and other forms of cross-cultural engagements are inevitable in a cosmopolitan space. In *Cosmopolitanism*, Appiah reminds us that cultural purity, even when desired by some sections of the community, is impossible and that the term designating it is a contradiction:

> We do not need, have never needed, [a] settled community, a homogeneous system of values, in order to have a home. Cultural purity is an oxymoron. The odds are that, culturally speaking, you already live a cosmopolitan life, enriched by literature, art, and film that come from many places, and that contain influences from many more. (2006, 113)

The Quiet Violence of Dreams is a celebration of ethnic and racial impurities. Through his main character (Tshepo), Duiker distances himself from Afrocentric and antiwhite artistic practices, favoring a more cosmopolitan urban space where diverse races and sexual orientations coexist. The pursuit of authenticity is mocked as the easiest conduit of degenerative cultural fiction in the financial ignorant Western tourists.

At the same time, Duiker underlines that the Western pursuit of hybridity should consider the contribution of peripheral populations to the construction of mosaic cultural objects that form international culture. Although the polemics through which Tshepo utters his critical and theoretical literary statements to himself are bland, the novel manages to signal through Tshepo's center of consciousness as he observes the artistic objects and books on a gay friend's shelves that the Western arts, seen as the most revolutionary, were "a blatant type of artistic plagiarism" (280). It is not lost on the reader that the Western artistic objects copying African arts are in close proximity to "a large contingency of gay literature" (280). Through this conflation of objects via Tshepo's perspective, the novel registers that even gay desire is not alien to Africa, a position that the character repeats by insisting that homosexuality is authentically African, and that homophobia is a construction of modernity.

The main argument in Duiker's fiction is that postapartheid South Africa is guilty of causing some of the problems facing it, due to parochial and homophobic nationalism. Osita Ezeliora is correct, then, when he observes that "Duiker's vision is an implicit request that South Africans should confront their self-inflicted negative perception through a collective national reassessment of their humanity and moral identity rather than continually shifting blame to the imagined Other" (2005, 170). Instead of blaming the sordid conditions in South Africa on white and black foreigners, Duiker's novels, like Mpe's *Welcome to Our Hillbrow*, provoke postapartheid South Africans to see their complicity in producing an oppressive order and to try to transcend that order by embracing that which they have always supposed to be their opposite. Largely unarticulated directly, it is a "third" identity that can be grasped through a close study of speech. Duiker does not seek to universalize or minoritize homosexuality; he situates it as a complex practice with both negative and positive effects on individuals and social groups.

Duiker's novels emphasize that in an unjust society neither men nor women are spared the violence of rape. His *thirteen cents* is a narrative of urban decrepitude in South Africa, in which the reader is presented with squalid details of poverty, violence, drugs, and raw sex. It tells the story of Azure, a black boy, so named because of his blue eyes. The "thirteen" of the title signifies the boy's youth and the lowly earnings he nets from prostitution. Azure is discriminated against and sometimes envied for his blue eyes, a physiological pedigree of whiteness. He insists on his name being pronounced differently from the seemingly English spelling to underline his claim on a self-description that distinguishes him from the rest of the world. But this claim to independence is an illusion. The novel describes Azure's proclamation of adulthood with an intense sense of irony; there is a disjunction between his declaration that he is a mature man and the reality in which he dwells. In the short novel, Duiker starkly portrays the inhumanity of black people against fellow blacks and women against fellow women.

Yet like other narratives about racial violence and discrimination in South Africa, Duiker's novel envisions a Habermasian modernity in which racial antinomies are dissolved alongside apartheid. In making white and black commingle in Azure, Duiker seems set to construct a modernity that claims Africanness without negating other racial categories. Although Azure opens his first-person narrative by telling us that his name is pronounced differently from its English spelling, the name reminds the reader of Pecola Breedlove in Toni Morrison's *The Bluest Eye* (1970), a reference ironically affirmed when a gangster denies Azure his real name and identity and insists that he be called Blue. The story is rendered through the eyes of the thirteen-year-old child narrator observing the world of adults and expressing his own plight in postindependence South Africa. Azure's interaction with texts is limited to Western pop music, postmodern apparel, and brand-name footwear, and the surrealism he gives the novel's texture comes mainly from the naïveté of his point of view.

The novel's Cape Town setting enables it to explore the sexual underworld in a burgeoning urban space, where oppressed people are brutally exploited by the powerful, regardless of the race and gender of the latter. Informally addressing a street kid as its ideal embedded reader, the novel uses taboo words to express the world of violence in which Azure lives. He is sexually and financially exploited by almost everyone, and he naïvely registers the contradictions in his society. Duiker shows that rape is not a threat to women alone; men, too, can be subjects of sexual abuse by other men.[34] It is suggested in this novel of growing up that same-sex desire in adult males for young boys is a pathological reflection of the malaise facing postindependence African nations. The portrayal of the existence of such desire indicates that homosexuality is not completely unheard of in the postcolonies. But like Fanon's (1967) *Black Skin, White Masks*, Duiker's *thirteen cents* portrays homosexual desire as a pathological practice of white people; there is a very thin line between homosexuality and child abuse. Azure's enjoyment of gay sex is affected because he is a prostitute, and he confesses to the reader the revulsion he feels to the people with whom he sleeps.

Whether Fanon's evacuation of homosexuals from the Global South in *Black Skin, White Masks* is based on his inexperience with the discrete ways homosexuality is practiced in Africa and the Caribbean or on a heteronormative wish to cleanse the nation of perverse practices and by assigning those practices to the colonialist, the young narrator in *thirteen cents* demonstrates the existence of gays who may pass as the "he-men" Fanon claims to be the real identity of the men from Martinique who pass as homosexuals. Especially ruthlessly deconstructed in the novel is the heteronormative marriage institution, as the boy narrates his sexual experiences with married men:

> The married ones are always the horniest and by far the roughest. He takes me in his family mini-bus to a dark beach near the V&A Waterfront. We are the only ones parked there. He takes me to the backseat and oils me with cooking oil before he takes me like a beast. I bite the seat in front of me while he grunts and moans. He goes at it at least for an hour before he comes into a condom. (30)

The observation with which Azure opens his description indicates that this man is just one of the many married people with whom Azure has had sex. Earlier in the story he has given the reader a catalogue of different kinds of men that he has met, describing their desires with ironic details to reveal their hypocrisy and exploitative nature. The experience described in this scene, frightening as it is, is not the worst because others subject him to unprotected sex.

In Azure, Duiker creates a victim who is also a keen analyst of his society's hypocrisy. Duiker shows us through Azure that the adults he sleeps with are pedophiles. Unlike in Abani's and Iweala's novels, where the sodomites are African men who epitomize the degradation and defilement of the nation, replacing the traditional presentation of the nation as a woman to accentuate the horror of disillusionment with postindependence politics in Africa, the sodomites in Duiker's *thirteen cents* are whites. In presenting Azure's victimizers as white males, it is possible that Duiker, who illustrates a few Fanonist theses in his work, is following Fanon's argument in *Black Skin, White Masks*, that a "Negrophobic man is a repressed homosexual" (1967, 156). But the novel aspires to a postracial society, and it suggests that the sexual relationships are more economic than racial. Azure's sexual victimizers are not presented as racists; he also is exploited, though not necessarily sexually, by people across racial lines. Furthermore, racist epithets are heard from nonwhite people who are uncomfortable with Azure's blue eyes.

Duiker's *thirteen cents* is on the surface homophobic in the way it conflates economic exploitation with sodomy, such as Armah's *Two Thousand Seasons* (1973) or Marechera's *The Black Insider* (1992). But toward the end, *thirteen cents* makes a move that would recuperate homosexuality as perhaps the only option for Azure despite his protests that he is not gay. In this moment in the narrative, it is suggested that either Azure, has been fully converted to homosexuality against his will, or that he has been gay all of his life. Delving into his own unconscious and revealing it to the reader, Azure says that he has never had a dream about heterosexual love and has lied to conform to the expectations of the other boys:

> I never dream of doing it with a woman. I'm not a moffie. One bastard once asked me if I was a moffie. And I told him I was not a moffie. But strange that I never dream of doing it with a woman, not even beautiful Toni Braxton. And the other guys are always saying it happens to them. I just lie about it and say it happens to me too, even though it never has. But this doesn't worry me too much. It worries me that I have never done it with a woman, and that I've only been doing it with men, even though I don't like them. (146)

Though he claims he is not a "moffie" (Cape Town slang for an effeminate/gay man), Azure is worried that gay inclinations might be ingrained in him, despite his wish to be straight.[35] Duiker here is not jumping on the constructionist bandwagon in sexuality studies, which argues that sexual identity is a construction by social and cultural factors. It might appear that Azure becomes gay because of the abuse he suffered as a kid in a pedophilic nation, but what Duiker seems to be stressing is that Azure can do little to change his emerging sexuality, whether inborn or constructed. He becomes gay because of a confluence of forces, including the environment (abuse) and biology (manifested by his feminine features). The story does not follow Azure's life beyond age thirteen, and there is little indication that his homosexual inclinations will change either for him or for the society in which he dwells. By situating the homosexuality in the unconscious, where it is censored from the conscious mind, the novel emphasizes that Azure has little choice in his sexuality. He can only suppress that which the environment, and perhaps his biology, has imposed on him. Thus one can say that the novel stages for homosexuality what Ross Chambers (2002) calls a "strategic constructivism," in the sense that it is not interested in delving into the social or environmental factors that lead to Azure's or his victimizers' homosexuality; rather, it is more focused on showing the role of homosexuality in the world and how it is exploited by the powerful to marginalize it even farther.

But although Azure is a child victimized by perverted male desire in *thirteen cents*, Tshepo, in Duiker's *The Quiet Violence of Dreams*, is at a later point in life a willing participant in alternative urban sexuality. Tshepo is sodomized as a kid by men hired by his father to rape and kill his mother. He is later gang-raped by his gay lover and the man's friends. Traumatized by these events, Tshepo suffers a mental breakdown and is hospitalized for drug-induced psychosis. Duiker uses the mental asylum to which Tshepo is confined to offer—as R. D. Laing, David Cooper, and Michel Foucault have—a liberationist critique of institutionalized psychiatry; the novel presents the institution as punitive of its own staff members, some of whom are portrayed as being as mentally unstable as their patients. The hospital is a site of brutality and dehumanization, and the critique of its practices in *The Quiet Violence of Dreams* conforms to the subversive tone that structures this narrative about urban sexuality.

Upon his release from the mental hospital, Tshepo shares an apartment with an ex-prisoner, but their relationship deteriorates with time. Desperate for income, Tshepo becomes a gay prostitute using the pseudonym Angelo. The mental instability of its central characters, their literary backgrounds, and the unorthodox practices around which the novel revolves combine to give the narrative a playful, surreal aura. *The Quiet Violence of Dreams* appears to be provoking the reader by mentioning what it considers unpalatable, while at the same time inserting the politics of canonization in its discourse, its main character being a socially rebellious student of fiction, drama, and poetry who loves cryptic narratives. The novel has sexually explicit descriptions and speeches that go against the grain of earlier foundational narratives but that, as I argue later, reduce the novel's effectiveness.

Mmbatho, Tshepo's female friend who has sex with women, is opposed to the canon. Her diatribe against "Shakespeare and other dead white writers" is an expression of the novel's disenchantment with the censored and established writing traditions:

> I take a taxi to town to attend a meeting at the Drama Department. There have been rumours about cutbacks of government subsidies and laying off of a few staff members. For us students it translates into fewer productions, which usually means doing less experimental work and more Shakespeare and other dead white writers that please the establishment. (178)

The novel's insistence on the inevitably hybrid nature of Cape Town, and its consistent deconstruction of racial and psychic dichotomies, indicates that it would not reject Shakespeare for being white; rather, it is more disappointed with the looming curtailment of experimental art.

In *The Quiet Violence of Dreams* Duiker tries to signify a sense of identity that goes beyond the South African nation and beyond racial divides to offer a layered examination of violence and postapartheid identities. The novel contains multiple intersecting narratives told in the first-person narrative voices of various characters as unmediated discourse. This stylistic choice enhances the novel's stated desire for a world free from control and imprisonment by social structures, some of which have all the weaknesses of the subjects they seek to treat and recover. Through the figure of the mental facility where Tshepo, the main character, is placed after he suffers a mental breakdown, the novel portrays imprisonment by social structures and norms as destructive not only to the victims but also to those charged with maintaining dominant practices. The asylum destroys its patients more than it benefits them, and the psychologists themselves suffer from the psychic illnesses they claim to be fighting.

The novel, then, is opposed to purism and welcomes the cultural mosaic that Cape Town is developing into. Its attitude toward "dead white writers" is not, then, an expression of opposition to Europe and whiteness per se. Through Mmbatho, the novel criticizes the new establishment in the universities for not only ignoring new writing but also for focusing on mechanical and scientific subjects as opposed to the arts: "They need scientists and mathematicians first, Andrew says, and a low discordant groaning goes out. How can you build a nation without telling its stories, someone says poignantly?" (178). It seems that Duiker's project is to write contemporary history, giving voice to those nationalist narratives have silenced.

According to the novel, the existence of homosexuality in contemporary Africa is a fact that we have to come to terms with. Tshepo eventually understands homosexuality as a human practice, not limited to a single race;

gay people also are capable of all of the human foibles that plague the rest of the society, including racism:

> I feel depressed and disillusioned, naïve for ever fooling myself that gay people are different. They are white people before they are gay, I tell myself bitterly. . . . Someone just tore a beautiful image I had in my mind. It is offensive, even ludicrous, to imagine that a gay person can be prejudiced when we live with so much fear and prejudice. It is a rude awakening. You are black. You will always be black. (343)

Tshepo tries to reclaim his identity from the superficiality of postmodern slippage, unaware that he is constructed by the very social circumstances from which he wants to run away. It is instructive to remember Jameson's warning in *The Political Unconscious* (1981), that even dialectical reversal involves a "painful 'decentering' of the consciousness of the individual subject, whom it confronts with a determination . . . that must necessarily be felt as extrinsic or external to conscious experience" (1981, 283). Tshepo thinks that he can master his Cape Townian identity while celebrating its multiplicity. For him, there are qualities that cannot be easily dispensed with because they are physical and biological; however, these idiosyncrasies peculiar to Cape Town should not be allowed to stand in the way of any form of freedom.

The novel rejects superficial interventions to bridge social division, especially if those interventions ignore the materiality of existence. Despite Tshepo's celebration of essence, he deconstructs the traditional beliefs that constrain human agency. He makes choices that run counter to expectations, but he cannot escape fully the past or the present that still prefers a socially sanctioned sexual orientation. His homosexuality, causally linked to his traumatic childhood, is constantly mentioned in the story, but it is after being raped in his adulthood in a society that silences male rape that Tshepo chooses to be a gay prostitute. The novel provokes the reader to see gay sexuality as a choice and not a mere adolescent experimentation, as presented in Mark Behr's *The Smell of Apples* (1995), in which the blued-eyed narrator, Marnus, engages in homosexual activity as a way of rejecting his sequestered, middle-class origins. Marnus's action contrasts markedly with the circumstance of Duiker's Azure in the sense that the latter character is forced into homosexuality by poverty. While we see in Tshepo a person's background as instrumental in shaping his or her sexuality, the novel insists that sexual orientation can be a choice. Sexuality is so much of a choice that although the female character, Mmbatho, has had interracial sexual encounters with an Asian woman with whom she occasionally meets, she does not consider herself a lesbian.

The epistemological binaries that Sedgwick (1990) observes as necessary to distinguish heterosexual norms from disruptive homosexuality are turned upside down in *The Quiet Violence of Dreams*. Duiker shows homosexual desire to pervade the society in repressed forms that turn brutally violent when given the chance to vent themselves. As the novel ends, it collapses the dichotomy between Tshepo and Angelo, his fictitious "Other." His identity slides neatly into African mythology, in which Tshepo sees himself as the Egyptian god Horus, a dancer and a painter. Directly citing the works by Ben Okri and Wole Soyinka—and seemingly abandoning imitation of phallic pre-Raphaelite art and opposition to Western canon—Tshepo foresees great hope for the African continent and the marginalized groups within it. The intricate intertextuality echoes Tshepo's cosmopolitan ethics; his ethnic identity is blurred, and he contests xenophobia and racism. The novel endorses homosexuality as the quintessential identity for the new cosmopolitan black South African male.

Belonging to the sub-genre of the African novel that focuses on the postcolonial student of English,[36] *The Quiet Violence of Dreams* conjoins creative writing with subtle literary commentary. The aesthetic is equated to the homoerotic, especially by "Angelo," Tshepo's identity, based on mystical pre-Raphaelite aesthetics, in the underworld gay community:

> To love a man? It is like feeling the roaring ocean inside you. It is like knowing the source of the north wind. It is like getting your reward at the top of the mountain, a breathtaking panorama. It is like running with wild horses, panting with excitement. It is like deep sea diving, with the water below being perfectly clear. It is like walking on the beach naked, sun licking your sweat. It is like falling backwards laughing after realizing there is nothing to fear. . . . To explore a man's body? It is like getting to know your own shadow intimately. It is like being a child again. It is like playing with fire without getting burned. It is like snowboarding without drugs, with skill as your high. It is like skiing in your own backyard . . . It is like rollerblading on the highway. It is like white water rafting the Zambezi. To love a man is not like loving a woman . . . To be with a man, to feel his strength. It is like a road whose twists and bends you know well . . . To know a man. It is like serenading yourself and all men . . . Oh, the infinite beauty of a man and his penis. (334–35)

The anaphoric parallelism with which Angelo praises homosexuality indicates artificial rhetoricity on his part and his blindness to the dangers to which he is exposing himself by protesting against "bigots, hypocrites, hetero-fascists who only want to further their own prejudices and intolerance of life" (334).

Instead of affirming his identity, Tshepo appears to be more interested in negating its opposite by performing different acts of alternative sexuality, including sadomasochism.

Although he manages to register his rejection of heterosexuality as the norm, Tshepo's main weakness lies in his reactive predisposition. Raped and sexually abused as a child, Tshepo is now responding to the world in an equally self-destructive manner. Invested in idealizing male homosexuality, the novel contains insidious misogynistic descriptions of women. Like the Lacanian infant who sets up mechanisms of identification with objects outside of himself—objects, other people, and the image in the mirror—Tshepo struggles to apprehend his own homosexuality by setting up binaries against which he can define himself, even if those oppositions are unfair to equally marginalized groups. He hates himself and the other sexual groups he looks down upon. He seems to recognize the unity between them and the female homosexuals he stereotypes. We might be tempted to criticize the character's view and justify the text as critiquing Tshepo's worldview. However, there is little aesthetic distance between Tshepo and the author, especially in the way women characters are presented. Mmbatho, the principal female character in the novel, comes through as a flat, stereotypical woman whose main role is to incubate and mother Tshepo.[37] She is devastated when her German lover is taken from her by Angelo, who is portrayed as a better sexual partner.

Told mainly from the perspective of Tshepo, whose agenda is to make a case for male homosexuality, sections that treat the theme of homosexuality in *The Quiet Violence of Dreams* fail to see the positive aspects of women's sexuality and ignore women's sexual responses:

> There is something comical about watching a woman having sex. They are let go completely. Really, it makes me laugh. I have [to hold] myself back as I watch her face twisted in comical expressions, moaning about things that only she knows about. I thrust quicker and deeper into her. Her expression becomes too much. (333)

The saving grace here is Tshepo's acknowledgment that he is ignorant about women's sexuality. Earlier his underlying misogyny is exposed because he is obsessed with gay men as opposed to gay women (254). But he still sees the lesbian as playing the traditional role of nurturer in passages that remind one of Catherine Acholonu's (1995) statements on motherism. Tshepo idealizes the lesbian as the new Mother Africa when he says: "Women's role is going to be greater than men's because society will revert to a reference for the earth mother" (254). As a gay male invested in reacting to heteronormativity and exposing its fundamental weaknesses, Tshepo fails to genuinely empathize with equally suppressed groups merely because they happen to be heterosexual. But through references to art, the novel hints of an optimistic future for alternative sexuality.

Issues of sexuality are brought forth through a hybrid narrative in which binaries are problematized and art is invoked to privilege the silenced gay male. At one point, Armah's *The Beautyful Ones Are Not Yet Born* (1968) is invoked as Tshepo's favorite novel. It is remarkable that the character around whom the narrative revolves is "rereading" (177) Armah's equally explicit novel. This signals its affiliation with the literature of disillusionment, especially with the status quo in newly independent nations. The "rereading" is located mainly in the hope that *The Quiet Violence of Dreams* generates. Tshepo is the Shona word for hope, and his survival against all odds moves the novel away from the pessimism of Armah's *The Beautyful Ones Are Not Yet Born*. Like Armah's *Osiris Rising* (1995), in which the phallus is invoked as the symbol of hope for societal regeneration, Duiker's *The Quiet Violence of Dreams* evokes African spirituality through references to the Egyptian god Horus, whom a regenerated Tshepo-Angelo uses as a personal icon to affirm his identity. While Armah uses Osiris as an icon of heterosexual phallic virility, Duiker deploys the son of the god as an icon of the homoerotic future. Hope resides not in raging against the adversary but in understanding where his "greatest treasures lie" (457). Seeing himself as an artist-God, Tshepo realizes, as the novel closes, that his greatest strengths "are within me."

Desire for More Figurative Discourse

In conclusion, we have seen in this chapter that contrary to the popular view that homosexuality is not an important issue in African discourses of identity, it has preoccupied a sizeable number of novelists writing in the postrealist mode. Even though Michel Foucault, despite the self-consciousness of his *The History of Sexuality*, is skeptical about the assumed agency of self-reflexivity that serves as "a shimmering mirage" (1981, 59), African novels that use metafiction as a mode of expression reveal self-reflexivity as both an articulation of the existence of the gay lifestyle and a marker of social constraints regarding alternative sexuality. Just as novels critical of dictatorships use indirect style to textualize the denial of the freedom to express oneself directly, metafiction is used in novels dealing with homosexuality to unmask the need to break out of the heteronormative limitations and the limitations facing agents trying to enact that unmasking.

The novels portray homosexuality as a practice that can only be expressed in self-reflexive jokes and figurative terms that performatively augment its suppression. Thus metafiction, as a nonrealist form, serves to highlight both the collective subjection of the society to heteronormative sex and serves also as an avenue through which the subaltern sexual orientation indicates its suppressed presence and struggles to emerge from the margins. Even if we are not to see homosexuality as the desirable practice that Foucault maintains it to be, the writers urge society to speak about it more openly and to critique its suppression.

Paradoxically, when metafictional novels use realist modes to treat homosexuality in an activist advocacy stance, they tend to weaken their effect. When the novel speaks against homophobia, one would hope that it does so in a more figurative discourse that is as stylistically subtle as the one employed to present other themes. Novels such as Duiker's *The Quiet Violence of Dreams* (2001) or Ghalib Shiraz Dhalla's *Ode to Lata* (2002), by using metafiction to treat other themes, project and name homosexuality openly and in representational forms as a means of reclaiming its space as an alternative sexual identity in the referential world. While the writers' alignment with pornographic language is perhaps a strategy of protest or of "writing back" to the literatures that erase homosexual desire or veil it in subtexts, it nevertheless risks creating the impression that homosexuality is simple, singular, and straightforward.

Furthermore, when the novels describe scenes of homosexual practice in a representational mode, and the rest in metafictional mode, they create a sense of bravura that entrenches the conventional belief that homosexuality is a monstrous and abnormal lifestyle that can only be talked about in a false show of bravery. A more indirect way of expressing the complexity and elusiveness of homosexual desire—as metafictionally staged by Soyinka's *The Interpreters* (1965) and Njau's *Ripples in the Pool* (1975) and *The Sacred Seed* (2003)—would, to me, be far more rhetorically effective than activist attempts to name and represent gay politics. To be sure, the conflation of madness with gay desire not only offers writers such as Njau and Duiker possibilities of experimentation with narrative to figure the neurotic state of the characters presented, but it also suggests that such identities are suppressed in society and can only come out in moments of audacity. The two novels by Njau, published almost three decades apart, indicate change in the way female homosexuality is presented. *The Sacred Seed* is much more sympathetic. *Ripples in the Pool* used metafiction to accentuate the disorientation of the lesbian character while subtly recuperating her as a victim of an intolerant society. *The Sacred Seed* not only indicts heteronormativity as complicit with rape and despotism, but it also shows female-female bonding to go beyond the corporeal to encompass economic and diasporic interests to improve the lives of women in Africa.

Sigmund Freud infamously linked narcissistic tendencies to women and homosexuals, viewing self-reflexivity and gay inclinations in pathological terms.[38] The correlation between metafiction and the figuring of homosexuality are apparent. The novels do not use self-reflexivity exclusively to present gay lifestyles. They exploit the possibilities of metafiction to portray gay issues, especially by referring to earlier texts that would provoke the reader to situate discourse within a homosexual context. Yet not all metafictional texts welcome gay identities, as exemplified by Armah's *Two Thousand Seasons* (1973)—in which homosexuality is associated with foreign predatory habits and local betrayal of indigenous agency—or Ngũgĩ's intensely metafictional *Wizard of the Crow* (2006), where, in passages absent from the English translation, Ngũgĩ associates some of the most repulsive characters with repressed homosexuality.[39] In most of the cases where homosexuality is referred to, it is not for the purpose of overthrowing heterosexuality but of exposing its contradictions. These novels suggest that homosexuality is not transhistorical; it is contingent, and its practitioners cannot be excused from the primary human duty of protecting equally underprivileged and marginalized groups.

Finally, I must state that even when writers have not presented homosexuality in their works, the more progressive among them have distanced themselves from the pervasive homophobia in their societies. A case in point is novelist and poet Marjorie Macgoye, who has adopted a liberal position on homosexuality in her essays, although her fiction's plots are energized by heterosexual relations. These relations may not flourish, but they never become homosexual. As Roger Kurtz argues in his apt analysis of Macgoye's work, *Nyarloka's Gift* (Kurz 2005), this Kenyan writer of English ancestry has called for retention of African institutions such as motherhood, to which mainstream Western feminists seem hostile. To her, in a modern Africa where sex and procreation are no longer tightly linked, homosexuality can no longer be called "unnatural." She openly argues that homosexuality should be legalized:

> It is surely better to acknowledge consenting adult behaviour, homosexual or heterosexual, than to drive it underground and risk mystification, blackmail, and violence. Where homosexual relations are against the law, people who do not feel that they are committing sin have to conceal them. This makes them easy targets for blackmail. It also makes them insecure and so prone to violence against people they feel are snooping on them or trying to provoke them. Sometimes it tempts them to seek under-age partners. (Macgoye 1996, 34)

This is a fairly radical position for a writer whose novels are based on conservative family values and to whom "abortion is murder" (Macgoye 1996, 38). Kurtz observes that Macgoye's view on homosexuality may have been influenced by her friendship with Jonathan Kariara. Kariara (1935–1993) is a poet and publisher whose work never treated the theme of homosexuality, although there are many hints in the poems and short stories of the insecurities of heterosexual unions and the alienation of the unmarried individual.[40] Macgoye's position definitely marks a break from the norm-guarding writers. Respect for family values and motherhood should not translate into the insensitive treatment of homosexuals or the denial of gay rights. The next chapter offers a synthetic summary of African feminist positions of family, motherhood, and homosexuality as a way of recalibrating the theory of African literature.

Chapter 8

Gendered Theoretical Recalibrations

This brief chapter tries to come to terms with the neglect of formal properties of African literature, the disregard for gender issues in postcolonial readings of African literature, and the obsession with the "writing back to the center" paradigm in the reading of literatures from the Global South. I further provide a synthetic summary of African women's statements on gender as a way of undoing the systematic silencing of African theories of gender. I focus on self-conscious, theoretical statements by African students of gender, whom postcolonial scholarship has largely ignored in its consideration of African culture.

John Guillory accurately observes in *Cultural Capital* (1993) that the incorporation of non-Western texts into Western humanities departments in the late 1960s coincided with the rise of deconstruction, which became the synonym for "literary theory," thus excluding feminist and other political voices in favor of textualist preoccupations. I specifically take issue with the foreclosure of African feminist theorists, whose meditations on gender relations have been silenced. The growth of African criticism may not have caught up with the proliferation of writing from the continent, but there are womanist voices that need to be taken into account if we are to apprehend the general perception of gender in African societies.

Overdramatizing the Margins

Ashcroft and colleagues (2002) adopted the phrase "writing back" from a 1982 newspaper article by Salman Rushdie in *The Times* (London) reporting on the conference of Asian writers on the weekend of the first week in July 1982. It is useful to dwell for a moment on this article because, although it is frequently relegated to footnotes or taken as a given in postcolonial studies, it serves as a palimpsest of the "writing back to the center" paradigm. The title of the article ("The Empire Writes Back with a Vengeance") is itself a pun on the popular American movie *Star Wars: The Empire Strikes Back*. It appears that the editor's pun on Rushdie's tongue-in-cheek reference to "the empire striking back" changes the conventional meaning of "writes back" (responding to a letter) to connote a retaliation or riposte to Western literature.[1] It usually goes unmentioned in postcolonial theories that describe non-Anglo-Saxon aesthetics as an antinomic rejection of the West that the underlying argument in Rushdie's article is that language use by immigrant and postcolonial writers in English is not equivalent to rejection or deformation of the English language or of metropolitan culture; rather, Rushdie foresees the extension and revitalization of the English language by diasporic and postcolonial writers operating within the frontiers of the English language. He highlights the insertion of local dialects and indigenous languages such as the Gĩkũyũ language used by Ngũgĩ wa Thiong'o to express indigenous perspectives rather than to assault Western aesthetics. In effect, Rushdie is celebrating an aesthetics in which writers from the non-Western world, whether writing in or translated into English, "infuse English with new rhythms, new histories, new angles on the world" to offer perspectives other than the mainstream Anglo-Saxon point of view (1982, 8).[2]

The impression of rebellion and insurgency against the West foregrounded by postcolonial theory is articulated less in Rushdie's article itself than in its more graphologically visible paratexts—the bold-type headline and the caption accompanying photos of three of the many wrtiers mentioned in the article. The caption lumps together Samuel Beckett, James Baldwin, and V. S. Naipaul as "rebels" against the classical Anglo-Saxon tradition. At the graphological level, gender is erased; the focus is on male writers, even though the article mentions prominent women novelists such as Nadine Gordimer and Toni Morrison. Although the article is tucked away on page eight of the paper and positioned in the right-hand corner of the broadsheet, away from the page's focal point, the page layout, the headline, the pull quote, and the photo captions reveal a desire to capture the reader's attention by dramatizing the difference between Anglo-Saxon writers and writers from colonial outposts. Hidden in the subtext is the xenophobia that informs the caption and the headline, in which non-native English language writers, regardless of their ideology, are presented as "rebels." The reader is expected to feel threatened. In Beckett's photo, placed above the other two, his gaze is slightly averted from the block of text containing Rushdie's words, as if to signal to the reader that, despite Rushdie's claims in the article, Beckett himself does not belong among that category of writers who Rushdie characterizes as "writing back." Read in relation to the photographic representation of Beckett, Naipaul's and Baldwin's photographs come through as more relevant to the story. Suggested by this positioning is that nonwhite writers such as Naipaul and Baldwin are the ones who best epitomize the postcolonial "writing back."

Seeming to follow the copy editor's paratextual cue, postcolonial theorists in Western academies overdramatize difference by subconsciously literalizing the idiomatic expression in the title, *writing with a vengeance* (writing with great force and energy), to connote writing in pursuit of revenge.[3] In a later essay in which he echoes some of the phrases he uses in *The Times* article, Rushdie reveals his discomfort with the "writing back to the center" theory: "I don't think it is always necessary to take up the anti-colonial—or is it post-colonial?—cudgels against English. What seems to me to be happening is that those peoples who were once colonized by language are now rapidly remaking it, domesticating it, becoming more and more relaxed about the way they use it—assisted by the English language's enormous flexibility and size, they are carving out large territories for themselves within its frontiers" (1991, 64). While I would be reluctant to celebrate English as the most important language for decolonizing non-Western cultures as Rushdie does here, I am suspicious of over-dramatized difference that seems to fascinate the Western academy. This perception of difference reinstates the West as the center of inquiry.[4]

Granted, "writing back," as used in some postcolonial theory, has more nuanced meanings than sheer antinomy between Africa and the West. Borrowing the term *counterdiscourse* from Richard Terdiman (1985), Helen Tiffin has stressed the intricate and dynamic qualities of the dialogue between peripheral and metropolitan texts: The operation of postcolonial counterdiscourse is dynamic, not static: it does not seek to subvert the dominant with a view to taking its place, but to, in Wilson Harris's formulation, "evolve textual strategies which continually 'consume' their '*own* biases' at the same time as they expose and erode those of the dominant discourse" (Tiffin 1987, 18, emphasis in original). In fact, in her reading of Jean Rhys's counterdiscursive revision of Bronte's *Jane Eyre* (1947) in the novel *Wide Sargasso Sea* (1966), Tiffin does not seek to show the two novels as radically antithetic to each other.[5] Counterdiscourse, in Terdiman's terms, emerges as a form of symbolic resistance in which canonical texts are inevitably reinscribed in the new texts that subvert them. Thus in the postcolonial context envisioned by Ashcroft and colleauges (2002), "counterdiscourse" involves rewriting metropolitan texts in a way that marks the new texts as permeated by that which they resist. However, overall, the most dominant interpretation of "writing back" and "counterdiscourse" is that postcolonial literature is a project of insurrection against the West.

But are there other forms of "counterdiscourse" in which *local* texts permeate and deconstruct one another? I submit that Tiffin is too rushed in her dismissal of the persistence of "the national or the regional" in postcolonial literatures. As we have already seen, African texts are much more in dialogue with one another than with Western art. Intriguingly, despite Tiffin's insistence on a multidirectional border crossing, the general subtext running through the "writing back to the center" discourse implies that African literature treats European culture and aesthetics with menace. Even a perceptive critic such as Sara Suleri sees postcolonial literatures as "reactive," despite her position against binary oppositions that produce monolithic interpretations of texts and culture. Suleri is right in her assertion that if we are to understand postcolonialism, we should consider the "multiplicity of histories that are implicated in its emergence" (1992b, 21), but non-Western literature is not necessarily a repercussive counter-discourse in which Western categories are the primary objects of denunciation, retaliation, or mimicry.

Indigenous Theorists and "Writing Back" to Europe

Oyekan Owomoyela (2002) succinctly observes that the criticism and theorizing of African literature by African critics have not achieved the same prestige as the literature itself, despite the fact that there have been important developments in African criticism since the 1980s. Reading a small set of African novels by women writers, postcolonial theory has developed since its inception in the 1980s a penchant to either ignore African critical statements on gender or to dismiss them as inconsequential. Despite a growing body of womanist criticism by African women,[6] postcolonial theory as practiced in the West seems to assume that Africans can provide the raw materials for theorizing gender and sexuality, but that they are not capable of theorizing the subject. For example, in *The Empire Writes Back*, Ashcroft and colleagues (2002) offer acute insights into the main issues in African literary theories and the vexed and tentative relationship between postcolonial theory and feminism, but they leave out gender as an analytical category in African literary theorizing. When the African study of gender is acknowledged in this text, it is in novels, such as Buchi Emecheta's, that seem to be serving as raw material for the Western critical industry. In other cases, any non-Western gender theory is seen as applicable to the African situation, with critics prioritizing the West-East dyad. In Tina Chanter's *Gender: Key Concepts in Philosophy* (2007), for instance, the conflicts between Western and postcolonial theorizing of gender are seen in terms of an East-West typology, while John McLeod's *Beginning Postcolonialism* (2000) and Bart Moore-Gilbert's *Postcolonial Theory* (1997) include well-argued statements on gender and postcolonialism, but while noting the need to consider feminist positions from non-Western cultures as a way of avoiding false universalizations when speaking about Third World women, they occlude African theorizations of gender.

Yet gender is at the heart of African politics. Achille Mbembe notes in "Ways of Seeing: Beyond the New Nativism—Introduction" that "sex and gender norms have historically been central to the structure of power relations and to the organization of cultural categories in Africa" (2001b, 7). But while the performance and representation of sex form a vital part of Mbembe's understanding of the grotesque, gender is a peripheral issue in Mbembe's analyses of state power. To dismiss African feminism as a practice in "notorious," "philosophical poverty" the way Mbembe does in his "On the Power of the False" (2002b) is to fail to appreciate the nuanced dialogues that African feminists have staged with both philosophical and feminist texts from across global divides. Mbembe joins mainstream postcolonial theory in silencing the positions of indigenous African theorists when he dismisses them without identifying or discussing the supposed philosophical weaknesses of the theorists' arguments.

Contrary to popular misconception, African feminist statements are neither necessarily anti-Western nor obsessed with duplicating Western feminism. Indeed, Rosemary Marangoly George (2006) observes that, since the 1980s, feminist postcolonial theory has moved away from examining the distortion of "Third World" feminism in Western discourses in order to focus more on the representation of the female subject in "Third World" texts and on how subaltern female intersubjectivity is recovered in texts about women in non-Western spaces. Because non-Western cultural categories are seen, to use Olakunle George's apt term, as "contrastive enablers" of the Western meditation on its specific condition in modernity (2003, 30), African notions of gender are presented as the Other of Western feminism without attention being given to the specificity and diversity of theoretical statements. Yet to conceive non-Western feminism as a contrary axiomatic to Western feminism is to fail to see the interdetermined and interdetermining relationships between the two categories of thought and practice. A leading African feminist from Nigeria, Obioma Nnaemeka, has warned against the tendency to conceptualize African feminism in terms of how it is different from practices and theories from the West:

> A major flaw of feminists to tame and name the feminist spirit in Africa is their failure to define African feminism *on its own terms* rather than in the context of Western feminism. Such a contexualization of African feminism argues in effect that African feminism is what Western feminism is not. In other words, that African feminism establishes its identity through its

> resistance—it *is* because it resists. (Nnaemeka 1998a, 6, emphasis in original)

Here Nnaemeka echoes Mohanty (1991), who argues that the color of one's skin and one's nationality are not, in themselves, a solid basis for identitarian resistance. Feminism in Africa should be a transnational intervention based on reciprocity and negotiation because, for Nnaemeka, "the language of African feminism is less a response to the language of Western feminism and more a manifestation of the characteristics (balance, connectedness, reciprocity, compromise, etc.) of the African worldview as demonstrated in the encoding in many African languages of gender-neutral, third-person singular pronouns whose etymologies are mindful of gender neutrality and balance" (Nnaemeka 1998a, 9). Although Nnaemeka tends to suppress the separatist voices (those that call for the exclusion of white women from Africana womanist intervention, or advocate nonheterosexual relationships), what she clearly stresses throughout her work is that Africa does not construct its identity from resistance to the West.[7]

Nkiru Nzegwu, in *Family Matters* (2006), and Oyèrónkẹ́ Oyewùmi, in *The Invention of Women* (1997), argue that precolonial African societies were ungendered. Ogunyemi (1996) documents that the organizing principle in the Oyo Yoruba culture of Nigeria was seniority, not gender, while Nzegwu sees as a gross distortion of the portrayal of precolonial Ibo society as patriarchal, even in postcolonial novels such as Chinua Achebe's *Things Fall Apart* (1958). Nzegwu particularly criticizes the feminist assumption that African societies are patriarchal, and that they are defined by "a history and tradition of gender oppression" (2006, 13). However, despite Oyewùmi's and Nzegwu's sustained contention that the particular precolonial societies they discuss were ungendered, and that we should examine them outside of the feminist framework, the two theorists acknowledge that colonial modernity distorted the traditional relationships between men and women, and that the study of unequal power relations should not be abandoned. We may add that while the study of ungendered societies in precolonial Africa is in itself fascinating, the present is intensely gendered. These gender hierarchies, and their deconstruction, are manifest in the fiction and arts of African modernity.

The problem that most African female scholars have with "Western feminism" (often perceived as radical, lesbian, and anti-motherhood) is its failure to consider the historical and social specificities in which African women struggle to determine their individual and collective destinies. On the whole, African feminisms cannot be characterized as negating feminisms from other parts of the world but as reclaiming the defamiliarizing local differences that underline the uniqueness of African experiences. Emphasizing plurality, Nnaemeka asserts that "to meaningfully explain the phenomenon called African feminism, it is not to Western feminism but rather to the African environment that one must refer. African feminism is not reactive; it is proactive. It has a life of its own that is rooted in the African environment. Its uniqueness emanates from the cultural and philosophical specificity of its provenance" (Nnaemeka 1998a, 9). In coining the term *nego-feminism* to designate an African analysis of gender that is malleable and accommodative, Nnaemeka uses Mbembe's notion of a historically instantiated configuration of positions within a given space, which Mbembe elaborates in "At the Edge of the World" (2000), to enable her to create an adaptive feminism that is "goal-oriented, cautious, accommodating, adaptable, and open to diverse views" (2003, 382). Like most African feminists, Nnaemeka highlights the importance of considering contexts in which even the most inimical patriarchal practices, such as female genital cutting, are not approached in an insurrectionary and a Western salvationist mind-set that further dehumanizes African women.[8]

It must be noted that the option for confrontation is not foreclosed in African feminism, but, as Nnaemeka (1998b, 369) stresses, dialogue is to be given priority over insurgency. Some at the first Women in Africa and Diaspora (WAAD) conference in Nsukka, Nigeria, called for the exclusion of men and white women, but Nnaemeka interprets gender in cultural rather than biological terms.[9] Men and white women can be co-opted to uplift the welfare of African women. This does not mean that rebellion is ruled out. According to Nnaemeka, if dialogue proves ineffective, then African women can consider insurgency against men and white women as a strategy of resistance. Most African students of gender do not feel that they have reached this stage, and despite their skepticism toward the Western agenda, their approach to gender equality is not "writing back" or theoretical insurgency. Nnaemeka's form of feminism is dynamic in a way that would fragment and decenter boundaries to empower the African female subject without accepting shifts of boundaries that would roll back African women's agency at the mercy of globalization. If some African woman theorists such as Oyèrónké Oyewùmi, Chikwenye Okonjo Ogunyemi, Amede Obiora, and Nkiru Nzegwu view with suspicion theorists who dismiss Afrocentric perspectives as nativist by showing that the theorists are themselves nativists viewing Africa from a differently positioned strand of nativism, it must be stated that African feminisms are not necessarily anti-West and undiscriminating in their criticism of dominant paradigms. For instance, Ifi Amadiume's rejection of the misinterpretation of gendered practices in her Ibo community in *Male Daughters, Female Husbands* (1987) is based on a detailed engagement with both Western and Igbo students of gender in a way that cannot be dismissed as ethnocentric, despite its recovery of African interpretation of the relations between men and women.

Furthermore, the positive terms in which African feminists cite "Western" feminists, such as Simone de Beauvoir, Mary Daly, Adrienne Rich, Josephine Donovan, Minecke Schipper, Alice Jardine, Elaine Showalter, Kate Millet, Patricia Sparks, and Helene Cixous (to mention just a few of the most recurring names), contradict the general assumption that Africans feminists "write back" to the Western students of gender in an ethnocentric exercise against the Euro-American feminist tradition. Reading Mariama Bâ in a mode that echoes Elleke Boehmer and Florence Stratton, Ajayi-Soyinka, a strong critic of Western liberal feminism who would naturally dissociate herself from Boehmer's and Stratton's creeds, criticizes male negritude poets for their flattening of the mother figure by representing colonized Africa as a woman defiled. She is not against motherhood, but she exposes the patriarchal assumptions behind the use of the idealized figure of the mother to represent a continent.[10]

Considering that Western feminists disagree amongst themselves, in overplaying the differences in African theorists' approach vis-à-vis Western feminism as dramatic departures, there is an uncomfortable conjecture that the African feminist is not expected to disagree with formulations from the Western academy. If Chikwenye Okonjo Ogunyemi, in her *Africa Wo/Man Palava* (1993), finds de Beauvoir's, Cixous's, and Katherine Frank's brands of feminism "curious," then it is because these feminists tend to look down on Africans or to treat them as a uniform group (Ogunyemi 1993, 106–26). She disagrees with their particular presentations without dismissing indiscriminately the Western feminist movement, some of whose tenets she uses in rephrased and nuanced ways to study women's writing in Nigeria.

Therefore, Mbembe's claim that African feminism suffers from "philosophical poverty" has been negated by the presence of multiple, well-argued analyses of the relations between Euro-American theoretical categories and the lived experience of African women and men. It was similarly dismissive and condescending pronouncements, without engagement with the positions being dismissed, that Carole Boyce Davies, in "Introduction: Feminist Consciousness and African Literary Criticism" (1986), saw as the main culprit in the exclusion of women's thought and aesthetics in the study of African literature. African feminists do not always agree with one another, but the splintering differences usually are presented with sophistication and an acute understanding of the circumstances in which African women live. The initial reluctance of major African women writers such as Ama Ata Aidoo, Buchi Emecheta, Lauretta Ngcobo, and Marjorie Oludhe Macgoye to describe their work as feminist is indicative of their wish to break from a single conception of women's experiences privileging Western women as the norm.

Dramatic and interesting as it is, the view of the two categories of feminism as antinomic fails to recognize the differences among African scholars of gender relations and politics. As noted by women scholars of gender, such as Micere Mugo (1998), Amina Mama (1995, 2001), and Helen Mugambi (2007), the practice of feminism in Africa is diverse and multiple. The creation of such words as "Stiwanism" (Ogundipe-Leslie), "Womanism" (Ogunyemi and Kolawole), "Kwenu" (Ogunyemi), "Nego-feminism" (Obioma Nnaemeka) and "Motherism" (Catherine Acholonu), "Uhamili" (Juliana Nfah Abbenyi), and "Umoja" (Kolawole) to designate African women's understanding of relations between men and women and describe women's movements and struggles are not necessarily total negations of Western feminisms. The terms signify the contingency of feminism as it is practiced in different parts of the world and Africa. Evoking Alice Walker's retrieval of the term *womanism*, in *In Search of Our Mothers' Gardens: Womanist Prose* (1983), to designate a racially and class-contingent practice of feminism, Ogunyemi and Kolawole emphasize the particularity of African women's experience. These alternatives to Western feminism emphasize that African women's efforts to improve their livelihood and to claim their basic rights are "predominantly family oriented" (Kolawole 1997, 13). Ogunyemi may have arrived independently at the coinage "womanism," which she uses in "Womanism: The Dynamics of the Contemporary Black Female Novel in English" (1985), but her use of the term parallels its use by Alice Walker and Clenora Hudson-Weems to distinguish black women's understanding of gender rights from the way they are theorized by mainstream/white feminist traditions. Ogunyemi's main argument against the African American practice of feminism is based on the fear that, located in relatively more powerful academic spaces, African American feminism can easily be taken as representative of all black women across the world, thus silencing marginalized female voices in Africa. Ogunyemi departs from Walker on the issue of lesbianism; while Walker defines womanism to include women's love for other women "sexually and/or nonsexually" (Walker 1983, xi), Ogunyemi highlights instead "the African obsession with children as the silence on or intolerance of lesbianism" (Ogunyemi 1993, 133). Ogunyemi therefore sees African societies as too natally oriented to practice lesbianism, a position that, as I demonstrate presently, is disputed by other thinkers.[11]

Catherine Acholonu makes a point similar to Ogunyemi's when, distinguishing African feminism from dominant Western paradigms, she emphasizes that African feminist consciousness is "anchored on the matrix of *motherhood* which is central to African metaphysics and has been the basis of the survival and unity of the black race through the ages" (Acholonu 1995, 3, emphasis in original). Invoking the eco-critical imperative to preserve world resources, Acholonu says that "whatever Africa's role may be in the global perspective, it could never be divorced from her quintessential position as the Mother Continent of humanity, nor is it coincidental that motherhood has remained the central focus of African art, African literature (especially women's writing), African culture, African psychology, oral traditions, and empirical philosophy" (3).[12] Like the negritudists, Acholonu valorizes nature and sees the potential of the African woman to be anchored in the environment as opposed to Western modernity.

Yet to argue that Acholonu is not a feminist is to overlook the intensely feminist themes she covers in her writing, which she uses as a forum for examining the problems African women have endured, such as rape and violence, in a male-dominated present political reality that is different from the precolonial Africa that she idealizes in her theorizing of gender. In her poetry, Acholonu self-consciously presents herself as the indigenous mother drum that, while venerating male contributions to the society, seeks spaces for women and castigates men, whose proclivity for corrupt politics seems inborn. For example, the newborn infant in the title poem of the futuristic *Nigeria in the Year 1999* (1985) pronounces a manifesto that outlines how he will cheat in exams, how he will amass wealth through corrupt deals, and how he will usurp power through antidemocratic practices:

> chapter one—how to run without walking
> chapter two—education made simple
> expo 2000
> chapter three—how to make billions without
> sweat
> the secret of ten percent
> chapter four—rig yourself into life-presidency (Acholonu 1985, 54–55)

In the poem, Acholonu expresses her eschatological fear of a postmodern Nigeria in which exploitation will be conducted blatantly and with technological precision. The male-dominated politics will have positioned itself to dominate the society without regard to feminine fears. What is clear from Acholonu's artistic work is that despite the polemical stances she takes against "Western feminism," she is vocal in her criticism of the sorry state to which women in Africa have been reduced by the current leadership. Using slang that can be understood within specific contexts—such as the expression *expo 2000* for cheating in exams and *goof* for cannabis—Acholonu emphasizes the different local politics that must be considered before rigid positions are taken.

This African Feminism That Is Not One

What keeps coming up in African commentaries on gender is that it is wrong to see African feminism in monolithic terms; there are intense splintering differences between feminists, with scholars and practitioners placing different emphases on various practices and issues. For example, Nigerian theorists Molara Ogundipe-Leslie and Oyèrónkẹ́ Oyewùmi have argued for an African feminism that is not obsessed with differences between men and women. They also have contended that the precolonial African woman was not a passive victim of patriarchy, as Western perceptions, out to demonize Africa, might indicate. However, Ogundipe-Leslie and Oyewùmi part ways when Ogundipe-Leslie champions a feminism that is tolerant of homosexuality (1994, 215, 219) and criticizes "the way African writers enthuse about motherhood . . . [as] if there are no women who hate childbirth or have undeveloped maternal instincts" (58). Like Ogunyemi, Nkiru Nzegwu, and L. Amede Obiora, they both bemoan the racism in the international women's movement, whereby the identities and situated interventions of women of color are erased by white feminists. Yet Ogundipe-Leslie, who accepts the biological facticity of gendered formations in culture, deemphasizes physiological racial characteristics as an important consideration in seeking alliances to better women's lives. Ogundipe-Leslie and Oyewùmi both contend that feminism need not be seen as oppositional to men, and that women's conditions should be understood within particular scenarios that involve men and children without overlooking the issues of race and class. Yet Ogunyemi opposes what she views as Ogundipe-Leslie's extrapolation of the Western theoretical archive into African contexts.

Furthermore, while motherhood and the reluctance to talk about female homosexuality are, as Ogunyemi notes, central markers of African novels, the issues are nevertheless signified through metafictional devices, as we have seen. Contradicting Ogunyemi's position is Ugandan feminist lawyer and academician Sylvia Tamale who, in "Out of the Closet: Unveiling Sexuality Discourses in Uganda" (2003), documents the existence of homosexuality in Africa since precolonial times and bemoans the erasure of lesbian identities from Ugandan laws that have explicitly criminalized male homosexuality as an act "against the order of nature" and "unAfrican" (Tamale 2003, 44). Although she is focusing on a particular society within Uganda, Tamale claims that the nonrecognition by the law is a conspiracy orchestrated by the increasingly fundamentalist religious organizations and populist authoritarian regimes in order to avoid acknowledging the existence of homosexuality.[13]

Micere Githae Mugo, a Zimbabwean feminist poet and dramatist of Kenyan origins, also has criticized homophobia as a form of political intolerance comparable to the worst systems of governance in Africa and the world. Like Ogunyemi and Acholonu, Mugo champions African-centered discourse, the institution of motherhood, and womanism, but in her metafictional poems in *My Mother's Poem and Other Songs* (1994), which self-consciously combine creative writing and literary theorizing, Mugo enunciates a form of African feminism that equates homophobia with nationalist and ethnocentric political practices such as apartheid and tribal cleansing. Resonating with a socialist analysis of culture and gender, Mugo's poems in the collection retrieve for immediate memorialization the forgotten "Mother Afrika's matriots," whom racism, classism, and sexism have attempted to erase from memory. Mugo emphasizes the need to examine colonialism and neocolonialism in any attempt to comprehend gender issues in Africa. In her condemnation of homophobia in the poem entitled *To Be a Feminist Is*, Mugo uses a register that connotes the militant struggle against colonialism and neocolonialism:

> For me
> to be a feminist is
> to unhood racism
> to decry zionism
> to detonate apartheid
> to obliterate "tribalism"
> it is to
> necklace homophobia
> to drown fanaticism
> to strangulate classism
> to fumigate ethnic cleansing. (Mugo 1994, 37)

The use of a refrain in the poem and the poet's deviation from norms of punctuation indicate that the poem is an oral performance communally enacted, complete with call-and-response, in which the community is in agreement about the issues being raised. The active verbs that the collective persona uses to describe interventions against political and social outrages signify the urgency and militancy with which the evils should be fought.

In this poem, the break in the anaphoric parallel structures (beginning with "to") when articulating homophobia serves both to emphasize the urgency of fighting the social weakness and to acknowledge that not everyone might recognize homophobia as an urgent problem in Africa. The inclusion of homophobia among ethnocentric practices in Africa, despite the poet's celebration of motherhood and biological femininity, is not only a call for toleration of diverse sexual practices but an insistence that this diversity should be openly embraced.[14] Indeed, novels of the 1990s also have broached the issue of same-sex women's relationships more openly than the texts Acholonu and Ogunyemi use to arrive at their conclusions. Ogunyemi's notion of "post-womanism," which she develops in a reading of a fabulist metafictional narrative, *Maru* (1971), by Bessie Head, might lie not only in the reclamations of the magical *juju* against "extreme rationalism, realism, and other phenomena that ignore life shrouded in mystery" (2005, 9) but also in women writers' use of magical realism to transcend boundaries and discuss hitherto taboo topics, as Head ably does in *Maru* in her metafictional signification of queer identities.

Mugo's wide-ranging essay "The Woman Artist in Africa Today" (1998) observes the neglect of African women writers both by publishers and critics, despite women's skills for storytelling honed by traditions, where women are treasured as the custodians of communal narrative art. Like Aidoo, Mugo stresses the need to recover the voices of women that have been silenced by colonialism and patriarchy. She particularly stresses the necessity to consider oral literature and texts in indigenous languages because these are areas where women have made significant contributions. This would call for further consideration of class issues because women have been relegated to lower social classes and have limited access to modern education. Without being antagonistic to Western practices of feminism, Mugo insists on the correction of unequal economic relations between the North and the South if African women are to have any hope of liberation. What comes up frequently in her appeal is the need to appreciate multiplicity among women artists because they "have never constituted a uniform group" (Mugo 1998, 48).

Thus contrary to Gwendolyn Mikell's claim that African gender politics is "distinctly heterosexual," "intrinsically heterosexual," "pronatal," and focused on economics (1995, 412; 1997, 4), the articulation of gendered subjectivities in Africa is multiple and advocates different positions regarding mothering and sexual orientation. This is even more true of metafiction, where socially stigmatized identities can be presented through defamiliarized techniques that may not be available in face-to-face interviews and peer group discussions that Mikell relies on in drawing her conclusions. If there are African feminists who are critical of certain strands of Western feminisms, then they are also oppositional to each other. Although a group of African students of gender, such as Obiora, Oyewùmi, Nzegwu, and Ogunyemi, is suspicious of Western feminism as an extension of white imperialism, and although this group emphasizes the heterosexual nature of African gender practices, others such as Ogundipe-Leslie, Tamale and Mugo admit to the existence of alternative sexualities. Even within a single country such as South Africa there are multiplicities of feminist positions, as shown by the various clashing and blending voices in Margaret Daymond's anthology of essays *South African Feminisms: Writing, Theory, and Criticism, 1990–1994* (1996). These essays study not only the differences between various feminisms among South African writers (such as the intergenerational differences between white women writers Nadine Gordimer and Olive Schreiner) but also the differences between various Western feminisms in relation to South African writing.

The thread unifying the essays is the observation that no single body of feminism can be transposed onto African literature and manage to do justice to the complex class and race issues covered in South African feminist texts; feminism, seen by the essays as arriving in Africa from Britain, France, and America, in different forms, would have to be modified to suit local artistic expressions. Calling for inclusiveness that a single feminist approach cannot offer, the essays reject homogeneity in favor of a heterogeneous cultural and theoretical matrix. The tendency to see African feminisms as one block of theory against a similarly homogenous body of statements from an opposing culture is a misstatement of the diversity of non-Western feminisms and the diversity of impulses that give impetus to the theorizing of non-Western women.

Asian gender theorist Chandra Talpade Mohanty is arguably the most influential scholar in rethinking the relationship between gender studies and African cultural discourse. While revealing the localized situatedness of non-Western feminism, Mohanty does not insist on non-Western feminism as being antithetical to Western feminism. She points to "Third World" feminisms' multiple points of departure from Western (white, middle-class) feminism, but she also sees the possibilities of a transnational struggle against patriarchal and colonial domination. In her "Cartographies of Struggle," Mohanty makes it clear that "Third World" feminisms oppose "racism, sexism, colonialism, imperialism, and monopoly capital" (1991, 4). What is perceived as Western feminism comes under Mohanty's critique only if individual texts are complicit with the social offenses that "Third World" feminisms are set against.

In an earlier essay that has served as a benchmark for theorizing non-Western feminism, "Under Western Eyes: Feminist Scholarship and Colonial Discourses" (1984), Mohanty criticizes the colonialist hegemony governing the study of non-Western women in European and American academies. She sees bourgeois white feminism as complicit in a patronizing, Eurocentric view of women from non-Western societies as a singular and monolithic subject. For her, non-Western women are not a coherent group with identical interests, experiences, and goals. Western feminists treat non-Western women as "outsiders," and local economic, religious, and familial structures are judged by Western standards. Through a Western feminist lens, the "typical Third World" woman is seen as religious, family oriented, illiterate and domestic, and a legal minor, while the Western woman is presented as sexually liberated models for the non-Western women to emulate. Western feminism, Mohanty points out, assumes a universal notion of patriarchy in which all men oppress women. Counterpoising the subject/object dichotomy in which Western women view themselves as liberated subjects with a duty to save objectified "Third World" women from patriarchy, Mohanty argues that non-Western women have their own moments of empowerment.

All in all, Mohanty argues against oversimplification of the condition of non-Western women, to whom Western feminists rush for proof of the powerlessness of "Third World" women. In the essay that was to become the benchmark for non-Western feminism, Mohanty aligns herself with critics of liberal humanism, which tends to impose a false universalism on particular historical and social conditions. Her problem is with the failure of liberal, middle-class, white feminists to grasp the local particularities that inform the universal. She qualifies that the problem is not simply one of location of the theorist in terms of West versus the rest; "Third World" theorists in urban spaces in the "Third World" are themselves inclined to see rural and poor women in their own societies through Western feminist lenses. Viewed as against Western feminism and universal sisterhood, Mohanty's essay has been misread as an ethnocentric argument against the West.[15] But in a chapter entitled "Under Western Eyes Revisited" in *Feminism without Borders* (2003), first published as a journal article in *Signs* in 2002, Mohanty downplays the opposition between Western and non-Western feminisms, underlining their entangled nature. For her, the focus should be on forging transnational solidarity against unequal power relations engendered by global capitalism. The enduring quality of Mohanty's works resides not so much in her strident criticism of Western feminists but in her celebration of the work done on behalf of non-Western women by feminists who are attentive to the structures of inequality imposed on women from marginalized regions by various forces that govern local and international economies.[16] This is where African feminisms' main agenda rests—to liberate African women without using Western gender theories as the center of their gaze.

Why Colonialism Is Not Africa's Father

In sketching an ethics of theory, Richard Terdiman remarks in *Body and Story* that "theories *never* agree . . . , they will *always* be in contention. For any given theory there will be antagonists whose claims are not distinctly less forceful or less widely held" (2006, 200, emphases in original). At the heart of controversies surrounding postcolonial theory is whether its language can express the realities in formerly colonized regions, and whether its emphasis on textuality and language obscures the harsh material realities in which formerly colonized people live. Suffice it to say that African women theorists have been particularly uneasy with mainstream postcolonial theory due to what they describe as the suppression of the voices of African female subjects. Ghanaian novelist, playwright, and critic Ama Ata Aidoo states that the word "postcolonial" is inappropriate because it seeks to obscure with ambivalence the continued imperialist subjugation of Africa by Western capitalism. For her, "Colonialism has not been posted anywhere at all . . . Ask any village woman how postcolonial her life is" (quoted in Chreachain 1991, 5–6). From Aidoo's skepticism toward metropolitan theory, she looks at African cultures and literatures through the prism of the ordinary people rather than through terms that have been coined in elite Western universities. It is in this context that we should read Nigerian Omofolabo Ajayi-Soyinka's confrontation with Gayatri Spivak at the "Feminism and Cultural Imperialism" conference in 1989 over the usefulness of deconstruction in apprehending the lived experiences of African women. Ajayi-Soyinka is angry that Spivak characterized her "opinions on Eurocentric theories for African conditions as a genetic fear on the part of Africans for theory and an inability to conceptualize ideas," inferring "that Africa has never contributed and will never contribute significantly to human progress and knowledge" (2005, 48). In Ajayi-Soyinka's terms, postcolonial theory perpetuates the colonialist erasure of Africa as a viable site of epistemological self-determination. To her, it privileges Eurocentric and male-centered ways of perception and further tries to subordinate African theorists to Asiatic modes of thinking in a hierarchized order that places Africans at the bottom of intellectual capabilities.

According to Bill Ashcroft and colleagues (2002), for imperialist discourse to claim authority over the colonized, it has to delineate "the Other as radically different from the self, yet as the same time it must maintain sufficient identity with the Other to valorize control over it. The Other can, of course, only be constructed out of the archive of 'the self,' yet the self must also articulate the Other as inescapably different" (102). Within the colonial perspective, when similarity with the colonial subjects is acknowledged at all, it must be seen as both derivative and new to maintain the relation of dependence that Abdul JanMohamed notes in *Manichean Aesthetics* (1983). Postcolonial studies tend to see African literature in opposition to Western aesthetics, even when that opposition is not explored in any detail because the difference is taken as a given; the similarities and cross-cultural entanglements are celebrated with an intensity of enthusiasm that indicates them as an oddity. The underlying assumption that African literatures are the "Other" of European literature but at the same time intersect with it in hybrid formations has a similar implication for the study of African cultural arts: subordinating indigenous literatures to Western value systems. It is for this reason that critics of postcolonial theory have complained about the theory's liberal humanist complicity in silencing non-Western literatures while pretending to claim agency for those literatures. For example, criticizing postcolonial theory's subordination of gender as an analytical category, Anne McClintock (1995) has ably criticized the propensity of postcolonial theorists to regard colonialism, an Eurocentric event, as "history proper," relative to which events in formerly colonized regions prior to and after colonialism are to be explained.[17] For McClintock, such a retrospective approach not only subordinates the colonized to the linear time of colonial enlightenment and progress but also fails to acknowledge the factors that distinguish the colonized both from Westerners and from one another.[18] Although colonialism is a critical discursive reference point in the study of Africa, using it to define cultural phenomena not only sets back the ideological liberation of the continent but also distorts the realities addressed in African literatures.

A rethinking of the relationship between older art and new expression enables us to see that African literature is not necessarily antagonistic to colonial art, and to bring about the possible autonomy of African literature from the Western gaze that dominates postcolonial studies and insists on viewing African literature in terms of its break from colonialism. Harold Bloom observes in *The Anxiety of Influence* (1973) that the deconstruction of earlier literature is a project of all imaginative art; for him, poets have to eradicate their predecessors in order to escape from the suffocating influence of earlier foundational art. In this sense, modern African writers such as Chinua Achebe, Zakes Mda, Tsitsi Dangarembga, Yvonne Vera, Ngũgĩ wa Thiong'o, and Mary Okurut, to mention but a few, have deconstructed colonial and patriarchal narratives to claim a voice for marginalized racial and gender groups. Indeed, Bakhtin, in *The Dialogic Imagination* (1981), sees insurgency as the defining feature of the novelistic discourse, whereby individual texts reject any form of generic monologue by undermining previous novels and existing classes of language. For Bakhtin, the novel is always anticanonical and self-reflexive, with an impulse to reject the monologism of hierarchy and hegemony.[19] Theorists who critique Bloom's model at least agree that texts are related to one another in some ways, even if the networks of relations between some texts are not as Oedipal, neurotic, and adversarial as Bloom's theory of intertextuality suggests.[20] Thus "writing back," even when we see it in Bloom's narrow terms as a temporal practice, is not a literary novelty because all literature is about revisioning and augmenting earlier texts; what is crucial is the nature and function of that "writing back."[21]

The primary question for us, then, is: Is African literature's "writing back" dependent on colonialism? Does Freud's universal, transhistorical, and transcultural conception of the Oedipus complex apply to African literature in such a way that African texts would be seen in masculinist terms, as adversarial to a masculine Western canon? And who is the mother figure with whom it would identify? As we have seen, African texts, especially since the 1980s, have "written back" to itself; to these authors, colonialism is a secondary but pervasive concern.

The antagonism and polarization that Bloom's model suggests are radically downplayed in the appreciation of African literature by critics such as Nana Wilson-Tagoe, who insists that texts by male and female African writers do not simply revise or imitate one another; for her, the writers engage in "a complex discourse with several intersecting points, criss-crossing and interrogating each other continually" (1997, 26, 27). To look at the literature in terms of "anxiety of influence" or "writing back" is to ignore the multiple points of convergence, the internal heteroglossia, and the self-interrogation in which the texts engage in their relationship to other texts and to their own narratives. If African writing has from the beginning been a "literature of victims," as Emmanuel Obiechina notes in *Language and Theme* (1990, 150), it nevertheless underscores that victimizers are not limited to European colonizers; it criticizes in uncompromising terms the complicity of local elites in the dilapidation of the continent, especially in the decades following constitutional independence.

Without exonerating colonialism and enslavement for their terrorization of African societies and the trauma they caused across Africa and its diaspora, Obiechina notes that the victimizer is not exclusively the European colonizer; the indigenous societies depicted in folktales from precolonial African cultures have their share of victimizers of individuals and groups. African novels are less interested in waging a tirade against the European victimizer than in celebrating the efforts of the victim toward self-realization and self-empowerment. Obiechina follows a markedly Afrocentric trajectory here when he points out that the indebtedness of African literature to the Western canon is exaggerated. To him, while the influence of the West on African literature cannot be discounted, it is more indebted to indigenous oral traditions and to indigenous scripts, especially Arabic writing.

In enunciating a postprotest aesthetics in his criticism and creative writing, especially in the novel *The Cry of Winnie Mandela* (2003), South African theorist Njabulo Ndebele underscores the need to abandon the victim mode and calls for a "change of discourse from the rhetoric of oppression to that of process and exploration" (1991, 71). By sidelining the oppressors, the literature would not be vindicating their actions. For Ndebele, such a postprotest symbolic economy in which the oppressor is displaced as an active, dominant actor in the imagination of the oppressed would tactically enable the African artist to "consolidate the sense of a viable, psychologically self-sufficient community among the oppressed" (1991, 71). What is clear is that hinging the relevance of African literature on its negation of Western and colonial practices has disempowered the marginalized people. The focus should be on how the marginalized are self-conscious actors against oppression from its diverse sources.

Demanding Ethical Inclusion

Granted, postcolonial literature involves what Ato Quayson appropriately terms "hegemonic/counter-hegemonic dialectic," which is now spreading to other disciplinary spheres where, as in postcolonialism, there is a set of unequal relations engendering hegemony and resistance between different contradictory forces (2005, 253). This tells us that "writing back" is not an exclusive project of postcolonial literature. The contestation that Quayson identifies here should not be confined to the colonizer/colonized province; it can productively be put to use to transform postcolonialism's view of the metropolitan, former colonial center as the Other against which it must define itself. African literature is not merely "writing back" to hegemonic metropolitan centers but also to hegemonic institutions within postcolonial societies. Similarly, literatures in the metropolitan centers write back to each other.

In this chapter, I have sought to demonstrate that African female theorists have all along emphasized the multiplicity and variedness of their perspectives on gender and sexuality, whereas the Western academy still lumps them together as the ontological polar opposite of Western feminism. The assertion by African feminists that they are different from one other has been repeated so often that it is redundant. But the utter disregard for African feminists' wishes not to be assigned positions they do not hold indicates that the status quo is likely to be maintained, and the powerful metropolitan academy will continue to see African theorists as a single block that is ontologically opposed to Western feminism. What is most worrying is the fact that, as noted by Fanon in the chapter "The Negro and Recognition" in *Black Skin, White Masks* (1967), during colonialism, misrecognition of the African was the emblematic expression of racial contempt and the will of the colonialist to impose European values on the colonized people and to destroy their self-esteem.[22] The misrecognition of the African feminist by researchers of gender in African texts smacks of the kind of racism that Fanon speaks about.

Spivak also notes the ethical malpractice in the Western academy, where "the putative center welcomes selective inhabitants of the margin in order better to exclude the margin" (1988, 107). This means that through tokenism, non-Western cultures can be excluded from the curriculum by welcoming only those texts that affirm Western perspectives. Therefore, a discussion of African women's texts that systematically excludes the African female theorists easily falls within the paradigmatic tokenism Spivak discusses, where a few women's texts are included in order to exclude African theories of gender. With the continued celebration of this form of academic impunity, one would have to be naïve to expect the metropolitan academy to recognize African feminists just because they demand that recognition. African scholars would be better off discussing literary texts and each other's theories in planetary and global/local terms, as exemplified by Nana Wilson-Tagoe's work on African and Caribbean literature, than appealing for recognition in metropolitan institutions of interpretation. However, conscientious students of African literature should read with skepticism any feminist analysis of African texts that ignores African feminist theorists. Such a reading is likely to be committing a similar kind of epistemic violence decried by Fanon by entrenching Western stereotypes about African gender studies without paying attention to the variedness of the indigenous theoretical statements on gender and sexuality.

Finally, in seeking to debunk the heavily masculinist Oedipal connotations in the "writing back to the center" theory, I am not trying to reinstate the discredited part of the universalist paradigm that sees all literatures as the same. Rather, my argument is that there is no novelty in seeing works of art as different from one another; so long as a work of art is original it must, to an appreciable degree, be different form any other. What matters is a detailed analysis of the differences and similarities between the texts without treating one set of texts as superior because of their racial or geographical origins. Students of African literatures should be wary of scholarship that directly or indirectly presents Western art as the norm against which other literatures must deviate to be authentic or to which they must "write back" to affirm the identity of African subjects.

Conclusion

In a talk presented at the International Literature Conference in Cologne, West Germany, in 1982, Kenyan writer Ngũgĩ wa Thiong'o underscored that the African writer must continuously remind audiences in developed nations of their complicity in the exploitation of non-Western working classes. For Ngũgĩ, the writer "must expose to his Western audience the naked reality of the relationship between the North and the South. He has to show to his European reader that, to paraphrase Brecht, the water he drinks is often taken from the mouths of the thirsty in the third world and the food he eats is snatched from the mouths of the hungry in Asia, Africa, and South America" (1983, 74).

In other words, Ngũgĩ contends that one of the duties of African writers is to address the Western reader in terms that provoke guilt about the reader's participation (even if unknowingly) in creating the sorry state of the nations in the Global South. Postcolonial literature, then, should continue to show how the wrongs against humanity in the formerly colonized world are, to use Robert Young's words, "a product of the economic dominance of [the] north over the south" (2001, 6). This is a project the contemporary novel in Africa has embraced, as writers, especially those operating from a Marxist perspective, such as Said Mohamed, Ngũgĩ, Kyallo Wamitila, Katama Mkangi, and Seithy Chachage, trace the roots of the current dispossession to the capitalism of the late colonial period. These writers are aware that even decades after the Bandung Conference of the 1950s, where African and Asians sought to liberate themselves from the Soviet Communist and Western capitalist control and form a nonaligned "third force," their governments have remained puppets of Western capital or, if socialist, are structured by a level of greed similar to capitalism. It is also clear that despite the leaders' resolution to respect human rights and uphold peace, the Global South is dominated by human rights abuse and internecine wars.

Therefore, while African writers continue to expose the inequities between the North and the South, their primary audience is the indigenous community. Indeed, in the same talk, Ngũgĩ catalogues some of the most horrendous abuses that African communities suffer at the hands of their ruling elites and the need for the local communities to resist their oppressive national rulers. The subtext of Ngũgĩ's argument, then, is that if the writer is to address the Western audience at all, it should be in terms of the West's continued exploitation of Africa. I have shown in this book that literature in local languages such as Kiswahili and Gĩkũyũ (probably inaccessible to Western readers) satirizes Western institutions for their continued plunder of African societies. Nevertheless, more sharply criticized in these texts are the local elites that facilitate the exploitation, a group of villains whom Tanzanian novelist Chachage contemptuously dismisses in the sexually suggestive title of one of his Kiswahili novels as *Makuadi wa Soko Huria* (the pimps of the free market). The fact that this literature is written in local languages and published by local presses and is not available even in some of the best libraries in the West indicates that the butt of the narratives' laughter is not the West but local agents of capitalism that facilitate the exploitation of their societies.

Although the Africanness of African literature does not reside in the literature's non-Westernness, there is a persistent tendency to see African art to be nothing but a rant against colonialism and a counterpoint to Western aesthetics. This is mainly because African literature has been slowly received in Western academies, and the few times it does appear in "World Literature" or "Postcolonial Studies" courses, it is the pioneer nationalistic texts in European languages that are read. While the colonial discourse finds its way into all aspects of African life, African literatures, especially those produced in the 1980s and after, tackle emergent and contemporary issues. These new issues help us understand the nature of colonial violence while focusing on the emerging challenges in the society.

It is postcolonial theory's claim that African literature is preoccupied with responding to European texts that I have sought to debunk here by showing that the literature has become increasingly inward-looking in its reassessment of postcolonial conditions in local cultures. Insurrection against Europe is never ruled out, but writers seem more focused on forging alliances that would help solve local problems, especially in the realm of gender activism, than in protesting Western aesthetics. I have followed Ashcroft and colleagues' view that the future of postcolonial theory resides in a consideration of local conditions and the influence of the global moments on particular instances and spaces (2002, 210). Reading specific local texts in context helps us move beyond assigning African literature a blanket insurrectional, retaliatory, and subversive role. Examination of recent texts in English and local languages indicates that the literature is not a secondary and derivative production responding to a primary foundational colonial canon.

I have stressed throughout this book that to view African postcolonial literature as preoccupied with "writing back" to Europe, as has been the case in conventional studies of the postcolonial cultures, is to ignore those sublimated moments when the art actually does examine its own status as a social institution capable of bringing about change in the material world and critiquing junctures of internal forms of colonialism. Gerald Gaylard's (2005) reading of African postrealist fiction in *After Colonialism* rightly notes that contemporary novels do not oppose cultural products from elsewhere. Tim Woods makes an equally valid argument in *African Pasts: Memory and History in African Literatures*, when he argues that the postrealist literatures are "enganged in establishing their own history, their own models, their own structures" (2007, 265). Gaylard notes that postrealist fiction is politicized postmodernism that is based on cosmological beliefs and indigenous myths as opposed to Western technological advancement.

While claiming autonomy for this situated postmodernism from its Western counterpart, I have argued for ways of reading African literature that do not privilege colonialism as the reference point of the artistic projects that happen in Africa. It is apparent that even when African texts "write back" to the metropolis, colonialism is just one of the phenomena that African literature deconstructs. The literature is not silent to equivalents of colonialism in the form of class, gender, and sexual repression—what Ben Okri's metafictional novel *In Arcadia* calls "invisible imperialism spreading the cancer all over the earth" (2002, 218). There is thus a need to deconstruct postcoloniality's monolithic fascination with the way African literature differs from or relates to European literature. In the metafictional novels, we see a readiness to use Western texts and languages to deconstruct power structures that threaten to stifle local freedoms. Equally deconstructed are local texts, including oral literature, traditionally privileged as the site of indigenous authenticity.

We should be aware that if metropolitan theory regards African literatures as constantly resisting the metropolitan center all the time, then it is possible that, after arrogating to itself the position of normativity in relation to non-Western cultures, the Western academy expects African literatures to be like Western texts and is thus startled by an art with a different aesthetic. Indeed, though appearing on the surface as emancipatory, nonhierarchized, and nonexclusionary because it celebrates hybridity and border-crossing, the view of African literatures as "writing back" to metropolitan Europe compounds the silencing of African texts, the majority of which are interested in refiguring identities by negotiating with other literatures within Africa rather than arguing with a supposedly adversarial cultural and aesthetic category. If Western cultures, as Homi Bhabha accurately observes, definitionally bind themselves to the non-West because of their complicity with imperialism, African literatures attempt to see themselves in their own terms rather than as a derivative of, or a response to, Western cultural practices.

I must confess that I do not fully comprehend why the Western academy would for decades focus on the "writing back to the European center" paradigm, even when the literature on the ground indicates quite the opposite. My guess is that at the heart of the metropolitan university's celebration of "writing back to the center" there is a wish to evoke unease in the Western critic and to assuage the West's guilt for the material plunder of Africa. Turning itself into the new victim of the postimperial dispensation (in which it is being struck back), the West implies that formerly colonized people have already retaliated for the wrongs committed against them during imperialism. That is, it is suggested that Africa has already taken sweet revenge against its exploiters by "writing back to Europe with a vengeance." To the West, the discursive rebellion in which African discourse supposedly mangles Western cultures is much more psychologically reassuring than material or physical revenge, hence the eagerness to foreground the linguistic and symbolic rebellion that leaves intact material structures of domination.

I have argued that the metafictional/nonmetafictional dichotomy that we are tempted to resort to by maxims of discourse as a way of defining each of the terms is an illusory project. Realist texts deploy metafictional gestures to ground their illusion of realism and to enhance textual coherence. Although metafictional devices intensified in African fictions in the 1980s, a period that coincided with the advent of the postmodern, earlier novels have displayed a strong antirealist mode. Tutuola's narratives of the early 1950s, which constitute some of the earliest texts to come out of sub-Saharan Africa, are defined by phantasmagoric excursions mainly because of their location in folkloric traditions of the Yoruba community. However, earlier phantasmagoric narratives such as Tutuola's tried to explain the reasons for their departures from reality, always at great pains to recuperate a causal relationship among the events presented. Later novels are much bolder in their violation of the rules of realism, and the normalization of the abnormal seen in earlier fantastical narratives, including folktales, is largely absent. The use of metafictional devices does not in itself make a work of art superior to realist fiction. To be sure, the nonmetafictional tradition remains alive well into the twenty-first century in the remarkable works of Marjorie Oludhe Macgoye, Meja Mwangi, Ken Walibora, Goretti Kyomhendo, and Henry ole Kulet, to mention but a few.

The notion of hybridity, submitted by Homi Bhabha, and the theory of the subaltern, championed by Gayatri Chakravorty Spivak as a means of comprehending the postcolonial subject, are challenged by the novels' metafictional modes. The novels mimic their own discourse and society as opposed to

Bhabha's contention that this mimicry is directed at imperial power. Mimicry is redeployed to deconstruct nationalism and patriarchy rather than to remonstrate the West. Resistance in postcolonial texts goes beyond the discursive to the celebration and reproduction of material and the militant rejection of hegemony. The "subaltern" that Spivak sees in the postcolonial is not an overwhelmed individual with an erased subjectivity. The postcolonial subject seizes the power of speech and performance to criticize local enactments of hegemony without sparing the colonial past from critique.

From the metafictional novels, it is apparent that African literature is defined as that art which, through the resources of languages, patois, and dialects spoken in Africa, presents the conditions and the possibilities in Africa. While Ngũgĩ and Obi Wali severally insist that African literature must be written in an indigenous African language spoken on the continent before colonialism, metafictional literature indicates that even colonial languages can be Africanized to present the anxieties and hopes of the continent. Ngũgĩ's metafictional texts, especially those he has written in Gĩkũyũ, present the reader with main characters and narrators who speak a polyglot language in which the Gĩkũyũ/non-Gĩkũyũ boundary is breached. The purism suggested in Ngũgĩ's polemical statements on the defining characteristic of African literature is deconstructed by his own fiction that champions a reduced antagonism toward the English language.

Comparative approaches to African literatures are productive, especially the comparison and contrast of African texts from different authorial, geographical, gender, generic, and sexual backgrounds. Legitimate also are comparisons of African literatures with artistic production from non-African societies. But as Edward Said has argued in *Culture and Imperialism*, the field of comparative literature in world institutions of interpretation and cultural theory tends to hierarchize cultural production, placing "Europe and its Latin Christian literatures at the top" (Said 1993, 45). Other scholars have criticized the political tendentiousness of the system in which "comparatists" are those who specialize in Western literatures, while students of non-Western literatures are treated as part of area studies.[1] But what I find most inadmissible, as has been underlined by African critics since the infancy of the criticism of African literatures in the 1960s, is the use of literatures from outside Africa as the yardstick against which we measure the Africanness of African literature or the value of individual texts. Just as we do not bother to find out how, for instance, Phillip Roth uses Kafka in his *Professor of Desire* (1977) differently from J. M. Coetzee in *Life and Times of Michael K* (1983), we should not ground the Africanness of Coetzee's text in the way it is different from Roth's. Both are autonomous texts, and their similarities and differences cannot be used to evaluate their African and American authenticity. Comparison is useful only if the texts are treated on equal terms as primarily self-contained artistic products that nevertheless share certain characteristics with other texts and literatures.

I have shown African theorists' discomfort with the primacy given to precolonial arts in Western spaces as the expression of an uncontaminated and pure Africa. Such stratagems deny Africa's participation in modernity, arresting it in its own antiquity. After the facts of colonialism and globalization, "authentic" precolonial Africa exists only in artificial spaces, where it is performed for locals and foreigners alike by individuals who revert to a different modern lifestyle after the performance. K. Sello Duiker's *The Quiet Violence of Dreams* (2001) contains a scene in which a South African indigenous performance is laced with gestures borrowed from the Maasai of East Africa. This signals the artificiality of what might be presented as authentic Africa. Most of the texts discussed here depict modern Africa either in English or local languages. The two sets of languages have contaminated each other in such a way that Ngũgĩ's Gĩkũyũ, for instance, is Anglophone. It is futile, then, to search for "authentically" African texts in the narrow sense of how the African text differs from the "colonial" Western one.

A reading of East African literature against the background of wider continental literature has revealed the diversity of the presentations of gender beyond the stereotype of African feminism as exclusively heterosexual and pronatal. I also tried to take advantage of my knowledge of East African indigenous languages, drawing examples especially from Gĩkũyũ and Kiswahili. There is a need to study more texts in African languages, which metropolitan theories of literature have tended to ignore. Texts in local languages seem to challenge in a fundamental way the "writing back to the European center" paradigm. By writing in local languages, African writers are not protesting against English; rather, they are using the language that local populations would understand. The writers pepper these narratives with English words in a way that indicates that the hostility assumed in a people's use of their indigenous language is but a figment of the dominant group's imagination. More studies need to be done on texts in African languages in other artistic genres because postrealist fiction in African languages, as texts in Kiswahili and Gĩkũyũ indicate, tends to be dominated by male novelists, with women working much more in drama and popular music, probably because it is difficult to break into the publishing world with a novel in an indigenous African language.

It must also be reiterated that the fact that later African texts are not preoccupied with colonialism or "writing back" to the colonial metropolitan centers does not mean that these contemporary texts justify colonialism or imperialism. A critique of colonialism is persistent in those texts that criticize local forms of hegemony. The texts, especially those by Mda, Wamitila, Khamis, Ngũgĩ, and Chachage, draw the reader's attention to globalization as a euphemism for the continued Western domination of poor nations. As a part of history with parallels in the current experiences in Africa, colonialism remains a discursive reference point in African cultural production. Indeed, it can truly be said that colonialism runs as a subtext in most of the literature, serving as a master metaphor for other forms of oppression, exploitation, and repression that have taken root in Africa since independence. These new forms of colonialism are figured in sexual terms, with rape and voyeurism featuring strongly as metaphors in novels.

Lastly, the study of metafictional texts should avoid the ahistorical emphasis tacitly endorsed in most postcolonial readings of African literature. The 1990s witnessed the growth of useful studies on postcolonial literature as a cultural field of inquiry. The interest has grown unabated well into the twenty-first century, with critics engaging each other and texts from formerly colonized regions to explain power relations as refracted and signified in those texts. In spite of my discomfort with some aspects of postcolonial theory, I have chosen to remain within it and criticize it from within. This is because, for all of my skepticism toward some of its unconscious metanarratives, postcolonial theory still seems to me the best model of interrogating the limits of nationalism and Western hegemony. No other theory has been as successful in surveying and probing the complex forces underlying artistic production in formerly colonized regions. Creative works continue to present, in both realist and nonrealist modes and in different literary genres, the plight of African child soldiers, street children, and minorities caught up in interethnic conflicts. Ethnic minorities such as Asian communities in Africa have intervened through narrative to reclaim their suppressed identity.[2] However, the application of postcolonial theory to individual African texts and to bodies of literature must be attentive to local specificities if the theory is to be of use in explaining the prevailing conditions, anxieties, and possibilities in Africa. What is most crucial is that postcolonial critics avoid being as teleological and transhistorical as the forces of colonialism that they have spilled so much ink critiquing.

Notes

Introduction

1. A note on terminology is in order here because of the recurrence of the terms "Global South" and "self-fashioning" in this discussion. By the "Global South," I mean the formerly colonized societies of Africa, Asia, and South America, or what has been referred to since the 1950s as the Third World. Most African critics use the term in nonpejorative contexts, but it is now considered racist and inaccurate. For a discussion of the terms "Global South" and "Third World" and their genealogy, see the fifth chapter of Dirlik (2007), also available at http: //www.humnet.ucla.edu/mellon/Global%20South.pdf. See also Young (2001, 4–6). I use Stephen Greenblatt's term "self-fashioning" loosely to describe the process of constructing one's identity and public persona (Greenblatt 1980). The process which I use the term to describe here does not necessarily, as in Greenblatt's formulation, have to follow the dominant social norms. I use it to mean any form of constituting one's identity, even if the actions transgress the general code of behavior.

2. Critiques of postcolonial theory in metropolitan institutions are too numerous to list. Appiah (1992) draws attention to the disjunction between actual cultural production in Africa and postcolonial theorizing in the West. Arif Dirlik (1994) sarcastically conjoins postcolonial theory with the Western academy; for him, it is an academic practice of Third World critics in Western institutions. Amoko (2006), Dirlik (1994), and Hardt and Negri (2000) have called attention to the conservatism behind some of the seemingly progressive radical critiques of colonialism. Karin Barber (1995a, 1995b) and Karin Barber and Graham Furniss (2006) have criticized postcolonial theory for ignoring oral texts, and Alain Ricard and Flora Veit-Wild have noted the exclusion of texts in "autochthonous Africa languages" (2005, xi). Ahmed's well-known complaint against postcolonial readings of Indian literature is, in part, their tendency to treat texts in English as national and those in local Indian languages as "regional, hence minor and forgettable" (1992, 75). Ramazani (2006) has questioned the postcolonial theorists' tendency to see the relation between literatures from formerly colonized regions as adversarial to Western cultural forms. In a reading of Derek Walcott, Reed Way Dasenbrock (2005) perceptively sees less tension than cross-fertilization between Caribbean and European art.

3. Chukwuma Okoye (2007) has posited a similar critique of the "writing back" orthodoxy in postcolonial studies. The essay is limited in scope and does not address formal choices in the works of Promise Okekwe that it uses to illustrate its

claims. Invested in contesting "Western feminists and their non-Western acolytes" (Okoye 2007, 68), the essay tends toward the very weaknesses for which it criticizes postcolonial theory.

4. The location of self-reflexivity and postrealist techniques in indigenous art forms is variously emphasized by Helen Tiffin (1987, 171), Derek Wright (1997, 205), Gerald Gaylard (2005, 44–46), and Tim Woods (2007, 243–48), who suggest the need to see metafiction in African novels as independent of both Latin American magical realism and Western modernist and postmodernist aesthetics. (See also Linguanti, Casotti, and Concilio [1999], Bowers [2004], Sánchez [2002], Zamora and Faris [1995], Faris [2004], and Cooper [1998].) These critics are almost unanimous in their belief that metafiction from the Global South is inspired by indigenous forms, such as folklore and journalism. While the studies emphasize continuities between modern subversive fiction and folklore, my analysis focuses more on breaks with the oral literatures to which the texts refer. Cooper suggests this shift when she remarks that the writers, for all their claims to authenticity, are modern subjects who are "not inserted within these indigenous, pretechnological cultures that provide their inspiration" (1998, 16).

5. In her oft-quoted definition of a metafictional text, Patricia Waugh claims that it is the one "which self-consciously and systematically draws attention to its status as an artifact in order to pose questions about the relationship between fiction and reality" (1984, 2). In a different analysis of the Kiswahili novel, while stressing the oral-literature basis of postrealist fiction, Khamis (2007) uses the terms "metafiction," "metafictional," and "postmodern" to describe a strain of new novels, including his own *Babu Alipofufuka* (When Grandpa Came Back to Life, 2001) and *Dunia Yao* (Their World, 2006), written under the name Said A Mohamed.

6. For a concise description of the various critical positions on the use of postmodern terminology in relation to African literature, see Tim Woods's *African Pasts: Memory and History in African Literatures* (2007, 243–48).

7. A similar argument is proffered regarding modernism in the essays in Doyle and Winkiel's *Geomodernisms: Race, Modernism, Modernity*, especially in the editor's introduction, in which the writers note that modernist practices across the globe are "refracted through the local-global dialectic of inside and outside, belonging and exile, in ways that disrupt conventional poetics" (Doyle and Winkiel 2005, 3). Metafiction, as an aspect of postmodernism, heightens the awareness of woven links and ruptures among similar practices across cultures.

8. Kiswahili literary theorists have adopted the term *metabunilizi* from the word "metafiction" to dialogue much more easily with global institutions of criticism and literary theory because the suffix *piku* (heightened) may not be immediately clear.

9. See Stratton (1994, 58). The novel was published the same year as Flora Nwapa's *Efuru* (1966). Stratton argues that the reason the novel was not canonized by the male-dominated literary academies while it deals with similar wider themes as novels by male writers such as Ngũgĩ and Achebe is that Grace Ogot is more invested in deconstructing patriarchal privileges than in staging nationalist liberation rhetoric.

10. See also Adélékè Adéèkó's *Proverbs, Textuality, and Nativism in African Literature* (1998), in which he appropriately reads Ayi Kwei Armah's *Two Thousand*

Seasons (1973) as a metafictional text in the way it uses African orality and nativist mythologies to thematize the creative role of the modern artist. Adéèkó's reading of Armah is sobering, especially in the way it demonstrates that the novel's use of metafictional devices can be seen as an index of Fanon's prophesy in *The Wretched of the Earth* (1963) that postcolonial intellectuals will wield the modern methods obtained from Western academies to validate the independence of postcolonial cultures. According to Adéèkó, Armah's text, written before metafiction became a dominant mode, questions "the mimeticism dominant in postindependence Anglophone African writing" (Adéèkó 1998, 98). Other foundational texts that display metafictional impulses include Nadine Gordimer's *The Lying Days* (1953), in which the relevance of the canon of African literature is presented from the perspective of a partially unreliable first-person narrator.

11. Critics have emphasized the progenitor status of Equiano's narrative with regard to the locally produced literary canon. S. E. Ogude shows this relationship between Equiano and later artists by indicating similarities between him and twentieth-century writers: "Certainly here is a common attitude in the works of Achebe, Laye, and Equiano. It is quite possible to see some of the passages in the first chapter of Equiano's *Narrative* in the same light as Achebe's novels, especially *Things Fall Apart* and *Arrow of God*. Or Camara Laye's *African Child*" (quoted in Ikiddeh 1978, 130). Ngũgĩ wa Thiong'o invokes Equiano's narrative in *Writers in Politics* to show the continuity between Equiano and Achebe in producing a literature that "celebrated the struggle against colonialism and asserted the African presence in the world" (1981, 22). Further, Ngũgĩ uses the narrative to demonstrate that "even during the era of slave trade, there were those who refused to espouse the slave mentality and the ruling class ideologies and articulated instead a consciousness of emancipation and liberation" and to emphasize the continuity between Equiano and later nationalists such as "Edward Blyden, Kwame Nkrumah, Jomo Kenyatta, and Nhamdi [*sic*] Azikiwe" (Ngũgĩ 1981, 41–42).

12. "Orature" is a term coined by Ugandan linguist Pio Zirimu in the 1960s to mark artistic forms that used verbal communication and live performance. It is counterpoised to "literature" which, as written discourse, is relatively new in Africa. The term is used mainly to resolve the contradiction in the nomenclature "oral literature," but we use the two terms here interchangeably.

13. Although his approach is not comparative, Said Khamis (2005) observes a rupture with the tradition in Kiswahili novels published in the 1990s. While the novels in English have executed radical gestures that challenge the customary ontological boundaries, novels in Kiswahili and other local languages are more adventurous in stylistic innovativeness than the novels in English.

14. Achebe, in the essay "Africa and Her Writers" sees art for art's sake as a luxury that only certain Western schools of aesthetics can afford. For Achebe, "Art for art's sake is just another piece of deodorized dog-shit . . . In other words, I will still insist that art is, and was always, in the service of man" (Achebe 1975, 19). The philosophy of art for art's sake, according to Achebe, is a new European development.

15. See Achebe's essay "The African Writers and the English Language" (1975). In this essay, first published in 1963, Achebe underlines that "you cannot

cram African literature into a small, neat definition," and that "any attempt to define African literature in terms that overlook the complexities of the African scene at the material time is doomed to failure" (Achebe 1975, 56). For him, as long as English is modified to carry the experiences of Africans, it qualifies as a language for African literature to be written in. For Ngũgĩ's position, see *Decolonising the Mind* (1986a).

16. For a particularly well-argued review of Morrison's and Fuss's practice of essentialism in racial politics, see the chapter "Speaking the Unspeakable," in McBride's *Why I Hate Abercrombie and Fitch* (2005).

17. For example, see Wilson-Tagoe's "Reading towards a Theorisation of African Women's Writing" (1997) and "Narrative, History, Novel: Intertextuality in the Historical Novels of Ayi Kwei Armah and Yvonne Vera" (1999). Equally reflective in her call for formal analysis is Mary E. Modupe Kolawole's observation that African women's writing is marked by a sense of self-reflexivity that is inflected with the sociopolitical conditions in the extratextual world even if there is no immediately veridical relationship between the signifier (the fiction) and the signified (the presented phenomena). Kolawole (1997) offers a good guide to the reading of gender in African metafiction in a brief discussion of the strategy in Tsitsi Dangarembga's *Nervous Conditions* (1988), urging readers to examine the underlying realism even in Dangarembga's choice of symbolic names for her characters.

18. Emphasizing literary language's deviation from habitual usage, Shklovsky argues that "the purpose of art is to impart the sensation of things as they are perceived and not as they are known. The technique of art is to make objects 'unfamiliar,' to make forms difficult, to increase the difficulty and length of perception because the process of perception is an aesthetic end in itself and must be prolonged. Art is a way of experiencing the artfulness of an object; the object is not important" ([1917] 2005, 800). For a restoration of the revolutionary and the political to the historical study of the practice and theorization of estrangement, see Cristina Vatulescu's "The Politics of Estrangement: Tracking Shklovsky's Device through Literary and Policing Practices" (2006).

19. Wendy Faris has noted the affinity between magical realism—instances in which realism is mixed with the fantastic—and minority discourse, such as postcolonial and feminist writing. See, for example, her "The Question of the Other: Cultural Critiques of Magical Realism" (2002), "Scheherazade's Children: Magical Realism and Postmodern Fiction" (1995), and *Ordinary Enchantments* (2004). Like Slemon, Faris sees the radical incongruity of magical realism as signifying material conditions in society.

20. Although Jameson's demonstrated cogency would not allow him to hold such a reductive view of the world as some of his harshest critics have implied, he perhaps falls short of his critics' expectations in his failure to emphasize strongly enough that Western literature is not necessarily the opposite of what he views as Third World literature; some of the Western narratives are national allegories in which the Marxist (collective) and the Freudian (individual) perceptions merge in intricate ways. At the same time, Third World literature, especially through its metafictional devices, contests the traditional idea of the nation, especially when notions of a unitary nationhood are used to suppress ethnic, gender, and sexual minorities.

21. The point that needs to be emphasized here is that African literature is not designated as "African" simply by virtue of the fact that it is not Western. The tendency to view art in terms of how it is different from Western literature is as culturally arrogant as the already discredited approach that evaluates African texts in terms of how they approximate Western ones.

22. Refer to the opposition to "postcolonial" theory by the Subaltern Group of India, which views the term "postcolonial" as too limiting. Their sentiments are shared by Edward Said and Gayatri Spivak.

23. Natalie Melas underscores the inevitability of comparison in some subjects of discussion because the supposed opposite is always implied, even if it is not the immediate focus of discussion, whereby even to talk of comparison would appear redundant. She, however, notes that the binary between West and non-West is non-equivalent and problematic (2007, 2–3). Melas's approach to non-Western literatures such as the texts of Derek Walcott and Aime Cesaire is exemplary because she does not oppose that literature to an outside aesthetics or treat it as a mere addition to comparative literature in order to give the discipline a sense of inclusivity or sensitivity to local particularism.

24. Such studies include Brenda Cooper's *Magical Realism in West African Fiction* (1998), Azodo and Eze's *Gender and Sexuality in African Literature and Film* (2007), William Spurlin's *Imperialism within the Margins* (2006), Catherine Cole and others' *Africa after Gender* (2007), Cheryl Stobie's *Somewhere in the Double Rainbow: Representations of Bisexuality in Post-Apartheid Novels* (2007), and Neville Hoad's *African Intimacies: Race, Homosexuality, and Globalization* (2007). I build on the work of these critics while offering an East African perspective.

Chapter 1

1. By the "experimental turn" Attwell means literature written in the modernist or postmodern mode to foreground its own devices, departing from conventional realism.

2. In South Africa, the discussion about whether to include local literatures in the curriculum began in 1956, as recorded by Michael Chapman in *Southern African Literatures* (1996). A University English conference held at the University of Witwatersrand broached the "issue of teaching local SA literature; anxious about the status of English in Afrikaner-dominated state" (Chapman 1996, 455). Notable is the paper by R. G. Howarth, "Indigenous Literature and Its Place in University English Studies" (1957), in which he argues that "indigenous literature rightfully claims a place in English courses" (1957, 50). One of the ways of inserting local literature into the curriculum was to conduct judicious comparative studies in which British canonical writers would be analyzed alongside South African, Commonwealth, and American literatures. For historical developments in East Africa, see Carol Sicherman (1995, 1998).

3. The Bandung Conference, held in Bandung, Indonesia, in April 1955, brought together twenty-nine Asian and African states representing half the planet's

population. In its Communiqué issued after the conference, the delegates condemned colonialism and underlined the right to self-determination, inter-South cooperation, and the respect for human rights. Although it stressed decolonization as one of its agendas, speakers such as Indian Prime Minister Jawaharlal Nehru mentioned the mistakes his nation had made in the past and emphasized the futility of being an "anti" person in relation to other cultures and political ideologies. The conference is hailed by Robert J. C. Young in *Postcolonialism: An Historical Introduction* (2001) as "the beginning of the production of 'the postcolonial' as an ideological and political position, beyond its historical descriptive reference" (190).

4. See Keith Smith's "Who Controls Book Publishing in Anglophone Middle Africa" (1975) for a discussion of the role of foreign firms in the production of books in Africa.

5. A case in point is Rebeka Njau's *Ripples in the Pool* (1975), which was published in the series in 1978 and was soon dropped from the African Writers Series list. In my own reading of *Ripples of the Pool* later in this book, I agree with Andrade that these novels of private and domestic experience have an allegorical dimension that treats public themes. The female novelists were astute in collapsing the binary between the domestic and the national.

6. For a history of the African Writers Series, see Alan Hill's *In Pursuit of Publishing* (1988). For claims about the centrality of African Writers Series in creating a canon of African literature, see *Africa Writes Back* by publisher James Currey (2008), who served as an editor of the series between 1967 and 1984. Currey's text came out when mine was already in production. Although the term "writing back" is unexplained in his book, Currey's observation that the series provided African writers with a forum where "they really could write back" connotes that they could resist Western canon (Currey 2008, 296). For a quick review of Currey's book, see Gray (2009, 177–80). For a critique of the series as a neo-colonialist enterprise that in effect stifled indigenous African writing and publishing besides promoting a Eurocentric gaze at African cultural production in the Western metropolis, see Camile Lazarribar's dissertation, "Something Else will Stand Beside It: The African Writers Series and the Development of African Literature" (1998) and Gail Low's "In Pursuit of Publishing: Heinemann's African Writers" (2002).

7. A similar argument is suggested in C. L. Innes's *The Cambridge Introduction to Postcolonial Literatures in English* (2007), in which she further notes an attempt by later writers such as Abdulrazak Gurnah to produce texts that portray the relationship between the colonizers and the colonized in a more complex fashion than earlier texts, such as Achebe's *Things Fall Apart* (1958), which cast the relationship between the colonizer and the colonized in dichotomous or contrasting terms.

8. For an incisive account of this kind of "thematic nativism" and skepticism toward modernist aesthetics, see the first chapter of Adélékè Adéèkó's *Proverbs, Textuality, and Nativism in African Literature* (1998).

9. The early and more accessible novels were published in the West by multinational companies such as Heinemann, Cambridge University Press, Macmillan, and Oxford University Press because "there were no publishing houses in Africa at the time most of the African writers started publishing" (Egejuru 1980, 55). The writers were bound by contracts with Western venues, and if the publishers felt that

"a book may not appeal to the foreign market, that book would not be published" (Egejuru 1980, 55). The tendency, then, would be to create and circulate texts that had some relevance to Western readers, for example, because they deconstructed the Western canon. If these texts consciously write back to the colonial center, then there are other noncanonized texts that, published locally in Africa by small firms, express other forms of relations.

10. The prostitute and the brothel are used in African literature as the figure of the fallen nation. They signal the moral collapse that Westernization has brought in its wake. For a discussion of this topic, refer to *The Prostitute in African Literature* (1982) by Fikeni Senkoro. The male is rarely seen as wrong in exploiting women in the sex industry. Among other things, the title of the novel *Petals of Blood* (Ngũgĩ 1977) refers to the color of the fire that consumes Wanja's brothel.

11. Achebe was not rejecting universalism per se, only the misuse of the term. For example, in "The African Writer and the English Language," he supports writing in the colonial language because of the "universal currency of English" (1975, 58); for him, English had to be "at once universal and able to carry his peculiar experience" (1975, 62). Ngũgĩ expresses a similar argument about universality in his essay "The Universality of Local Knowledge." Here he criticizes the tendency of the West to generalize "its experience of history as the universal experience of the world. What is Western becomes universal and what is Third World becomes local. Locality becomes measured by the degree of its distance from the metropolis of the Western world" (1993, 25).

12. For a discussion of the poor quality of the materials in which popular fiction in the 1970s was printed, see Chapter 2 of Larson's *The Ordeal of the African Writer* (2001). The problem persists in locally published works that rarely get international readership, despite their more updated reassessment of attitudes and practices in African societies.

13. Maillu changed into a "serious" writer in the 1990s, but these later novels, such as *Broken Drum* (1991), contain thinly veiled references to his earlier works.

14. Other examples from East Africa include Tanzania Publishing House, established in 1966 in Dar es Salaam with assistance from Macmillan to publish local literature. Mkuki na Nyota of Dar es Salaam was established by Walter Bogya in 1991, while Focus is owned by the Opus Dei and produces novels with catholic teachings. Femrite of Uganda publishes work by women writers, and its works so far lean more toward realist prose than metafiction. The publishers are not uniform in relation to their choice of nonrealist prose, probably as a result of a divergence in editors' tastes. For example, E&D Publishers in Dar es Salaam seems to produce realist prose, including its director Eliesh Lema's novel *Parched Earth*. Considered the first feminist novel from Tanzania, *Parched Earth* presents the silencing of women in a fairly realist mode without seeking to disrupt the heterosexual union between its principal characters. Femrite's novels are largely realist. By contrast, Mkuki na Nyota tends toward fiction based on spiritual and magical realism, such as S. N. Ndunguru's *A Wreath for Fr. Mayer* (1997) and Anthony Hokororo's *Salma's Spirit* (1997), in which inexplicable and bizarre preternatural forces intervene in the actions and experiences of the characters.

15. For a literary history of writing in African languages, see Albert Gerard's *African Language Literatures* (1981).

16. For a detailed examination of the unreliability of the Gichaandi oral artist in *Devil on the Cross*, see Mwangi (2007).

17. For instance, Gordimer's *The House Gun* (1998) is particularly lucid in its portrayal of postapartheid violence. Her other postapartheid novel, *The Pickup* (2001), subtly subverts the idea of the desert as presented in other African novels, especially Aye Kwei Armah's *Why Are We So Blest?* (1972). Armah sees the desert as a site of mortification, where Modin has his genitals cut by Westerners, signifying emasculation and the racially implicated destructiveness of white people. In Gordimer's novel, the white/nonwhite, rich/poor, native/foreigner, legal/illegal dichotomies are disturbed to allow a romantic union between a rich girl, Julie, and an illegally employed menial worker of Arab extraction. Gordimer makes the desert a site of the possible. It is in the desert that Julie and Ibrahim are likely to conceive a child in their interracial union.

18. For a succinct summary of the "mixed nature" of the regimes that succeeded the "transition to democracy" in Africa, see Richard A. Joseph's "Oldspeak vs. Newspeak" (1998).

19. The first novel by the playwright Imbuga, *Shrine of Tears* (1993), is a metafictional examination of the role of theatre and literature in African politics. Imbuga's stage works, which deploy the play-within-a-play technique and have been in the Kenyan syllabus since the 1980s, could account for the proliferation of the "novel-within-a-novel" technique in the works of younger writers in the country; they may be emulating Imbuga's technique in a different genre.

20. Fanon's study was first published in French in 1961 as *Les Damnés de la Terre*. Many novels reflect Fanon's thesis. Armah's *The Beautyful Ones Are Not Yet Born* (1968), *Fragments* (1969), and *Why Are We So Blest* (1972), Ngũgĩ 's *A Grain of Wheat* (1967) and *Petals of Blood* (1977), Farah's *Sweet and Sour Milk* (1979), *Sardines* (1981), and *Close Sesame* (1983), Aidoo's *No Sweetness Here* (1979), Leonard Kibera's *Voices in the Dark* (1970), and Achebe's *No Longer at Ease* (1960) and *Anthills of the Savannah* (1988) express in their various ways the rottenness and corruption eating at the vitals of the African state. Peter Nazareth's remarkable novel *In a Brown Mantle* (1972a) captures the racism and dictatorship in Uganda and how colonialism and its aftermath have affected the identity of Asians in Africa. At the heart of the novel is a disappointment with the bureaucratic and political elites who have betrayed the hopes of a multiracial Uganda. The novel has an inner self-reflexivity that questions realism as it treats the theme of the place of Asians in East African culture and politics. Although Nazareth (1981, 59) seems to encourage us to see his novel as a nonrealist text belonging in the phantasmagorical conjurations of Indian R. K. Narayan, Colombian Garcia Marquez, and Mexican Juan Rulfo, *In a Brown Mantle* remains, without reducing its forcefulness as an aesthetic object, anchored in the realist tradition.

21. Some of the writers who openly show Fanon's influence include Ngũgĩ, Kibera, and Armah. Other writers, such as Achebe, portray the disillusionment with classical independence without endorsing the model of violence suggested in Fanon's work as an inevitable consequence of colonial and neocolonial violence. Yet other writers, such as Tsitsi Dangarembga in *Nervous Conditions* (1988), critique Fanon's notion of a split personality by figuring a more engendered consequence of colonial

violence, in which women bear the brunt of colonial and patriarchal violence in settler communities. In the novel, whose title and epigraph invoke Fanon's *The Wretched of the Earth* (1963), Dangarembga subverts Fanon's monolithic construction of African women and his prioritization of nationalist decolonization at the expense of the liberation of women from colonialism as well as precapital and precolonial patriarchy.

22. There is a way that Mazrui's *The Trial of Christopher Okigbo* (1971) can be characterized metafictional. It is not only set in the preternatural world in which characters stand trial for their actions in the real world, but it also thematizes the tension between individualism and communal duty in an African writer through the work and experiences of a poet. Hybridity and intertextuality form an integral part of the theme of poetic production across epochs and cultures; however, the novel remains largely realist in texture. Notwithstanding its commentary on aesthetics, politics, and interpretation, *The Trial of Christopher Okigbo* seems to go to great lengths to naturalize the preternatural world it conjures into existence. It treats the themes of aesthetics, writing, criticism, and hybridity, but its language is transparent. Its experimentalization resides in paralinguistic features, such as the setting and characterization. I must state that although it has not been given the critical attention it deserves, and despite the fact that Achebe's foundational essay "Thoughts on the African Novel" seems to take issue with Mazrui's arguments about Okigbo, *The Trial of Christopher Okigbo* should not be described as a lesser work of art merely on the basis of its realist technique. To do so would be to overlook its handling of a theme that would render it amenable to metafiction and more intense self-deconstruction.

23. In Okurut's novel about the Ugandan experience under Idi Amin's dictatorship, the ruling class is uneducated and has deliberately run down the academy. Makerere University, a symbol of academic culture, deteriorates by the day. At one point in *The Invisible Weevil* (1998), Achebe's classic *Things Fall Apart* serves as wrapping paper alongside "Top-Secret" government documents (109). The novel's mention of the canonical African text as one of the documents destroyed by the government signals the complete collapse of intellectual cultural practices in Idi Amin's Uganda. The students of culture, such as the novel's main characters, become sexual victims of the military regime. Macgoye's *Coming to Birth* (1986) cites Ngũgĩ wa Thiong'o's detention without trial by the Kenyan government in 1977 as one of the events symbolized by the miscarriages that happen in the story. The character Martin's growth is marked by an event in which he reads Ngũgĩ's then newly politically conscious novel *Petals of Blood* (1977). It is in a similar context that Tsitsi Dangarembga's narrator, Tambudzai, in *Nervous Conditions* (1988) and its sequel *The Book of Not*, makes fun of herself for having arrogantly dismissed a radically anticolonial novel by Ngũgĩ before reading it. As a schoolgirl steeped in Christian missionary education and the British literary tradition, she regarded the Fanonist novel as "rather than being revolutionary seemed to be about agriculture for it was called *A Grain of Wheat*, written as far as I could see by someone like poor Bongo in the Congo, a starving Kenyan author" (2006, 117). At the present time she is saying this to the reader in *The Book of Not*, Tambudzai is already a mature woman and seems to know better; she is mocking her earlier self.

24. *Ujamaa* (Kiswahili for "extended family" or "familyhood") was the concept that formed the basis of Julius Nyerere's social and economic development policies in

Tanzania just after it gained independence from Britain in 1964. President Nyerere published his development blueprint, titled the "Arusha Declaration," in 1967. In it, he pointed out the need for an African model of development, and it formed the basis of African socialism. One of the pillars of *Ujamaa* was the fostering of the nation's self-reliance through the transformation of economic and cultural attitudes.

25. Macgoye's *Chira* (1997) is written in the realist mode but draws allegorical parallels between the AIDS scourge in Africa and the seemingly incurable malaise faced by African nations. Another novel employing a similar mode is Mary Karooro Okurut's *The Invisible Weevil* (1998), which suggests that the problems facing post-Amin Uganda result from an unnamed virus. Caroline Adalla's *The Confessions of an AIDS Victim* (1993) uses a powerfully autobiographical mode which, like Mariama Bâ's *So Long a Letter* (1981), relies on the epistolary form to anchor its realism. Yusuf Dawood's *Water under the Bridge* (1991) and Wamugunda Geteria's *Nice People* (1992) present the AIDS condition as a punishment for the sinful. Meja Mwangi's *The Plague* (2000) focuses on AIDS in powerfully realist prose. Lutanga Shaba's *Secrets of a Woman's Soul* (2005) tackles what it seems to see as the ineffectiveness of the fight against AIDS while women remain powerless. *Waste Not Your Tears* (1994) by Violet Kala is about the failure of African societies to acknowledge deaths from AIDS and, strikingly, it uses the realist mode in sections focalized by its male villain, Roderick, and a more hallucinatory prose in sections told from the perspective of its heroine, Loveness. Phaswane Mpe's *Welcome to Our Hillbrow* (2001), like Zakes Mda's *The Madonna of Excelsior* (2003a), is metafictional and bases its tragic end on an AIDS death. For a survey of Kenyan novels on AIDS, refer to Marie Kruger's "Narrative in the Time of AIDS: Postcolonial Kenyan Women's Literature" (2004).

26. Though revolving around a revolutionary poet in apartheid South Africa, Nkosi's postapartheid novel, *Underground People* (2002), is more realist than the author's earlier novel, *Mating Birds* (first published in Nairobi in 1983, then in New York in 1986, and finally in Johannesburg in 1987), but I would not describe the nonfabulist text as a lesser work of art on account of its realist rendition. *Underground People*, however, joins the metafictional novels in casting doubts on cheap, propagandistic commitments. In the novel, the "committed" nationalistic poet is phony and joined the revolution by accident; he is little different from the antihero in Ngũgĩ's *A Grain of Wheat* (1967), who is widely respected for feats he has never achieved. Nkosi's *Mandela's Ego* (2006) returns to a more fabulist mode to narrate the myths about Mandela as a legendary figure in rural South Africa.

Chapter 2

1. Noting that popular literature affected the way serious literature was written in the 1970s, Kurtz observes that Ngũgĩ's first post-1970 novel, *Petals of Blood* (1977), "was clearly influenced by the new detective stories" (102–103). This is an acknowledgment of the porous boundary between the canonical nationalist novels and noncanonical popular literature.

2. These authors are seen as a threat to canonical African literature because of their popularity, especially in the 1970s and 1980s. They focus on sex and crime,

and they border on the pornographic. While David Maillu's works used African idiom and situations, Chase's were better packaged, with glossy cover pictures of gun-totting beauties. Ngũgĩ's *Devil on the Cross* (1982) figures ideological and experiential naïveté in terms of reading "novels by James Hadley Chase, Charles Mangua, and David Maillu" (1980, 17). Mangua is also a writer in the popular vein. In Ngũgĩ's *Wizard of the Crow* (2006), the remarkable ideological maturity of the principal female character, who works as a secretary, is underscored by the fact that she is reading the Kiswahili translation of Ngũgĩ's own *Devil on the Cross* instead of pulp fiction, as might be expected of women of her caliber.

3. The phrase "petals of blood" thus indicates the victims of agents of capitalism, who have made the nation barren through the plunder of national resources. In the first instance in which the title is referred to, the "petal" is described as having the color of blood because it is unhealthy. Postindependence Kenya is viewed as barren and unable to deliver the promised freedoms for which the society fought. The title also, as indicated by its metaphorical reference to the fire in which Wanja's brothel burns to the ground, refers to acts of liberation that countermand oppression by burning the blooming flowers of capitalism. Blake's poem also can be read as a statement against Puritanism, a project that *Petals of Blood* also engages by claiming more space for the African canon in African schools.

4. In a scene of indigenous performance that recalls the circumcision songs in Ngũgĩ's *The River Between* (1965), it is the Gitiiro artists who at one point in *Petals of Blood* perform an "opera of eros" in which they engage in "a full battle in an erotic war of words and gestures and tones suggestive of many meanings and situations" (208).

5. See Soyinka's account in "On the Trail of Transition" (1997, 416). Soyinka had used the term earlier in a cyclostyled student magazine, *The Horn*. He pursued the same idea at the 1964 Berlin Conference on African Arts. In *The Burden of Memory: The Muse of Forgiveness* (1999), Soyinka takes back his dismissive remarks on negritude.

6. While more critical of Soyinka in their avowedly Afrocentric *Toward the Decolonization of African Literature* (1980), Chinweizu, Onwuchechua Jemie, and Ihechukwu Madubuike criticize some of Okigbo's early poetry for its inaccessibility.

7. Armah's novel, uncompromising in its presentation of the dilapidation facing Ghana in the 1960s, has been a reference point in the discussions of the literature of disillusionment in Africa. Like Armah's other fiction of the 1960s and early 1970s, the novel presents a bleak vision of Africa. Armah's perspective changes in later fiction, especially after *The Healers* (1978).

8. Nongolot, the site where rape and tribal cleansing are staged by the government in Rebeka Njau's *The Sacred Seed* (2003), is an anagram for "Longonot," the name of a real geographical place around Mt. Longonot, a dormant stratovolcano located southeast of Lake Naivasha in the Great Rift Valley of Kenya. Like Henry ole Kulet's *Bandits of Kibi* (1999), Njau's novel thematizes sporadic, state-sponsored ethnic cleansing without mentioning directly any details that would give away the ethnic communities involved. We see a similar strategy in Zimbabwean novelist Yvonne Vera's *The Stone Virgins* (2002) in which the novelist avoids apportioning blame to either the Shona or the Ndebele community. Ole Kulet makes references

to writing in *Is It Possible?* (1971) and *Daughter of Maa* (1987), both novels about the conflict between modernity and traditions among the pastoralist Maasai community. However, continues to write in the realist mode. The play on the Maasai word for Nairobi (etymologically from "Enkare Nyrobi," which means "place of cold water") to produce Nairoua (Maasai language for "place of hot water") indicates the novel's intention to draw attention to extratextual references to places such as Mai Mahiu (Gĩkũyũ language for "hot water") affected by tribal cleansing and therefore to locate the narrative in the Moi-era Kenya.

9. Though journalistic in its register and highly documentary in its style, Wahome Mutahi's *Three Days on the Cross* (1991) is set in a dystopian nation characterized by intolerance of political dissent. The novel is also humorous in tone, as it ruthlessly satirizes the abuse of power by the African government under threat of being swept out of power by the wave of democratization occasioned by the collapse of the Soviet Union in the late 1980s. The name Kigoi, which the novel chooses for one of the victims of state repression it portrays, not only reminds readers of the Gĩkũyũ word for a species of arrowroot (an indigenous staple food in central Kenya, which is recurrently and playfully referred to in Mutahi's *Whispers* humor columns) but also seems to be a play on the name of Koigi wa Wamwere, a political prisoner in the Moi-era Kenya, the time the novel was written. Although Kigoi, the professor in exile in the novel, reminds readers of Ngũgĩ wa Thiong'o, the novel's play on Koigi's name indicates to the reader the material political conditions in the Kenya of the 1990s. The other prisoner's name in the novel, Ndimu Nduru, is a Gĩkũyũ translation of "Bitter Lemon," a brand of soda manufactured by Schweppes and one of the alternatives to Coca-Cola products. Therefore, although the novel claims to be set in an unknown country and despite the fact that the events it presents have parallels in Africa and the Third World in general, it uses names borrowed from the Gĩkũyũ language to cheekily indicate to the reader that the repressive Moi-era Kenya (1978–2002) is the primary target of its satire.

10. Karanja's *Dreamer's Paradise* (2001) announces its metafictionality right in the prologue to signal its use of folkloric materials to thematize ideological ignorance in a society battered by dictatorship and neocolonialism. Like Rebeka Njau's *The Sacred Seed* (2003) and Ngũgĩ's *The Wizard of the Crow* (2006) and *Matigari* (1988), Karanja's novel claims to be set in no particular nation, but it has numerous hints that it is about Moi's Kenya.

11. In a subsequent work, *Maps of Englishness*, Gikandi sees "decolonized situations" as marked by "the trace of the imperial pasts they try to disavow" (1996, 15). Literary texts from Africa undermine the colonial/postcolonial binary without reinstating imperial aesthetics.

Chapter 3

1. Quayson notes that literatures in local languages use similar strategies to signal social and political transformation. The advantage of Europhone texts, according to Quayson, is that they facilitate, via their transethnic accessibility, the appreciation of a different culture by outsiders (1997, 158).

2. In a reading of Salman Rushdie, Tim Brennan describes magical realism as a liberatory mode of writing that can be misused by being turned into "saleable 'Third-Worldism' " (Brennan 1989, 65). This would involve the peddling of a bizarre non-Western world to a rich and metropolitan readership too ready to see other cultures in exotic terms. For a critique of magical realism as "exoticism," see Gerald Gaylard's *After Colonialism* (2005, 176–80).

3. These nonrealist novels include Kezilahabi's *Nagona* (The Gazelle-Woman/The Insight, 1990) and *Mzingile* (The Labyrinth, 1990), Mkangi's *Mafuta* (Oil/Fuel/Ointment, 1984) and *Walenisi* (Those-Are-Us, 1995), Mbogo's *Vipuli vya Figo* (Kidney Trafficking, 1996), Mkufya's *Ziraili na Zirani* (Angel of Death and Zirani, 1999), Mohamed's *Babu Alipofufuka* (When Grandpa Came Back to Life, 2001) and *Dunia Yao* (Their World/Their Globe, 2006). If we consider that Said A. M. Khamis (the critic) and Said A. Mohamed (the novelist) are the same person, then it is easy to see that Mohamed (the author) is aware of engaging in metafictional games in his writing.

4. Said A. M. Khamis is the same person as the novelist, playwright, and poet Said A. Mohamed. This is most evidently betrayed in a lapse in the paratexts of his *Dunia Yao* (Their World, 2006), in which the cover page and title page indicate the author as "Said A. Mohamed," while the blurb on the back cover talks about the author of the novel as "Said A. M. Khamis." He has written criticism on his own novels, discussing their postrealist imperatives. See Khamis's comments on Mohamed's novels in his survey of the Kiswahili novel (Khamis 2005) and his online review of Mohamed's *Babu Alipofufuka*.

5. Grace Ogot's novels in Dholuo were published by her Anyange Press, while Asenath Bole Odaga is published by her own firm, Lake Publishers.

6. There have been remarkable African language poetic and dramatic productions by women artists such as Tanzania's Amandina Lihamba and Penina Muhando Mlama and Kenya's Ari Katini Mwachofi. Most of the women's works in local languages have limited circulation because they are published by small firms that have gone out of business. Although his first experimental novel *Bina-Adamu!* was published by a more established firm (Wamitila owns the firm), Vide Muwa now publishes his novels. He too is a university professor in Nairobi.

Chapter 4

1. Kevin Paul Smith's *The Postmodern Fairytale* (2007) finds a link between postmodern metafictional texts and oral narratives. He sees the foregrounding of narrators and storytelling in novels as diverse as Rushdie's *Midnight's Children* (1980) and Conrad's *Heart of Darkness* (1999) to be founded on attempts to question the primacy of the written discourse. The use of the structures of the fairytale is liberating. In this chapter, I focus on how the oral modes of communication are exploited but the contents of oral literature are undermined to suggest the need to liberate contemporary Africa from its feudal past.

2. In an examination of contemporary Luganda radio songs, Mugambi (1994) argues that the societies' founding myth is manipulated to produce gendered spaces

that empower women, depending on the competence and gender sensitivity of the artist.

3. The dynamic nature of orature has been noted by many scholars. For instance, Albert B. Lord correctly observes that despite a certain degree of fixity in its structure, oral literature is "neither a rigidly monolithic nor a static body of story or song." For him, a piece of orature "contains within itself much that is subject to change, though at differing rates, from one period to another" (1995, 8).

4. South African poet Masizi Kunene, whose poetry borrows from Zulu oral literature and cosmology, insists that it is standard practice in African literature to forge a connection between traditional philosophy and modern reality: "Whereas some literatures make the cosmic purpose their goal, African literature begins from the premise that the cosmic setting is the primary basis of all literature" (Kunene 1980, 200). But Kunene notes too that writers from other societies, such as "Homer, Milton, Tu Fu, Nguyen Du, and others, have used similar techniques that are seen as the primary elements in African literature (Kunene 1980, 191).

5. Studies of nonrealist "magical realism" also emphasize the centrality of oral literature in this form of self-expression. These authoritative texts include Elsa Linguanti, Francesco Casotti, and Carmen Concilio's *Coterminous Worlds: Magical Realism and Contemporary Post-Colonial Literature in English* (1999), Gerald Gaylard's *After Colonialism* (2005), and Brenda Cooper's *Magical Realism in West African Fiction* (1998). I would like to emphasize the departures from the oral forms that the novels evoke, especially following Cooper's warning that these novelists are not bound to the pretechnological cultures that inspire their writing (1998, 16).

6. Also see Winfried Siemerling's *The New North American Studies* (2005), in which she argues that minority—Native and African American—discourses are mediated through translated orality and a preoccupation with vernacular arts in modern writing.

7. In his examination of modern African poetry that employs traditional incantatory techniques, Charles Bodunde (2001b) emphasizes continuity and the transfer of oral literature into modern poetry. However, he suggests that the recourse to oral literature is made in order to critique systems of governance that deny ordinary people avenues of self-expression.

8. Lisa Mcnee holds a similar position in her reading of oral and written women's autobiographical discourses in *Selfish Gifts* (2000, 10) but, like Eileen Julien (1992), she tacitly contests the notion of authenticity in the modern use of orature. Besides Julien, others who have disagreed with Scheub's "unbroken continuity" argument include Margaret Daymond, especially in her reading of Sindiwe Magona's use of orature, "Complementary Oral and Written Narrative Conventions" (2002), and Maurice Taonezvi Vambe (2004) who, like Julien, emphasizes that modern writers are "not mere slaves to tradition, passively influenced by previous literary creations. They identify some aspects of tradition and fuse these with new ideas that confirm, modify, or reject these elements in their bid to forge new relations between orality and the novel and the past traditions and emergent aspects of the cultures with which they are working" (Vambe 2004, 236). It is worth noting that Scheub is not as reductive as his critics suggest. In his essay, he notes some differences in the way various writers deploy orality. He particularly observes that in order for more recent

writers to "probe the hero's psyche, they deviate from the basic movements of the oral tradition, and the cyclical romanticism of the ancient works is replaced by a realistic open-endedness" (Scheub 1985, 41). Elsewhere, in a study of postapartheid narratives, Scheub argues that some of the discourses, though seemingly celebrative of African traditions, "express their qualms and misgivings about traditions in their interstices and subtexts" (1996, 367).

9. For instance, the Tuareg, a diffuse group of Berber nomadic peoples who live in the Sahara and its fringes in Mali, Niger, and Algeria, have their own ancient alphabet and written script. Equally remarkable is the Ethiopian literature in Ge'ez and modern Amharic, whose script is indigenously African.

10. In *Penpoints, Gunpoints, and Dreams* (1998), Ngũgĩ has drawn attention to the elements of orality in cyber-culture and cinematic discourse, thus underlining the possibilities of conjoining orature with new, technological modes of transmitting culture. For Ngũgĩ, new modes of transmission do not necessarily turn older means of expression "into relics of the past" (1998, 109).

11. A case in point is Aaron Mushengyezi (2004), who suggests that myths of creation were used to inspire the Rwanda genocide of the 1990s. However, Mushengyezi goes on to state that African myths and legends "can still be used to positively inspire us in our struggles against all forms of injustice in our society" (2004, 41). A similar position is held by Okot Benge (2004), who argues that although oral literature maintains the dominant ideology and entrenches a "herd mentality," "there are many forms in which orature is used to contest patriarchy" (2004, 120). Benge's overall argument seems to be that despite some weaknesses in indigenous oral literature, recourse to foreign forms cannot provide a viable solution to problems of gender, human rights, and environmental degradation in Africa. Africans should summon indigenous arts and change them to address contemporary issues.

12. Penina Mlama (1995) similarly offers a critique of the co-option of indigenous artistic forms by the Tanzanian socialist government to maintain the status quo, while Hubert Chimhundu (1995) discusses the use of oral forms in modern popular culture to enforce a submissive femininity. Mlama particularly notes "the manipulation of oral art for the benefit of the ruling classes, leading to its domestication and disempowerment" (1995, 25).

13. While exposing the ideology of control that informs traditional oral narratives, Wanjiku Mukabi Kabira notes that there are counter-currents to these entrenched artistic practices in the sense that there are "forces of resistance among other artists who struggle within the same genre to address gender-based oppression. For every dominant ideology, there must be a resistant ideology that consistently works against the mainstream search of a better and just society" (Kabira 1994, 83). Essays by Wangari Kimani Mwai (1997) and Ciarunji Chesaina (1997) explain the positive role of oral literature, especially among women performers, in debunking patriarchy. Similarly useful studies of the complex relationship between gender and orature include Helen Nabasuta Mugambi (1994, 1997, 2007). Mugambi lucidly demonstrates how Luganda folklore can be and has been transformed in various performative spaces and used for women's liberation despite the stereotypes that some items have traditionally been used to circulate and entrench.

14. For a critique of Chinweizu and colleagues, see Appiah's essay "Topologies of Nativism" in *In My Father's House* (1992).

15. Coetzee's references are limited to written texts; for example, he refers to Defoe's *Robinson Crusoe* in *Foe* (1986), Konstantinos Kavafis's poetry in *Waiting for the Barbarians* (1980), and Dostoyevsky's writing in *The Master of Petersburg* (1994).

16. As already noted, Hegel's (1990) stereotype in *The Philosophy of History*, that Africans are more emotional than rational, and that they are oversexed, was taken as an advantage for the African by negritude poets, who celebrated as unique manifestations of black strength those ostensible African weaknesses that the West had denigrated as evidence of degenerate racial alterity. Egudu seems to be living out this stereotype.

17. Since *From a Crooked Rib* (1970) Farah has treated with rare sensitivity the abuse of women by traditional cultures and the resilience with which female characters, often Somali women, have fought against marginality.

18. In a controversial statement that has generated considerable opposition from African scholars, Finnegan contends in *Oral Literature in Africa* (1970) that "epic hardly seems to occur in sub-Saharan Africa" (Finnegan 1970, 108). She bases her criteria on length and verse but still ignores poetic texts from different parts of the continent. For initial opposition to Finnegan's conclusion, see, for example, Bird (1974, 1976), Biebuyck (1972, 1978), Johnson (1978, 1980), Mbele (1986), Okpewho (1977, 1979), and Mulokozi (1983). See also Mulokozi's *The African Epic Controversy: Historical, Philosophical, and Aesthetic Perspectives on Epic Poetry and Performances* (2002).

19. For a detailed discussion of the epic elements in *The River and the Source*, see Mwangi's "Gendering Genre" (2003).

20. The Kenyan African National Union (Kanu) ruled the country from independence in 1963 under Jomo Kenyatta and Daniel Moi until 2002. The two regimes were known for their high-handedness, especially toward the end of each reign. Kenyatta ruled until his death in 1978.

21. *Miaha* is the Dholuo word for the "first wife"; "strange bride" in the title seems to be a rather creative interpretation on the part of the translator.

22. Anderson contends that a reader feels solidarity with "thousands (or millions) of others of whose existence he is confident, yet of whose identity he has not the slightest notion" (1991, 35). For him, the particular systems of communication characterizing societies with popular literacy allow the population of the imagined community to be extended far beyond the bounds of the knowable or face-to-face community of societies characterized by traditional oral forms [of] communications (1991, 88–92). Thanks to the hegemonic nature of the state, in African literature there is a disjunction between what the people read and what is considered the national literature. See Chatterjee's critique of Anderson in *The Nation and Its Fragments* (1993).

23. The average literacy rate is about 50 percent. Zimbabwe has an adult literacy of 90 percent, but in some countries, literacy is below 20 percent. Women account for about two thirds of the nonliterate population in Africa. In some African countries, literacy is fairly high. See the World Health Organization figures in *World Health Report 1999* (1999, 84–87). The literacy reflects the ability to read basic texts, and literary materials remain the preserve of an elite minority.

24. Charles Larson observes in "Who Reads African Literature?" that "in spite of enormous advances in literacy and education in most African countries, the potential readers of African literature are no longer homegrown" (2002, 222). He cites the deterioration of African economies since the 1980s as one of the possible reasons behind the deterioration in reading habits. I would add that the growth of new media, as a result of the liberalization of airwaves that have witnessed a proliferation of entertainment television and FM radio stations, has compounded the problem of poor reading. However, postmodern and cosmopolitan venues have been used to encourage reading culture in, for example, open-mic reading sessions conducted by such groups as Kwani Trust in Kenya under the leadership of Binyavanga Wainaina.

Chapter 5

1. It is in a similar context that Chantal Zabus reads the African novel in her majestic *The African Palimpsest* (2007). She sees a modern African text to be comprised of several layers of different texts in different languages. Although written in European languages, the African novel has beneath the surface Europhone text a more profound text in indigenous languages. Zabus shows the effects of this confluence of languages in facilitating discourse among postcolonial writers, who enact the survival of their indigenous cultures that were threatened by colonialism. In my reading of the palimpsest in the current chapter, I focus on intertextuality between written texts and the way gender relations are played out in the interface between the dialoguing texts.

2. For Derrida in *Of Grammatology*, there is a mutual replication between the superinscription and the supposed original (1976, 61).

3. In reality the "indirectness" of British colonial rule did not mean voluntary submission to colonial practices or noncoercive methods of governance. Rather, the focus was more on economic exploitation than cultural transformation except in instances where culture threatened economic and political domination. Indeed, historian Bruce Berman (2004) reads the British colonial state as a "palimpsest of contradictions" in that it is haunted both by the past and the confusions and paradoxes of the present.

4. Okri's more metafictional *Astonishing the Gods* (1995) inverts Ralph Ellison's notions of invisibility in *Invisible Man* (1952) to indicate that invisibility can be a source of agency. It presents a pilgrim who travels to utopian places without being discovered because of his invisibility. It is because he discovers that he is invisible in official history that he starts exploring the powers of invisibility: "It was in books that he first learnt of his invisibility. He searched for himself and his people in history books he read and discovered to his youthful astonishment that he didn't exist. This troubled him so much that he resolved, as soon as he was old enough, to leave his land and find the people who did exist, to see what they looked like" (Okri 1995, 3).

5. For Riffaterre, intertextuality generates matrices of indebtedness that enable the reader to benefit from the transaction between the texts (1978, 85–86). What little is recoverable from the dialogue among texts enables the reader to negotiate through the meanings the text generates.

6. Other novels published in the series around the same time, such as Calixthe Beyala's *Thy Name Shall Be Tanga* (1996b) and *The Sun Hath Looked Upon Me* (1996a), Ghanaian Amma Darko's *The Housemaid* (1999) and *Beyond the Horizon* (1995), and Namibian Neshani Andreas's *The Purple Violet of Oshaantu* (2001), highlight the plight of African women by using narrative perspectives that prioritize the female center of consciousness, mainly those of the narrators and embedded addressees. They treat themes that earlier male writers had addressed in a cavalier manner—themes such as domestic violence, female genital cutting, and abuse of women's rights and its implications regarding the spread of HIV/AIDS.

7. I'm calling Enitan's optimistic declaration utopian because there appears no firm logical basis in the story to support her optimism.

8. Tutuola's narratives try to normalize the abnormal by offering the causal logic for the event. For example, the entry into the "bush of ghosts" is explained in a causal relationship in *My Life in the Bush of Ghosts* (1954), and all the major events in the story, strange as they may appear, are explained in order to restore the logical and causal relationships between events. Tutuola appears at pains to, if we may use Roland Barthes's term in *Image-Music-Text* (1977), "naturalize the narrative" by discovering for the reader the reason behind the seemingly unreasonable order of things.

9. For a reading of Ngũgĩ's use of Conrad, see Peter Nazareth's "Out of Darkness: Conrad and Other Third World Writers" (1982) and *Literature and Society in Modern Africa: Essays on Literature* (1972); Ponnuthurai Sarvan's "Conrad's Influence on Ngũgĩ" (1977) and "Under African Eyes: Joseph Conrad" (1990); Andrea White's "Conrad's Legacy in Postcolonial Literature" (1996); Jacqueline Bardolphe's "Ngũgĩ wa Thiong'o's *A Grain of Wheat* and *Petals of Blood* as Readings of Conrad's *Under Western Eyes* and *Victory*" (1987); Ebele Obumselu's "*A Grain of Wheat*: Ngũgĩ's Debt to Conrad" (1974); and David Cook and Michael Okenimkpe's Ngũgĩ *wa Thiong'o: An Exploration of His Writing* (1997).

10. The passage echoes Chinua Achebe's description of the Africans' initial reaction to the Europeans in *Things Fall Apart*: "But stories were already gaining ground that the white man had not only brought a religion but also a government. It was said that they had built a place of judgment in Umuofia to protect the followers of their religion. It was even said that they had hanged one man who killed a missionary" (Achebe 1958, 110).

11. For example, Judith Cochrane notes that in connecting Mumbi with Wangu (a negative reference), the novel recreates "the last of the great Gĩkũyũ women" but contradicts the figures of the compelling women Ngũgĩ projects in his fiction. Even positive characters such as Wangari, Mumbi, and Wambui turn out to be politically weak characters because the women's rule is largely figured as a misrule that is part of the historical past (Williams 1999, 65).

12. Carol Sicherman, in "Ngũgĩ wa Thiong'o and the Writing of History," and Patrick Williams, in *Ngũgĩ wa Thiong'o*, have severally discussed the revisions, but gender is not an analytic category in their arguments regarding the changes Ngũgĩ effects in the new narrative.

13. Maughan-Brown compares Ngũgĩ with other writers who have dealt with the Mau Mau struggle. For him, Ngũgĩ inserts Koinandu's negative aggression, "because Ngũgĩ is the most 'serious' of the writers" (1985, 245).

14. Ngũgĩ's novels published after *A Grain of Wheat* (namely, *Devil on the Cross* in 1982 and *Matigari* in 1986) tend to implicate the wives of capitalists with the evil activities of their husbands, or to show them as subservient victims of the masculinist abuse of power. *Wizard of the Crow* gives more agency to women by showing the wives of government officials as being capable of revolt against their all-powerful husbands.

Chapter 6

1. By making this claim, Jegede's argument here, I think, is that contemporary African art is no different from arts from the West, as Western scholars would want to insist in order to arrest African art within the confines of the precolonial "primitive" realms. An individualistic drive in producing art is scoffed at by Achebe, Ngũgĩ, and Armah. For instance, in *Why Are We So Blest?* (1972), a novel about writing and revolution, Armah makes Solo's voice the supposed binary between Western individualism and African revolutionary imperatives: "The Western artist is blest with that atrophy of vision that can see beauty in deliberately broken-off pieces of a world sickened with oppression's ugliness. . . . But in the world of my people that most important first of creation, that rearrangement without which all attempts at creation are doomed to falseness, remain to be done. . . . In my people's world, revolution would be the only art, revolutionaries the only creators. All else is part of Africa's destruction" (Armah 1972, 231).

2. Soyinka develops this idea further in the wider context of African literature in the essay "New Frontiers for Old," which he delivered at Cambridge University in 1990 and published in the later edition of *Art, Dialogue, and Outrage* (1993). For a similar skepticism toward notions of an authentic Africa in visual arts, see Harrow (2007), especially chapter 5 of the book.

3. Mudimbe expresses a similar sentiment in *The Invention of Africa* (1988) when he suggests that the overzealousness of inventing an authentic primordial Africa is a tacitly racist move to present the continent as perpetually arrested in premodernity. There is a similar critique of anthropologists' fascination with the "authentic" and disappointment with modernized non-Western cultures in the second chapter ("Where Have All the Natives Gone?") in Rey Chow's *Writing Diaspora* (1995). Guy Ossito Midouhouan (1991) voices similar concerns in an African context when he argues that the tendency to present Africa anthropologically as a mummified and fossilized space was meant to "provide a sanction for the colonial enterprise by affirming the cultural superiority of the West and by presenting colonialism as the impregnation of an essentially passive Africa, vegetating in its own degradation and threatened with sterility, by a male West—a sort of artificial insemination" (Midouhouan 1991, 94).

4. For a similar critique of the tendency to evacuate modernity from African art by insisting on an authentic tribal essence, see Salah Hassan's "The Modernist Experience in African Art" (1999) and Sidney Kasfir's "One Tribe, One Style" (1984) and "African Art and Authenticity" (1999).

5. Referred to in Ngũgĩ wa Thiong'o's *Petals of Blood* (1977), Elimo Njau is a Kenyan-based Tanzanian artist and the founder of Paa ya Paa Gallery. Founded in 1965 as the oldest and most important arts center in black Africa, Paa ya Paa was a

haven for African artists, writers, and critics, including Rebeka Njau, Hillary Ng'weno, Jonathan Kariara, Ngũgĩ wa Thiong'o, Taban lo Liyong, and Okot p'Bitek. In December 1997, a fire at the Paa ya Paa Arts Center in Nairobi destroyed Njau's work, alongside murals and paintings by Ethiopian, Kenyan, Tanzania, Uganda, and Sudanese artists. The fire also destroyed videos, books, cassettes, and computers at the Paa ya Paa Art Center, renowned for its wide acceptance of artists from Africa, America, Europe, and Asia who often held lectures, seminars, and workshops there.

6. Okri's *Astonishing the Gods* (1995) and *The Starbook* (2007) are set in a mythical world, but their invocation of the same *abiku* myth that structures his *The Famished Road* (1991) recuperates them within a particularly Yoruba cosmological belief system.

Chapter 7

1. William Atwood and William Murdoch were consecrated in Nairobi, Kenya, by Bishop Benjamin Nzimbi in August 2007, joining a group of conservative American bishops pledging allegiance to African bishops who take a tough line against homosexuality. Nigerian Archbishop Peter Akinola raised a storm of controversy in May of the same year when he consecrated Martyn Minns as bishop in the Convocation of Anglicans in North America, which is linked to the Church of Nigeria. The "Global South" (Africa, Asia, and Latin America) is pitted against the North (Europe and America) for the latter's tolerance of homosexuality.

2. See, for example, Dunbar T. Moodie (1988) on the one hand, and Hugh McLean and Linda Ngcobo (1995), on the other, over the Zulu term *hlabonga*. A similar debate rages between Arno Schmitt's "Different Approaches to Male-Male Sexuality/Eroticism from Morocco to Usbekistan" (1992) and Stephen O. Murray's "The Will Not to Know: Islamic Accommodations of Homosexuality" (1997).

3. See Munro's "Queer Futures: The Coming Out Novel in South Africa" (2007).

4. Following Spivak's and Bhabha's skepticism about forms of nationalism that survive on elision of disputes and differences, Spurling has, throughout *Imperialism within the Margins* (2006), offered a convincing critique of postcolonial theory that is premised on national boundaries.

5. For a materialist critique of the occlusion of the postcolonial from queer theory, see Rob Cover's "Queer with Class" (2005). Cover faults queer theory for ignoring non-Western societies. William Spurlin's "Broadening Postcolonial Studies/Decolonizing Queer Studies" (2001) provides a critique of Marxist and Althusserian studies of homosexuality in Southern Africa. Spurlin notes the elision of insurgent sexuality from nationalistic and critical postcolonial discourses. Neither study pays sufficient attention to literary materials, but each provides ways queer theory and postcolonial studies can inform one another. Valuable texts on the intersection of queer theory and postcolonialism include John Hawley's *Postcolonial and Queer Theories* (2001b) and *Postcolonial Queer* (2001a) and Spurlin's *Imperialism within the Margins*. These texts, however, seem more interested in how Western queer studies can bring on board non-Western practices of homosexuality rather than studying literary texts

in their own terms. Neville Hoad's *African Intimacies* (2007) takes a step in the right direction by incorporating literary texts in the study of homosexuality. Hoad's close reading of Mpe's *Welcome to Our Hillbrow* (2001) and Duiker's *The Quiet Violence of Dreams* (2001) astutely teases out the intersection of postapartheid nationalism, belated pan-Africanism, and insurgent sexuality in constituting cosmopolitan identities in South Africa.

6. A claim to a gay identity, for Foucault, would be as stifling as efforts to erase gay pleasure.

7. For a survey of the treatment of homosexuality in earlier African literature, see Chris Dunton's " 'Wheyting Be Dat?' The Treatment of Homosexuality in African Literature" (1989). Gaurav Desai's "Out in Africa" (2001) discusses the subtler ways in which homosexual desire is presented in some novels that earlier had been seen as homophobic. Stephen O. Murray and Will Roscoe's *Boy-Wives and Female Husbands: Studies of African Homosexualities* (1998) shows the existence of same-sex passion and practices in African societies since the precolonial times. Mwangi Gicheru's *Across the Bridge* (1979), a realist novel, mentions in a rare antirealist moment a he-goat mounting other he-goats. Gicheru's *The Mixers* (1991), another realist novel, contains moments of transgressive lesbian desire among cows from racially divided farms in colonial Kenya. In both cases, homosexuality in the animals symbolizes lack of the ideal outlet for desire. But it is ironic that in *Across the Bridge*, Gicheru uses his name, a common moniker for he-goats in Gĩkũyũ folklore, to name the transgressive he-goat in the novel (1979, 13).

8. For a critique of Fanon's views on homosexuality, see Desai's "Out in Africa" and Hoad's *African Intimacies*.

9. Furthermore, criticizing Micere Githae Mugo's mention of homophobia as a social ill in Mugo's poem *To Be a Feminist Is*, Ama Ata Aidoo argues in "Literature, Feminism, and the African Woman Today" (1998) that "it would be a violent untruth to assert that in the last decade of the twentieth century, the major preoccupation of the majority of African women was the debate on society's perception of female (or male) homosexuality" (Aidoo 1998, 27). Other critics who have been critical of finding of homosexuality where there supposedly is none include Ifi Amadiume, who argues that reading homosexuality into some cultural practices in Africa results from Western ethnographers imposing their homoerotic desires on heterosexual African cultures. For an explanation of the supposed paucity of (homo)sexuality as an abiding theme in African literature, see the various essays in Azodo and Eke's *Gender and Sexuality in African Literature and Film* (2007).

10. Ghanaian novelist Amma Darko, in *Beyond the Horizon* (1995), has used Germany, a setting used by Ama Ata Aidoo in *Our Sister Killjoy* (1979), to link homosexuality to the Western exploitation of African women. In *Beyond the Horizon* (1999), male homosexuals exploit hapless African women who need visas to stay in Europe as prostitutes. While homosexuality is largely seen as an importation from a perverted West, it is presented as a precolonial phenomenon in Armah's *Two Thousand Seasons* (1973) and in Marechera's metafictional novel *The Black Insider* (1992). Both Armah and Marechera conflate homosexuality with the authoritarian and degenerate tendencies of feudalistic leaders. Promise Okekwe presents both male and female homosexuality as perverse in *Fumes and Cymbals* (2003) but is

more sympathetic to lesbian Rebecca in *Women from the Crystal Deep* (2002b). The very broaching of sexuality issues in Okekwe's fiction joins similar presentation in Tess Onwueme (Nigeria), Titilola Shoneyin (Nigeria), Unoma Azuah (Nigeria), and Ken Bugul (Senegal) in demonstrating that alternative sexuality is a theme worth exploring in African fiction. Novels and short stories by these writers do not necessarily uphold lesbianism as do novels by Calixthe Beyala, but their courage in treating the theme is an indication of the acceptance of the existence of lesbianism in Africa and the disagreement with the denial that tends to define women-women solidarity as purely asexual.

11. For an equally engaging reading of the novel's treatment of same-sex desire, see Chapter 2 of Hoad's *African Intimacies*. Hoad considers the sexual ambivalence of some of the precolonial symbols to which Soyinka refers in the novel, including the figure of deities whose sexualities are blurred.

12. The same linguistic processes that construct the identity of a homosexual male to mark him off from heterosexuals can be used to assign a gay identity to a nonhomosexual character. We see this in Zakes Mda's (2003) *She Plays with the Darkness*, where Trooper Motsohi is mocked at as a gay person, although the text is clear that these rumors are unfounded. Radisene, another character in the novel who associates with Trooper Motsohi, is implicated in the imagined homosexuality when he gives Trooper refuge from his violent wife. Equally, Monicah Genya's (2004) *The Other Side of Love* reveals in a very brief scene the stereotypes that circulate in society about homosexuality. Genya's novel calls, in a gossipy dialogue scene, for toleration of the gay lifestyle but, as in Mda's novel, the female characters seem to think that homosexuality embodies a waste of good looks on gay men. The novel further presents homosexuality as something that happens among TV and sports celebrities, as opposed to ordinary people. Then it emerges that homophobia, being part of an arbitrary and irrational construction of male homosexuality, does not spare anyone, even those who are not gay. Through rumors, the society has the power to assign anybody a gay identity and condemn them. We emphasize the social construction of sexuality in which individuals act in a way that would conform to the society's expectations and those who do not are seen as aberrant and driven to alienation unless they forcefully challenge the society. Great care should be taken when dealing with the texts from heteronormative societies because homosexual identity is at times expressed through exaggerated heterosexuality or staged homophobia by individuals who want to appear socially "normal."

13. While women writers such as Charity Waciuma and Muthoni Likimani criticized Westerners for their attitude toward African traditionalists who performed female circumcision, Rebeka Njau was critical of the bodily marks on a woman's sexual organs as an index of her maturation. Her play *The Scar* (1965) criticizes this practice at a moment of euphoric nationalism when all precolonial practices would be upheld against missionary and colonial projects. Her *The Sacred Seed* (2003) names the practice as "mutilation" that women should resist. The novel seems to see the practice as the most basic of human rights abuses in Africa.

14. In *The African Novel in English: An Introduction* (1998), M. Keith Booker reads the novel as a precursor of the magical realist genre that came to dominate African writing in the 1980s.

15. In an overview of the treatment of homosexuality in African discourse in *Boy-Wives and Female Husbands: Studies of African Homosexualities*, Murray and Roscoe remark that Rebeka Njau's *Ripples in the Pool* presents female-female passion "very negatively" (1998, 39). For them, "the view from Njau's novel is that female-female passion is possible but is not only wrong, it is also very dangerous" (Murray and Roscoe 1998, 40). The society presented is homophobic, but the novel distances itself from some of the social practices and beliefs the characters observe. Although Njau does not endorse female-female passion, she is sympathetic in her presentation of the woman in the story who falls in love with another woman.

16. Consider, for example, Bessie Head's *Maru* (1971) and Grace Ogot's *Promised Land* (1966). There is repressed sexual attraction between Maru and Moleka in Head's novel, and Ogot, though a fairly conservative novelist who believes radical feminism should be left to younger writers, suggests sexual possibilities between two women.

17. See T. G. Benson's *English-Kikuyu Dictionary* under the entry "calf" (1975, 47).

18. This seems to conform to Ifi Amadiume's observation in *Daughters of the Goddess, Daughters of Imperialism*, that same-sex relationships are a phenomenon of the city and are accompanied by a domineering attitude toward less economically powerful women (2000, 240, 260).

19. Here I am relying on my experience growing up in central Kenya. We were warned never to go round the tree because we could change into girls. See Elizabeth Waichinga's account of the tree for a mention of this myth of physical sexual transformation (Waichinga 2004). However, Jomo Kenyatta's more authoritative anthropological account indicates that the going round the trunk of the tree seven times the way the characters do in *Ripples in the Pool* is part of the ancestral worship among the Gĩkũyũ community and has nothing to do with gender changes. According to Kenyatta, the "procession goes round the sacred tree seven times, moving from right to left, and, at the same time, sprinkling the milk and the honey-beer around the trunk of the sacred tree" (1937, 317; 1938, 248). Most probably the myth that people would be transformed to the opposite sex if they went round the tree seven times was a mere scare tactic to keep kids from playing at the prototypal sacred tree. However, the taboo not only kept the children away from the tree but entrenched the fear of possible cross-gender behavior.

20. See Taasisi ya Uchunguzi wa Kiswahili's *Kamusi ya Kiswahili* under the entry *chinusi* (1981, 34) and *chunusi* (1981, 38). See also Taasisi ya Uchunguzi wa Kiswahili's *Swahili-English Dictionary* under *chunusi* (2001, 51).

21. Armah presents a female African American, Ast, as an important force in the regeneration of Africa. She comes to the continent to recover the history of the community that the local leadership has joined former colonizers in suppressing. She rejects academic honors in the West because such recognitions are based on the willful distortion of black people's history.

22. Ngũgĩ invokes the figure of Sojourner Truth to criticize the ignorance and cynicism of postcolonial leadership. Through the principal female character, Nyawira, we are shown the need to study literatures from the diaspora, including texts from nonblack diasporas that treat feminist themes.

23. In Gĩkũyũ language, *mwera* is a young hen, in the transition from a chick to an adult. Although the word is omitted from T. G. Benson's *Kikuyu-English Dictionary* (1964), see the entry "hen" in his *English-Kikuyu Dictionary* (1975).

24. The narrator reminds the writer about how fictional works have affected the way he responds to real-life situations: "And you spent the rest of the night trying to read yourself back to sleep with John Maxwell Coetzee's *Waiting for the Barbarians;* seeing *Confessions* and *Apologies* filling every page that you turned" (Mpe 2001, 53). There are references to Zakes Mda's equally playful *Ways of Dying* (1995) as contrasted to the works of Joyce, Wilde, Shaw, and Deane. Though Mda's novel is recommended with national pride, to show that South Africa "had not been left behind when it came to quality literary output" (Mpe 2001, 107), there is no attempt to denigrate Western literature.

25. The narrator notes that Hillbrow is itself a mixture of the rural and the urban: "You discovered, on arriving in Hillbrow, that to be drawn away from Tiragalong also went hand-in-hand with a loss of interest in Hillbrow. Because Tarangalong was in Hillbrow. You always took Tiragalong with you in your consciousness whenever you came to Hillbrow or any other place. In the same way, you carried Hillbrow with you always" (Mpe 2001, 49).

26. A similar technique is effectively used in Nuruddin Farah's *Maps* (1986) and Benjamin Kwakye's *The Sun by Night* (2006), two other metafictional novels in which the narrator addresses himself in the second person in large segments of the narrative. For a discussion of Kwakye's novel, see Palmer's "African Jekyls and Hydes" (2007).

27. Like Mpe's novel, David Karanja's *Dreamer's Paradise* (2001) criticizes the use of the English language as the medium of expression, although it is itself in English and although it celebrates the liberatory potential of literary works in English such as George Orwell's *Animal Farm*. Karanja's work is less subtle in its metafictional tendencies.

28. A similar text in the presentation of reality as fiction is Dangor's *Kafka's Curse* (1997).

29. Mpe died at age thirty-four in December 2004. Like his novelist-character, he was born in a rural area and went to Johannesburg for college education. Due to his lack of money, he ended up living in the economically deprived inner-city area of Hillbrow, the setting of *Welcome to Our Hillbrow* (2001).

30. The South African novel participates in the language debate without taking as radical a position as Ngũgĩ's in *Decolonising the Mind* (1986a) because indigenous languages have been used by the apartheid system as a divisive tool against liberation efforts. The writer-narrator justifies the use of English as opposed to his native Sepedi by suggesting that English works would receive a wider readership and can be later translated into indigenous languages (Mpe 2001, 30–31, 57, 59). Note how Mda's novel, *The Madonna of Excelsior* (2003a), handles the topic in a moment when a town council in postapartheid South Africa is "quibbling over irrelevances" (Mda 2003a, 189). The metafictional preoccupation with which the language discourse should be conducted indicates that the novels, including Mda's, do not consider the language debate irrelevant.

31. *thirteen cents* was awarded the 2001 Commonwealth Prize for first book in the African region, and *The Quiet Violence of Dreams* won the Herman Charles Bosman Prize for English Literature. *The Hidden Star* was published posthumously in 2006.

32. A similar treatment of interracial sex is seen in Omondi Mak'Oloo's *Times Beyond* (1991), in which the main character, Waweru Njuhia, performs a penile conquest of Hungarian women. This novel is not as explicit as Onyeama's but, like Tayeb Salih's classic and more sophisticated novel *Season of Migration to the North* (1969), Mak'Oloo's *Times Beyond* captures the voyeurism of European women gazing at an African man as an oversexed source of pleasure to be exploited. In Mak'Oloo's novel, the females' ignorance is expressed through their lack of knowledge about obvious African literary texts. They view Waweru as a worldly embodiment of Achebe's masculine character Okonkwo, an object to be exploited sexually. However, Waweru views himself, like Mustafa in *Season of Migration to the North*, as avenging colonial crimes against Africa, although Hungary had no colonies in Africa. Unlike Salih's novel, this penile conquest of Europe through the sexual subjection of white women to sexual penetration with the African phallus is not treated with any disapproval or irony in Mak'Oloo's and Onyeama's novels.

33. For example, Ngũgĩ wa Thiong'o's *A Grain of Wheat* (1967) is revised in a 1986 edition to, among other things, erase an instance in which a Mau Mau freedom fighter rapes a white woman. Novels that have treated rape as a theme include Coetzee's *Disgrace* (1999), Vera's *The Stone Virgins* (2002), Mda's *The Madonna of Excelsior* (2003a), and Achmat Dangor's *Bitter Fruit* (2005). In these novels, rape is used to foreground the use of the female body as a site to inscribe male and nationalistic supremacy. Mark Behr's *The Smell of Apples* (1995) depicts the sexual exploitation of the male child. Incidentally, the novels that boldly present rape come from the southern parts of the continent.

34. Male-against-male rape is explored in recent fiction, especially from Nigeria. See, for example, Uzodinma Iweala's *Beasts of No Nation* (2005), in which boy soldiers are raped by seniors in the ragged armies, and Chris Abani's *Graceland* (2004), in which the principal character, Elvis, is raped in a scene reminiscent of Arundhati Roy's *The God of Small Things* (1997).

35. Although derogatory in everyday usage, *moffie* is the term South African writer Andre Carl van der Merwe chooses as the title of his semiautobiographical novel about gays in the South African military. Merwe attempts to retrieve the word from its derogatory status and reassign it value as a descriptor of males who do not fit into the heterosexual, macho stereotype.

36. Other prime examples of this genre are Gordimer's *The Lying Days* (1953), Achebe's *No Longer at Ease* (1960), and Austin Bukenya's *The People's Bachelor* (1972). In each of these, the principal characters are students of literature through whom the novels theorize about art and postcolonial existence.

37. For an incisive critique of the novel's presentation of women and race, see Cheryl Stobie's (2005) "Between the Arches of Queer Desire and Race." See also Annie Gagiano's (2004) "Adapting the National Imaginary: Shifting Identities in Three Post-1994 South African Novels," in which she reads the problematic of patriarchal and misogynistic overtones in Tshepo's gay identity. Stobie's *Somewhere*

in the Double Rainbow (2007) offers a more extensive analysis of bisexuality in South African fiction.

38. See, for example, "On Narcissism," in which he associates narcissism with "people whose libidinal development has suffered some disturbance, such as perverts or homosexuals" (1914, 88).

39. The English translation of Ngũgĩ's novel in Gĩkũyũ has elided the dictatorial characters' discussion of suppressing "ucoga." Borrowed from the Kiswahili *shoga* (nonsexual female friends or gay males), the reference indicates the desire of the government agents to police sexuality. It is apparent that the characters are referring to possible lesbianism. The novel suggests that the two characters are repressed homosexuals.

40. See, for example, Kariara's (1963) poem *A Leopard Lives in a Muu Tree* and the short story "Karoki" (1988).

Chapter 8

1. This is the reading Feroza Jussawalla and Reed Way Dasenbrock arrive at when they remark that postcolonial literature, according to Rushdie, has its own independent and original voice: "The writing that emerges in this process issues from a remarkably complex combination of cultures, as the postcolonial writers draw on indigenous traditions and languages of their own as well as on the resources of the traditional writing in English" (Jussawalla and Dasenbrock 1992, 4). For a similar argument, see Brian Shaffer (2006, 21–22). Writing differently, however, continues to be seen primarily as a subversion of Western aesthetics rather than as an expression of local culture and politics.

2. In underlying indigenous remodeling of English to express local ethnicities, Rushdie speaks in Achebean terms: "English, no longer an English language, now grows from many roots, and those whom it once colonized are carving large territories within the language/The empire is striking back" (1982, 8). Achebe's well-known position in the 1964 talk at the University of Ghana, "The African Writer and the English Language," is that even if the African writers choose English instead of their mother tongues in order to reach a global audience, they can manipulate the language to express African experiences (Achebe 1975, 62).

3. Chantal Zabus seems aware of this literalization of the headline when in the revised edition of her African palimpsest, she says, citing Rushdie and Ashcroft and others, the African novelist writes "with an accent" not "with a vengeance" (2007, xvi). Zabus here is using Iranian-born American writer Taghi Modaressi's claim that she writes "with an accent."

4. In the article, Rushdie claims that the cosmopolitanism that he celebrates in the international writers can "perhaps only happen in English; I don't think there's any other language that is large or flexible enough to include so many realities" (1982, 8). However, some of the novels he cites, such as Ngũgĩ's *Devil on the Cross*, were originally written in native languages and away from the Western metropolitan centers.

5. Elsewhere, Tiffin has countered the colonialist notion that Third World writers are offshoots of colonial literature (Tiffin 1984, 27–28). Also see Woods (2007, 246).

6. See, for example, Helen Nabasuta Mugambi (2007, 290) for some of the major works on African women's theorizing of gender. She demonstrates the diversity and richness of the positions these scholars hold.

7. Other critics following a similarly inclusive line of argument, despite their nonchalance toward Western feminist paradigms and practices as exclusionary, include Abena Busia and Filomena Chioma Steady. While critical of Western feminists, Busia (quoted in Kolawole 1997, 8) is skeptical toward what she calls the divide-and-rule philosophy of North American feminism, but she discourages the wholesale rejection of feminist principles. For her part, Steady criticizes mainstream feminism but sees African feminism as "a more inclusive brand of feminism" (Steady 1987, 4). I must qualify that some of the antiwhite feminism positions by African women from the diaspora are based on resistance to the exclusionary tendencies of mainstream feminism in the West; in other words, they are not so much in support of separationism and essentialism as they are an indictment of the exclusionary and essentialist practices defining mainstream feminism.

8. See Nnaemeka's essays on female circumcision in her edited collection *Female Circumcision and the Politics of Knowledge* (2005), especially the chapter "The Challenges of Border-Crossing: African Women and Transnational Feminisms."

9. The WAAD Conference was attended by over 800 participants from across the globe. Sabine Jell-Bahlsen notes that "*some, not all,* African American participants demanded the exclusion of white participants. In fact, those who demanded exclusion were the minority" (1998, 442, emphases in original).

10. See Ajayi-Soyinka's "Negritude, Feminism, and the Quest for Identity: Re-Reading Mariama Bâ's *So Long a Letter*" (1997) and "Transcending the Boundaries of Power and Imperialism: Writing Gender, Constructing Knowledge" (2005).

11. Olabisi Aina argues that homosexuality is peripheral to African women's concerns. For her: "African feminism is only thinking about social relations within the heterosexual relations . . . Issues of gays and lesbians are outside its agenda. This is because for many African societies lesbianism and homosexuality are nothing but abominations" (1998, 72). Abena Busia too warns that even if we have to campaign against the discrimination of childless women, the institution of motherhood should be protected from assault from radical Western feminists because "for most African women, the place of mothering remains central" (Busia 1988, 9).

12. Aidoo warns against the womanism/feminist binary opposition, noting its essentialization of African women. By arguing that African women were the first feminists, Obioma Nnaemeka contests the rejection of the term *feminist* to describe strategies of fighting for space and equality among black women. Amina Mama and Sylvia Tamale see the term *feminism* as more empowering than its alternatives. For a polemical argument against the view that "feminism and feminists are un-African," see Simidele Dosekun's "Defending Feminism in Africa" (2007).

13. Elsewhere Tamale has argued that the banning of erotic cultural productions such as *The Vagina Monologue* by the Ugandan government as "offensive

to cultural sensibilities" by being "obscene" in a way that "promoted lesbianism in Uganda" is an expression of the patriarchal fear of women's sexual liberation (2005, 20).

14. In "Literature, Feminism, and the African Woman Today," Ama Ata Aidoo disagrees with what she perceives as the poem's equation of "feminism with lesbianism" (1998, 27). However, to be fair to the poem, the persona does not collapse all feminisms into lesbianism. Rather, Mugo's poem denounces different forms of oppression and intolerance without specifying whether sexual preference is in male or female members of the society.

15. For instance, Sara Suleri argues that Mohanty advocates the authenticity of female racial voices in arguing that "only a black can speak for a black; only a postcolonial subcontinental feminist can adequately represent the lived experiences of that culture" (1992b, 760). Although Mohanty seems to favor local voices in the expression of circumstances in the postcolonial world, she does not exclude theorists and intellectuals in and from other spaces. She is indeed against the "devastating rhetoric of 'us and them' " that Suleri sees to beleaguer "issues of identity formation today" (1992b, 756).

16. Ketu H. Katrak inspires a similar response to "Third World" literature in *Politics of the Female Body: Postcolonial Women Writers of the Third World* (2006). In the book, she destroys any rigid dichotomy between Western and non-Western gender categories. She shows how social norms have been used unquestioningly to interpellate individuals as exiles within their society. For her, the process of socialization as reflected in texts cannot be fully grasped without paying attention to sociological data within particular societies.

17. See also Osundare's argument that the term *postcolonial* gives the content word colonial an "originary privilege" as the most significant moving force in African cultural production (2000, 118). For him, postcolonial and poststructural approaches assume a linear "chronology" that "constructs progression as a process in which ideas are used and discarded, then superseded and supplanted by new ones" (Osundare 2000, 113). For a critique of poststructuralist theorizing of women's writing in Africa, see Chukwuma Okoye's "Posting the Agenda in African Women's Writing" (2007). Like Uzo Esonwanne (1993), Okoye seems to favor an anticolonial, culture-specific, and politically engaged paradigm for the study of gender relations in Africa.

18. McClintock argues that colonialism is present in Africa in different guises long after flag independence. The single binary opposition between colonialism and postcolonialism does not reflect the reality of Africa, where structures of colonialism are intact. She has problems with the term *postcolonial* because it privileges "colonialism" as the single marker of history. For her, the prefix "post" reduces the cultures of peoples beyond colonialism to prepositional time. Other cultures share only the chronological relation to a Eurocentric epoch that is over (post) or not yet begun (pre). In other words, the world's multitudinous cultures are not positively marked by what distinguishes them but by a subordinate, retrospective relation to linear European time (1995, 11). For a further critique of the nonlinear model of history that fails to analyze the splintering differences within local political and artistic movements' opposition to Western categories, see Makdisi (2000), Gaonkar (2001), and Subrahmanyam (1998). Makdisi particularly notes that while novelists such as

Tayeb Salih and Naguib Mahfouz reject notions of modernity based on Western enlightenment or linear progress, they also problematize *nahda*, the Arab-world alternative to Western modernism.

19. Bakhtin observes in *The Dialogic Imagination* that "language in the novel not only represents but itself serves as an object of representation. Novelistic discourse is always criticizing itself" (1981, 49). For the interpretation of Bakhtin arguing that the novel is anticanonical and insurrectionary, I am indebted to Michael Holoquist's introduction to Bakhtin's essays in *The Dialogic Imagination* (Bakhtin 1981, xxxi). See also Hoy (1992, 778) and Parrinder (1991, 293).

20. Utilizing the Freudian concept of "Oedipus complex," Bloom argues that poets have a subconscious urge to depose their predecessors. Bloom focuses too much on the poet/father as an author and not on the texts themselves. The father-son relationship is sexist and leaves out women's texts. It is also single-linear, while contemporaries can deconstruct each other. For a discussion of the ways Bloom's model has been critiqued by feminists and students of multiculturalism, see Chapter 4 of Madelyn Jablon's *Black Metafiction* (1996). She favors the Bakhtinian model of dialogism, which attends not only to both revision and dialogue between texts but also to the social dimensions of aesthetic choices. McDowell (1990) reads the "female bonding" between Frances Harper and Alice Walker rather than the masculine oedipal tension that Bloom's model would find.

21. Beyond the temporal, writing back also could be understood in terms of the contesting representations by contemporaries in a spatial sense. Lindfors notes that the growth of much of East African literature involves "a dynamic dialectic of mutation, with each fresh thrust moving in a direction counter to that of its immediate predecessor, even when preoccupied with similar thematic concerns" (2002, 75).

22. Charles Taylor's "The Politics of Recognition" (1994) and Beatrice Hanssen's "Ethics of the Others" (2000) offer astute readings of Fanon in terms of ethics of multiculturalism in Western institutions. Spivak's "Who Claims Alterity" (1989) and *Death of a Discipline* (2003) also raise issues about literature's ethical vocation, especially in giving marginalized cultures a voice.

Conclusion

1. See Mitsuhiro Yoshimoto's "Questions of Japanese Cinema" (2002). Rey Chow's *The Age of the World Target* (2006), especially the third chapter, offers an excellent summary of this tendency.

2. Consider, for example, the meticulous novels of M. G. Vassanji, which focus on the Asian in the diaspora in Africa and elsewhere and subtly deconstruct the negative images of the Asian presented in some African texts, such as Ngũgĩ's works.

Works Cited

Abani, Chris. 2004. *Graceland*. New York: Picador.

———. 2007. *The Virgin of Flames*. New York: Penguin.

Achebe, Chinua. 1958. *Things Fall Apart*. London: Heinemann.

———. 1960. *No Longer at Ease*. London: Heinemann.

———. 1964. Arrow of God. London, Heinemann.

———. 1966. *A Man of the People*. London: Heinemann.

———. 1973. "The Role of the Writer in a New Nation." In *African Writers on African Writing*, ed. D. G. Killam, 7–13. London: Heinemann.

———. 1975. *Morning Yet on Creation Day*. London: Heinemann.

———. 1988. *Anthills of the Savannah*. London: Heinemann.

———. 2000. *Home and Exile*. Oxford: Oxford University Press.

Acholonu, Catherine. 1985. *Nigeria in the Year 1999*. Owerri: Totan.

———. 1995. *Motherism: The Afrocentric Alternative to Feminism*. Owerri: AFA Publications.

Adalla, Caroline. 1993. *The Confessions of an AIDS Victim*. Nairobi: Spear Books.

Adéèkó, Adélékè. 1998. *Proverbs, Textuality, and Nativism in African Literature*. Gainesville: University Press of Florida.

———. 2005. *The Slave's Rebellion: Literature, History, Orature*. Indianapolis: Indiana University Press.

Adejunmobi, Moradewun. 2004. *Vernacular Palaver: Imaginations of the Local and Non-native Languages in West Africa*. Buffalo, NY: Multilingual Matters.

Adepegba, Cornelius. 2000. "The 'Otherness' Syndrome and the Study of African Visual Art." In *Rethinking African Arts and Culture*, ed. Dele Layiwola, 5–21. Cape Town, South Africa: Center for Advanced Studies of African Society.

Adichie, Chimamanda Ngozi. 2003. *Purple Hibiscus*. Chapel Hill, NC: Algonquin Books of Chapel Hill.

Ahmed, Aijaz. 1992. *In Theory: Classes, Nations, Literatures*. London: Verso.

Aidoo, Ama Ata. 1979. *No Sweetness Here*. London: Longman.

———. 1998. "Literature, Feminism, and the African Woman Today." In *Challenging Hierarchies: Issues and Themes in Colonial and Postcolonial African Literature*, ed. Leonard A. Podis and Yakubu Saaka, 15–35. New York: Peter Lang.

Aina, Olabisi. 1998. "African Women at the Grassroots: The Silent Partners of the Women's Movement." In *Sisterhood: Feminisms and Power: From Africa to the Diaspora*, ed. Obioma Nnaemeka, 65–88. Trenton, NJ: Africa World Press.

Ajayi, J. F. Ade. 1965. *Christian Missions in Nigeria, 1841–1891: The Making of a New Elite*. Essex: Longman.

Ajayi-Soyinka, Omofolabo. 1997. "Negritude, Feminism, and the Quest for Identity: Re-Reading Mariama Bâ's *So Long a Letter*." *Women's Studies Quarterly* (25)3/4: 35–52.

———. 2005. "Transcending the Boundaries of Power and Imperialism: Writing Gender, Constructing Knowledge." *Female Circumcision and the Politics of Knowledge: African Women in Imperialist Discourses*, ed. Obioma Nnaemeka, 47–77. Westport, CT: Praeger.

Alter, Robert. 1975. *Partial Magic: The Novel as a Self-Conscious Genre*. Berkeley: University of California Press.

Althusser, Louis. 1969. *For Marx*. Middlesex: Penguin Books.

Amadiume, Ifi. 1987. *Male Daughters, Female Husbands: Gender and Sex in an African Society*. London: Zed Books.

———. 2000. *Daughters of the Goddess, Daughters of Imperialism: African Women Struggle for Culture, Power, and Democracy*. London: Zed Books.

Amodio, Mark C. 2004. *Writing the Oral Tradition: Oral Poetics and Literate Culture in Medieval England*. Notre Dame, IN: University of Notre Dame Press.

Amoko, Apollo. 2002. "The Problem with English Literature: Canonicity, Citizenship, and the Idea of Africa." *Research in African Literatures* 32(4): 19–43.

———. 2006. "Race and Postcoloniality." In *Routledge Companion to Critical Theory*, ed. Simon Malpas and Paul Wake, 127–40. New York: Routledge.

Amuka, Peter S. O. 1997. "The Romance of Nationhood: Kenya as Word and Desire." In *Writers Speak: Essays on Literature and Democracy*, ed. Kitula King'ei and Henry Indangasi, 89–99. Nairobi: Writers Association of Kenya.

———. 2000. "The Play of Deconstruction in the Speech of Africa: The Role of Pakruok and Ngero in Telling Culture in Dholuo." In *African Philosophy as Cultural Inquiry*, ed. Ivan Karp and D. A. Masolo, 89–104. Bloomington: Indiana University Press.

Anderson, Benedict. 1991. *Imagined Communities: Reflections on the Origin and Spread of Nationalism*. 1983. 2d ed. London: Verso.

Andrade, Susan A. 2007. "Rioting Women and Writing Women: Gender, Class, and the Public Sphere in Africa." In *Africa after Gender?*, ed. Catherine M. Cole, Takyiwaa Manuh, and Stephan F. Miescher, 85–107. Bloomington: Indiana University Press.

Andreas, Neshani. 2001. *The Purple Violet of Oshaantu*. London: Heinemann.

Appiah, Kwame Anthony. 1992. *In My Father's House: Africa in the Philosophy of Culture*. Oxford: Oxford University Press.

———. 1995. *Another Death in Venice*. London: Constable.

———. 2006. *Cosmopolitanism: Ethics in a World of Strangers*. New York: Norton.

Argan, Guilio Carlo. 1974. "Ideology and Iconology." In *The Language of Images*, ed. W. J. T. Mitchell, 15–23, trans. Rebecca West. Chicago, IL: University of Chicago Press.

Armah, Ayi Kwei. 1968. *The Beautyful Ones Are Not Yet Born*. Boston, MA: Houghton Mifflin.

———. 1969. *Fragments*. Boston, MA: Houghton Mifflin.

———. 1972. *Why Are We So Blest?* London: Heinemann.
———. 1973. *Two Thousand Seasons*. Nairobi: East African Publishing House.
———. 1977. "Larsony or Fiction as Criticism of Fiction." *New Classic*, 4: 33–45.
———. 1978. *The Healers*. Nairobi: East African Publishing House.
———. 1995. *Osiris Rising*. Popenguine: Per Ankh.

Arnold, Matthew. 1866. "The Study of Celtic Literature." *The Eclectic Magazine of Foreign Literature, Science, and Art* 3: 728–39.

Ashcroft, Bill, Gareth Griffiths, and Helen Tiffin. 2002. *The Empire Writes Back: Theory and Practice in Postcolonial Literatures*. 1989. 2nd ed. London: Routledge.

Atta, Sefi. 2005. *Everything Good Will Come: A Novel*. Northampton, MA: Interlink Books.

Attridge, Derek. 2004. *J. M. Coetzee and the Ethics of Reading: Literature in the Event*. Chicago, IL: University of Chicago Press.

Attwell, David. 2006. *Rewriting Modernity: Studies in Black South African Literary History*. Athens: Ohio University Press.

Azodo, Ada Uzoamaka, and Maureen Ngozi Eke. 2007. *Gender and Sexuality in African Literature and Film*. Trenton, NJ: Africa World Press.

Azuah, Unoma N. 2005. "The Emerging Lesbian Voice in Nigerian Feminist Literature." In *Body, Sexuality, and Gender*, ed. Flora Veit-Wild and Dirk Naguschewski, 129–42. Amsterdam: Rodopi.

Ba, Mariama. 1981. *So Long a Letter*. Translated by Modupé Bodé-Thomas. Oxford: Heinemann.

Bahri, Deepika. 2003. *Native Intelligence: Aesthetics, Politics, and Postcolonial Literature*. Minneapolis: University of Minnesota Press.

Bakhtin, Mikhail. 1981. *The Dialogic Imagination: Four Essays*. Ed. Michael Holquist and translated by Caryl Emerson and Michael Holquist. Austin: University of Texas Press.

———. 1984a. *Problems of Dostoyevsky's Poetics*. Translated by Caryl Emerson. Minneapolis: University of Minnesota Press.

———. 1984b. *Rabelais and His World*. Translated by Helene Iswolsky. Bloomington: Indiana University Press.

Baldwin, James. 1962. *Another Country*. New York: Dial Press.

Barber, Karin. 1995a. "African-Language Literature and Postcolonial Criticism." *Research in African Literatures* 26(4): 3–30.

———. 1995b. "Literacy, Improvisation, and the Public in Yoruba Popular Theatre." In *The Pressures of the Text: Orality, Texts, and the Telling of Tales*, ed. Stewart Brown, 6–27. Birmingham: Birmingham University Press, African Studies Series.

Barber, Karin, and Graham Furniss. 2006. "African-Language Writing." *Research in African Literatures* 37(3): 1–14.

Bardolphe, Jacqueline. 1987. "Ngũgĩ wa Thiong'o's *A Grain of Wheat* and *Petals of Blood* as Readings of Conrad's *Under Western Eyes and Victory*." *The Conradian: Journal of the Joseph Conrad Society* 12(1): 32–49.

Barnard, Rita. 2006. "The Place of Beauty: Reflections on Elaine Scarry and Zakes Mda." In *Beautiful-Ugly: African and Diaspora Aesthetics*, ed. Sarah Nuttall, 102–21. Durham, NC: Duke University Press.

Barthes, Roland. 1974. *S/Z*. Translated by Richard Miller. New York: Hill and Wang.

———. 1977. *Image-Music-Text.* Translated by Stephen Heath. London: Fontana.

BBC. 2005. "Achebe: Oral Tradition Not Needed." http: //news.bbc.co.uk/2/hi/africa/4380400.stm, accessed November 3, 2007.

Behdad, Ali. 1994. *Belated Travelers: Orientalism in the Age of Colonial Dissolution.* Durham, NC: Duke University Press.

———. 2000. "Une Pratique Sauvage: Postcolonial Belatedness and Cultural Politics." In *The Pre-Occupation of Postcolonial Studies*, ed. Fawzia Afzal-Khan and Kalpana Seshadri-Crooks, 71–85. Durham, NC: Duke University Press.

Behr, Mark. 1995. *The Smell of Apples.* New York: Picador.

Belcher, Stephen. 1999. *Epic Traditions of Africa.* Bloomington: Indiana University Press.

Belsey, Catherine. 1980. *Critical Practice.* London: Methuen.

Benge, Okot. 2004. "Orature and Contemporary Issues: Purveyor, Mediator, or Inventor?" In *Africa in World Affairs: Challenges to Humanities*, ed. Edward Wamala et al., 115–26. Kampala: Makerere University, Faculty of Arts.

Benjamin, Walter. 1992. "The Work of Art in the Age of Mechanical Reproduction." 1936. In *Illuminations*, trans. Harry Zohn, 211–44. London: Fontana.

Benson, T. G. 1964. *Kikuyu-English Dictionary.* Oxford: Oxford University Press.

———. 1975. *English-Kikuyu Dictionary.* Oxford: Oxford University Press.

Berman, Bruce J. 2004. "A Palimpsest of Contradictions: Ethnicity, Class, and Politics In Africa." *International Journal of African Historical Studies* 37(1): 13–31.

Bertoncini-Zúbková, Elena. 1989. *Outline of Swahili Literature: Prose Fiction and Drama.* Leiden: E. J. Brill.

Beyala, Calixthe. 1996a. *The Sun Hath Looked Upon Me.* Translated by Marjolijn de Jager. Oxford: Heinemann.

———. 1996b. *Thy Name Shall Be Tanga.* Translated by Marjolijn de Jager. Oxford: Heinemann.

Bhabha, Homi. 1994. *The Location of Culture.* London: Routledge.

Biebuyck, Daniel P. 1972. "The Epic as a Genre in Congo Oral Literature." In *African Folklore*, ed. Richard M. Dorson, 257–73. Bloomington: Indiana University Press.

———. 1978. *Hero and Chief Epic Literature from among the Banyanga.* Berkeley: University of California Press.

Bird, Charles S. 1974. *The Songs of Seydou Camara. 1: Kambili.* Bloomington: Indiana University Press.

———. 1976. "Poetry in the Mande: Its Form and Meaning." *Poetics* 5: 89–100.

p'Bitek, Okot. 1966. *Song of Lawino.* Nairobi: East African Publishing House.

Bloom, Harold. 1973. *The Anxiety of Influence: A Theory of Poetry.* New York: Oxford University Press.

Bodunde, Charles. 2001a. ed. *African Languages Literature in the Political Context of the 1990s.* Beyreuth: Beyreuth University.

———. 2001b. *Oral Traditions and Aesthetic Transfer: Creativity and Social Vision in Contemporary Black Poetry.* Beyreuth: Beyreuth University.

Boehmer, Elleke. 2005a. *Colonial and Postcolonial Literature: Migrant Metaphors*, 1995. 2nd ed. Oxford: Oxford University Press.

———. 2005b. *Stories of Women: Gender and Nation in Postcolonial Literature.* Manchester: Manchester University Press.

Booker, M. Keith. 1998. *The African Novel in English: An Introduction*. Portsmouth, NH: Heinemann.

Bowers, Maggie Ann. 2004. *Magic(al) Realism*. London: Routledge.

Boyd, Michael. 1983. *The Reflexive Novel: Fiction as Critique*. Lewisburg, PA: Bucknell University Press.

Brennan, Timothy. 1989. *Salman Rushdie and the Third World: Myths of the Nation*. London: Macmillan.

———. 1990. "The National Longing for Form." In *Nation and Narration*, ed. Homi K. Bhabha, 41–70. London: Routledge.

———. 1997. *At Home in the World: Cosmopolitanism Now*. Cambridge, MA: Harvard University Press.

Brontë, Charlotte. 1947. *Jane Eyre*. 1847. Harlow, Essex: Longman.

Brydon, Diana, and Helen Tiffin. 1993. *Decolonising Fictions*. Sydney: Dangaroo Press.

Buchanan, Ian. 2006. "National Allegory Today: A Return to Jameson." In *On Jameson: From Postmodernism to Globalization*, ed. Caren Irr and Ian Buchanan, 173–88. Albany: State University of New York Press.

Bukenya, Austin. 1972. *The People's Bachelor*. Nairobi: East African Publishing House.

Busia, Abena. 1988. "Words Whispered over Voids: A Context for Black Women's Rebellious Voices in the Novel of the African Diaspora." In *Studies in Black American Literature*, vol. 3, ed. Joe Weixelmann and Houston A. Baker Jr., 1–41. Greenwood, FL: Penkevill.

Cancel, Robert. 1993. "African-Language Literatures: Perspectives on Culture and Identity." In *A History of Twentieth-Century African Literatures*, ed. Oyenkan Owomoyela, 285–310. Lincoln, NE: University of Nebraska Press.

Cary, Joyce. 1947. *Mister Johnson*. London: M. Joseph.

Casanova, Pascale. 2004. *The World Republic of Letters*. Translated by M. B. DeBevoise. Cambridge, MA: Harvard University Press.

Chachage, C. S. L. 1991. *Almasi za Bandia*. Dar es Salaam: Dar es Salaam University Press.

———. 2002. *Makuadi wa Soko Huria*. Dar es Salaam: E & D Ltd.

Chambers, Ross. 2002. "Strategic Constructivism? Sedgwick's Ethics of Inversion." In *Regarding Sedgwick. Essays on Queer Culture and Critical Theory*, ed. Stephen M. Barber and David L. Clark, 165–80. New York: Routledge.

Chanter, Tina. 2007. *Gender: Key Concepts in Philosophy*. New York: Continuum.

Chapman, Michael. 1996. *Southern African Literatures*. London: Longman.

Chatterjee, Partha. 1993. *The Nation and Its Fragments: Colonial and Postcolonial Histories*. Princeton, NJ: Princeton University Press.

Chesaina, Ciarunji. 1994. "Images of Women in African Oral Literature: A Case Study of the Kalenjin and Maasai Oral Narratives." In *Understanding Oral Literature*, ed. Austin Bukenya, Wanjiku M. Kabira, and Okoth Okombo, 85–91. Nairobi: Nairobi University Press.

———. 1997. "The Song as a Medium of Expression of Gender Solidarity for Embu and Mbeere Women." In *Contesting Social Death: Essays on Gender and Culture*, ed. Wanjiku M. Kabira, Masheti Masinjila, and Milton Obote, 191–207. Nairobi: Kenya Oral Literature Association.

Chimhundu, Hubert. 1995. "Sexuality and Socialization in Shona Praises and Lyrics." In *Power, Marginality, and Oral Literature*, ed. Graham Furniss and Liz Gunner, 188–205. Cambridge: Cambridge University Press.

Chinweizu et al. 1980. *Toward the Decolonization of African Literature: African Fiction and Poetry and Their Critics*. Enugu: Fourth Dimension Publishing.

Chow, Rey. 1995. *Writing Diaspora: Tactics of Intervention in Contemporary Cultural Studies*. Bloomington: Indiana University Press.

———. 2006. *The Age of the World Target: Referentiality in War, Theory, and Comparative Work*. Durham, NC: Duke University Press.

Chreachain, Fi Rinne. 1991. " 'Post-Colonialism' or Second Independence?" *African Literature Association Bulletin* 17(3): 5–6.

Cixous, Helene. 1981. "The Laugh of the Medusa." In *New French Feminisms*, ed. Elaine Marks and Isabelle de Courtivron, 254–64. New York: Schocken.

Clarkson, Carrol. 2005. "Locating Identity in Phaswane Mpe's *Welcome to Our Hillbrow*." *Third World Quarterly* 26(3): 451–59.

Clingman, Stephen. 1986. *The Novels of Nadine Gordimer: History from the Inside*. London: Allen & Unwin.

Coetzee, J. M. 1980. *Waiting for the Barbarians*. London: Secker & Warburg.

———. 1983. *Life and Times of Michael K*. London: Secker & Warburg.

———. 1986. *Foe*. London: Secker & Warburg.

———. 1994. *The Master of Petersburg*. London: Secker & Warburg.

———. 1999. *Disgrace*. New York: Vikings.

———. 2003. *Elizabeth Costello*. London: Secker & Warburg.

———. 2005. *Slow Man*. London: Secker & Warburg.

Cole, Catherine M., Takyiwaa Manu, and Stephan F. Miescher, eds. 2007. *Africa after Gender?* Bloomington: Indiana University Press.

Conrad, Joseph. 1999. *Heart of Darkness*. 1902. New York: Columbia University Press.

———. 2003. *Under Western Eyes*. 1911. Mineola, NY: Dover.

Cook, David, and Michael Okenimkpe. 1997. *Ngũgĩ wa Thiong'o: An Exploration of His Writing*, 2nd ed. London: Heinemann.

Cooper, Brenda. 1998. *Magical Realism in West African Fiction*. London: Routledge.

Cooper, Fredric. 2005. *Colonialism in Question: Theory, Knowledge, History*. Berkeley: University of California Press.

Cover, Rob. 2005. "Queer with Class." In *Linked Histories: Postcolonial Studies in a Globalized World*, ed. Pamela McCallum and Wendy Faith, 45–60. Durham, NC: Duke University Press.

Currie, Mark. 1995. Introduction. In *Metafiction*, ed. Mark Curie, 1–18. New York: Longman.

Currey, James. 2008. *Africa Writes Back: The African Writers Series and the Launch of African Literature*. Oxford: James Currey.

Damrosch, David. 2003. *What Is World Literature?* Princeton, NJ: Princeton University Press.

Dangarembga, Tsitsi. 1988. *Nervous Conditions*. London: Women's Press.

———. 2006. *The Book of Not: A Novel*. Banbury, UK: Ayebia Clarke.

Dangor, Achmat. 1997. *Kafka's Curse*. Cape Town, South Africa: Kwela.

———. 2005. *Bitter Fruit*. New York: Black Cat.

Darko, Amma. 1995. *Beyond the Horizon*. Portsmouth, NH: Heinemann.

———. 1998. *The Housemaid*. Portsmouth, NH: Heinemann.

———. 2003. *Faceless*. Accra, Ghana: Sub-Saharan Publishers.

Dasenbrock, Reed Way. 2005. "Imitation versus Contestation: Walcott's Postcolonial Shakespeare." *Callaloo* 28(1): 104–13.

Davies, Carole Boyce. 1986. "Introduction: Feminist Consciousness and African Literary Criticism." In *Ngambika: Studies of Women in African Literature*, ed. Carole Boyce Davies and Anne Adams Graves, 1–23. Trenton, NJ: Africa World Press.

Davis, Lennard J. 1998. "Who Put the 'The' in 'the Novel'?: Identity Politics and Disability in Novel Studies." *Novel: A Forum on Fiction* 31(3): 317–34.

Dawood, Yusuf. 1991. *Water under the Bridge*. Nairobi: Longhorn.

Daymond, Margaret J. 1996, ed. *South African Feminisms: Writing, Theory, and Criticism, 1990–1994*. New York: Garland.

———. 2002. "Complementary Oral and Written Narrative Conventions: Sindiwe Magona's Autobiography and Short Story Sequence, 'Women at Work' " *Journal of Southern African Studies* 28(2): 331–46.

Delgado, Celeste Fraser. 1997. "Mother Tongues and Childless Women: The Construction of Kenyan Womanhood." In *The Politics of (M)othering: Womanhood, Identity, and Resistance in African Literature*, ed. Obioma Nnaemeka, 130–46. London: Routledge.

de Man, Paul. 1979. *Allegories of Reading: Figural Language in Rousseau, Nietzsche, Rilke, and Proust*. New Haven, CT: Yale University Press.

Derrida, Jacques. 1976. *Of Grammatology*. Translated by Gayatri Chakravorty Spivak. Baltimore, MD: Johns Hopkins University Press.

———. 1979. "Living On: Border Lines." In *Deconstructionism and Criticism*, ed. Harold Bloom et al., 75–176, trans. James Hulbert. New York: Seabury Press.

Desai, Gaurav. 2001. "Out in Africa." In *Post-Colonial Queer: Theoretical Intersections*, ed. John C. Hawley, 139–64. Albany: State University of New York Press.

Dhalla, Ghalib Shiraz. 2002. *Ode to Lata*. Los Angeles: Really Great Books.

Dirlik, Arif. 1994. "The Postcolonial Aura: Third World Criticism in the Age of Global Capitalism." *Critical Inquiry* 20(2): 328–56.

———. 2007. *Global Modernity: Modernity in the Age of Global Capitalism*. Boulder, CO: Paradigm.

Doane, A. N. 1991. "Introduction." In *Vox Intexta: Orality and Textuality in Middle Ages*, ed.. A. N. Doane and Carol Braun Pasternack, xi–xiv. Madison: University of Wisconsin Press.

Dosekun, Simidele. 2007. "Defending Feminism in Africa." *postamble* 3(1): 41–47.

Doyle, Laura, and Laura Winkiel, eds. 2005. *Geomodernisms: Race, Modernism, Modernity*. Bloomington: Indiana University Press.

Duiker, K. Sello. 2000. *thirteen cents*. Cape Town, South Africa: David Philip.

———. 2001. *The Quiet Violence of Dreams*. Cape Town, South Africa: Kwela.

———. 2006. *The Hidden Star*. Johannesburg: Umuzi.

Dunton, Chris. 1989. " 'Wheyting Be Dat?' The Treatment of Homosexuality in African Literature." *Research in African Literatures* 20(3): 422–44.

Echeruo, Michael. 1973. *Joyce Cary and the Novel of Africa*. Harlow: Longman.
———. 1978. *The Conditioned Imagination from Shakespeare to Conrad*. London: Macmillan.
Edelman, Lee. 1994. *Homographesis: Essays in Gay Literary and Cultural Theory*. New York: Routledge.
Egejuru, Phanuel Akubueze. 1980. *Towards African Literary Independence: A Dialogue with Contemporary African Writers*. Westport, CT: Greenwood Press.
Ellison, Ralph. 1952. *Invisible Man*. New York: Random House.
Emecheta, Buchi. 1979. *The Joys of Motherhood*. New York: Braziller.
Equiano, Olaudah. 1998. *Interesting Narrative of the Life of Olaudah Equiano, or Gustavus Vassa, the African*. London: Black Classics.
Esonwanne, Uzo. 1993. "The Nation as a Contested Referent." *Research in African Literatures* 24(4): 49–62.
Ezeliora, Osita. 2005. "The Novels of K. Sello Duiker and Phaswane Mpe." In *Words Gone Too Soon: A Tribute to Phaswane Mpe and K. Sello Duiker*," ed. Mbulelo Vizikhungo Mzamanc, 164–75. Pretoria: Umgangatho.
Fanon, Frantz. 1963. *The Wretched of the Earth*. 1961. Translated by Constance Farrington. New York: Grove Press.
———. 1967. *Black Skin, White Masks*. 1952. Translated by Charles Lam Markmann. New York: Grove Press.
Farah, Nuruddin. 1970. *From a Crooked Rib*. London: Heinemann.
———. 1979. *Sweet and Sour Milk*. London: Allison & Busby.
———. 1981. *Sardines*. London: Allison & Busby.
———. 1983. *Close Sesame*. London: Allison & Busby.
———. 1986. *Maps*. New York: Penguin.
———. 1999. *Gifts*. New York: Arcade.
———. 2000. *Yesterday, Tomorrow: Voices from the Somali Diaspora*. London: Cassell.
———. 2002. "Why I Write." In *Emerging Perspectives on Nuruddin Farah*, ed. Derek Wright, 1–13. Trenton, NJ: Africa World Press.
———. 2003. *Links*. Cape Town, South Africa: Kwela.
Faris, Wendy B. 1995. "Scheherazade's Children: Magical Realism and Postmodern Fiction." In *Magical Realism: Theory, History, Community*, ed. Lois Parkinson Zamora and Wendy B. Faris, 163–90. Durham, NC: Duke University Press.
———. 2002. "The Question of the Other: Cultural Critiques of Magical Realism." *Janus Head* 5(2): 101–19.
———. 2004. *Ordinary Enchantments: Magical Realism and the Remystification of Narrative*. Nashville, TN: Vanderbilt University Press.
Finnegan, Ruth H. 1970. *Oral Literature in Africa*. London: Clarendon.
Foucault, Michel. 1970. *Order of Things: An Archeology of Human Sciences*. New York: Vintage.
———. 1977. *Discipline and Punish*. London: Penguin.
———. 1981. *The History of Sexuality: An Introduction*. Harmondsworth: Penguin.
———. 1989. "Friendship as a Way of Life." In *Foucault Live*, ed. Sylvère Lotringer, 308–12. New York: Semiotext(e).
Franco, Jean. 1997. "The Nation as Imagined Community." In *Dangerous Liaisons: Gender, Nation, and Postcolonial Perspectives*, ed. Anne McClintock, Aamir Mufti, and Ella Shohat, 130–37. Minneapolis: University of Minnesota Press.

Freud, Sigmund. 1914. "On Narcissism: An Introduction." In *Standard Edition* 14, ed. James Strachey, 73–102. 1959. London: Hogarth Press.

Furniss, Graham, and Liz Gunner, eds. 1995. *Power, Marginality, and Oral Literature*. Cambridge: Cambridge University Press.

Gagiano, Annie. 2004. "Adapting the National Imaginary: Shifting Identities in Three Post-1994 South African Novels." *Journal of Southern African Studies* 30(4): 811–24.

Gakwandi, Shatto Arthur. 1977. *The Novel and Contemporary Experience in Africa*. New York: Africana Publishing.

Gaonkar, Dilip Parameshwar. 2001. "On Alternative Modernities." In *Alternative Modernities*, ed. Dilip Parameshwar Gaonkar, 1–23. Durham, NC: Duke University Press.

Gates, Louis Henry Jr. 1988. *The Signifying Monkey: A Theory of African American Literary Criticism*. New York: Oxford University Press.

Gaylard, Gerald. 2005. *After Colonialism: African Postmodernism and Magical Realism*. Johannesburg: Witwatersrand University Press.

Genya, Monicah. 2004. *The Other Side of Love*. Nairobi: East African Educational Publishers.

George, Olakunle. 2003. *Relocating Agency: Modernity and African Letters*. Albany: State University of New York Press.

George, Rosemary Marangoly. 2006. "Feminists Theorize Colonial/Postcolonial." In *The Cambridge Guide to Feminist Literary Theory*, ed. Ellen Rooney, 211–31. Cambridge: Cambridge University Press.

Gerard, Albert. 1990. *Contexts of African Literature*. Amsterdam: Rodopi.

Gerard, Albert S. 1981. *African Language Literatures: An Introduction to the Literary History of Sub-Saharan Africa*. Harlow, Essex: Longman.

Geteria, Wamugunda. 1992. *Nice People*. Nairobi: African Artefacts.

Gibbon, Peter. 1997. "Prawns and Piranhas: The Political Economy of a Tanzanian Private Sector Marketing Chain." *Journal of Peasant Studies* 24(4): 1–86.

Gicheru, Mwangi. 1979. *Across the Bridge*. Nairobi: Longman.

———. 1991. *The Mixers*. Nairobi: Longman.

Giddens, Anthony. 1990. *The Consequences of Modernity*. Cambridge: Polity Press.

Gikandi, Simon. 1984. "The Development of the East African Novel." In *The Writing of East and Central Africa*, ed. G. D. Killam, 231–46. London: Heinemann.

———. 1991. *Reading Chinua Achebe*. London: Heinemann.

———. 1992. *Writing in Limbo: Modernism and Caribbean Literature*. Ithaca, NY: Cornell University Press.

———. 1996. *Maps of Englishness: Writing Identity in the Culture of Colonialism*. New York: Columbia University Press.

———. 2000. "Reading the Referent: Postcolonialism and the Writing of Modernity." In *Reading the "New" Literatures in a Postcolonial Era*, ed. Shusheila Nasta, 87–104. Cambridge: D. S. Brewer.

———. 2002. "Globalization and the Claims of Postcolonialism." *South Atlantic Quarterly* 100(3): 627–58.

Gordimer, Nadine. 1953. *The Lying Days: A Novel*. New York: Simon and Schuster.

———. 1990. *My Son's Story*. New York: Farrar, Straus, and Giroux.

———. 1998. *The House Gun*. New York: Farrar, Straus, and Giroux.

———. 1999. *Living in Hope and History: Notes from Our Century*. New York: Farrar, Straus, and Giroux.

———. 2001. *The Pickup*. London: Bloomsbury.

Graeber, Laurel. 1990. "Ordinary Loves, Extraordinary Times." *New York Times Book Review* (October 21): 20.

Grant, Stirling. 2000. "Neurotic Narrative: Metafiction and Object-Relations Theory." *College Literature* 27(2): 80–103.

Gray, Stephen. 2009. Review. *Africa Writes Back: The African Writers Series and the Launch of African Literature*. *Research in African Literatures* 40(1): 177–80.

Green, Robert. 1988. "From the *Lying Days* to *July's People*: The Novels of Nadine Gordimer." *Journal of Modern Literature* 14(4): 543–63.

Greenblatt, Stephen. 1980. *Renaissance Self-Fashioning: From More to Shakespeare*. Chicago, IL: University of Chicago Press.

Greenstein, Susan M. 1993. "My Son's Story: Drenching the Censors the Dilemma of White Writing." In *The Later Fiction of Nadine Gordimer*, ed. Bruce Alvin King, 191–209. Basingstoke: Macmillan.

Gromov, Mikhail D. 2004. "Postmodernistic Elements in Recent Swahili Novels." *The Nairobi Journal of Literature* 2: 28–36.

Guillory, John. 1993. *Cultural Capital: The Problem of Literary Canon Formation*. Chicago, IL: University of Chicago Press.

Gurnah, Abdulrazak. 1994. *Paradise*. New York: New Press.

———. 1996. *Admiring Silence*. London: Hamish Hamilton.

———. 2001. *By the Sea*. London: Bloomsbury.

Habila, Helon. 2002. *Waiting for an Angel*. London: Hamish Hamilton.

Hall, Stuart. 1990. "Cultural Identity and Diaspora." In *Identity: Community, Culture, Difference*, ed. Jonathan Rutherford, 222–37. London: Lawrence & Wishart.

———. 1991. "Ethnicity, Identity, and Difference." *Radical America* 23(4): 9–20.

Halm, Ben B. 2003. "Atalanta's Apples: Postcolonial Theory as a Barrier to the 'Balance of Stories.'" *Research in African Literatures* 34(4): 155–73.

Halperin, David M. 2002. *How to Do the History of Homosexuality*. Chicago, IL: University of Chicago Press.

Hanssen, Beatrice. 2000. "Ethics of the Others." In *The Turn to Ethics*, ed. Marjorie Garber, Beatrice Hanssen and Rebecca L. Walkowitz, 127–79. New York: Routledge.

Hardt, Michael, and Antonio Negri. 2000. *Empire*. Cambridge, MA: Harvard University Press.

Hardy, Thomas. 1993. *Jude the Obscure*. 1895. Hertfordshire, England: Penguin.

Harrow, Kenneth W. 2007. *Postcolonial African Cinema: From Political Engagement to Postmodernism*. Bloomington: Indiana University Press.

Hassan, Salah. 1999. "The Modernist Experience in African Art: Visual Expressions of the Self and Cross-Cultural Aesthetics." In *Reading the Contemporary*, ed. Olu Oguibe and Okwui Enwezor, 214–35. London: Institute of International Visual Arts.

Hawley, John C., ed. 2001a. *Postcolonial Queer: Theoretical Intersections*. Albany: State University of New York Press.

———, ed. 2001b. *Postcolonial and Queer Theories: Intersections and Essays*. Westport, CT: Greenwood Press.

Head, Bessie. 1971. *Maru*. London: Heinemann.

Head, Dominic. 1994. *Nadine Gordimer*. Cambridge: Cambridge University Press.

Hegel, Georg Wilhelm Friedrich. 1990. *The Philosophy of History*. New York: Prometheus Books.

Hill, Alan. 1988. *In Pursuit of Publishing*. London: John Murray and Heinemann Educational.

Hoad, Neville. 2007. *African Intimacies: Race, Homosexuality, and Globalization*. Minneapolis: University of Minnesota Press.

Hokororo, Anthony. 1997. *Salma's Spirit*. Dar es Salaam: Mkuki na Nyota.

Howarth, R. G. 1957. "Indigenous Literature and Its Place in University English Studies." In *Proceedings of a Conference of Writers, Publishers, Editors, and University Teachers of English Held at the University of Witwatersrand, Johannesburg from 10–12 July 1956*, 46–54. Johannesburg: Witwatersrand University Press.

Hoy, Mikita. 1992. "Bakhtin and Popular Culture." *New Literary History* 23(3): 765–82.

Hulme, Peter. 1986. *Colonial Encounters: Europe and the Native Caribbean, 1492–1797*. New York: Methuen.

Hussey, Eric R. J. 1932. "The Languages of Literature in Africa." *Africa: Journal of the International African Institute* 5(2): 169–75.

Hutcheon, Linda. 1988. *A Poetics of Postmodernism: History, Theory, Fiction*. London: Routledge.

Ikiddeh, Ime. 1978. "African Literature and the Generation Gap: Aspects of Contemporary Response to West African Anticolonial Literature." In *Teaching of African Literature in Schools*, ed. Eddah Gachukia and S. Kichamu Akivaga, 127–38. Nairobi: Kenya Literature Bureau.

Imbuga, Francis. 1976. *Betrayal in the City: A Play*. Nairobi: East African Publishing House.

———. 1979. *The Successor*. Nairobi: Heinemann Educational.

———. 1993. *Shrine of Tears*. Nairobi: Longman.

———. 2004. *Miracle of Remera*. Nairobi: Africawide Network.

Innes, C. L. 2007. *The Cambridge Introduction to Postcolonial Literatures in English*. Cambridge: Cambridge University Press.

Irele, Abiola. 1981. *The African Experience in Literature and Ideology*. London: Heinemann.

———. 2001. *The African Imagination: Literature in Africa and the Diaspora*. Oxford: Oxford University Press.

Isegawa, Moses. 2001. *Abyssinian Chronicles*. New York: Random House.

———. 2004. *Snakepit*. New York: Random House.

Iweala, Uzodinma. 2005. *Beasts of No Nation: A Novel*. New York: HarperCollins.

Jablon, Madelyn. 1996. *Black Metafiction*. Iowa City: University of Iowa Press.

Jameson, Frederic. 1972. *The Prison House of Language*. Princeton, NJ: Princeton University Press.

———. 1981. *The Political Unconscious: Narrative as a Socially Symbolic Act*. New York: Cornell University Press.

———. 1986. "Third World Literature in the Era of Multinational Capitalism." *Social Text* 15 (Autumn): 65–88.

———. 1991. *Postmodernism, or, the Cultural Logic of Late Capitalism*. Durham, NC: Duke University Press.

JanMohamed, Abdul R. 1983. *Manichean Aesthetics: The Politics of Literature in Colonial Africa*. Amherst: University of Massachusetts Press.

Jegede, Dele. 1990. "African Art Today: A Historical Overview." In *Contemporary African Artists: Changing Tradition*, ed. El Anatsui et al., 29–43. New York: The Studio Museum in Harlem.

Jell-Bahlsen, Sabine. 1998. "WAAD Conference at ASA." In *Sisterhood, Feminisms, and Power: From Africa to the Diaspora*, ed. Obioma Nnaemeka, 441–43. Trenton, NJ: Africa World Press.

Jeyifo, Biodun. 1990. "The Nature of Things: Arrested Decolonization and Critical Theory." *Research in African Literatures* 21(1): 33–48.

———. 2006. "Politics and Literature in Nigeria." *Nigeria 2007: Political, Social, and Economic Transitions* Conference, November 24. Evanston, IL: Northwestern University.

Johnson, John William. 1978. "The Epic of Sunjata: An Attempt to Define the Model for African Epic Poetry 1–3." PhD dissertation, Indiana University.

———. 1980. "Yes, Virginia, There Is an Epic in Africa." *Research in African Literatures* 11(3): 308–26.

Johnson, Lemuel A. 2002. "(En)countering Traditions of the Erotic in African Narratives." In *African Writers and Their Readers: Essays in Honor of Bernth Lindfors Volume II*, ed. Toyin Falola and Barbara Harlow, 167–218. Trenton, NJ: Africa World Press.

Jonet, Catherine. 2007. "She Doesn't Know about Me": "[T]he Shaping Presence" of the Closet in Amma Darko's *Beyond the Horizon*." In *Gender and Sexuality in African Literature and Film*, ed. Ada Uzoamaka Azodo and Maureen Ngozi Eke, 199–211. Trenton, NJ: Africa World Press.

Joseph, Richard. 1998. "Oldspeak vs. Newspeak." *Journal of Democracy* 9(4): 55–61.

Julien, Eileen. 1992. *African Novels and the Question of Orality*. Bloomington: Indiana University Press.

Jussawalla, Feroza, and Reed Way Dasenbrock. 1992. "Introduction." In *Interviews with Writers of the Post-Colonial World*, ed. Feroza Jussawalla and Reed Way Dasenbrock, 3–23. Jackson: University of Mississippi Press.

Kabira, Wanjiku Mukabi. 1994. "Gender and Politics of Control: An Overview of Images of Women in Gĩkũyũ Oral Narratives." In *Understanding Oral Literature*, ed. Austin Bukenya, Wanjiku M. Kabira, and Okoth Okombo, 77–84. Nairobi: Nairobi University Press.

Kafka, Franz. 1922. *The Castle*. New York: A. A. Knopf.

Kala, Violet. 1994. *Waste Not Your Tears*. Harare: Baobab.

Karanja, David. 1996. *The Girl Was Mine*. Nairobi: Spear Books.

———. 2001. *Dreamer's Paradise*. Cape Town, South Africa: Kwela.

Kariara, Jonathan. 1963. A *Leopard Lives in a Muu Tree*. In *The Penguin Book of Modern African Poetry*, ed. Gerald Moore and Ulli Beier, 145–46. Harmondsworth: Penguin.

———. 1988. "Karoki." In *An Anthology of East African Short Stories*, ed. Valerie Kibera, 21–28. Nairobi: Longman.

Kasfir, Sidney. 1984. "One Tribe, One Style? Paradigms in the Historiography of African Art." *History in Africa* 11: 163–93.

———. 1999. "African Art and Authenticity: A Text with a Shadow." In *Reading the Contemporary*, ed. Olu Oguibe and Okwui Enwezor, 88–112. London: Institute of International Visual Arts.

Katrak, Ketu H. 2006. *Politics of the Female Body: Postcolonial Women Writers of the Third World*. New Brunswick, NJ: Rutgers University Press.

Kenyatta, Jomo. 1937. "Kikuyu Religion, Ancestor-Worship, and Sacrificial Practices." *Africa: Journal of the International African Institute* 10(3): 308–28.

———. 1938. *Facing Mount Kenya: The Traditional Life of the Gĩkũyũ*. 1978. Nairobi: Kenway Publications.

Ker, David. 1998. *The African Novel and the Modernist Tradition*. New York: Peter Lang.

Kezilahabi, Euphrase. 1971. *Rosa Mistika*. Nairobi: East African Literature Bureau.

———. 1990a. *Mzingile*. Dar es Salaam: Dar-es-Salaam University Press.

———. 1990b. *Nagona*. Dar es Salaam: Dar-es-Salaam University Press.

Khamis, Said A. M. 2001. "Fabulation and Politics of the 90s in Kezilahabi's Novel *Nagona*." In *African Languages Literature in the Political Context of the 1990s*, ed. Charles Bodunde, 119–33. Bayreuth: Bayreuth African Studies.

———. 2005. "Signs of New Features in the Swahili Novel." *Research in African Literatures* 36(1): 91–108.

———. 2007. "The Swahili Novelist at the Crossroads: The Dilemma of Identity and Fecundity." *Swahili Forum* 14: 165–80. http: //www.ifeas.uni-mainz.de/SwaFo/SF_14_09%20Khamis.pdf, accessed February 10, 2008.

Kibera, Leonard. 1970. *Voices in the Dark*. Nairobi: East African Publishing House.

———. 1979. "Pessimism and the African Novelist: Ayi Kwei Armah's *The Beautyful One's Are Not Yet Born*." *Journal of Commonwealth Literature* 14(1): 64–72.

Kibugi, Wairimu. 1997. *Painful Tears*. Nairobi: Jomo Kenyatta Foundation.

King-Aribisala, Karen. 1998. *Kicking Tongues*. London: Heinemann.

Kolawole, Mary E. Modupe. 1997. *Womanism and African Consciousness*. Trenton, NJ: Africa World Press.

Krishnaswamy, Revathi. 2005. "Mythologies of Migrancy: Postcolonialism, Postmodernism, and the Politics of (Dis)location." In *Linked Histories: Postcolonial Studies in a Globalized World*, ed. Pamela McCallum and Wendy Faith, 91–108. Durham, NC: Duke University Press.

Kruger, Marie. 2004. "Narrative in the Time of AIDS: Postcolonial Kenyan Women's Literature." *Research in African Literatures* 35(1): 108–29.

Kulet, Henry Ole. 1971. *Is It Possible?* Nairobi: Longman Kenya.

———. 1987. *Daughter of Maa*. Nairobi: Longman Kenya.

———. 1999. *Bandits of Kibi*. Nairobi: Longhorn.

Kunene, Mazisi. 1980. "The Relevance of African Cosmological Systems to African Literature Today." *African Literature Today* 11: 190–205.

Kurtz, J. Roger. 1998. *Urban Obsessions, Urban Fears*. Trenton, NJ: Africa World Press.

———. 2005. *Nyarloka's Gift: The Writing of Marjorie Oludhe Macgoye*. Nairobi: Mvule.

Kwakye, Benjamin. 2006. *The Sun by Night*. Trenton, NJ: Africa World Press.

Larson, Charles R. 2001. *The Ordeal of the African Writer*. London: Zed.

———. 2002. "Who Reads African Literature?" In *Palavers of African Literature: Essays in Honor of Bernth Lindfors Volume 1*, ed. Toyin Falola and Barbara Harlow, 221–28. Trenton, NJ: Africa World Press.

Laye, Camara. 1965. *The African Child*. Translated by James Kirkup. London: Collins.

Lazarus, Neil. 1990. *Resistance in Postcolonial African Fiction*. New Haven, CT: Yale University Press.

———. 1999. *Nationalism and Cultural Practice in the Postcolonial World*. Cambridge: Cambridge University Press.

———. 2005. "Politics of Postcolonial Modernism." In *Postcolonial Studies and Beyond*, ed. Ania Loomba et al., 423–38. Durham, NC: Duke University Press.

Lewis, William Arthur. 1965. *Politics in West Africa*. Toronto: Oxford University Press.

Li, Victor. 2006. *The Neo-primitivist Turn: Critical Reflections on Alterity, Culture, and Modernity*. Toronto: University of Toronto Press.

Lindfors, Bernth. 1973. "The Rise of African Pornography." *Transition* 42: 65–71.

———. 1979. "East African Popular Literature." *Journal of Popular Culture* 13(1): 106–15.

———. 1994. "A Basic Anatomy of East African Literature in English." In *Comparative Approaches to East African Literatures*, ed. Bernth Lindfors, 75–91. Amsterdam: Rodopi.

———. 2002. *Africa Talks Back: Interviews with Anglophone African Authors*. Trenton, NJ: Africa World Press.

Linguanti, Elsa, Francesco Casotti, and Carmen Concilio. 1999. *Coterminous Worlds: Magical Realism and Contemporary Post-Colonial Literature in English*. Amsterdam: Rodopi.

Lizarribar, Camile. 1998. "Something Else will Stand Beside It: The African Writers Series and the Development of African Literature." PhD dissertation, Harvard University.

Lord, Albert B. 1995. "Oral Composition and 'Oral Residue' in the Middle Ages." In *Oral Tradition in the Middle Ages*, ed. W. F. H. Nicolaisen, 7–30. Binghamton, NY: Center for Medieval and Early Renaissance Studies, State University of New York at Binghamton.

Low, Gail. 2002. "In Pursuit of Publishing: Heinemann's African Writers Series." *Wasafiri*. 37: 31–35.

Macgoye, Marjorie O. 1986. *Coming to Birth*. Nairobi: East African Educational Publishers.

———. 1996. *Moral Issues in Kenya: A Personal View*. Nairobi: Uzima Press.

———. 1997. *Chira*. Nairobi: East African Education Publishers.

Macherey, Pierre. 1978. *A Theory of Literary Production*. Translated by Geoffrey Wall. London: Routledge.

Magona, Sindiwe. 1990. *To My Children's Children*. D. Philip: Claremont, South Africa: 1990.

Maillu, David G. 1973a. *My Dear Bottle*. Nairobi: Comb Books.

———. 1973b. *Unfit for Human Consumption*. Nairobi: Comb Books.

———. 1974. *After 4:30*. Nairobi: Comb Books.

———. 1975. *Kommon Man*. Nairobi: Comb Books.

———. 1976. *No!* Nairobi: Comb Books.

———. 1991. *Broken Drum*. Nairobi: Jomo Kenyatta Foundation and Maillu Publishing House.

Makdisi, Saree. 2000. "Postcolonial Literature in a Neocolonial World: Modern Arabic Culture and the End of Modernity." In *The Pre-Occupation of Postcolonial Studies*, ed. Fawzia Afzal Khan and Kalpana Seshadri-Crooks, 266–91. Durham, NC: Duke University Press.

Mak'Oloo, Omondi. 1991. *Times Beyond*. Nairobi: East African Educational Publishers.

Makotsi, Ruth. 1988. "Book Trade in Africa: Potential and Problems." *African Publishing Review* 7(4): 1–3.

Mama, Amina. 1995. *Beyond the Masks: Race, Gender, and Subjectivity*. London: Routledge.

———. 1997. "Sheroes and Villains: Conceptualizing Colonial and Contemporary Violence against Women in Africa." In *Feminist Genealogies, Colonial Legacies, Democratic Futures*, ed. M. Jaqui Alexander and Chandra Talpade Mohanty, 46–62. New York: Routledge.

———. 2001. Talking about Feminism in Africa." *Women's World*. http: //www.wworld.org/programs/regions/africa/amina_mama.htm, accessed January 6, 2007.

———. 2005. "Gender Studies for Africa's Transformation." In *African Intellectuals: Rethinking Politics, Language, Gender, and Development*, ed. Thandika Mkandawire, 95–116. London: Zed Books.

Mann, Thomas. 1924. *Death in Venice*. 1965. Translated from the German by Kenneth Burke. New York: Knopf.

Marais, Michael. 1996. "The Hermeneutics of Empire: Coetzee's Post-colonial Metafiction." In *The Critical Perspectives on J. M. Coetzee*, ed. Graham Huggan and Stephen Watson, 66–81. Basingstoke: Macmillan.

Marechera, Dambudzo. 1980. *The Black Sunlight*. London: Heinemann.

———. 1992. *The Black Insider*. London: Lawrence and Wishart.

Maraire, Nozipo J. 1996. *Zenzele: A Letter for My Daughter*. London: Weidenfeld.

Martinez-Alier, Juan. 2002. *The Environmentalism of the Poor: A Study of Ecological Conflicts and Valuation*. Northampton, MA: Edward Elgar.

Maughan-Brown, David. 1985. *Land, Freedom, and Fiction: History and Ideology in Kenya*. London: Zed Books.

Mazrui, Alamin M. 2004. "The Swahili Literary Tradition." In *The History of African and Caribbean Literature Volume 1*, ed. F. Abiola Irele and Simon Gikandi, 199–226. Cambridge: Cambridge University Press.

———. 2007. *Swahili beyond Boundaries: Literature, Language, Identity*. Athens: Ohio University Press.

Mazrui, Ali. 1971. *The Trial of Christopher Okigbo*. London: Heinemann.

Mazrui, Ali A., and Alamin M. Mazrui. 1995. *Swahili, State, and Society: Political Economy of an African Language*. Nairobi: East African Educational Publishers.

Mbele, Joseph. 1986. "The Hero in the African Epic." PhD dissertation, University of Wisconsin, Madison.

Mbembe, Achille. 2000. "At the Edge of the World: Boundaries, Territoriality, and Sovereignty in Africa." Translated by Steven Rendall. *Public Culture* 12(1): 259–84.

———. 2001a. *On the Postcolony*. Berkeley: University of California Press.

———. 2001b. "Ways of Seeing: Beyond the New Nativism—Introduction." *African Studies Review* 44(2): 1–14.

———. 2002a. "African Modes of Self-Writing." *Public Culture* 14(1): 239–73.

———. 2002b. "On the Power of the False." *Public Culture* 14(3): 629–41.

Mbogo, Emmanuel. 1996. *Vipuli vya Figo*. Nairobi: East African Educational Publishers.

Mbonde, John P. 2004. "Seithy L. Chachage: Makuadi wa Soko Huria (2002): Uchambuzi na Uhakiki." *Swahili Forum* 11: 211–26.

Mbotela, James. 1934. *Uhuru wa Watumwa* (Freedom of the Slaves). London: Sheldon.

McBride, Dwight A. 2005. *Why I Hate Abercrombie and Fitch*. New York: New York University Press.

McCaffery, Larry. 1982. *The Metafictional Muse: The Works of Robert Coover, Donald Barthelme, and William H. Gas*. Pittsburgh, PA: University of Pittsburgh Press.

McCallum, Pamela, and Wendy Faith, eds. 2005. *Linked Histories: Postcolonial Studies in a Globalized World*. Durham, NC: Duke University Press.

McClintock, Anne. 1995. *Imperial Leather: Race, Gender, and Sexuality in the Colonial Context*. New York: Routledge.

McDowell, Deborah E. 1990. " 'The Changing Same': Generational Connections and Black Women Novelists." In *Reading Black, Reading Feminist: A Critical Anthology*, ed. Henry Louis Gates Jr., 91–115. New York: Penguin.

McFadden, Patricia. 1990. "The Condition of Women in Southern Africa: Challenges for the 1990s." *Southern African Political and Economic Monthly* 3(10): 3–9.

McLean, Hugh, and Linda Ngcobo. 1995. "Abangibhamayo Badhi Ngimnandi (Those Who Fuck Me Say I'm Tasty): Gay Sexuality in Reef Townships." In *Defiant Desire: Gay and Lesbian Lives in South Africa*, ed. Mark Gevisser and Edwin Cameron, 158–85. New York: Routledge.

McLeod, John. 2000. *Beginning Postcolonialism*. Manchester: Manchester University Press.

Mcnee, Lisa. 2000. *Selfish Gifts: Senegalese Women's Autobiographical Discourses*. Albany: State University of New York Press.

Mda, Zakes. 1995. *Ways of Dying*. Cape Town, South Africa: Oxford University Press.

———. 2000. *The Heart of Redness*. New York: Picador.

———. 2003a. *The Madonna of Excelsior*. Oxford: Oxford University Press.

———. 2003b. *She Plays with the Darkness*. New York: Picador.

Melas, Natalie. 2007. *All the Difference in the World: Postcoloniality and the Ends of Comparison*. Stanford, CA: Stanford University Press.

Merwe, Andre Carl van der. 2006. *Moffie*. Hermanus, South Africa: Penstock.

Midouhouan, Guy Ossito. 1991. "Modern Literature and the Flourishing of Culture in Black Africa." *Research in African Literatures* 21(1): 93–99.

Mikell, Gwendolyn. 1995. "African Feminism: Toward a New Politics of Representation." *Feminist Studies* 21(2): 405–24.

———. 1997. "Introduction." In *African Feminism*, ed. Gwendolyn Mikell, 1–50. Philadelphia: University of Pennsylvania Press.

Mitchell, W. J. T. 1994. "Ekphrasis and the Other." In *Picture Theory*, ed. W. J. T. Mitchell, 151–81. Chicago, IL: University of Chicago Press.

Mkangi, Katama. 1984. *Mafuta*. Nairobi: Heinemann.

———. 1995. *Walenisi*. Nairobi: East African Educational Publishers.

Mkufya, W. E. 1999. *Ziraili na Zirani*. Dar-es-Salaam: Hekima.

Mlama, Penina. 1995. "Oral Art and Contemporary Cultural Nationalism." In *Power, Marginality, and Oral Literature*, ed. Graham Furniss and Liz Gunner, 23–34. Cambridge: Cambridge University Press.

Mohamed, Said A. 2001. *Babu Alipofufuka*. Nairobi: The Jomo Kenyatta Foundation.

———. 2006. *Dunia Yao*. Nairobi: Oxford University Press.

Mohanty, Chandra Talpade. 1984. "Under Western Eyes: Feminist Scholarship and Colonial Discourses." *Boundary 2* 12(3)/13(1): 333–58.

———. 1991. "Cartographies of Struggle: Third World Women and the Politics of Feminism." In *Third World Women and the Politics of Feminism*, ed. Chandra Talpade Mohanty, Ann Russo, and Lourdes Torres, 1–47. Bloomington: Indiana University Press.

———. 2003. *Feminism without Borders: Decolonizing Theory, Practicing Solidarity*. Durham, NC: Duke University Press.

Moodie, Dunbar T. 1988. "Migrancy and the Male Sexuality on the South African Gold Mines." *The Journal of Southern African Studies* 14(2): 228–56.

Moore-Gilbert, Bart. 1997. *Postcolonial Theory: Contexts, Practices, Politics*. London and New York: Verso.

Morrison, Toni. 1970. *The Bluest Eye: A Novel*. New York: Washington Square Press.

Mpe, Phaswane. 2001. *Welcome to Our Hillbrow*. Pietermaritzburg: University of Natal Press.

Mudimbe. V. Y. 1988. *The Invention of Africa: Gnosis, Philosophy, and the Order of Knowledge*. Bloomington: Indiana University Press.

Mugambi, Helen Nabasuta. 1994. "Intersections: Gender, Orality, Text, and Female Space in Contemporary Kiganda Radio Songs." *Research in African Literatures* 25(3): 47–70.

———. 1997. "From Story to Song: Gender, Nationhood, and the Migratory Text." In *Gendered Encounters: Challenging Cultural Boundaries and Social Hierarchies in Africa*, ed. Maria Luise Grosz-Ngaté and Omari H. Kokole, 205–22. New York: Routledge.

———. 2007. "The 'Post-Gender' Question in African Studies." In *Africa after Gender?* ed. Catherine M. Cole, Takyiwaa Manuh, and Stephan F. Miescher, 285–301. Bloomington: Indiana University Press.

Mugambi, Stephen. 2005. *Wait for Me Angela*. Nairobi: Kenya Literature Bureau.

Mugo, Micere Githae. 1994. *My Mother's Poem and Other Songs*. Nairobi: East Africa Educational Publishers.

———. 1998. "The Woman Artist in Africa Today: A Critical Commentary." In *Challenging Hierarchies: Issues and Themes in Colonial and Postcolonial African Literature*, ed. Leonard A. Podis and Yakubu Saaka, 37–61. New York: Peter Lang.

Mulokozi, Mugyabuso M. 1983. "The Nanga Bards of Tanzania: Are They Epic Artists?" *Research in African Literatures* 14(3): 283–311.

———. 2002. *The African Epic Controversy: Historical, Philosophical, and Aesthetic Perspectives on Epic Poetry and Performances*. Dar es Salaam: Mkuki na Nyota.

Munro, Brenna. 2007. "Queer Futures: The Coming Out Novel in South Africa." In *African Literature: An Anthology of Criticism and Theory*, ed. Tujemola Olaniyan and Ato Quayson, 752–64. Malden, MA: Blackwell.

Murray, Stephen O. 1997. "The Will Not to Know: Islamic Accommodations of Homosexuality." In *Islamic Homosexualities: Culture, Literature, and History*, ed. Stephen Murray and Will Roscoe, 14–54. New York: New York University Press.

Murray, Stephen O., and Will Roscoe. 1998. *Boy-Wives and Female Husbands: Studies of African Homosexualities*. New York: St. Martin's Press.

Mushengyezi, Aaron. 2004. "Folklore and Contemporary Ideology in Africa: An Assessment of Ankole Myths and Legends." In *Africa in World Affairs: Challenges to Humanities*, ed. Edward Wamala et al., 41–49. Kampala: Faculty of Arts, Makerere University.

Mutahi, Wahome. 1991. *Three Days on the Cross*. Nairobi: Heinemann Kenya.

Mwai, Wangari Kimani. 1997. "Power of the Song for the Swahili Women." In *Contesting Social Death: Essays on Gender and Culture*, ed. Wanjiku M. Kabira, Masheti Masinjila, and Milton Obote, 84–102. Nairobi: Kenya Oral Literature Association.

Mwangi, Evan. 2003. "Gendering Genre: Issues of Feminist Identity and Subversion of the Epic in Margaret Ogola's *The River and the Source*." *Nairobi Journal of Literature* 1: 42–54.

———. 2007. "Gender, Unreliable Oral Narration, and the Untranslated Preface in Ngũgĩ wa Thiong'o's *Devil on the Cross*." *Research in African Literatures* 38(4): 28–46.

Mwangi, Meja. 1973. *Kill Me Quick*. London: Heinemann.

———. 2000. *The Plague*. Nairobi: East African Educational Publishers.

Nazareth, Peter. 1972a. *In a Brown Mantle*. Nairobi: East African Literature Bureau.

———. 1972b. *Literature and Society in Modern Africa: Essays on Literature*. Nairobi: East Africa Literature Bureau.

———. 1981. "Practical Problems and Technical Solutions in Writing My Two Novels." *Callaloo*, 11–13: 56–62.

———. 1982. "Out of Darkness: Conrad and Other Third World Writers." *Conradiana: A Journal of Joseph Conrad Studies* 14(3): 173–87.

Ndebele, Njabulo. 1991. *Rediscovery of the Ordinary: Essays on South African Literature and Culture*. Johannesburg: COSAW.

———. 2003. *The Cry of Winnie Mandela: A Novel*. Claremont, CA: David Philip.

Ndunguru, S. N. 1997. *A Wreath for Fr. Mayer*. Dar es Salaam: Mkuki na Nyota.

Newell, Stephanie, ed. 1997. *Writing African Women*. London: Zed Books.
Newman, Beth. 1990. "The Position of the Looker-on: Gender, Narration, and Gaze in *The Wuthering Heights*." *PMLA* 105(5): 1029–41.
Nfah-Abbenyi, Juliana Makuchi. 1997. *Gender in African Women's Writing*. Bloomington: Indiana University Press.
Ngaboh-Smart, Francis. 2004. *Beyond Empire and Nation: Postnational Arguments in the Fiction of Nuruddin Farah and B. Kojo Laing*. Amsterdam: Rodopi.
Ngũgĩ wa Thiong'o. 1964. *Weep Not, Child*. London: Heinemann.
———. 1965. *The River Between*. London: Heinemann.
———. 1967. *A Grain of Wheat*. London: Heinemann.
———. 1972. *Homecoming: Essays in African and Caribbean Literature, Culture, and Politics*. London: Heinemann.
———. 1977. *Petals of Blood*. London: Heinemann.
———. 1980. *Caitaani Mũtharaba-inĩ*. Nairobi: East African Educational Publishers.
———. 1981. *Writers in Politics*. Nairobi: Heinemann.
———. 1982. *Devil on the Cross*. Nairobi: East African Educational Publishers.
———. 1983. *Barrel of a Pen: Resistance to Repression in Neo-Colonial Kenya*. Trenton, NJ: African World Press.
———. 1986a. *Decolonising the Mind: The Politics of Language in African Literature*. London: Heinemann.
———. 1986b. *A Grain of Wheat*. 2nd ed. London: Heinemann.
———. 1986c. *Matigari ma Njiirũngi*. Nairobi: East African Educational Publishers.
———. 1988. *Matigari*. Nairobi: East African Educational Publishers.
———. 1993. *Moving the Centre: The Struggle for Cultural Freedoms*. London: James Currey.
———. 1998. *Penpoints, Gunpoints, and Dreams: Towards a Critical Theory of the Arts and the State in Africa*. Oxford: Oxford University Press.
———. 2004. *Mũrogi wa Kagogo*. Nairobi: East African Educational Publishers.
———. 2005. "Homecoming: Address at the University of Nairobi, August 2004." *The Nairobi Journal of Literature* 3: 62–67.
———. 2006. *Wizard of the Crow*. New York: Pantheon.
———. 2009. *Something Torn and New: An African Renaissance*. New York: Basic Civitas Books.
Njambi, Wairimu Ngaruiya, and William E. O'Brien. 2005. "Revisiting 'Woman-Woman Marriage': Notes on Gĩkũyũ Women." In *African Gender Studies: A Reader*, ed. Oyèrónkẹ́ Oyewùmi, 145–65. New York: Palgrave.
Njau, Rebeka. 1965. *The Scar: A Tragedy in One Act*. Moshi, Tanzania: Ibo Art Gallery.
———. 1975. *Ripples in the Pool*. Nairobi: Transafrica.
———. 2003. *The Sacred Seed*. Nairobi: Books Horizon.
Njogu, Kimani. 1997. *Uhakiki wa Riwaya za Visiwani Zanzibari* [A Critical Examination of Novels from the Zanzibar Island]. Nairobi, Kenya: Nairobi University Press.
Nkosi, Lewis. 1986. *Mating Birds*. New York: St. Martin's Press.
———. 2002. *Underground People*. Cape Town, South Africa: Kwela.
———. 2006. *Mandela's Ego*. Johannesburg: Umuzi.

Nnaemeka, Obioma, ed. 1997. *The Politics of (M)othering: Womanhood, Identity, and Resistance in African Literature*. London: Routledge.

———. 1998a. "Introduction: Reading the Rainbow." In *Sisterhood, Feminisms, and Power: From Africa to the Diaspora*, ed. Obioma Nnaemeka, 1–35. Trenton, NJ: Africa World Press.

———. 1998b. "This Women's Studies Business: Beyond the Politics and History (Thoughts on the First WAAD Conference)." In *Sisterhood, Feminisms, and Power: From Africa to the Diaspora*, ed. Obioma Nnaemeka, 351–86. Trenton, NJ: Africa World Press.

———. 2003. "Nego-Feminism: Theorizing, Practicing, and Pruning Africa's Way." *Signs: Journal of Women in Culture and Society* 29(2): 357–85.

———. 2005. ed. *Female Circumcision and the Politics of Knowledge: African Women in Imperialist Discourses*. Westport, CT: Praeger.

Nwapa, Flora. 1966. *Efuru*. London: Heinemann.

Nzegwu, Nkiru. 2006. *Family Matters: Feminist Concepts in African Philosophy of Culture*. Albany: State University of New York Press.

Obiechina, Emmanuel N. 1968. "Cultural Nationalism in Modern African Creative Literature." *Africa Literature Today* 1: 24–35.

———. 1990. *Language and Theme: Essays on African Literature*. Washington, DC: Howard University Press.

Obumselu, Ebele. 1974. "*A Grain of Wheat*: Ngũgĩ's Debt to Conrad." *Benin Review* 1: 80–91.

Ogola, Margaret. 1994. *The River and the Source*. Nairobi: Focus.

———. 2002. *I Swear by Apollo*. Nairobi: Focus.

———. 2005. *Place of Destiny*. Nairobi: Paulines Publications.

Ogot, Bethwell Allan. 1973. "A Man More Sinned Against than Sinning: The African Writer View of Himself." In *Black Aesthetics: Papers from the Colloquium Held at the University of Nairobi, June 1971*, ed. Pio Zirimu and Andrew Gurr, 20–31. Nairobi: East African Literature Bureau.

Ogot, Grace. 1966. *Promised Land*. Nairobi: East African Publishing House.

———. 1968. "Elizabeth." In *Land without Thunder*, ed. Grace Ogot, 189–204. Nairobi: East African Publishing House.

———. 1976. "The Middle Door." In *The Other Woman*, ed. Grace Ogot, 16–35. Nairobi: TransAfrica.

———. 1983a. *Miaha*. Nairobi: Heinemann Educational.

———. 1983b. *Simbi Nyaima*. Kisumu: Anyange Press.

———. 1989. *The Strange Bride*. Translated by Okoth Okombo. Nairobi: East African Educational Publishers.

Ogude, James. 1999. *Ngũgĩ's Novels and African History: Narrating the Nation*. London: Pluto.

Oguibe, Olu. 2004. *The Culture Game*. Minneapolis: University of Minnesota Press.

Ogundipe-Leslie, Molara. 1994. *Re-Creating Ourselves: African Women and Critical Transformations*. Trenton, NJ: Africa World Press.

Ogunyemi, Chikwenye Okonjo. 1985. "Womanism: The Dynamics of the Contemporary Black Female Novel in English." *Signs: Journal of Women in Culture and Society* 11(1): 63–79.

———. 1993. *Africa Wo/Man Palava: The Nigerian Novel by Women*. Chicago, IL: University of Chicago Press.

———. 2005. "Tête-à-tête with the Chief: Post-Womanist Discourse in Bessie Head's Maru." In *Body, Sexuality, and Gender*, ed. Flora Veit-Wild and Dirk Naguschewski, 3–14. Amsterdam: Rodopi.

Ojaide, Tanure. 1992. "Modern African Literature and Cultural Identity." *African Studies Review* 35(3): 43–57.

Okekwe, Promise Ogochukwu. 2002a. *Groaning Passage*. Lagos: Oracle.

———. 2002b. *Women from the Crystal Deep*. Lagos: Oracle.

———. 2003. *Fumes and Cymbals*. Lagos: Oracle.

Okoye, Chukwuma. 2007. "Posting the Agenda in African Women's Writing: The Postcolonial Condition in Promise Okekwe's Novels." In *Gender and Sexuality in African Literature and Film*, ed. Ada Uzoamaka Azodo and Maureen Ngozi Eke, 57–71. Trenton, NJ: Africa World Press.

Okpewho, Isidore. 1975. *The Epic in Africa: Toward a Poetics of the Oral Performance*. New York: Columbia University Press.

———. 1977. "Does the Epic Exist in Africa? Some Formal Considerations." *Research in African Literatures* 8(8): 171–200.

———. 1979. *The Epic in Africa: Toward a Poetics of the Oral Performance*. New York: Columbia University Press.

———. 1992. *African Oral Literature: Backgrounds, Character, and Continuity*. Bloomington: Indiana University Press.

Okri, Ben. 1991. *The Famished Road*. London: Cape.

———. 1995. *Astonishing the Gods*. London: Phoenix House.

———. 1998. *Infinite Riches*. London: Phoenix House.

———. 2002. *In Arcadia*. London: Weidenfeld & Nicolson.

———. 2007. *The Starbook*. London: Rider.

Okurut, Mary Karooro. 1998. *The Invisible Weevil*. Kampala: Femrite.

Olaniyan, Tejumola. 1995. *Scars of Conquest/Masks of Resistance: The Invention of Cultural Identities in African, African American and Caribbean Drama*. Cambridge, MA: Harvard University Press.

Onyeama, Dilibe. 1976. *Sex is a Nigger's Game*. London: Satellite.

O'Reilly, Sally O. 2005. "Self-Reflexivity." *Art Monthly* (September): 7–10.

Osundare, Niyi. 2000. "African Literature and the Crisis of Post-Structuralist Theorizing." In *Rethinking African Arts and Culture*, ed. Dele Layiwola, 113–27. Cape Town, South Africa: Center for Advanced Studies of African Society.

Ottaway, Marina. 2003. *Democracy Challenged: The Rise of Semi-Authoritarianism*. Washington, DC: Carnegie Endowment for International Peace.

Ousmane, Sembene. 1976. *God's Bits of Wood*. Translated by Francis Price. London: Heinemann.

Owomoyela, Oyekan. 2002. "Socialist Realism and African Knowledge." In *Tongue and Mother Tongue*, ed. Pamela J. Olubunmi Smith and Daniel Kunene, 90–102. Trenton, NJ: Africa World Press.

———. 2008. "Lost in Transit: Africa in the Trench of the Black Atlantic." *Recharting the Black Atlantic: Modern Cultures, Local Communities, Global Connections*, ed. Annalisa Oboe and Anna Scacchi, 238–55. New York: Routledge.

Oyewùmi, Oyèrónkẹ́. 1997. *The Invention of Women: Making an African Sense of Western Gender Discourse*. Minneapolis: University of Minnesota Press.

Palmer, Eustace. 2007. "African Jekyls and Hydes: Benjamin Kwakye's Study of Double Personalities in the *Sun by Night*." *Jala: Journal of African Literature Association* 1(1): 127–51.

Parkin, David. 1978. *The Cultural Definition of Political Response: Lineal Destiny among the Luo*. London: Academic Press.

Parrinder, Patrick. 1991. *Authors and Authority: English and American Criticism, 1750–1990*. New York: Columbia University Press.

Press, Karen. 1990. "Building a National Culture in South Africa." In *Rendering Things Visible: Essays on South African Literary Culture*, ed. Martin Trump, 22–40. Johannesburg: Ravan Press.

Prince, Gerald. 1988. "The Disnarrated." *Style* 22(1): 1–8.

Quayson, Ato. 1997. *Strategic Transformations in Nigerian Writing: Orality and History in the Work of Rev. Samuel Johnson, Amos Tutuola, Wole Soyinka, Ben Okri, and Ato Quayson*. Bloomington: Indiana University Press.

———. 2000. *Postcolonialism: Theory, Practice, or Process?* Cambridge: Polity Press.

———. 2003. *Calibrations: Reading for the Social*. Minneapolis: University of Minnesota Press.

———. 2004. "Modernism and Postmodernism in African Literature." In *The Cambridge History of African and Caribbean Literature, Volume Two*, ed. Simon Gikandi and F. Abiola Irele, 824–52. Cambridge: Cambridge University Press.

———. 2005. "Transnational and National Pre-and Postcolonial." In *Postcolonial Approaches to the European Middle Ages: Translating Cultures*, ed. Ananya Jahanara Kabir and Deanne Williams, 253–68. Cambridge: Cambridge University Press.

———. 2007. *Aesthetic Nervousness: Disability and the Crisis of Representation*. New York: Columbia University Press.

Quint, David. 1993. *Epic and Empire: Politics and Generic Form from Virgil to Milton*. Princeton, NJ: Princeton University Press.

Radhakrishnan, R. 1993. "Postcoloniality and the Boundaries of Identity." *Callaloo* 16(4): 750–71.

———. 2003. *Theory in an Uneven World*. Malden, MA: Blackwell.

Ramazani, Jahan. 2006. "Modernist Bricolage, Postcolonial Hybridity." *Modernism/Modernity* 13(3): 445–63.

Ravenscroft, Arthur. 1976. "The Novels of Bessie Head." In *Aspects of South African Literature*, ed. Christopher Heywood, 174–86. London: Heinemann.

Rhys, Jean. 1966. *Wide Sargasso Sea*. London: Deutsch.

Ricard, Alain, and Flora Veit-Wild. 2005. "Introduction: Local Literatures versus Global Cultures." In *Interfaces between the Oral and the Written: Interfaces entre l'ecrit et l'oral*, ed. Alain Ricard and Flora Veit-Wild, ix–xiv. New York: Rodopi.

Richards, Sandra L. 1999. "Yoruba Gods on the American Stage: August Wilson's *Joe Turner's Come and Gone*." *Research in African Literatures* 30(4): 92–105.

Riffaterre, Michael. 1978. *Semiotics of Poetry*. Bloomington: Indiana University Press.

Rose-Innes, Henrietta. 2004. *The Rock Alphabet*. Cape Town, South Africa: Kwela.

Roth, Philip. 1977. *Professor of Desire*. New York: Farrar, Straus, and Giroux.

Roy, Arundhati. 1997. *The God of Small Things*. London: Flamingo.

Ruganda, John. 1972. *The Burdens*. New York: Oxford University Press.

Rushdie, Salman. 1980. *Midnight's Children*. New York: Avon.

———. 1982. "The Empire Writes Back with a Vengeance." *The Times*, July 3, p. 8.

———. 1991. *Imaginary Homelands: Essays and Criticisms 1981–1991*. London: Granta Books.

Ryan, William E., and Theodore E. Conover. 2003. *Graphic Communications Today*. Clifton Park, NY: Thomson/Delmar Learning.

Said, Edward. 1991. "The Politics of Knowledge: Imperialism, Intellectuals, and Nationalism." *Raritan* 11(1): 17–31.

———. 1993. *Culture and Imperialism*. London: Chatto and Windus.

———. 1994. *Orientalism: Western Conceptions of the Orient*. 1978. 2d ed. New York: Vintage.

Salih, Tayeb. 1969. *Season of Migration to the North*. Translated by Denys Johnson-Davies. Portsmouth: Heinemann.

Sánchez, María Ruth Noriega. 2002. *Challenging Realities: Magic Realism in Contemporary American Women's Fiction*. Valencia: Universitat de Valencia.

Sangari, Kumkum. 1987. "The Politics of the Possible." *Cultural Critique* 7: 157–86.

Sarvan, Ponnuthurai. 1977. "Conrad's Influence on Ngũgĩ." *Kucha* 1: 39–44.

———. 1990. "Conrad's Influence on Ngũgĩ" and "Under African Eyes: Joseph Conrad." In *Third World Perspectives*, ed. Robert Hamner, 153–60. Washington, DC: Three Continents Press.

Scheub, Harold. 1985. "A Review of African Oral Traditions and Literature. *African Studies Review* 28(2/3): 1–72.

———. 1996. *The Tongue Is Fire: South African Storytellers and Apartheid*. Madison: University of Wisconsin Press.

Schipper, Mineke. 1987. "Mother Africa on a Pedestal: The Male Heritage in African Literature and Criticism." *African Literature Today* 15: 35–54.

———. 1996. "Emerging from the Shadows: Changing Patterns in Gender Matters." *Research in African Literatures* 21(1): 155–71.

Schmitt, Arno. 1992. "Different Approaches to Male-Male Sexuality/Eroticism from Morocco to Usbekistan." In *Sexuality and Eroticism among Males of Moslem Societies*, ed. Arno Schmitt and Jeheodar Sofer, 1–24. New York: Haworth.

Scott, David. 1999. *Refashioning Futures: Criticism after Postcoloniality*. Princeton, NJ: Princeton University Press.

Sedgwick, Eve Kosofosky. 1990. *Epistemology of the Closet*. Berkeley: University of California Press.

Senkoro, Fikeni E. M. K. 1982. *The Prostitute in African Literature*. Dar es Salaam: Dar es Salaam University Press.

Shaba, Lutanga. 2005. *Secrets of a Woman's Soul.* Harare: Lutanga Shaba.

Shaffer, Brian W. 2006. *Reading the Novel in English, 1950–2000.* Malden, MA: Blackwell.

Shklovsky, Victor. 2005. "Art as Technique." 1917. In *Critical Theory since Plato,* ed. Hazard Adams and Leroy Searle, 797–805. Boston, MA: Thomson Wardsworth.

Sicherman, Carol. 1989. "Ngũgĩ wa Thiong'o and the Writing of History." *Research in African Literatures* 20(3): 347–70.

———. 1995. "Ngũgĩ's Colonial Education: "The Subversion . . . of the African Mind." *African Studies Review* 38(3): 11–41.

———. 1997. "Literary Studies at the University of Dar es Salaam: A Mirror of Tanzaman Socialism." *Ufahamu* 25(1): 107–29.

———. 1998. "Revolutionizing the Literature Curriculum at the University of East Africa: Literature and the Soul of a Nation." *Research in African Literatures* 29(3): 129–47.

Siemerling, Winfried. 2005. *The New North American Studies: Culture, Writing, and the Politics of Re/cognition.* New York: Routledge.

Simatei, Tirop Peter. 2001. *The Novel and the Politics of Nation Building in East Africa.* Bayreuth: Bayreuth African Studies.

Sironi, Mario. 2005. "The Manifesto of Muralism." Appendix to "Flash Memories." In *Donatello among the Blackshirts: History and Modernity in the Visual Culture of Fascist Italy,* ed. Claudia Lazzaro and Roger Crum, 238–40. Ithaca, NY: Cornell University Press.

Slemon, Stephen. 1990. "Modernism's Last Post." In *Past the Last Post: Theorizing Post-Colonialism and Post-Modernism,* ed. Ian Adam and Helen Tiffin, 1–11. New York: Harvester Wheatsheaf.

Smith, Keith. 1975. "Who Controls Book Publishing in Anglophone Middle Africa?" *Annals of the American Academy of Political and Social Science* 421: 140–50.

Smith, Kevin Paul. 2007. *The Postmodern Fairytale: Folkloric Intertexts in Contemporary Fiction.* Basingstoke: Palgrave.

Snead, James. 1990. "European Pedigrees/African Contagions: Nationality, Narrative, and Communality in Tutuola, Achebe, and Reed." In *Nation and Narration,* ed. Homi Bhabha, 231–49. London: Routledge.

Soyinka, Wole. 1965. *The Interpreters.* London: Heinemann.

———. 1968. "The Writer in a Modern African State." In *The Writer in Modern Africa,* ed. Per Wastberg, 14–21. Uppsala: The Scandinavian Institute of African Studies.

———. 1975. *Myth, Literature, and the African World.* Cambridge: Cambridge University Press.

———. 1981. *Aké: The Years of Childhood.* London: Collings.

———. 1990. "Foreword." In *Contemporary African Artists: Changing Tradition,* ed. El Anatsui et al., 7–9. New York: The Studio Museum in Harlem.

———. 1993. *Art, Dialogue, and Outrage: Essays on Literature and Culture.* New York: Pantheon.

———. 1997. "On the Trail of Transition." *Transition 1961–1976* 75–76: 414–19.

———. 1999. *The Burden of Memory, The Muse of Forgiveness*. New York: Oxford University Press.

Spivak, Gayatri Chakravorty. 1985. "Can the Subaltern Speak?: Speculations on Widow Sacrifice." *Wedge* 7–8: 120–30.

———. 1988. *In Other World. Essays in Cultural Polotics*. New York: Routledge.

———. 1989. "Who Claims Alterity?" In *Remaking History*, ed. Barbara Kruger and Phil Mariani, 269–92. Seattle, WA: Bay Press.

———. 1999. *A Critique of Postcolonial Reason: Toward a History of the Vanishing Present*. Cambridge, MA: Harvard University Press.

———. 2003. *Death of a Discipline*. New York: Columbia University Press.

Spurlin, William J. 2001. "Broadening Postcolonial Studies/Decolonizing Queer Studies: Emerging 'Queer' Identities and Cultures in Southern Africa." In *Postcolonial, Queer: Theoretical Intersections*, ed. John C. Hawley, 185–205. Albany: State University of New York Press.

———. 2006. *Imperialism within the Margins: Queer Representation and the Politics of Culture in Southern Africa*. New York: Palgrave.

Stander, Christell. 1999. "Desiring the Undesirable: Developing a Mythology of Queer Reading." In *Bodies, Identity, Sub-Cultures and Repression in Texts from Africa*, ed. Johannes A. Smit, 148–60. Durban: CSSALL, University of Durban-Westville.

Stanzel, Franz K. 1971. *Narrative Situations in the Novel*. Bloomington: Indiana University Press.

———. 1984. *A Theory of Narrative*. Cambridge: Cambridge University Press.

Steady, Filomena Chioma. 1987. "African Feminism: A Worldwide Perspective." In *Women in Africa and the African Diaspora* ed. Rosalyn Terborg-Penn, Sharon Harley, and Andrea Benton Rushing, 3–24. Washington, DC: Howard University Press.

Stobie, Cheryl. 2005. "Between the Arches of Queer Desire and Race: Representing Bisexual Bodies in the Rainbow Nation." In *Body, Sexuality, and Gender*, ed. Flora Veit-Wild and Dirk Naguschewski, 65–87. Amsterdam: Rodopi.

———. 2007. *Somewhere in the Double Rainbow: Representations of Bisexuality in Post-Apartheid Novels*. Scottsville: University of KwaZulu-Natal Press.

Stoler, Ann Laura. 1997. "Sexual Affronts and Racial Frontiers: European Identities and the Cultural Politics of Exclusion in Colonial Southeast Asia." In *Tensions of Empire: Colonial Cultures in a Bourgeois World*, ed. Frederick Cooper and Ann Laura Stoler, 198–237. Berkeley: University of California Press.

Stratton, Florence. 1994. *Contemporary African Literature and the Politics of Gender*. London: Routledge.

Subrahmanyam, Sanjay. 1998. "Hearing Voices: Vignettes of Early Modernity in South Asia, 1400–1750." *Daedalus* 127(3): 75–104.

Suleri, Sara. 1992a. *The Rhetoric of English India*. Chicago, IL: University of Chicago Press.

———. 1992b. "Woman Skin Deep: Feminism and the Postcolonial Condition." *Critical Inquiry* 18(4): 756–69.

Taasisi ya Uchunguzi wa Kiswahili (TUKI). 1981. *Kamusi ya Kiswahili*. Nairobi: Oxford University Press.

———. 2001. *Swahili-English Dictionary*. Dar es Salaam: Dar es Saalam University Press.

Tamale, Sylvia. 1999. *When Hens Begin to Crow: Gender and Parliamentary Politics in Uganda*. Boulder, CO: Westview Press.

———. 2003. "Out of the Closet: Unveiling Sexuality Discourses in Uganda." *African Feminist* 2: 42–49.

———. 2005. "Eroticism, Sensuality, and "Women's Secrets' Among the Baganda: A Critical Analysis." *African Feminist* 4: 9–36.

Taylor, Charles. 1994. "The Politics of Recognition." In *Multiculturalism*, ed. Amy Gutmann, 25–73. Princeton, NJ: Princeton University Press.

Terdiman, Richard. 1985. *Discourse/Counter-Discourse*. Ithaca, NY: Cornell University Press.

———. 2006. *Body and Story: The Ethics and Practice of Theoretical Conflict*. Baltimore, MD: Johns Hopkins University Press.

Tiffin, Helen. 1984. "Commonwealth Literature and Comparative Methodology." *World Literature Written in English* 23(1): 26–30.

———. 1987. "Post-Colonial Literature and Counter-Discourse." *Kunapipi* 9(3): 17–38.

Tobin, Steven. 1997. "The Poetics of Revolution: Ngũgĩ wa Thiong'o's *Matigari*." *Critique* 38(3): 163–76.

Tutuola, Amos. 1952. *The Palm-Wine Drinkard and His Dead Palm-Wine Tapster in the Deads' Town*. London: Faber and Faber.

———. 1954. My *Life in the Bush of Ghosts*. London: Faber and Faber.

Vambe, Maurice Taonezvi. 2004. "Orality in the Black Zimbabwean Novel in English." *Journal of Southern African Studies* 30(2): 235–49.

Vassanji, M. G. 1996. *The Book of Secrets: A Novel*. New York: Picador.

Vatulescu, Cristina. 2006. "The Politics of Estrangement: Tracking Shklovsky's Device through Literary and Policing Practices." *Poetics Today* 27(1): 35–66.

Vera, Yvonne. 2002. *The Stone Virgins*. Harare: Weaver.

Visagie, Andries. 1999. "Flaunting the Gay Male Body: Slagplaas by Koos Prinsloo." In *Bodies, Identity, Sub-Cultures, and Repression in Texts from Africa*, ed. Johannes A. Smit, 184–90. Durban: CSSALL, University of Durban-Westville.

Wade, Michael. 1978. "Nadine Gordimer and Europe-in-Africa." In *The South African Novel in English: Essays in Criticism and Society*, ed. Kenneth Parker, 131–63. London: Macmillan.

Waichinga, Elizabeth Mumbi. 2004. "The Mugumo Fig Tree of Kenya." *Szirine*. September 20. http://www.szirine.com/2004/09/20/the-mugumo-fig-tree-of-kenya, accessed October 20, 2006.

Walcott, Derek. 1965. "The Swamp." In *The Castaway and Other Poems*, ed. Derek Walcott, 11–12. London: Jonathan Cape.

Walker, Alice. 1983. *In Search of Our Mothers' Gardens: Womanist Prose*. San Diego, CA: Harcourt Brace.

———. 1992. *Possessing the Secret of Joy*. New York: Harcourt Brace Jovanovich.

Wamitila, Kyallo Wadi. 1997. "Contemptus mundi and Carpe Diem in Kezilahabi's Works." *Kiswahili* 60: 15–24.

———. 1998. "A Philosophical Labyrinth: Tracing Two Critical Motifs in Kezilahabi's Prose Works. *Afrikanistische Arbeitspapiere Swahili Forum* 55(5): 79–91.

———. 1999. "What's in a Name?: Towards Literary Onomastics in Kiswahili Literature." *Afrikanistische Arbeitspapiere Swahili Forum* 60(4): 35–44.

———. 2001. "Contextualization of Politics and the Politics of Contextualization: The Case of the Swahili Novel." In *African Languages Literature in the Political Context of the 1990s*, ed. Charles Bodunde, 135–51. Bayreuth: Bayreuth African Studies.

———. 2002. *Bina-Adamu!* Nairobi: Phoenix.

———. 2007. *Dharau ya Ini*. Nairobi: Vide-Muwa.

Wanjala, Chris L. 1978. *The Season of Harvest: Some Notes on East African Literature*. Nairobi: Kenya Literature Bureau.

———. 1980a. *For Home and Freedom*. Nairobi: Kenya Literature Bureau.

———. 1980b. "Imaginative Writing since Independence: The East African Experience." In *The East African Experience: Essays on English and Swahili Literature/2nd Janheinz Jan Symposium*, ed. Ulla Schild, 9–24. Berlin: Dietrich Reimer Verlag.

Ward, Cynthia. 1997. "Bound to Matter: The Father's Pen and Mother Tongues." In *The Politics of (M)othering: Womanhood, Identity, and Resistance in African Literature*, ed. Obioma Nnaemeka, 114–29. London: Routledge.

Ward, Ida. 1941. "Note on Vernacular Literature." *Journal of the Royal African Society* 40: 88–91.

Waugh, Patricia. 1984. *Metafiction: The Theory and Practice of Self-Conscious Fiction. London:* Methuen.

Weinhouse, Linda. 1993. "The Paternal Gift of Narration: Nadine Gordimer's *My Son's Story*." *Journal of Commonwealth Literature* 29(2): 66–76.

White, Andrea. 1996. "Conrad's Legacy in Postcolonial Literature." In *Under Postcolonial Eyes: Joseph Conrad after Empire*, ed. Gail Fincham and Myrtle Hooper, 195–208. Cape Town, South Africa: University of Cape Town Press.

Whitman, Walt. 1966. *Leaves of Grass*. 1855. New York: Eakins.

Williams, Patrick. 1999. *Ngũgĩ wa Thiong'o*. Manchester: Manchester University Press.

Wilson-Tagoe, Nana. 1997. "Reading Towards a Theorisation of African Women's Writing: African Women Writers within Feminist Gynocriticism." In *Writing African Women: Gender Popular Culture and Literature in West Africa*, ed. Stephanie Newell, 11–28. London: Zed Books.

———. 1999. "Narrative, History, Novel: Intertextuality in the Historical Novels of Ayi Kwei Armah and Yvonne Vera." *Journal of African Cultural Studies* 12(2): 155–66.

———. 2003. "Representing Culture and Identity: African Women Writers and National Cultures." *Feminist Africa* 2: 25–41.

Woods, Tim. 2007. *African Pasts: Memory and History in African Literatures*. Manchester: Manchester University Press.

World Health Organization. 1999. *World Health Report 1999: Making a Difference*. New York: Stationery Office Books.

Wright, Derek. 1997. "Postmodernism as Realism: Magic History in Recent West African Fiction." In *Contemporary African Fiction*, ed. Derek Wright, 181–207. Bayreuth: Bayreuth University.

Yeats, W. B. 1916. *Responsibility and Other Poems*. New York: Macmillan.

Yoshimoto, Mitsuhiro. 2002. "Questions of Japanese Cinema: Disciplinary Boundaries and the Invention of the Scholarly Object." In *Learning Places: The Afterlives of Area Studies*, ed. Masao Miyoshi and H. D. Harootunian, 368–401. Durham, NC: Duke University Press.

Young, Robert J. C. 2001. *Postcolonialism: An Historical Introduction*. Malden, MA: Blackwell.

Zabus, Chantal. 2007. *The African Palimpsest: Indigenization of Language in the West African Europhone Novel*. 1991. Amsterdam: Rodopi.

Zamora, Lois Parkinson, and Wendy B. Faris, eds. 1995. *Magical Realism: Theory, History, Community*. Durham, NC: Duke University Press.

Index